for Barbara Laman
with b...

Dec. 2006

# The Future without a Past

# THE FUTURE WITHOUT A PAST

## The Humanities in a Technological Society

John Paul Russo

University of Missouri Press    Columbia and London

Library of Congress Cataloging-in-Publication Data

Russo, John Paul.

  The future without a past : the humanities in a technological society / John Paul Russo.

    p.  cm.

  Summary: "Argues that technological imperatives like rationalization, universalism,
monism, and autonomy have transformed the humanities and altered the relation between
humans and nature. Examines technology and its impact on education, historical memory, and
technological and literary values in criticism and theory, concluding with an analysis of
the fiction of Don DeLillo"—Provided by publisher.

  Includes bibliographical references and index.

  ISBN 0-8262-1586-6 (alk. paper)

  1.  Humanities—Philosophy.  2.  Technology and civilization.  3.  Science and the
humanities.  4.  Humanities—Study and teaching (Higher)  5.  Learning and scholarship—
History.  I. Title.

  AZ103.R87  2005

  001.3'01—dc22

                                                                    2005002031

∞™This paper meets the requirements of the
American National Standard for Permanence of Paper
for Printed Library Materials, Z39.48, 1984.

Designer: Jennifer Cropp

Typesetter: Crane Composition, Inc.

Printer and Binder: Thomson-Shore, Inc.

Typefaces: Minion, Dyadis

To Robert Casillo

# Contents

# Acknowledgments

The first essay was the Dean's Lecture at Purdue University in 1998, and I wish to thank Anthony Julian Tamburri for his invitation and hospitality; the lecture was printed in *Humanitas* and subsequently translated into Spanish and published in *Valores en la Sociedad Industrial*. Previous portions of this work have also appeared in slightly different form in *Da Ulisse a . . . : Il viaggio nelle terre d'oltremare,* ed. Giorgetta Revelli; *Modern Language Quarterly; Texas Studies in Language and Literature; Letterature d'America; Culture a contatto nelle Americhe,* ed. Michele Bottalico and Rosa Maria Grillo; *Dal romanzo alle reti: Soggetti e territori della grande narrazione moderna,* ed. Alberto Abbruzzese and Isabella Pezzini; and *Bulletin of Science, Technology and Society.*

I owe a collective debt of gratitude to fellow panelists at the annual conferences of the International Association for Science, Technology and Society: Richard Stivers, Kim A. Goudreau, Willem H. Vanderburg, and James van der Laan. W. Terrence Gordon's studies of Marshall McLuhan and C. K. Ogden were an inspiration. The staff of the University of Miami's Otto G. Richter Library and especially its Inter-Library Loan Department have been extraordinarily helpful in support of my work.

I want to extend my thanks to those from whom I have profited in discussing the humanities and technological society: Alberto Abruzzese, Carol Bonomo Albright, Massimo Bacigalupo, Casey Nelson Blake, Michele Bottalico, Bruce Boucher, Andrea Carosso, Giuseppe Castorina, Russ Castronovo, Terry N. Clark, David Cowart, Maria Vittoria D'Amico, Hans de Salas-del Valle, Ian Duncan, Ferdinando Fasce, Priscilla Parkhurst Ferguson, Giovanna Franci, Patrizia Fusella, Dana Gioia, Valeria Giordano, Iain Halliday, William Bruce

Johnson, Elena Lamberti, Mario Maffi, Andrea Mariani, Ezequiel Morsella, Franco Mulas, Gigliola Nocera, Frank Palmeri, Maria Parrino, David Perkins, Giorgetta Revelli, Jeffrey Robbins, Perri Lee Roberts, Vincent Sherry, David Simpson, Federico Siniscalco, Thomas Skipper, the Right Honourable Chris Smith (MP), Gregory D. Sumner, Mihoko Suzuki, Arnaldo Testi, Lina Unali, and David Walter.

For their penetrating observations on the issues raised in these pages, and for their unfailing goodwill, I am grateful to Lorna C. Ferguson, Cristina Giorcelli, and Richard Shiff. Conversations and correspondence over many years with Giuseppe Sertoli helped shape the initial discussion and subsequently broadened the scope of the investigation. My brother, J. Edward Russo, challenged my readings in science and technology and alerted me to new perspectives and avenues of inquiry. Robert Ferguson contributed insightfully at every stage of the project, besides lending his always generous encouragement. My colleague Robert Casillo commented extensively on the manuscript and sharpened its focus with his searching criticism and good judgment.

Thinking about the future leaves one particularly prone to error; there is no shortage of false prophets; but the mistakes and misconceptions that remain here are my own.

# THE FUTURE WITHOUT A PAST

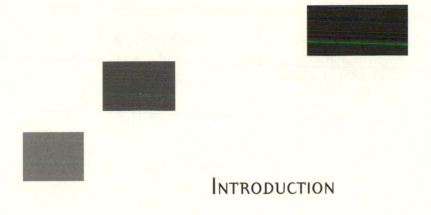

# INTRODUCTION

In 1831 John Stuart Mill declared that the Western world was entering an age of transition without equal in historical memory. Paul Johnson's *Birth of the Modern World* contains a wealth of illustration from the period 1815–1830 showing some of the more immediate causes. A few decades afterward, Matthew Arnold's "Stanzas from the Grande Chartreuse" (1867) portrayed the mid-Victorian generation in terms of a stalled transition: "Wandering between two worlds, one dead, / The other powerless to be born." Though writers and thinkers in succeeding generations spoke of accelerated, disorienting change, no one could specify when the pace would slacken and a new society would achieve stability.[1] For well over a century, with invention following invention, it even seemed that the state of transition would be permanent. But in the last decades of the twentieth century, in spite of all relativistic skepticism and ideological conflict, the transition that Mill had announced had reached its end. Change will not cease, yet the future has taken shape. We now have students raised and educated wholly within the hard shell of the technological environment, a generation for whom the great transition is finally over.

If one wants to know the future, Lord Bacon said, consult people in their twenties. This generation, born in the mid-1980s, was reared not only under conditions of mass culture, which had been true for at least the previous fifty years, but also in the midst of a communications revolution and its decisive impact on all fields of technology and globalization. "Today's children are growing up in the computer culture," notes Sherry Turkle. "All the rest of us are at best its naturalized citizens."[2] For many, the computer was their first big toy; for all, beginning with the elementary grades, it served as the key educational influence—"a computer on every desk," as former President Clinton liked to campaign. They played video games, listened to Walkmans, and downloaded multimedia CDs; they watched VCRs and DVDs; they browsed the Web and hyper-linked through cyberspace; they acquired an arcane vocabulary and learned by interactivity simulations, PowerPoint, CD-ROMs, and virtual communities. In the process, they became thoroughly technicized.

Now their cell phones interrupt them constantly so that their experience is broken into bits and pieces. E-mail, Net surfing, chat rooms, portable digital devices, electronic bulletin boards, and instant messaging erode the boundaries of personal privacy, while issues of surveillance do not appear overly to disturb them. Contemporary students are said to exhibit "decivilizing (or 're-tribalizing') processes, as indicated, for example, by major shifts in manners, morals, dress";[3] they are unaware of the nineteenth-century bourgeois distinction between private and public space, which they cross indiscriminately. Because they grew up after the collapse of the Soviet Union, they recall no time when the Western way of life was seriously threatened. Their understanding of history is minimal; its lessons present little of immediate usefulness in a society that differs so markedly from any previous epoch. They view the past as strange, confusing, tedious, and unnecessary. Mario Rigoni Stern talks of Italian students for whom the First World War is "as distant as the moon." Commenting on the results of a survey of eighteen- to twenty-four-year-old Britons, the *Guardian* went out of its way to excuse them for not knowing who Winston Churchill was—"maybe they do not need to know, in 'a world of information overload.'"[4]

In *Reading at Risk,* a survey conducted over the past twenty years, the National Endowment for the Arts (NEA) found that literary reading "is fading as a meaningful activity" among all groups; young adults, between age eighteen and twenty-four years, registered the most dramatic loss: minus 28 percent (since 1982). A drop of 10 percent is the equivalent of twenty million readers. As Dana Gioia, chair of the NEA, commented on the "dire" findings, the decline of literary reading correlates not only with the "massive shift" toward electronic media but also with decreased civic and cultural participation.[5] The diminishing percentage of history and humanities majors starting in the 1960s has been catastrophic. In 1984, one higher education study reported that "since 1970 the number of majors in English has fallen by 57 per cent, in philosophy by 41 per cent, in history by 62 per cent, and in modern languages by 50 per cent." In 1995 "only about 9% of American college freshman declared themselves interested in Arts and Humanities majors."[6] Nearly all students of the present generation are convinced that the technological wonders of the moment and the immediate future offer them a felicity unparalleled by anything in the past.

Educated to adapt to an ever impinging technological world—as seductive and soothing as it can be importunate and violent—the current student generation has become accustomed to think within the framework of a technical mentality, which enables them to find a linear path through the most complicated digital designs and apparatuses with surpassing ease, almost as if they were being entertained. The icon of the age is the person absorbed before a computer screen, scanning its luminous surfaces, peering into window behind window, interacting, customizing, constructing, working, playing. Hegel said, "There is nothing behind the curtain other than that which is in front of it." The mind being what it is, inevitably the outside becomes the inside. Where Marshall McLuhan wrote that technologies are "extensions of ourselves," now one inquires "to what extent we ourselves have become cyborgs, transgressive mixtures of biology, technology, and code."[7] Analyzing image transmission from the invention of photography in 1839, Peter Weibel describes the present stage (the seventh) as one of telerobotics and "interactive," "telematic culture"; eighth is the stage of "advanced sensory technologies": "the development of 'brain-chips' or 'neuro-chips' in order to bypass classic electronic surfaces and link the brain as directly as possible to the digital realm." What might this hold in store? Brain waves picked up and read by an implant connected to a wireless system? "Once a container, technology now becomes a component of the body," comments one artist. "As an instrument, technology fragmented and de-personalized experience—as a component it has the potential to split the species. It is no longer of any advantage either to remain 'human' or to evolve as a species." No longer advantageous to evolve because the process would take far too long: technology speeds up evolution to accomplish in years what might have taken eons. One is no longer fully human but a combination of the human and the machine—a cyborg. And this is far from the wildest speculation. "The cyborg is a creature in a post-gender world," contends Donna Haraway. "It has no truck with bisexuality, pre-oedipal symbiosis, unalienated labour, or other seductions to organic wholeness"; it is "the illegitimate offspring of militarism and patriarchal capitalism, not to mention state socialism. But illegitimate offspring are often exceedingly unfaithful to their origins."[8]

In the past twenty years a stream of books (and e-books) and journals have appeared with such titles as *The Age of the Internet; The New Renaissance: Computers and the Next Level of Civilization;*[9] *Digital Age; Electronic Age; The Information Age; The Computer Era; This Era of Microcomputers; The Rise of Network Society; CyberSociety 2.0; Posthumanism; The New Technoculture;* and *The Age of Spiritual Machines*—titles that make the age of Aquarius and postmodernism seem distinctly quaint and passé. Most writers salute the computer revolution under the banners of freedom, democracy, consumer choice, and empowerment from below, and with metaphors of exploration, religion, and communalism.

"As we immerse ourselves ever more deeply in our own technologies; as the boundaries between our technologies and ourselves continue to implode," Allucquère Rosanne Stone awaits the "high adventure" of the future. "For centuries," comments Hugh Kenner, "routines of trivial order-giving were preparing Western society for computerization: a list-comparing, paper-copying, bill-collecting society which had already turned vast numbers of people into machines when real machines began being invented to set them more or less free."[10] Although it is true (as Lewis Mumford said) that people had to turn themselves into machines before machines could dominate them, Kenner misconceives the nature and historical evolution of technology by treating it piecemeal in terms of labor-saving devices and by ignoring its totalizing systemic power, subtlety, and pervasiveness. He thinks that more and more technology, at some point, miraculously liberates us from technology.

Recalling McLuhan's global village, Howard Rheingold delights in the prospect of overcoming alienation in *The Virtual Community* with its cozy subtitle, *Homesteading on the Electronic Frontier.* Some writers have confused the feelings aroused by technology with the awe inspired by the divine. In *The Web of Text and the Web of God,* Alan C. Purves glamorizes an electronically mediated theophany.[11] (Don DeLillo's *Underworld* [1997] concludes with an immanent revelation in cyberspace.) One book carries a messianic title, *Online Eden: Reinventing Humanity in the Technological Universe.* Not everyone shares the enthusiasm, as shown by books like *Trapped in the Net, Out of Control, Let Them Eat Data,* and *The Robot's Rebellion.* Not that one should be unduly elated or depressed: it is a fairly well-known constant that books on the future have a terribly short shelf life.

Why focus on communications and technology in the 1980s as the critical divide rather than the noisier political and social unrest of the 1960s? For many reasons the "greater 1980s" are the decisive decade, the real break with the past. According to Marvin Lister and the coauthors of *New Media: A Critical Introduction,* economically, to enlarge the frame for the moment, the 1970s underwent a deep worldwide recession, brought on by an oil crisis and ending in weak economic growth, high unemployment, and high inflation. Daniel Bell's *Coming of Post-Industrial Society* appeared in 1973. Politically, traditional government responses (social welfare, entitlements, union protection) gave way under the ideology of neoliberalism to policies of deregulation, monetarism, and privatization that spread throughout the Western world in the 1980s and '90s. Globalization took on new intensity as foreign investment in individual economies went from 4 percent in the period 1981–1985 to 24 percent in the years 1986–1990. The "replacement, in the West, of an industrial age of manufacturing by a 'post-industrial' information age" involved a "shift in employment, skill, investment and profit, in the production of material goods to service and information 'industries.'"[12] Universities also underwent intensive corporatization in the 1980s. On the international scene, this decade witnessed the breakup of the Eastern bloc; the cold war ended, an enormous ice floe melting away; and the Iranian Revolution (1979) brought Islamic fundamentalism to the forefront of attention in the West.

Within this setting, and linked to it in many ways, occurred the astonishing advances in communications technologies that spread through many fields: new techniques in recording—CD (1970); VCR (1971); cell phone (1973);[13] CD-ROM (1978); Walkman (1980); new technologies in printing, storage, and digital photography (1986); expansion of biogenetic engineering, video surgery, magnetic resonance imaging (1977–1980), DNA fingerprinting (1984), and gene therapy; home video games, high-definition digital television, wireless cable systems; and the ubiquitous computer. "The 1980s marked the passage from an era of large, centralized computer installations to a world in which vast numbers of more inexpensive machines, distributed widely among users, are tied to one another and to a shrinking number of specialized, centralized computer resources."[14] If one needs dates, in 1982 *Time* announced not a person, but a machine of the year: the personal computer. "In the decade since the release of the first Web browser [1990], information technology has insinuated itself into virtually every corner of higher education"—and almost every other corner as well.[15]

Though many breakthroughs date from the 1960s and 1970s (the Internet [1969], silicon chip [1971], and personal computer [1974]), only in the 1980s did these innovations interact with one another to produce something much vaster than the individual technologies on their own.[16] The personal computer began as a glorified typewriter, turned into a screen for receiving images, soon served as a mail room, hosted chat-room encounters, opened a shopping mall, and became an information service, business office, auction block, travel agent, library catalog (not just for one's own library but for thousands of others as well), and so on. Likewise, the mobile phone meant that there was no place where one could be out of reach—technology follows one everywhere if one allows it to do so. As DeLillo writes in *Underworld,* a novel that captures the spirit of the age, "everybody is everywhere at once."[17] By the rule of miniaturization, video cell phones now do what the personal computers did ten years ago and mainframes twenty years earlier. Globalization in political and economic terms on the scale we are considering would have been inconceivable without the communications revolution.

With their complex histories, the new media were not entirely new; television, for example, had prepared the way for home-screen viewing. But to read

Lister and his coauthors, there are strong reasons that *new* is the appropriate modifier and not merely an ideological weapon or advertising tag for "social progress as delivered by technology." These media delivered new textual experiences in both genre and entertainment such as computer games, hypertexts, and special-effects cinema. They offered innovative ways of representing reality such as virtual environments and screen-based interactive media. We are not just seeing images; we are "immersed *within* images." The present world of visual media is one in which "images, still and moving, in print and on screens, are layered so thick, are so intertextual, that a sense of what is real has become problematic, buried under the thick sediment of its visual representations" (for example, the average urban American, it is said, sees some three thousand advertisements each day). There were also "new relationships between subjects (users and consumers) and media technologies" (voice-image transmission, the Web, CD-ROMs, virtualities); "shifts in the personal and social experience of time, space, and place (on both local and global scales)"; and new ways of conceiving the biological body's relation to technology with cyborgs, prostheses, and so on.[18] These media ran on the same technological principles—least effort, speed, miniaturization, digitization over analogue, interactivity, hypertextuality, virtuality—concepts that have come to dominate and will continue to dominate, until the next era.

It may appear foolish to generalize over an epistemic shift when the greater 1980s are not so far behind. By Ortega y Gasset's definition of an intellectual generation as a mere fifteen years, the '80s are scarcely one generation away. If one adopts Fernand Braudel's tripartite historical model of brief, medium, and long duration, one could argue that the decade of the '80s contains a brief event *(événement):* the communications revolution. This event occurs toward the end of a fifty-year *conjuncture:* postwar economic and cultural globalization. Beneath the conjuncture, however, lie the enormous, determinative, slow-moving *structures* of *longue durée:* secularizing, rationalizing modernity, from the late Renaissance to the present.[19] The '80s revolution constitutes an *événement* that is carved so deeply into the historical terrain that it has not only forged a division between midlevel *conjunctures* but also produced a tectonic shift in the underlying *longue durée.* Many historians of civilizations are pessimistic over the medium- or long-term future of the West.

In 1941, Pitirim Sorokin said that Western society was undergoing a "tragic" disintegration of its "six-hundred-year-long Sensate day" (*sensate* meaning materialist, sensual, relativist, narrowly particularistic, seeking immediate gratification). "The night of a transitory period begins to loom before us and the coming generations," a "*dies irae, dies illa* of transition to a new Ideational or Idealistic phase" (*ideational* meaning supersensory, mystical, ascetic, truths of reason). In 1957, he reaffirmed his belief that the West was in its "darkest hour . . . with its nightmares, gigantic destruction, and heartrending horrors." Arnold Toynbee wrote that the Third Italistic Age of Western civilization ended in 1875, with a twilight period through 1945. These are remarkably accurate figures, given that humanistic education was fading by 1914. (Compare travel writing before and after the First World War.) For him, civilizations decline mainly from internal causes and an inability to respond to challenges, internal and external. Western civilization was suffering a "spiritual breakdown" from the extremes of sensate culture (he might have prophesied '60s culture), a time of troubles, though there was a possibility of renewal.[20]

Carroll Quigley employed an economistic model of core-periphery relations, instruments of expansion (good), institutionalization (wasteful), and periodic expansion-stagnation cycles. He determined that Western civilization is in "profound crisis," not yet resolved into a fourth age of expansion or fallen into another age of conflict, an uncertainty expressed in one of his books, *Tragedy and Hope*. Like Toynbee, Quigley examined the issues from all sides; so vast is the amount of data to marshal and digest, so many and independent are the variables, that a slight emphasis in one place can have enormous consequences in another. But there is a difference between indecisive and undecided. The communications revolution, making capitalism more efficient, could be the economic instrument needed to propel the fourth expansion age. Quigley (who died in 1977) concluded his last lectures on a dark note. He condemned the destruction of community and the family by state power; the "commercialization of all human relationships"; the "technological acceleration" of weaponry, communications, and transportation; and the "dualism of almost totalitarian imperial power and an amorphous mass culture of atomized individuals." "And if a civilization crashes, it deserves to."[21]

Other historians have reached similar conclusions. For Matthew Melko, advanced technology means more specialization and less time for persons "to develop their total capacities" and hence less possibility for "new creative phases." If a "giant world technology" emerging from the West were to falter, "it would bring a world civilization down with it, and the results could be so prolonged and frightful that nuclear destruction would seem like social euthanasia." Stephen K. Sanderson predicts that the "Capitalist-Sensate" culture of the West will survive for "a few more decades." "When solutions are finally attempted, they will come too late. . . . It does not have to happen, but it will happen." "It" is either a nuclear holocaust, as suggested by W. Warren Wagar in *A Short History of the Future* (1992), or economic, demographic, and ecological disaster. "We are on the brink of a great historical shift," Sanderson comments dryly. "Not enough people are paying attention."[22]

The points of view of these civilizationist historians allow for a certain distance and objectivity on the present generation. Some, known by the Swiftian term *endists,* specialize in the pathology of culture. Yet the most pessimistic among them do not think that Western civilization is vanishing overnight, whereas the optimists or meliorists (admittedly few and far between) believe that the major world systems are moving toward a low-cost, polycultural, quadrilingual, conciliatory, global technocracy that will take another hundred years or so to establish itself—low-cost because interest in ethnicity and any specific culture will lack genuine intellectual or emotional investment.[23]

But whatever the time scale, a deep chasm has been crossed between the 1980s and the present day. There is a phenomenology as well as a history of technology. Having lived on both sides of the epistemic period shift, one notes the alterations in consciousness and physical life so much more acutely than if one had lived wholly on one or the other side—the generation now coming to its maturity has not felt this dislocation. Western civilization is evolving on grounds other than its own, or on one highly specialized version of its own, the technological, and it will soon cease resembling itself.

Any explanation, however speculative, of the deeper forces that govern the period shift since the 1980s should take into account at least three current views: first, technological determinism, which maintains that the technological system is grinding the world together; second, the clash of civilizations that maintains antithetically that there are cultural forces that are driving the world apart; and a third view, which embraces a combination of factors, some technological, others not. It is perhaps too strong to call the second and third positions antideterminist—there are degrees of determinism from hard to soft[24]—but both positions leave scope for human intention, freedom, and rational calculation.

From the appearance of *The Technological Society* in 1954 Jacques Ellul has been associated with hard technological determinism. His central thesis is premised on the fact that we have undergone a transformation—not only in Western culture but in nearly every other one as well—through technological characteristics such as rationalization, speed, universalism, monism, and self-augmentation. Technology is not a mere neutral, ad hoc instrument, but a substantive force that permeates every aspect of our lives, from politics, economics, management, psychology, and medicine to food, education, sports, travel, and leisure. To emphasize this notion of totality, Ellul employs the word *technique* (*la technique:* the ensemble of means, procedures, and above all the technical mentality) rather than *technology* or the machines and specific practices per se. "The machine could not integrate itself into nineteenth-century society; technique integrated it. Old houses that were not suited to the workers were torn down; and the new world technique required was built in their place."[25]

In earlier periods technical advances were added to human culture gradually and in piecemeal fashion, to the extent that technical products and values could be humanized and assimilated. Now the technological system has become overwhelming, runaway, and autonomous; far from being humanized in the process of assimilation, it has had the effect of eroding human values or technologizing them. Propaganda, too, is a technique, along with one of its most lethal forms, advertising. Nor can education be counted upon to oppose propaganda, because education, which in Ellul's view has become a means of technological adaptation, is propaganda for the technological system. Oddly enough, the more education people have, the more they render themselves susceptible to propaganda and advertising—intellectuals most of all. As Ellul states with Cartesian verve, technique "clarifies, arranges, and rationalizes; it does in the domain of the abstract what the machine did in the domain of labor. It is efficient and brings efficiency to everything." Intrinsic and normative, the technological phenomenon "shapes the total way of life."[26] Our powers to intervene are approaching nil.

Similar to Ellul, Marshall McLuhan takes a "plenary approach to technology" in which the whole is vaster than, and qualitatively different from, the sum of its parts. "When the globe becomes a single electronic computer" begins a typical sentence (in 1960!). Ellulian too is his belief that the technological interface between ourselves and nature has thickened to such a degree that we live increasingly within a technological, not a natural, world and that we derive normative values from the relentlessly self-aggrandizing imperatives of the technological system. "The new media are not bridges between man and nature; they are nature." McLuhan furthers an understanding of the period shift in his treatment of the communications media as paradigmatic of technology itself and as the dominant agents of change. Not simply the press or television, the media in his expanded sense of the term are all "go-betweens" or "in-betweens," that is, "extensions of man" such as speech, clothing, the shoe and car (extensions of the foot), money, gunpowder, and so on. His famous tag, *the medium is the message,* indicates that the means of communication, though often invisible, are ultimately more important than any "message" (content, information) could possibly be in determining the milieu.[27] His further spin, *the medium is the massage,* implies that technology insinuates itself into every aspect of our lives, either by force, by seduction, or by tacit consent; the massage is "the shaping, the twisting, the bending of the whole human environment by technology . . . a violent process, like all new technologies, often revolting, as well as revolutionary."[28] A violent massage captures the oxymoronic nature of the condition.

A second view on the shaping of the global scene is Samuel P. Huntington's clash of civilizations, which has enjoyed great notoriety since it was first proposed in *Foreign Affairs* in 1993. Huntington argues that religious, ethnic, linguistic, and cultural values and other supranational factors now weigh—and have weighed for several decades—more heavily as historical determinants than nationalism, economics, class, or technology. Though still powerful, nation-states are no longer the shaping forces they were in the period 1800–1960; instead, the seven or eight greater civilizations (Western, Chinese, Islamic, Hindu, Slavic-Orthodox, and others) are the real players in the historical drama. As the world grows smaller through travel, communications, business, and other cultural pressures, these civilizations come into increased conflict, revealing geopolitical fault lines with vivid precision. Relatively speaking, the West has declined with the emergence of a multipolar, multicivilizational world order. "The survival of the West depends on Americans reaffirming their Western identity and Westerners accepting their civilization as unique not universal and uniting to renew and preserve it against challenges from non-Western societies." Huntington's preference for multiculturalism on the global scale requires at least a minimal standard of accepted values, "not only in order to restrict the clash of civilizations but also in order to strengthen civilized behaviour generally."[29] Of particular interest to theorists of civilization, Huntington also notes that the West was stronger relative to the other civilizations at the beginning of the twentieth century than at the end of it. He expresses from the political center or just right of center what Jacques Ellul in *The Betrayal of the West* advances from the left of center. Events of the past decade seem to have lent some credence to the Huntington thesis.

Soft technological determinism is the third explanatory view. With only slight exaggeration it may be said that hard determinists are all alike, but soft determinists are soft after their own fashion. Some are so soft that they occasionally say things that are virtually antideterminist. Others seek a middle ground, dangerous because they can collect fire from both extremes. For all soft determinists, however powerful are technology and communications in the shape of things to come, these are second-level factors compared to culture, ideology, politics, or religion. In this view, the main problems with hard technological determinism are its monocausality, reductiveness, and insufficient embeddedness in the social and political framework.

In his *Autonomous Technology: Technics-Out-of-Control as a Theme in Political Thought,* Langdon Winner, one of Ellul's foremost interpreters, might seem to have aligned himself with a reductionist hard determinism. "We do not *use* technologies as much as *live* them," he comments. "Complex technologies are tools without handles or, at least, handles of extremely remote access." But Winner does not yield up the middle ground of choice and personal intervention, calling technology "a political phenomenon." "It is somnambulism (rather than determinism) that characterizes technological politics—on the left, right, and center equally." Perhaps, as Merritt Roe Smith notes, technology for Winner is not out of control so much as are the contemporary theories that thematize "technology-out-of-control." Still, Winner's soft approach to technological determinism is not completely convincing, as when he pleads that "we should try to imagine and seek to build technical regimes compatible with freedom, social justice, and other key political ends." The very idea of a regime implies an incompatibility with freedom. Winner believes that political debate requires an informed, democratic society that grants the "claims of technical expertise." But one questions how to educate a vast, global society on technological choices, especially when the very means to reach and educate society must of necessity be technological. Nonetheless, Winner concludes "on a hopeful note."[30]

For Peter C. Perdue, technology is one of the future's constraints. In his "flexible equilibrium" model the "interrelationship of all the elements, rather than any single one, determines the whole." Human freedom, which "includes the recognition of necessity," is one element; another is "humility." And we must fend off "despair."[31] Lynn White Jr., a single-factor hard determinist in his early works, eventually included medieval Christianity as a factor in the technological progress of the High Middle Ages.

A soft determinist, Albert Borgmann admires modern technology for bringing forth "the most complex and the most imposing creations in human history," and if one thinks solely in terms of material achievement (flying through the rings of Saturn), one cannot deny it. The modern history of technology has been characterized by the availability of more and more devices, gadgets, and commodities, "instantaneous, ubiquitous, safe, and easy." Once these devices were miniaturized and their machinery concealed, their relation to production and nature became virtually invisible. Now a commodity makes "no demands on our skill, strength, or attention." A hundred years ago, it took considerable work to withstand winter—by chopping trees, splitting and hauling wood, and making the fire (Borgmann lives in Montana). Heating can be a "focal thing" (the word *focus* is Latin for *hearth*); it once centered the efforts of a whole family; today we raise the thermostat. Technological expansion has consisted in whittling away focal things and substituting commodities to the point where "nature in its pristine state now consists of islands in an ocean of technology." Though Borgmann does not want to return to a pretechnological world, he believes that if we rely less on gadgets and devices and more on focal things and practices, we can "challenge *the rule of technology*" with a new philosophy of living; we can "prune back the excesses of technology and restrict it to a supporting role." Technology will be "a way of proceeding that we follow at certain times and up to a point." Reinstated, focal things should not be seen as mere coping mechanisms; they are a means to fullness of being; their end is embodied in their very means. His examples betray a homespun world distant from modern urban lifestyles and the thin but immensely powerful electronic culture: instead of eating a TV dinner, the careful preparation of an elaborate meal; gardening; hiking in the wilderness; running so that one can better appreciate sports on television. "The technological environment heightens rather than denies the radiance of genuine focal things" because we recognize the disparity between them. In *Power Failure: Christianity in the Culture of Technology* he recommends miniutopias where we have "citizen-based decision making, communal celebrations, and a vital connection with the table and the Word through daily shared meals and the discipline of reading."[32] In every American is a bit of Brook Farm.

Ellul has also defended himself against the charge of hard determinism. Even in his early work, which never denies freedom of choice, he was not nearly so hard as his numerous critics had supposed. In the preface to *The Technological Society,* whose original title is *Technique ou l'enjeu du siècle* (Technique or the wager of the century), he said that humanity made a decision and bet on technology in the twentieth century. Technology had won the bet and proceeded to beat the house.[33] Yet Ellul always believed that we have cards to play—reason, will, and choice. Even with propaganda and advertising, resistance is possible: "propaganda ceases where simple dialogue begins."[34] Toward the end of his life he wrote that "with the new developments in computer science *(informatique)* and everything organized around it, we have new alternatives, different ways to organize society" that were not present in the postwar period.[35] Whether his expectations from the computer revolution are misplaced remains to be seen. In his theological writings, as impressive as his books on technology with which they are interrelated, Ellul proposes an ethics of restraint: human beings should "agree not to do everything they are able to do":

> Nevertheless, there is no more project, nor value, nor reason, nor divine law to oppose technology from the outside. It is thus necessary to examine technology from the inside and to recognize the impossibility of living with it, indeed of just living, if one does not practice an ethics of nonpower. . . . [W]e must search systematically and willingly for nonpower, which of course does not mean accepting impotence.[36]

Ellul, then, may be numbered among the soft determinists: "There are few possibilities, but one should never lose hope."[37]

Perhaps the most insightful of the soft determinists are Romano Guardini and Lewis Mumford. From both a philosophical and historical perspective, the Catholic theologian and critic Guardini expresses the strongest hope for the future, though it comes through full awareness of loss and tragedy. Influenced by German romantic philosophy, he had grown up before 1914 and lived though a twilight era. In a beautiful early work, *Letters from Lake Como: Explorations in Technology and the Human Race* (1927), the halcyon landscape of the Italian lakes forms the backdrop for meditations on preindustrial and industrial societies. In contrast to the German city in which he was teaching at the time, the region surrounding Lake Como was marked by human interventions and imbued with traditional social values, yet nature still remained norm-giving and in possession of itself. The sentiment of Virgilian piety spread in concentric circles from the home to the town and into the natural universe. The inhabitants had found a harmonious balance between themselves and nature, which was founded on a sense of self-limitation and fostered urbanity and civic community. "Here nature can pass over smoothly into culture. There is nothing alien or *antithetical* to culture that must wither away if this humanity, this *urbanitas,* this art of living is to come into being."[38]

Such an integration between people and nature took centuries to establish. In one valley, however, he came upon a large boxlike, smoking factory, and "everything fell apart." Then the motorboats began taking over the lake with their speed, noise, and smell, and a new road for automobiles changed the natural contours of the landscape, organizing everything around it. Modernity, which in northern Europe had already broken the continuity between the natural and the human, was doing the same around Lake Como. People were being uprooted from their own natural contexts and ultimately from their own human essence. "There is no feeling for what is organically possible or tolerable in any living sense. No sense of natural proportions determines the approach. . . . Machines are an iron formula that directs the material to the desired end."[39]

This was a startling turnaround from the romantic period; Guardini located the shift in northern Europe between 1830 and 1870. In the late nineteenth and early twentieth centuries technology remained largely under the command of a nontechnical mentality. Beginning with the arms race and World War I, and in the decades leading up to and including World War II, however, "the man motivated by technology broke into the field of history and took possession." Guardini could find no historical parallels for such domination, not even in the great hydraulic civilizations of the Near East. Individuals who had derived a sense of vitality from the natural world and interacted with it on a plane of parity were now surrounded by machines from which they were existentially divided. "Man today distrusts nature."[40]

In *The End of the Modern World,* written after World War II, Guardini endures a time of "final crisis," the "ominous spectacle of a human nature withering beneath the destructive hand of modernity." The choice is either to master the technological world or to cease being human, and if humanity does not make the choice, it would be made for it. A wide historical gulf separated his generation from the opposite bank, that is, the future. Previous ages in Western history—the classical, the medieval, and the post-Renaissance or modern—were related to one another in both real and symbolic terms; they followed one another organically. That historical development had come to an end. What for Guardini characterizes the coming age is its disassociation from the past, even its repudiation. Individuals no longer feel as if they belong to nature, or take their lessons from nature, or could establish a relation to it, except in highly artificial ways and always abetted by the very technological means that they hope to reduce, if not escape. Their sense of autonomy that expanded in the bourgeois epoch and penetrated through a large part of the population, larger than at any previous time in the history of the West, has diminished in a tightly regulated society. Above all, the technological system is slowly reshaping the forms of human consciousness. Norms now derive from technology: the mass is "fashioned according to the law of standardization, a law dictated by the functional nature of the machine"; "the most highly developed individuals of the mass, its elite, are not merely conscious of the influence of the machine; they deliberately imitate it, building its standards and rhythms into their own ethos." The impositions and distortions wrought by the technological system have resulted in a " 'non-cultural culture,' " a " 'non-natural nature,' " and a " 'non-human' man."[41]

Yet Guardini also acknowledges that technological society has increased personal and public freedom—not only *from* something (from hunger, poverty, ignorance, and drudgery) but also *for* something, on a higher plane of aspiration and moral significance. Technology, which could be used for the well-being of the human race, is being used for power and is changing the very nature of human nature. "Man as a human being is far less rooted and fixed within his own essence than is commonly accepted. And the terrible dangers grow day by day." Would the challenge of moral freedom be accepted? Guardini expresses a profound and simple faith in human nature, in the masses. Not the masses directed by a cadre of intellectuals, or governed by a wealthy elite, or courted by one of Burckhardt's terrible simplifiers: he has faith in the masses themselves. Although Guardini presents the bleakest vision of the end of the modern world, his Christianity prevents him from yielding to the sins of despair and pride. "We need stronger, more considered, more human technology"; "the emergence of a new, free, strong, and well-formed humanity is needed, one that would be a match for these forces."[42] In this way Guardini affirms his deep faith in the future.

Espousing a similar romantic organicism, though otherwise from a different intellectual tradition, Lewis Mumford was an early, if not uncritical, appreciator of the technological revolution. Yet after World War II he came to deplore the all-powerful effects of what he calls "megatechnics." The impact of technology and communications on mass society had been a nightmare: "Disorder, blight, dingy mediocrity, screaming neon-lighted vulgarity are spreading everywhere, producing, as I said, an empty life, filled with false vitality, expressed in occasional outbreaks of violence and lust, either in brutal action or in more frequent fantasy." *The Myth of the Machine* (volume 1, *Technics and Human Development;* volume 2, *The Pentagon of Power;* published 1966–1970) presents the strongest critique of the technological system produced by the English-speaking world since Ruskin on industrial Britain. "The bottom has dropped out of our life. . . . [T]he human institutions and moral convictions that have taken thousands of years to achieve even a minimal efficacy have disappeared before our eyes: so completely that the next generation will scarcely believe they ever existed." Like Guardini, Mumford never denies the positive value of technology, if it could only be controlled properly. He therefore urges that we abandon the "myth of the machine" (technology as all powerful and making all things possible) and that we adopt new myths, a "life economy," and an "organic ideology." One must begin with an "inner change": extricate oneself from the "power system" and assert one's "primacy as a person in quiet acts of mental or physical withdrawal, in gestures of non-conformity, in abstentions, restrictions, inhibitions," thereby liberating the self from "the domain of the pentagon of power."[43] Though he eschews politics, leaving specific plans to be worked out by others, and though he lacks Guardini's messianic faith in the masses, he has a liberal's conviction that individual reason can find solutions to the most intransigent problems and that the community can be restored to health. Others share this conviction.

At the end of *After Virtue* (1981), with its "chillingly pessimistic" view of late modernity, Alasdair MacIntyre draws a parallel between the decline of the Roman Empire in the fifth and sixth centuries and the present time. Drawing analogies between historical epochs is dangerous, yet the final act in the long Roman drama has exerted a lasting fascination over Western culture and provided its interpreters with a standard of comparison and a warning. Then, according to MacIntyre, persons of goodwill gave up identifying morality and civility with the continuation of the Roman state, as they had for centuries, and substituted new forms of community "so that both morality and civility might survive the coming dark ages of barbarism and darkness."[44] We are in a similar position, thinks MacIntyre, with the benefit of having the Roman historical example as well as the additional centuries of moral thought and experience between them and ourselves. Johan Galtung, Tore Heiestad, and Erik Rudeng note parallels between the decline of Rome and the contemporary West:

> increased rejection of the dominant cosmology and lifestyle, as expressed in the contemporary West, for instance, by increasing interest in Eastern religion and mysticism, as well as by increased interest in parapsychology, astrology, and occultist traditions; increasing anomie, as expressed by increases in crime and other deviance, drug use, alcoholism, and mental disorder; alienation, as expressed in such things as the increasing loss of confidence in governments and politicians; the promotion of "leisurism" as a new lifestyle; increasing social fragmentation; and ecological breakdown.

To this recital of woe Stephen K. Sanderson adds the "decline in the Protestant ethic" as well as in "a sense of pride in workmanship" and "a major decline in the quality of education." Carroll Quigley also compares the end of the Roman Empire with the present time when "all signs [point] to our violent, irreversible, devastating destruction." But there is hope: "When Rome fell, the Christian answer was, 'Create our own communities.' "[45]

So that morality and civility might survive: for MacIntyre, modernity is plagued by the weakened sense of the self, the choice among pleasure or utility or a narrow sense of self-fulfillment over the virtues (wisdom, justice, fortitude, honesty, courage, prudence, and so on), and the loss of civitas. His "provisional conclusion" stipulates a retrieval of the moral tradition, a recapturing of the classical virtues, and an attempt to reinstall Aristotle's notion of the good life as an end, with pleasure as a by-product of achieving that end. "What matters at this stage is the construction of local forms of community within which civility and the intellectual and moral life can be sustained through the new dark ages which are already upon us. And if the tradition of the virtues was able to survive the horrors of the last dark ages, we are not entirely without grounds for hope. . . . We are waiting not for a Godot, but for another—doubtless very different—St. Benedict." One should emphasize that "very different": however critical of contemporary moral relativism, like Max Weber and Michael Polanyi, MacIntyre does not romanticize the past. In his nonnostalgic view he wants a "modern conception that could endorse the 'progressive' social movements." For him, the past is an active engagement with tradition that can stand outside the present, to be observed and gleaned in a critical fashion. Specifically, the virtues may be seen tested and proved in moments of historical and social stress. "An adequate sense of tradition manifests itself in a grasp of those future possibilities which the past has made available to the present."[46]

Hope, despair, humility, imagination, freedom, possibility, dialogue: the language of these writers aims at keeping open a space for human intention that hard determinism might close off. In their social agenda, the legacy of religious thought is either manifest or is filtered through ethical humanism. Whatever separates Guardini, Ellul, Winner, Mumford, Borgmann, and MacIntyre in their analysis of the crisis (MacIntyre scarcely alludes to technology), they agree that there can be self-mastery, reasoned face-to-face encounters, humane values, a sense of limit, and small communities of like-minded individuals seeking solutions.

Nicola Chiaromonte, the friend of Camus and Malraux and a member of the New York *politics* circle, portrays such a group in his memoir of exile. Having fled Italy in 1934 and Paris in 1940, he found intellectual solidarity among fellow refugees in Toulouse: "enough for company, enough to feel among friends, but not so many that one would feel, in spite of their numbers and in their midst, alone."[47] His ideal "heretics" must subscribe neither to technocratic materialism, collectivist fads, nor self-interest masquerading as humanitarianism, and "must detach themselves without shouting or riots, indeed, in silence and secrecy; not alone but in groups, in real 'societies' that will create as far as is possible a life that is independent and wise, not utopian or phalansterian." These individuals must work at their craft, whatever it may be, "according to the standards of the craft itself, standards that in themselves are the simplest and strictest of moral principles and, by their very nature, cut out deception and prevarication, charlatanism and the love of power and possession." This is not detachment from politics "in the real sense of the word"; it is a means of rebuilding the model.[48] Yet, in secular terms, the virtues of patience and hope may feel like a waiting game, with little spiritual satisfaction and much ongoing frustration.

Now, after having crossed the gulf separating us from the past, we look back to the opposite shore on which Guardini and Mumford stood a half century ago. Next, we turn away from this Lethean verge and project ourselves into the unfolding vistas of the new epoch: mall culture, suburbs into exurbs, less urbanity; greater longevity and health-care delivery systems; the full-house atmosphere of the modern world (in Ortega's phrase) with the fear of being lost in the mass balanced by a fear of not being lost in it; one environmental crisis after another; propaganda succeeding effortlessly because (as Ellul says) it "is being used for amusement"; the media and publicity everywhere affirming our cultural imperatives, and corporate logos instead of living symbols; world megaevents seen by two to three billion people; and big cities that draw vast tourist markets, and smaller cities competing for growth or survival by what they can offer in consumerism and regimented leisure. As Michael Storper points out, though consumer products multiplied between six and ten times between the 1970s and 1990s, the idea of having a choice is partly an illusion: the products multiply to counter the often-heard complaints of loss of diversity and localism. Yet the very demand for diversity requires even more technology to implement it, thereby ensuring uniformity. "Throughout the advanced economies, and in the biggest cities of the rest of the world, there has been a considerable diffusion of certain similar dimensions of mass culture: fast food, films, youth fashion, and shopping centers come immediately to mind. Whether we go to a jazz club in Greenwich Village or Paris, to a gay disco in San Francisco or London, or to a big rock concert or standard symphony-hall high-culture event anywhere, the venues resemble each other. . . . [T]here is a definite convergence in certain kinds of consumerism and corresponding ways of life for certain social classes."[49] Children online can choose among 150 outfits for the virtual Barbie doll. In a way all the choices are the same, because the persons looking at the screen are becoming the same.

In sum, the first computer generation is now marching away from the shore of that deep chasm, of which they are scarcely aware, and into a world for which they may be well prepared in one sense but terribly ill-prepared in another. What, then, are the implications of this seismic shift into technoculture for the humanities, traditionally seen as the guardians of the human?

The essays that follow concern the at once defined though questionable shape of the future. Although few doubt its general contours, few question its worthiness for humankind. The essays explore how technological values have trumped all others, to begin with, how they have decimated historical memory and infiltrated education to the point of limiting the humanities and undermining their force. Education is rich in the training of techniques and poor in the development of the self, of inwardness, *Innigkeit;* the emphasis falls on passing, not on learning. What too frequently results is an individual captivated by fads and technological gadgets, blunted in perception, and abandoned to the mercies of the media and other organs of culture. At the same time I contend that the humanities in many instances have withstood the worst aspects of technologization, and can continue to do so. Without humanistic training in Cicero's capacious definition—the study of "every liberal art and branch of learning," from the arts to the sciences—one will not possess the critical ability to expose and resist the gaping deficiencies of the present condition and hope to correct them.

The first essay, "The Future of the Humanities in a Technological Society," presents the main arguments upon which subsequent essays elaborate. Although I am not monocausal with regard to the determinants of the contemporary world, it astonishes how little attention is paid to the technological system in which we live and move and have our being. Then one realizes that the illusion of invisibility is one of the hallmarks of technology—first, to miniaturize, then to become as viewless as the air, precisely what Mumford meant by his metaphor of etherialization. In the hope of rendering visible the so-called invisible, the essay outlines the components of the technological system, examining their impact on cultural habits and the way humanists go about the business of criticism and teaching. In my definition, humanism stands for the autonomy of the individual, the library of world culture and the arts, and an effort to translate the import of our studies into the moral world through teaching and other civic action.

A new academic field called the "history of memory" analyzes the modes in which the individual and society structure their accounts of the past, from personal memoir to the chronicle of empire. Should there not also be a history of forgetting? Its modes are as various; its materials are even more extensive. The second essay, "The Great Forgetting," explores the atrophy of memory in post-modern society, from its aggressive demotion in the classroom to the more or less unconscious abandonment of the entire historical past. David Lowenthal makes a comparison in the title of his book *The Past Is a Foreign Country.* The metaphor is almost comforting, because a foreign country may be visited and holds out mystery and fascination. It is more accurate to say that the past is another planet.

"The Circle of Knowledge," the third essay, refers both to the ancient concept of the interrelation of all knowledge, represented by the sisterhood of the nine Muses, and also to the "cycle" or "circle" of studies that must be "rounded" before moving on to the next level. The curriculum of Cicero and Quintilian and the one refashioned in the Renaissance included the sciences among the subjects considered humanistic, that is, capable of educating the self, of bringing forth the self's essential humanity. After the circle was broken by the impact of modern science and specialization, the sciences, social sciences, and technical subjects assumed the predominant role in education. In the centuries following the Renaissance the debate concerned the role of science in the humanistic curriculum; at present the debate concerns the role of the humanities in a science, social science, and technical curriculum.

Though education should prepare a student for self-education and civic responsibility, today's education has become a means of technical adaptation to society; thus, it mirrors its society. Ideally, the humanistic education holds the mirror up to nature, that is, to human nature over vast spans of time, enabling students to study their own age from critical vantage points, both within and (as far as possible) without the age. To go without, it believes in the power of an informed imagination and the questioning eternal mind to transport the self into distant times, different cultures, and other lives. In the light of such thinkers as Descartes, Vico, Newman, Mill, Arnold, Irving Babbitt, and Lionel Trilling, the essay examines the ancient debate over the circle of knowledge and the goal of the well-rounded individual.

"Belief and Sincerity," the fourth essay, concerns the response by I. A. Richards and other humanists to the decline of faith beginning in the mid-nineteenth century. The essay could almost be called "Belief *in* Sincerity," because the radical Protestant inwardness of these secularizing thinkers led them to invest their own deep-sworn sincerity with transcendent value.[50] In terms of humanistic education in a global culture, Richards treats how readers translate the import of writers whose beliefs and systems of thought have passed into history or are otherwise different from their own. One should not, he argues, suppress the problem by concentrating solely on formalist aesthetics or historical reconstruction of a work of art. Neither is suspension of belief a solution— pretending, say, to believe for a moment in Dante's angels or Milton's devils, then to drop the belief. What great writers and artists communicate ought to be assimilated by and modify one's consciousness and to penetrate to the depths of one's being. A supreme virtue of the critic and reader, sincerity is the feeling that accompanies accepting and speaking truth, bringing with it a sense of inner coherence and stability.

The fifth essay, "The Tranquilized Poem," takes its title from Robert Lowell's epithet "the tranquilized Fifties"; I refer to the crisis of the New Criticism in that pivotal decade. As we know, the New Critics excluded history, political ideology, biography, psychology, and external intentions from the analysis of the work of art; they were concerned with formal integrity and ironic wholeness. They taught generations of students how to read closely and aesthetically, if narrowly. Yet the emphasis on the skillful deployment of techniques in interpretation bears witness to the very technological modalities that were sweeping across the culture, blinding the professors of literature to the intellectual determinants of their own methodologies. Meanwhile, the poem would not lie tranquilized. Ironies and ambiguities would not resolve into tight unities; rather, they multiplied. In the aftermath of New Criticism, methods arose attempting to cope with the teeming ambiguities and pluralistic options—myth and symbol criticism, the Geneva school or critics of consciousness, structuralism, deconstruction, new historicism, and so on.

The trial of inwardness is the subject of the sixth essay. If the nineteenth century witnessed the so-called disappearance of God, the twentieth century saw the disappearance of the self. Its origins were examined by Wylie Sypher in *Loss of the Self in Modern Literature and Art* as long ago as 1962. One may take evidence from sources other than the arts—from sociology, psychology, and cultural studies—and one may rely on one's own pulse. All seem to point to the same conclusion: the humanistic self, if not dead, has been squeezed into a corner and utterly degraded. In this view, the current generation has lost its bearings, and the media onslaught hardly leaves it time to catch its breath. Many contemporary writers and critics actually welcome the loss of the self, connected in turn to the larger theme of the death of the West, because the concepts of the individual and personal freedom are inextricably tied to the history of the West. Also, in a somewhat hubristic way, many loss-of-the-self and death-of-the-West theorists do not appear to recognize the extent to which they are like vacationing passengers on the technological train, along for the ride, but not the principal factors in causation. In my essay the focus falls upon studies in American autobiography that reveal a growing sense of the self in dissolution.

The subject of the final essay is Don DeLillo's critique of technologism, for which he draws on the resources of his ethnicity, his Italian Catholicism with its immanent particularism, and his humanistic education. *Underworld,* his longest and most ambitious novel, explores the vast expansion of technological society in the second half of the twentieth century. I focus upon a contrast between two settings: the glowing twilight of a bustling ethnic neighborhood in New York in his and his narrator's youth in the 1940s and early '50s and the gleaming milieu of technological utopianism represented by the sprawling suburbs of contemporary Phoenix, Arizona. Though DeLillo does not romanticize Little Italy, it nonetheless stands against technological society for its vibrant plenum of sensation, communal values, economy of consumption, and the presence of the sacred. The many forms of waste containment depicted in the novel, from landfills and nuclear dumps and garbage bags to computer banks and cyberspace, figure as the end result of consumerist materialism, massification, the decline of community, the loss of diversity and historical memory, and the flattening of culture. Far more than a reprise, *Underworld* is a summa of DeLillo's thought on technology. As such, a study of his work helps review the themes of this book as a whole and give them a fitting conclusion.

These essays are written defensively, at the end of the transitional era that Mill announced in 1831 and at a point when Western humanism has declined to the point of irrelevance. For the current generation the humanities mean a few requirements on the margins of discourse mostly pursued antihumanistically, and in another two or three generations they will be lost forever. Library lobbies and reading rooms increasingly resemble technology centers with café bars (all barriers being permeable); it is hard to persuade students that all their research cannot be done online. A translator of Horace contends that his poetry is "immensely trustworthy, level-headed, compatible with almost any society."[51] This is a fine original way of saying Horace is universal, *almost.* Students today do not find Horace or the classical world or any premodern civilization compatible. Products of a technical world, they are not accustomed to thinking beyond its boundaries and are not expected to do so. And they do not feel lacking.

The humanities cannot bear the burden of value, guidance, and encouragement once placed upon them, existing as they do increasingly within a vacuum and receiving little help from the cultural environment. Technique has taken charge, setting parameters, directing choices, serving as inspiration—technique that includes medical breakthroughs, but also entertainment, propaganda, advertising, and global lifestyles.

Never in the five hundred–year history of humanism in the academy has it been more disadvantageous to be a humanist—intellectually, socially, culturally. One can only hope that Western humanism and its "traditions of civility," which have survived from age to age, will meet this latest, severest challenge to their survival.[52] Humanistic studies have been at their most effective when they did not withdraw into themselves but addressed the major questions of their age, as happened in the Renaissance with Valla and More and in subsequent centuries with Vico, Sainte-Beuve, Arnold, Burckhardt, and Trilling. Under present conditions one asks for a humanism sufficiently integral in its effort to interpret and evaluate not only its own past but also non-Western pasts, confronting the issues of its times while striving to remain whole, coherent, and faithful to itself. Could such a humanism exist? This book will have achieved one of its goals if it gives the reader one big headache—the same headache I have when I think of these issues.

# I

# The Future of the Humanities in a Technological Society

Physicists talk of two of the fundamental forces of nature as the strong and the weak forces. I am going to borrow these terms in an entirely metaphorical way to name the two fundamental forces in which I live my life as a professor of literature. The strong force is technology, not to be understood as this or that machine, or this or that branch of machinery, but as the entire organized and interdependent ensemble dictating the technicization of everyday life, from politics, economics, and bureaucratic administration to the media, advertising, fast food, transportation, and tourism. The technical-experimental state of mind dominates contemporary education, from the earliest grades through the university. Technology includes the three thousand advertisements that the average American sees each day and the thirty-five buttons I press or dials I turn from the moment I wake up to the moment I walk into my first class, which is at only eight o'clock. Over the past century the technological system has gradually become so intrinsic and all-pervasive that, like the air we breathe or the purloined letter, it often seems invisible. Either we mystify its presence as in so many Hollywood spectaculars, or we tend to think of it as neutral, a mere means toward freely chosen ends and not an end in itself that uses persons as *its* means. Technology, the strong force, is the central feature of modern life.

The weak force is essentially what I like to teach, literature. These two forces intersect in my daily life in the English Department.

Let me compare a visit to our departmental office twenty years ago and today. Then, there were three secretaries and seven machines (typewriters, telephones, and a mimeograph). Now, there are three and a half secretaries and forty-two machines (word processors, copiers, printers, scanners, fax machines, cell phones, and a microwave)—so many machines that the office next door was taken over to house them. Then, there were faculty gossip and the occasional discussion of literature. Now, there is anxiety over the university's sudden adoption of Microsoft Word or the backward incompatibility of a new program. Then, with its casual clutter of books and some old dusty plants, the office looked like an academic department. Now, when it no longer looks like itself, it ironically looks like so much else: with its light gray tones and jam-packed machines it could be a dentist's office, or a pharmacy, or the suburban branch of a corporation. One morning it reminded me of the Mir Space Station, which by chance I had just seen on the news—technological society does not know the horror of mixing. At a time when the words *difference, diversity,* and *multiculturalism* are on everyone's lips, and when postmodernism proclaims the end of totalizing systems, technology has been grinding the world relentlessly together. These events, I believe, are not unrelated.

As we are hustled through the technological system like a badly handled package, we tend to blame the ill-functioning of the system rather than inquire into its nature.[1] In countless ways human rhythms have succumbed to technological rhythms, which we attempt to humanize by such words as *user-friendly,* though they have a habit of ambushing us, like computer viruses. Technology is above all a use; if you have it, you use it. A recent faculty memorandum came to me via a fax machine from the Senate Office. It had been beamed up to a satellite a couple of hundred miles above the earth and back again; yet the Senate Office and the English Department are next door to each other in the same building. I asked myself what earlier forms of communication did such technological overkill replace: the photocopier, the typewritten letter, the handwritten letter . . . the *handshake*? Face-to-face contact has been replaced again by face-to-machine contact.

People who raise the faintest objections to technology are branded as Luddites. This term of opprobrium only goes to prove how incredibly naive technology's defenders can be about the subject. *Luddite* implies that one can smash up a specific machine or burn down a factory and "go back" to a pretechnological world. Technology, however, can no longer be understood in terms of single machines; it is the system in which we live and move and have our being. There is no question of "going back," but whether we have any control over how we go forward. I do not want to evoke pastoral nostalgia or to dream of a lost wholeness: those withered departmental plants! Such indulgence may be compared to reading old travelogues about a lovely country whose face has been scored by modernity. Yet it may be instructive to trace the recent histories of these strong and weak forces, technology and literature, and their convergence in the present moment, though *convergence* may suggest an equality of opportunity that they do not possess. At a time when the humanities have suffered greatly at the hands of technological society, they are more important to our social and ethical life than ever before in human history.

Today the humanities are under attack from many quarters. Far more students take courses in behavioral psychology to learn about interpersonal relations than in Shakespeare or the nineteenth-century novel. A report in the *New York Times* (October 9, 1996) chronicles the drop in foreign language majors from 1990 to 1995: Latin declined by 8 percent, Italian by 12, French by 25, and German by 28. Philosophy, English, and religious studies have declined steadily since the 1970s. It is sometimes said that the humanities will survive only as a plaything of technocrats or a mere adornment to life. At best they will be the private delight of the aesthete, the antiquarian, or the bibliophile.

Any assessment of the humanities in technological society should refer, if only briefly, to their foundations, to their concepts of freedom and the individual, *civitas* and *humanitas,* and the civilizing mission they have performed during their long history: in Eugenio Garin's words, "the formation of a truly human consciousness, open in every direction, through the historical and critical understanding of the cultural tradition."[2] From Isocrates, Cicero, and Quintilian to Guarino da Verona, Montaigne, and Matthew Arnold, the humanities have always helped frame certain choices: what kind of student are we producing, what type of mind, what configuration of ideals, what practical skills, what standard of conduct? In short, by whom in the future does society wish to be represented? The goal was to educate a person who knows not only many things but also how to rank them, who has the spark of wisdom to know where to look again for wisdom.

In the later nineteenth century, when science and technology were making their demands on the curriculum, Arnold correctly perceived that humanistic values had been undermined neither by the widening of the humanities to include modern languages nor even by nineteenth-century science. The physical sciences did not claim to address the subjects that concerned the humanities, and the differences between them could be resolved by applying, under the eye of the humanities, scientific discoveries to the improvement of life. Arnold conceded that the humanities would have to yield their "leading place" in education, though he also believed that they would find it again, that forces in human nature itself were working for them. He urged humanists to carry on "the disinterested pursuit of perfection," to construct a global culture founded upon the best that has been thought and said throughout history, to evaluate the results of science on the basis of their benefit to human needs and freedom, and to nourish the sense of beauty.

But Arnold was wrong in his prediction.[3] Not only have the humanities failed to regain their high status in education, but they have slipped even further behind. What Arnold could not have known was that a whole new body of academic disciplines, the social sciences, would soon emerge to fight for their own place in the curriculum and assert their right to relate the conclusions of the physical sciences, as well as their own theories and discoveries, to human needs in the modern world. The social sciences had encroached upon the traditional sphere of the humanities, interrogating the very same subjects and issues, claiming that they too could teach students how to lead an ethical, beneficial, and self-fulfilled life. Sociology examined the individual's relation to the community, once primarily a humanistic question. Psychology and psychoanalysis laid claim to the study of the inner life, another humanistic province. In a similar fashion, the new disciplines of political science, economics, and anthropology proposed to solve problems that had been the sovereign domain of the humanities. Furthermore, Arnold could not have predicted the transformative power of technology. Even Max Weber in the next generation, analyzing the "iron cage" of rationalized modernity, did not gauge the extent to which rationalization would involve the technicization of life.[4]

Throughout the twentieth century the debate over the role of the humanities has waxed and waned. High points include the reforms at Columbia and the University of Chicago in the 1920s and 1930s and those at Harvard after the Second World War and in the 1970s. With every new plan, the humanities yielded more ground. In the past decade or so the debate has been renewed with bitterness and desperation. Allan Bloom's *Closing of the American Mind,* E. D. Hirsch's *Cultural Illiteracy,* Robert Proctor's *Education's Great Amnesia,* Richard Gambino's *Racing with Catastrophe,* John R. Searle's *Is There a Crisis in American Higher Education?*—the titles invoke impending doom. "A fairly sizable number of professors in literature departments have lost interest in the study of literature as it has been traditionally construed," observes Searle. "My impression of neurobiology conferences is that the participants are deeply committed to neurobiological research. . . . [M]y guess is that many of the participants at the MLA have lost interest in doing what they are officially supposed to be doing."[5] Some literature professors would prefer that core humanities requirements, a shadow of their former selves anyway, be phased out, though without them their departments would shrink drastically, suffering the fate of classical studies three or four generations ago.

Rather than analyzing the decline of the humanities narrowly in terms of turf battles among disciplines, one ought to situate it within the larger social and historical panorama. Astonishingly, the debate proceeds with scant reference to the massive presence and continuing expansion of the technological system. Despite the postmodern belief in the continuousness between academe and the "real world," vestiges of the ivory-tower mentality may have induced us to think we are protected from the system, at least from its worst excesses. Nonetheless, the nature and impact of technology have been closely examined by such writers as Lewis Mumford and Jacques Ellul, Roderick Seidenberg, Gilbert Simondon, and Siegfried Gideon, not to mention Heidegger and Marcuse. They and others have tried to comprehend the unparalleled shift in adaptive behavior that has happened within the space of a hundred-odd years, from industrial to technological society.

Students of technology may be placed within two broad groupings: instrumentalists and substantivists. Instrumentalists believe that technologies are single tools that lie ready to hand as in a toolbox and that tools are neutral or value-free means to chosen ends. Typically, instrumentalists speak of technologies rather than technology, thinking they can pick and choose among options while keeping their hands on the reins of power. For them, technology is indifferent to politics.[6] A car is a car and a computer is a computer in any social or political context, and top-down management, bureaucratic expertise, and quality control are the same everywhere. In the instrumentalist view, technology differs from law and religion, "which cannot be readily transferred to new social contexts because they are so intertwined with other aspects of the societies in which they originate."[7]

By contrast, the substantivists, a minority that includes such figures as Ellul and the later Mumford, argue that technology is a monolithic phenomenon vastly greater than the sum of its parts. For Heidegger, human beings are mere "standing reserves," raw materials to serve the system. Far from being neutral, technology has become the *substance* informing more and more of life, like an implacable bureaucracy at the core of things that directs decisions at every turn. Thus, choosing technology entails "unwitting cultural choices": where instrumentalists might defend fast food as the most efficient way of getting calories, saving time, and avoiding social complexities, substantivists would recall the ritualistic aspects of the dinner hour, lament the breakdown of the family, and denounce the coarsening of taste.[8] They would decry the fact that French children prefer what they affectionately call the "MacDo" to French cuisine.

The technological paradigm of Jacques Ellul is admittedly extreme, but its very extremism focuses the issues in their clearest light.[9] According to Ellul, modern technology began with the machine, abstracted principles from it, then outstripped it, became independent, and finally turned itself into a political, economic, and social reality. For the essential concept and its all-embracing referent, Ellul uses the term *technique (la technique)*, defined as "the *totality of methods rationally arrived at and having absolute efficiency* (for a given stage of development) in *every* field of human activity."[10] Technique has five major features. The "prime characteristic"—indeed, the "supreme imperative"—is the principle of least effort or efficient ordering.[11] This includes rationalization, measurement, standardization (for instance, of the production process), linearity, segmentation, simplification, minimum waste, and speed. Human values are filtered out except where they facilitate the technical means that are omnipotent and often "unfriendly," thereby requiring the user-friendly convention. No real choice exists among technical methods: after all the necessary calculations are factored, the decision is obvious because technique dictates the *one best means* or least effort.[12] Rival technology signifies that the principle has yet to make its latest judgment on a case, which will not be final because improvements and breakthroughs are always in the offing.[13] If mistakes occur, technique intervenes to remove the defect and a new pathway is opened.

A second feature of technology is *self-augmentation:* machines keep making more and more machines. "Everything occurs *as if* the technological system were growing by an internal, intrinsic force, without *decisive* human intervention."[14] Progress is irreversible and unceasing, and the progression is geometric as opposed to arithmetic. A breakthrough in one field brings solutions on all sides, like the internal combustion engine, the laser, or the computer. "These solutions in turn create even more problems which in turn demand ever more technical solutions."[15] Paratechnologies quickly develop in response.[16]

A third characteristic of technology is *monism.* The parts of the system are united in one another and recombine easily because they do not vary in their essentials. Technique is acultural, ahistorical, ageographical; there is no Eastern or Western technology. We live inside a "transnational and *multi*-polar, interdependent, and highly interactive, capitalist economic *world order.*"[17] Monism imposes the good with the bad uses of technique. At the point when atomic energy had been harnessed, it was bound to be used for a bomb. Information-gathering services can be applied to scholarship or surveillance. "Technique never observes the distinction between moral and immoral use. It tends, on the contrary, to create a completely independent technical morality."[18] Robert Merton labels it the morality of "know-how": "Technique transforms ends into means. What had been prized in its own right now becomes worthwhile only if it helps achieve something else. And, conversely, technique turns means into ends. 'Know-how' takes on an ultimate value."[19] Further, monism entails linkage: techniques of communication combine with techniques of administration and militarism—to produce propaganda, which becomes a new technique that can be applied elsewhere, as in advertising.

Fourth, technique implies *universalism.* It grows on all sides, across the planet, and into space, and everyone wants it, and more and more of it, from the richest to the poorest peoples, from the capitalist nations to the socialist nations, from democracies to totalitarian regimes.[20] Once a part, now it is the envelope of the whole. Moreover, one can never do with just a little technology. A commitment to some of it inevitably brings in the rest: like a "universal language," it "shapes the total way of life."[21] In September 1997 China tried to justify its plan to privatize major industries by calling it "socialism with Chinese characteristics."[22] No one was taken in by such propaganda. Ideology is mere window dressing and tends to interfere with the smooth functioning of a worldwide system. Morning business news in the West begins with reports on the closing of the Hong Kong market. Technique subdues nature, a good example being the tentacular suburb that invades the environment and subjugates it. One is hard-pressed to think of a single aspect of human activity that has not been subjected to "a reflection of technological orientation": sports, entertainment, "speeded tests," food, law enforcement, sex, personal relations, religion—*how-to* books of myriad number.[23] The technological phenomenon crosses class lines, universalizes taste, and creates a global civilization. Megaevents such as the Olympic Games, the World Cup soccer championship, and Princess Diana's funeral, impossible without technology, are watched by people numbering more than a billion—and this is only the beginning.

*Autonomy,* the fifth characteristic of the paradigm, is the most controversial element because it is shadowed by fears that "somehow technology has gotten out of control and follows its own course, independent of human direction."[24] Technology has now reached the point where it is a law unto itself, "depends only on itself," and "maps its own route." Fifty years ago one might have spoken of the interdependence of technology and nature; now technology has the upper hand. In fact, it takes more technology to save nature from technology, and so its power spreads.[25] In a similar fashion, we speak of saving ourselves from governmental centralization by devolution toward the peripheries. Yet to enact this process and keep it functioning requires more technique, so that the system grows apace. "Inside the technical circle, the choice among methods, mechanism, organizations, and formulas is carried out automatically."[26] Individuals still play a role, they invent the various tools, they make new bureaucratic protocols, and so on, but what counts is the "anonymous accretion of conditions for the leap ahead." Generally speaking, only "minimal human intervention" is needed to create or improve something; "literally anyone can do the job, provided he is trained to it" (a point that would be supported by Heisenberg). The entire system should be understood as an "'organism' tending towards closure and self-determination." Soon supercomputers will alone be able to create programs for other supercomputers. The main issue is that, in its evolution toward an advanced state, technology tends more and more to dominate humanity itself. "Man," sums up Ellul, "is reduced to the level of a catalyst."[27] The sense of helplessness can be overwhelming.

No one doubts that technology saves lives and cuts down on drudgery, though not on work. The real moral problem of the system is that everything is situated in relation to it so that ultimately all choices become technological ones. "Technological advance will move faster and faster and can never be stopped," maintains Heidegger. "In all areas of his existence, man will be encircled ever more tightly by the forces of technology. These forces, which everywhere and every minute claim, enchain, drag along, press and impose upon man under the form of some technical contrivance or other—these forces . . . have moved long since beyond his will and have outgrown his capacity for decision."[28] Lewis Mumford and René Dubos have arrived at similar conclusions.

Left to itself, technology so thoroughly subordinates human ends to technical means that those ends are lost. Tools were formerly molded by the rhythms of the body, which conferred the primacy of the human over the artificial. When the tool was replaced by the clock, comments Franco Piperno, the human body had "the bewildering experience of being synchronized with the rhythm of the machine; the time of the machine builds a nest in the body of the worker—think for instance of Charlie Chaplin's film *Modern Times.* The advent of the computer, finally, introduces a time that escapes the very possibility of experience." In computer time a second is a "gigantic dilation" of the present; concepts of time and memory are transformed on mathematical lines. We no longer become caricatures of ourselves, as in Chaplin; we cease resembling ourselves. "The central aim of information knowledge is not the completeness and coherence of facts and judgments on the world, but rather the optimization of procedures, be they for decisions, diagnosis, management, or planning. Information knowledge incessantly transforms procedures so that the action may be more effective and, above all, faster."[29] Other graphic symptoms of this apparently unstoppable growth of technology are the global ecological crisis, intellectual devastation by the media and advertisement, bureaucratism, the strangulating and labyrinthine transportation system, architectural gigantism, and what Mumford calls "the suppression of personal, communal, and regional individuality by a kind of tasteless, homogenized universalism."[30]

One of the most effective ways that technique communicates is by images. Marshall McLuhan, Guy Debord, and Neil Postman have long since informed on our spectacle-oriented, audiovisual culture.[31] An avalanche of images from morning to night, via television, film, computer, and the rest of the mass media, have smothered the humanities, not to mention literary culture. Voracious consumers of images, we use them even where they are not strictly necessary. We blame the growth of visual culture for the surfeit of classroom miseries as students struggle to arrive at the meaning of not especially cryptic poems. But we fail to connect this failure with the underlying technological imperatives that we embrace elsewhere. What goes unexamined is how, at a deeper level, technology and visual culture share a common basis, have evolved alongside each other, and have drastically shrunk the domain of literary language. "Contemporary culture in its now global communications context," asserts Don Ihde, "is increasingly embodied through its instrumentarium . . . image technologies."[32]

To begin with, the continuous parade of images would be impossible without technology; this alone accounts for the nonstop invasion and multiplication of images within every corner of daily life. Like technology, images—still or moving, speaking images—operate on the principle of least effort. Useful, fast, and efficient, they enable us to grasp the total gist of something at a glance: "sight saves us the trouble of thinking and having to remember." Because of their association with vision, images pack a high degree of realism, currentness, and objectivity, even when on other grounds we are convinced of their falsehood (for example, in advertising). Images are "accepted as reality and identified with it," says Ellul. "We think we are reflecting on facts, but they are only representations."[33] Critical responses to Gulf War news broadcasts revealed "the simultaneous *immediate awareness of the viewers that the news was being 'cooked' and yet its planned effect was accepted and even celebrated.*" Image-mediated sight frames and detaches an object, diminishes depth, alters contrast; it is nonisomorphic with objects ("virtual reality" is more virtual than real), and it is constructive (time reversals, flashbacks, special effects, and discontinuities).[34] We are hurried along by the multiplicity of images and ride on their gleaming surfaces; like technology, they have no insides, no interiority. Images move us from stimulus to response in a flash, programmatically, without the discourse of reason, involving "a kind of direct communication of knowledge, as if it did not pass through the brain," like pressing a button or buying a product ("impulse buying").[35]

Instead of reading a book, children and teenagers prefer to play video games because it is easier, more immediate, "more fun": the whole mind does not have to work as hard to think up and imagine forth—the principle of least effort. Video games, so full of rules and operative procedures, and so relatively contentless, adapt the young not only to the physical apparatus but also to the formalisms and methods of technological society (one game rule book runs to forty pages). It is said that current college students are the Nintendo generation, having grown up with the computer as entertainment. The computer's real triumph arrives with the next generation, for whom the computer is primarily a "learning *tool*" and an "extension of the faculties," though what has happened is an introjection of the principles of technique into young minds and narrowed sensibilities.

Let it be granted that images can convey certain forms of knowledge quickly and easily—chiefly, scientific knowledge, which is today the model of knowledge. Ellul concedes that in some fields a picture *is* worth a thousand words; science and social science require sketches and diagrams since many of their propositions cannot be expressed in words. The issue is the dominance of image-based culture as a whole, not only the deluge of images but their quality as well: basic, ideographic, exaggerated, coarse by the standards of high art. Think of the computer-created Disney feature films. The content of these simplified cartoon images was determined by the forms of technology—efficiency, speed, economy, segmentation, conformity, and the like. Compare the industrial colors and standardized faces of these cartoon persons or animals with the real thing or, say, with an engraving of a rabbit by Albrecht Dürer. A rabbit by Dürer is beautiful and has much in common with a real rabbit. Yet people prefer a Disney rabbit to a Dürer rabbit or the real thing. Disney World in Orlando is the single most touristed spot on the globe, with more than thirty million visitors a year. All of Italy with its thirty splendid cities has only twenty-four million visitors a year.[36]

Currently, one of the more popular tourist spots in France is Cluny, not the real abbey of Cluny, which was destroyed in the early nineteenth century; rather, a virtual reconstruction of it viewable in a museum adjoining the original grounds. If people were genuinely interested in the history of Cluny or the monks of the Middle Ages, they could have read half a dozen books in half the time it took them to get there. They could have gone to see a *real* abbey. Instead, they chose to "experience" a visual stunt. As one advocate remarks on this new direction in entertainment:

> [T]he "virtuality" machine involves a full immersion in computerized programs that will provide contact in real time (i.e. the answers of the operator will interact with the human "proprioceptor system"). . . . The machine, which for all intents and purposes is a journey in itself, offers a wide range of getaway places and tourist settings. This type of anticipatory experience with its plausible interactive relationship could reinforce the *déjà vu* feeling even further and perhaps condition the psychology of perception in a way which one cannot yet foresee.[37]

One may recall the decadent Des Esseintes in Huysman's *À rebours:* to save himself the trouble of traveling to London, he simulates the feelings of being there, at a railway pub, listening to a few Englishmen, on a drizzly day, in Paris.

Ihde argues that image technologies overcome the conflict between high and popular cultures, delivering a "pluriculture" or "multiple otherness." News broadcasts comprise bits and pieces of information, countries, products; MTV transmits a "multicultural mix of musics, fashions, ethnic traditions, human races." The nonlinear, jumpy, novel content resembles the form, its technique; this has become the model for many kinds of programming. "Ordinary space-time is here technologically deconstructed and reconstructed in a *bricolage* image of space-time." The model both mirrors current experience and promotes it everywhere. "One may pick and choose culture fragments, multiply choices, and in the process reflectively find one's own standards often provincial or arbitrary." Given the superficiality of much programming, these choices are more often illusory than real. The image technologies, concludes Ihde, diffuse a relativizing spirit that is *"non-neutrally acidic to all traditional cultures."*[38] Because we live less and less in ordinary space-time and more and more in technologically mediated space-time, we may discern the lineaments of a wholly new type, the young man or woman of our time.

More than simply fabricating the hyperreal environment, technology constructs the technicized individuals that navigate through it. Here its image investment pays off enormously: a functional, simplified imagery, as on a computer screen, is the one best means to adapt people to the efficient, streamlined technological environment, which needs visually oriented people to expand and reticulate, if only for the sheer amount of information to be processed and disseminated. Technicization begins in earliest childhood (hence the power of Disney and the like) and then permeates all levels of the educational system. First, the goal was a television in every classroom; now it is a computer on every desk. Pictures in textbooks used to be ornamental and subservient to the content; "now the text has become the explanation of the images." Who could say that students are learning more? In current guidebooks, pictures and cutaways have seized the lion's share of the page. One series (significantly titled *Eye*witness) announces itself, "The Guides That Show You What Others Only Tell You" (one glossy cutaway glides down the Grand Canal in Venice). The audio-visual method, Deweyesque learning-as-doing, the denigration of memory as mere rote—all have set a premium on speaking a foreign language rather than reading it, though for most people speaking the language will be exceedingly rare, and meanwhile sacrificed is a reading of Leopardi, Baudelaire, and Rilke. What one receives from school is minimal by comparison to captivating home video and the computer screen. Without realizing it, those who have grown up in a technological society "have a need to live through images." Ellul underscores the evenness of the exchange: "Technique requires visually oriented people. And people living in a technical milieu require that everything be visualized."[39] In this way the system makes the very product it feeds upon.

The apotheosis of image technology is the Hollywood blockbuster. Everyone agrees that these films are aesthetically negligible and trivialize reality. Yet their producers and purveyors lavish immense sums on them. What takes place in this display of imagistic wizardry is a reinforcement of the audience to the principles of technique. These films are hymns to technique, representing built-in propaganda for the technological system. Who needs propaganda when one has Hollywood? In a stunning example of technological universalism, Hollywood has edged out all other national film industries. Japanese, Italian, and French cinema, which had once mounted an effective opposition, have succumbed. The independent filmmaker has all but lost the battle of independence.

What are some of the consequences of visual culture? In "Bowling Alone" and "The Strange Disappearance of Civic America" Robert D. Putnam examines the decline of civicness or social trust from the "long civic generation" born between 1910 and 1940 to the "post-civic" generations of baby boomers and after. Over the past thirty years, he notes, membership in voluntary organizations has fallen by a quarter to a half: from churches, community clubs, and labor unions (down 65 percent since 1954) to literary discussion groups, PTAs, the Red Cross, and bowling leagues. Newspaper home circulation has dropped by one-half from its peak in 1947. Though Putnam concedes that the downward trend is not monocausal, nonetheless one cause stands out: "the culprit is television." The long civic generation, which grew up without it, belongs to twice as many associations as the postwar generations, which grew up with it. Today, by conservative estimates, the average American watches television three hours a day, which amounts to about 40 percent of leisure time. Most homes by the late 1980s had more than one set, which means more private viewing. We have gone from being joiners to being viewers. Heavy readers tend to be joiners, whereas "heavy viewers are more likely to be loners."[40] Heavy television watching tends to make people overestimate crime rates and to sharpen skepticism regarding the benevolence of other people; it quite possibly increases aggressiveness in young people and lowers scholastic achievement. It certainly fascinates mainstream America with its sordid display of scandal and corruption—moral, social, political, religious.[41] Putnam cites Neil Postman's conclusion relating television and passivity.

In *Technologies without Boundaries,* Ithiel de Sola Pool predicts that the communications revolution will continue to fractionate and privatize American culture. "A society in which it becomes easy for every small group to indulge its tastes will have more difficulty mobilizing unity. A society where mass publishing has to compete with specialized information resources will have more trouble establishing coherence of intellectual debate." At the same time Pool, who defines himself as a "soft technological determinist," also thinks that

technology "will promote individualism." On the contrary, the evidence points
to the dwindling of autonomous selfhood under the superficial signs of privatism and lifestyles—styles bought and discarded like ready-made fashions.
In the tradition of William Morris and Patrick Geddes, Mumford argues that
"technological civilization destroys the individual's capacity to take part in the
craft of fabricating his world."[42]

Most significantly, the power of technology and the omnipresence of the
image have resulted in the subservience and devaluation of language. This does
not mean its absence—on the contrary, we are drowning in a sea of words.
Instead, technology establishes simple, unambiguous, utilitarian language as
its literary standard; this kind of language wins its way by excluding all or
nearly all but the referential and directional functions of words. Even the emotive or expressive function (prominent in advertisements) now takes a backseat, though its imagistic content is noisier and more importunate, like a
backseat driver. Language neutralized as information dominates the "knowledge culture." Thomas Sprat, the seventeenth-century historian of the Royal
Society, pleaded on behalf of a "close, naked" style of speech and writing,
"bringing all things as near the Mathematical plainness, as they can." His hope
is being realized by the computer: "for technique all language is algebraic"
(Philippe Roqueplo), and "technique's ambition is to make the whole world algebraic" (Marcel Jousse).[43] Diction, tone, figures of speech, metaphor, subtler
forms of syntax, connotation and etymology, sound and rhythm, all the arts of
language developed over the centuries to express intricate thought and emotional depth, get ironed out and suppressed. Technological society has no need
for them, or finds such literary strategies to be adversarial. Complex literary
language penetrates the imagistic surfaces, probes into the furthest recesses of
mind and feeling, breaks the force of habit, and draws patterns of coherence in
order to deepen and empower a self-determining, continuously developing
selfhood. Rightly to understand this language, one often needs to seek out its
origins on biographical, social, and historical grounds, for that is what gave
birth to it. So understood, literary language connects us to the past—personal,
communal, and historical. It may contain unbidden, unfathomable mysteries,
what Wordsworth meant by the word *invisible* in describing the secret inter-
change of mind and nature, what Coleridge meant by the word *magical* in portraying the imagination.

The decline in language studies affects much more than the reading of literature. Has anyone noticed how difficult it is to convince people by a solid argument, an argument constructed on the logic and rhetoric of forensic discourse?
Few people can interpret it, appreciate it, and hence listen to it. Such language
is becoming pointless.

When Kant set forth his concept of aesthetic autonomy as freedom from immediate utility and external controls, he was proposing a model for the autonomous self. A knowledge of complex literary language has traditionally been one of the liberating influences for the self, and so has been at the heart of the humanities. Present students have grown up on the use of formulaic computer language that refers generally to the reality of the technological environment, which seems complete in itself. The average video game does not have much language, and what little there is hardly varies from box-top directions. "Lack of interest in literature and the condemnation of philosophy reflect the inability of these disciplines to convert themselves into diagrams."[44] One should not wonder at students' turning away from complex language, which requires much more effort to decode and which must often seem utterly opaque compared to the luster of an image. Immediacy, currency, and entertainment define the image. By contrast, literary language calls for both an analytic rigor and a disciplined knowledge not only of aesthetic strategies and literary tradition but of the other humanities, history, and often the social and natural sciences as well. All this requires memory, one of the great reservoirs of selfhood.[45]

Although perhaps it cannot be proved, some hidden connection exists between the ahistoricism of the technological system and the utter lack of interest in memory as an educational value. Memory has become old-fashioned. But without the experience of literary language and the power of memory to retain it, interiority loses one of its best means of development. If we consider a child's or a student's potential, one could say that interiority shrinks before the computer, or, the same thing, it becomes procedural, formalistic, and conformist, a mirror of technique. Technology has no interiority; its windows are surfaces.

Within my own teaching career I have observed the English of Shakespeare becoming a foreign language to my students. Given all the publicity about word processors in the teaching of introductory writing courses, who would dare say that students write better today than they did twenty years ago? With all the means and resources they now have "at their fingertips," can they connect information and build upon it so that they can converse better? On the devaluation of language through its subordination to computer needs, Ellul states: "The conversation with a computer is not limited to that situation; it becomes the model for all conversation. . . . This covers an enormous proportion of language use, since it involves all sorts of technicians: administrators, jurists, economists, physicists, chemists, marketing experts, doctors, engineers, psychologists, publicity experts, film makers, programmers, etc. They represent nearly the totality of language use."[46]

One publisher recently announced the cancellation of 175 contracts for novels and paid off the writers. The publisher could not afford to bring out so many books on account of the competition, not from other publishers but from the visual media, whose products were easier and more marketable. The principle of least effort had inserted itself. Elvis Presley's Graceland in Nashville has seven hundred thousand visitors a year, charging nine dollars a head, whereas the White House has only a million, charging nothing. It takes infinitely less historical understanding to appreciate Graceland than it does the White House. Once again, the principle of least effort.

In 1930 C. K. Ogden proposed his Basic English as an international second language. This was based on 850 key words and simple grammatical patterns designed to give foreigners quick access to everything touched by English. His colleague I. A. Richards noted the parallels between this simplified language and the leveling nature of the media, which could therefore be employed to introduce such language as a first step toward literacy or second-language training (but *not* as a replacement of Standard English). Though it was a laudable goal, Richards was swimming in dangerous waters. In 1942 he went to the Disney Studios to learn how to make stick-figure drawings of people and things. Thus began his multivolume *Language through Pictures* in an expanded version of Basic English; the series eventually went into record, tape, television, and computer, easily adapting itself to the evolving media. He put seven other languages into the same diagrammatic patterns. The abstract generality of the original linguistic model permitted it, and all cultural specifics were plowed under. Although Basic offered an ideal of technological efficiency—it was supposedly quick and easy to learn—it tended to reduce language from a complex instrument of intellectual analysis into a collection of purely functional or operational phrases.[47]

Basic English was part of the global spread of English, an event that one must link to the technological principle of the one best means or least effort. English was the first language of telecommunications, aviation, modern science, and international business. When computers needed a kind of algebraic language to communicate on the information superhighways, it turned to something that resembled Basic English. What other language could a machine understand?[48] Just as technology in the environment has led to the reduction of species diversity, so too the technological system is reducing the overall number of languages. By the year 2050, in some estimates, the world will be getting on with ten languages, only four main ones.[49]

To mention Richards is to bring up the acknowledged founder of New Criticism, the first of the grand techniques that seized the academic high ground of literary studies after 1945. Paraphrasing Le Corbusier's "a house is a machine to think with," Richards said "a book is a machine to think with." The

New Critics of the 1940s and 1950s attempted to protect the verbal artifact from the pressures of historical necessity and mere utility, yet their method was a direct reflection of those pressures. New Criticism was a kind of synecdochic condensation of the technological system in its antihistoricism; its objective neutrality and treatment of the poem as a clinical specimen; its quasi-scientific emphasis on specialization and method together with a meager, mostly inconsequential theorizing; its myths of synthesis and entelechy; its metaphors for organization. The New Critics fostered a straightforward, roll-up-your-sleeves approach to criticism that valued technocratic expertise, teamwork, bureaucratized efficiency, and anonymity (though a few top stars always get the prizes). "Criticism, Inc." was John Crowe Ransom's dry reference to the enterprise of which he was a principal partner. However, the New Critics ended in contradiction. On the one hand, they posited Kantian aesthetic non-purposiveness and a residual concept of the integrated subject; on the other, they held to a technocratic ideal of instrumental purposiveness, objectivity, efficiency, and practice. Their very emphasis on ambiguity tended to break up the ideal of wholeness and mirrored as in shivering glass that "loss of the self," to borrow Wylie Sypher's phrase, in countless procedures and mechanical exercises. The expansion of intellectual and imaginative freedom won by irony and ambiguity lapses into a free fall of proliferating meanings. The loss of the self may have as much to do with the anonymity of the corporation man and the overadministered society than with the doctrine of austere impersonality in high modernism.

There is hardly a better example of technological monism than the conjunction of aims in post–World War II American politics, in the academy following its shake-up and the rapid expansion of colleges and universities, and in the New Criticism. In 1945 a Harvard committee on educational reform published *General Education in a Free Society,* which exerted a potent influence on American education. Their thinking had been shaped by issues such as "'why we fight,'" the "definition of democracy in a world of totalitarianism," the "need to provide a 'common learning' for all Americans as a foundation of national unity," and the "effort to fortify the heritage of Western civilization."[50] Richards, a member of the committee, was obviously the person who wrote the sections recommending the New Critical "close study of well-written paragraphs and poems" instead of "more knowledge about the past"; who dared suggest making "versions of great works cleared of unnecessary and unrewarding obstacles," decontextualizing to make them "more accessible to general readers"; and who urged the "fullest understanding of the work read rather than of men or periods represented, craftsmanship evinced, historic or literary developments shown, or anything else."[51] In this way literature could be taught "efficiently" to a "new, mass student body" which lacked a "common cultural background" ("and not just the student body but the new professors").[52]

The major theoretical movements that succeeded New Criticism—each with its own authorities, special problems, methods (especially methods!), literary terms, common texts, and objectives—shared the same fundamental interest in technique over content, while abandoning the last vestiges of the humanistic concept of the self. The offspring of the New Critics became the first generation of the so-called critics as theorists. How did they carry out the principles of technique and earn Ellul's rebuke for the *humiliation of the word*? First, the synchronic aspect of language was favored over the diachronic. Again, history was demoted (though it is hard to think how much lower history could sink), but this, too, registers the impact of the technological system, which over the course of the past century has fostered the grand forgetting of history. Like the New Critics, the poststructuralists exhibited, in Frank Lentricchia's words, a "tendency to dissolve literary history into a repetitious synchronic rhetoric of the *aporia*."[53] Second, language was divided between signifier and signified, with the signifier being vastly preferred on account of its greater observability and controllability—more technical values—compared with the historical, social, religious, cultural, and biographical signifieds. Moreover, the heavy stress on method predetermined the field of vision and even the results. As with technique, there was a loss of ends, a concentration on means. Such proceduralism had typified New Criticism, when all the moves were marked in advance, on behalf of irony and ambiguity; afterward, the terms were indeterminacy, difference, undecidability, *mise-en-abîme*, and so forth. Theorists also attacked language on account of its ability to exert quasi-magical power through, say, some outdated "great narrative," metaphysical idealism, a ruling class, religion, or high culture.[54] In every instance, literary language bore the brunt of the assault.

One might reply that to be an instrument of hegemony is but one of the many uses of language. It is closest to propaganda. With regard to technique and the principle of least effort, propagandists present one (and only one) big, simple thing at a time, in the simplest language, repeated again and again, until it seems like a fact of life. However, if literary language has served as an instrument of hegemony, ancient tyrants and twentieth-century dictators must have found it an extremely inefficient one. Such language has too much complexity, historical range, and inner resistance to be effective as propaganda. Jacob Burckhardt chose his words carefully when, in 1889, he warned that the "*terrible simplifiers . . .* are going to descend upon poor old Europe" in the coming era.[55] For Solzhenitsyn, language is what finds the cracks within the system.[56]

In the midst of the precipitous decline of the humanities, perhaps the most distressing fact is that those entrusted to their defense have unwittingly partic-ipated in their dismemberment. If by the laws of nature a force gives rise to a counterforce, the force must first be recognized as such. Postmodern critics ignore technological universalism and celebrate the play of difference—some-times differences so minimal that they make no difference or are indifferent—without noticing that real difference, which is individuality, is being eroded. The technological system permits such minor liberties as the floating signifier or verbal play as things of small consequence compared to itself. Nor are post-modernist claims to have robbed myths and ideologies of their power anything but self-flattering dreams; Marxism and Freudianism, to name two, collapsed from lack of empirical evidence over the long term. Yet one should not be amazed that intellectuals have been captured and controlled by the very fash-ionable instruments that they believe they are wielding so freely. Although they protest against "history" or "traditional" culture on the grounds of a political or cultural agenda, the real reason behind their protest is that they have be-come completely technicized. "Americans have been commonly instructed since the 1930s that education and intellectual analysis detect propaganda and immunize the citizenry against it," declares Michael R. Real. "Instead, Ellul sees education as a necessary precondition for propaganda and the intellectual as the most propagandized member of society because of his access to over-whelming amounts of information, his need to have an opinion on every sub-ject, and the conviction 'of his own superiority.' "[57] In *Software for the Self,* Anthony Smith refers to academics as the "pioneers" of the Internet.

Some critics are optimistic about the future of technology and culture. Middle-of-the-roaders as well as wholehearted proponents want to adapt tech-nology to the arts and education. Anthony Smith dreams of the combined re-sults of video on demand and virtual reality: "If you attempt to link these two tendencies—the public spectacle and the capacity for individual choice—you arrive at a medium of dial-up reality: individuals or small groups using inter-active techniques to gain access to an intangible but wholly enthralling experi-ence, giving the solitary individual the feeling of being present at a spectacle in the illusory company of a large number of others." It is difficult to see how such amusements, akin to daydreaming or doodling, can produce an intellec-tually and emotionally enriching experience, let alone lasting art. Here is an-other stunt and ought to be called by its right name, "enthralling" only in the imprisoning sense of the word. Still, such an outcome has everything going for it: mass curiosity, governments needing to fill up leisure time, monied inter-ests. One cannot persuade people they are losing anything, if they never had the opportunity to grapple with literary language. Smith misconceives T. S. Eliot's definition of culture in saying that it implies "a sense of the permanence of the industrial system and its universalizing values."[58] The author of *The Waste Land* left no doubt regarding his judgment on the "universalizing values" of industrialism, which are those of technique. Smith's title, *Software for the Self,* has an element of excruciating, cozy talk-show chatter: the *soft*ware undermines the very self that it supposedly supports and entertains.

To ponder the question "Is a technical culture possible?" one may invoke the old distinction between culture and civilization. To be certain, technology can give us a material civilization. Smith rightly points out that in the future people will want two things above all, entertainment and health care, that is, endless play and the longevity to enjoy it (though one thinks of Eliot's "Distracted from distraction by distraction"). But technology cannot give us a culture because of what it is doing to language—to literary language and symbolism, with their deep roots in the historical, cultural, and religious past. The technological system can gather and process information, can organize and control the planet, all more efficiently than anything hitherto; it cannot establish a humane standard of evaluation or provide a symbolism other than a desiccated, flattened imagery, for the most part parasitic on the culture it replaces. As the commitment to literary language fails, as computer language sweeps away other languages, we will lose an attachment to culture, "for culture has to rest on the specificity of a language."[59] When languages become obsolete, the cultures they enshrine will become obsolete with them.

One searches to avoid a counsel of despair. To whom can one turn? Lewis Mumford believes that a technical elite will produce a "uniform, all-enveloping, super-planetary structure, designed for automatic operation. Instead of functioning actively as an autonomous personality, man will become a passive, purposeless, machine-conditioned animal whose proper functions, as technicians now interpret man's role, will either be fed into the machine or strictly limited and controlled for the benefit of de-personalized, collective organizations." Still, Mumford sees a ray of hope: "The next move is ours: the gates of the technocratic prison will open automatically, despite their rusty ancient hinges, as soon as we choose to walk out." Andrew Feenberg believes that technology does not of itself exclude democracy but has been used to block it; that technology is not "*essentially* destructive" but is "a matter of design and social insertion." Langdon Winner advances a Scandinavian model that shows "the promise of creating citizen roles in places where private calculations of efficiency and effectiveness, costs, risks, benefits, and profits usually rule the day." Feenberg and Winner would take from both the instrumental and the substantivist theorists to forge a middle ground. In this category are Pool and Putnam: Pool's belief that "social values can condition the effects of technology . . . invites us not merely to consider how technology is privatizing our lives—if, as it seems to me, it is—but to ask whether we like the result, and if not, what we might do about it."[60]

At the optimistic end of the spectrum, Immanuel Wallerstein sees an ongoing battle between the forces promoting technology and the forces promoting the liberation of the underclass and oppressed everywhere: postmodernism is defined as "a mode of rejecting the modernity of technology on behalf of the modernity of liberation." Although he boldly predicts that the modern world system is in "terminal crisis" and will collapse within fifty years, curiously enough he does not say what will happen to technology. We are summoned in a utopian spirit to "the task of imagining, and struggling to create, this new social order."[61] All well and good, but the technological system is not going to vanish into thin air.

What does Ellul recommend? A clear look at the facts without a mystification of technology; personal self-transformation in religious terms; the promotion of anything that tends to oppose technological values: play, diversity, pluralism, and habits of anticonsumption.[62] In his late *Anarchy and Christianity* he aligns himself with the great high modernists in decrying the spiritual emptiness of modernity and gives the example of early Christians who withdrew from the world in apolitical autonomous communities. Protest in sufficient numbers, a policy of lowered consumption—these just might effect some change.[63] We can all point to pockets of resistance.

Although this may seem far-fetched, it is worthwhile to recall that monastic refuge happened once in Western culture and the humanities survived. The light of learning at Lindisfarne and Cîteaux, at St. Gall and Monte Cassino, could be rekindled by an apprenticeship to the word in the midst of our necessary participation in technological society. As Burckhardt said, the culture of the West may once again be saved by ascetics.[64]

# The Great Forgetting

## Library, Media Center, and Las Vegas

In Mark Strand's poem "Always," persons described as the "great forgetters" sit around a table in a bare room "lit by a single bulb." They are "hard at work" at the business of forgetting both culture and nature—nature at least as it has been imbued with human imagination if not nature itself. As one thing or another is forgotten, it simultaneously vanishes from the universe. First, a house and a man in a yard disappear, then the moon, Florida, and San Francisco. With each passing line, the world empties out. "And afterward Bulgaria was gone, and then Japan." It is only a matter of time before nothing is left:

> "Where will it end?" one of them said.
> "Such difficult work, pursuing the fate
> of everything known," said another.
> "Yes," said a third, "down to the last stone
> and only the cold zero of perfection
> left for the imagination."

At the conclusion, in a victorious climax for the great forgetters, one of them gazes from a window: "not a cloud, not a tree, / the blaze of promise every-where."[1]

The deeply held American belief that Strand invokes in this poem descends from Emerson (and ultimately from Puritan thought) through Whitman, Emily Dickinson, William James, and Wallace Stevens. As Harold Bloom formulates the motto of this tradition, "Everything that can be broken should be broken." The world must be shattered down to irreducible sense data, in order

43

to be reimagined by the individual, or we are captured by the past and not our own masters. For Bloom, this is the central tradition in American culture and literature, with its romantic desire for immediacy and its emphasis on the present and the future. Emerson said that "the soul is progressive" and that he sought an original relation to nature, and President James K. Polk (about the same time) asserted that America's history is the future.[2] The Emersonian line is opposed by the Europe-leaning tradition of Pound and Eliot, which descends from Longfellow and Charles Eliot Norton, Henry Adams, Henry James, and Santayana. They, too, desire immediacy in protesting the thick layers of mediation—technological, bureaucratic, legal, cultural—that are tied to the very definition of modernity. On that, William James and Henry James were in profound agreement.

Extreme representatives of the Emersonian line, the great forgetters turn their back on the previously imagined, humanized, and used-up world. Their agent, the imagination, in its calculating, modernist thrust toward "cold" perfection can both deny life (as in Keats's "Cold pastoral") and clear the ground for a fiery rebirth, the "blaze of promise" that comes with sunrise, that very promise conditioned by annihilation. The poem expresses an ascetic independence from the past, a scrupulous refusal of allusion, like the bare room lit by artificial light. The title "Always" calls attention to the permanent possibility of regeneration from "zero," highlighting an upbeat American optimism ("promise *everywhere*") over what might otherwise seem to be a tragic loss—all that history and culture. Poetically, "blaze of promise" is a curiously weak phrase; perhaps Strand wants the phrase to do more than it actually does. This weakness undermines confidence in the utopian future or, at least, indicates that any future is subject to the same destructive conditions that brought it into being. Twice in a short poem, the work of forgetting is called "hard" or "difficult," though nothing in the poem seems to show why. Rather, it looks almost as easy to forget as to do nothing. It is "late in the day"; the forgetters seem bored, "slouched" in their chairs; one of them "yawned." Will it happen again tomorrow?

When I heard Mark Strand recite the poem, he had the audience laughing, if not at the loss of the world, at least at the way the world was being lost. Do traditions die hard, as the cliché goes? Rather, it would seem they die easily.

The mentality of forgetting behind Strand's poem consorts so well with the technological society that it is impossible not to understand them except as emerging with and reinforcing each other. One does not mean the fading away of the near past, the inevitable result of the onrush of historical time, but a willed, aggressive, self-amputating, self-congratulatory, antihistorical *great forgetting*. Throughout the past century a smug air of condescension toward the past has pervaded the West, accelerating in recent decades. There have been minor protests, New Humanism, Third Humanism, endowments, national trusts, and of course the "self-justifying traditionalism" of right-wing movements—all of which, as David Lowenthal remarks in *The Past Is a Foreign Country*, is not the main issue. Rather, "we have lost the wellnigh universal tradition of the educated: intimate acquaintance with the classical and Scriptural past."[3]

Thematically, the "sense of the past" (the phrase is Kipling's) as an enriching, or steadying, or consoling influence characterized Western culture from time immemorial, with periods of greater or lesser intensity. Greek colonists living in Magna Graecia and becoming Italianized over the generations held an annual public festival to recall that "they were once Greeks."[4] English Benedictine monks following the Norman Conquest turned to historical studies to sustain their spirit: "They had a great past, but they were uncertain of their present and future."[5] When in 1416 Poggio Bracciolini found a damaged manuscript lying at the bottom of a dank tower in the monastery of St. Gall, he felt as if he were releasing a prisoner from a dungeon or bringing the dead to life: "If we had not brought help, he would surely have perished the very next day. There is no question that this glorious man, so elegant, so pure, so full of morals and of wit, could not much longer have endured the filth of that prison, the squalor of the place, and the savage cruelty of his keepers [the neglectful monks]." Jurists in the Renaissance problematized the notion of the past: "The image of antiquity had been recovered," asserts Myron P. Gilmore, "but at the same time it ceased to speak directly to the modern world"; "history was becoming academic." In the aftermath of the industrial revolution the Victorians suffered a deep spiritual crisis with regard to their history: "When as a consequence the past ceased to be a repository of true doctrines and became an incoherent heap of errors and inhumanities," Robert W. Southern notes, "sensitive people were threatened with the most serious alienation from their past in the whole course of European history." The Victorians answered with nostalgic revivals in historical fiction, the arts, and architecture and by embracing antiquarianism and historical studies: "The doctrines of the past might be false, but the experiences which had given rise to the doctrines were indubitably true. By the imaginative appropriation of these experiences, people could still possess the past, while rejecting the intellectual structure."[6]

One doubts whether any of these crises can compare in scale with those of the past fifty years in the West. Perhaps one should not speak in terms of crisis, because it is not perceived as such. The past is disappearing without a struggle. So apparent are the signs of the great forgetting that one risks belaboring the obvious.

## Signs of the Times

Caroline Winterer observes that beginning in the 1960s the steep fall in classical studies and Western civilization courses "heralded the overall decline in the humanities."[7] In 1966, 20 percent of bachelor degrees were in the humanities; by 1990 the figure dropped to just under 10 percent.[8] From 1971 to 1991, the number of English majors declined by 28 percent, classics majors by 28 percent, history majors by a staggering 45 percent. From 1961 to 1976, high school Latin enrollments fell by 80 percent, from 695,000 to 150,000. "This drop in turn fed the ongoing decline in college level enrollments," though revivals have periodically taken place.[9] Greek course enrollments in colleges fell 32 percent from 1977 to 1986. Classics was the smallest of thirty-two graduate programs in 1982. "In the National Curriculum promulgated in England and Wales in 1988, no reference was made to classics," proving how far the humanities had been replaced by English and the sciences.[10] By one estimate, only six hundred bachelor degrees were awarded in classics in 1994 (out of one million overall).[11] "In the not-too-distant past a humanist was a person who knew classical languages," recalls E. H. Gombrich. "I do not claim that they are necessarily the only means of entry to our concerns, but given the fact that not only the Romans but also Dante and Erasmus, Milton and Newton wrote in Latin will lead to a grave loss of cultural memory."[12] Nor do faculty attitudes vary significantly from the students'. "What the plight of classics most dramatically illustrates is the sorry prospect of any field that deals with the *past*, especially the distant past. More and more, the long-standing student attraction to the present is seconded by scholarly obsession with contemporary cultural criticism."[13]

Lack of knowledge in foreign languages is another warning sign: compared with 16 of 100 college students in foreign language courses in 1960, only 7.6 were taking them in 1995. The avenues to understanding another culture are history and language. In four-year colleges, history majors fell in the 1960s and '70s from 10 to 2 percent of all majors and never rebounded. "The real struggle isn't over the history of a particular discipline," comments Kenneth Kitchell Jr., "but over the survival of historical study itself."[14]

Few students pay attention to the arts of memory, the result of a long campaign by public, private, and progressive schools. No one recommends that their pupils learn "by heart" (the phrase, a relic of an earlier culture of memory) a soliloquy by Shakespeare, a passage from Ecclesiastes, or a poem by Dickinson or Frost (though those pupils can recite the rules of complicated video games with precision). With the exception of the more traditionally religious colleges and universities, most students are almost completely ignorant of the

Bible. Yielding to the tide, colleagues shun the arts of memory as things of the past, vestigial organs. Yet as Gombrich points out, the original task of the humanities had been to preserve the memory of classical culture. Carved over the entrance to the Warburg Institute, London is MNEMOSYNE, Memory, the mother of the Muses. Nor did she preside over the mere rote functions and public duties of memory, but inspired the creative imagination. In his study of classical Mnemosyne in its relation to self-reflection Donald Phillip Verene cautions that memory, far from being just a passive storehouse, "has the inner form of remembering, imagining, and perceiving connections"; "[it] is not the thought of the past but thought that can connect what was, is, and is to come, that can allow us to be Masters of Time."[15] Such a lofty ideal seems to belong to another age.

People read, to be sure, or such vast bookstores as Borders, Dalton, and Barnes and Noble would not be sprouting up everywhere. But what do people read? *How-to* books, self-therapies, new age writing, and popular fiction. In *The Bonfire of the Humanities: Television, Subliteracy, and Long-Term Memory Loss,* David Marc summarizes the current situation: "Though children are taught to read in the school system beginning in the early grades, the role of literacy in their lives outside of the classroom becomes increasingly remote."[16] The National Endowment for the Arts (NEA) has been studying the reading of literature among adult Americans for more than twenty years, surveying more than seventeen thousand people in most demographic groups (gender, income, educational level, age, and race or ethnicity). The standard for "literary reading" was the bare minimum: a few pages of a novel or short story, play, or poetry in the previous year. The results are deeply disturbing. In the words of Dana Gioia, chair of the NEA, "Literary reading in America is not only declining rapidly among all groups, but the rate of decline has accelerated, especially among the young": down 18 percent in all groups and down 28 percent among the eighteen to twenty-four age group. Americans read literature much less than Europeans, falling in the bottom third of the fifteen European countries surveyed. Moreover, the decline correlates strongly with increased participation in electronic media (Internet, video games, portable digital devices, and the like) and with decreased civic involvement: "Literary readers are more likely than non-literary readers to perform volunteer and charity work, visit art museums, attend performing arts events, and attend sporting events." This in turn exerts a negative influence on political awareness and engagement. The report concludes that "a cultural legacy is disappearing"; "at the current rate of loss, literary reading as a leisure activity will virtually disappear in half a century."[17]

My on-the-pulse proof of the decline of high-cultural literacy also comes from the classroom. Good reading and writing have lost much of their useful-ness among students working in an online environment. Reading aloud can be a painful exercise for a surprisingly large number of students who cannot an-ticipate syntactical patterns, punctuation, or the rhythms of the sentences. Politicians regularly bewail the scores of state and national tests, a yearly ritual that fails to produce any real action. Students who seek careers in law might not acquire the necessary writing skills until they take a course in their first year, not of college, but of law school itself. At this point, writing has become an instrumental exercise, a technique, which, to be sure, has its rightful place in the student's education, but this exercise should not be mistaken for a human-istic discipline concerned with the study of artistic and cultural achievements.

The competition is as obvious as the decline in high-cultural literacy itself or the blurring of the line between high and popular culture: television, identi-fied by Robert D. Putnam a decade ago, and the new video and communication technologies.[18] Composition texts have become technical manuals increasingly preoccupied with visual aids. *Writing with Norton Textra* is a 250-page book, but one will look in vain for the way to mend a comma splice or employ the subjunctive; instead, page after page describe an online command system. "Textra" sounds like a sugar substitute—indeed, it is a substitute for the gen-uine text. In such books there is typically some obligatory moment of self-consciousness, a paragraph or two in a preface, when the writers plead that they have thought out these issues to their heart's core, that "we live in an age of media hype" and computers may be another "educational fad" (remember television?), that we "should be cautious" and perhaps "hold on to those edu-cational practices that have worked best in the past." But such moments of scrupulosity are short-lived, and the tides of history sweep us away: computer-based technologies have "firmly established themselves practically everywhere"; "most of us want to keep up"; technology "may be the key for our gaining that vital competitive edge"; and so forth.[19] One composition reader, *Seeing and Writing,* advertises itself: "Giv[ing] words and images equal weight . . . this in-novative reader is the first to provide students with numerous opportunities to practice the analytical skills they need to succeed in an increasingly visual world." Hardly neutral, the ideologically loaded word *equal* implies that it would not be fair-minded if a reader did not balance words with pictures.

*Privilege* is another loaded word that is drawn from the language of class hi-erarchy. "English composition teachers have continued to privilege alphabetic texts over texts that depend on visual elements"; so argue the authors of *Writ-ing New Media* who, on behalf of "visual literacy," urge adopting alternative ap-proaches to composition. A typical project for a "composer/designer" is to "create a visual argument" on the relations between humans and robots by

2050, using "at least" fifteen images. These can either be downloaded from Web sites for an online essay or be cut out of magazines to be pasted on a poster board. "There is something increasingly untenable about the integrated coherence of college essayist prose, in which the easy falseness of a unified resolution gets prized over the richer, more difficult, de facto text the world presents itself as." How can a re-presentation (not even a representation) of the world be "more difficult" than reflection, analysis, and resolution? The authors stipulate the overriding importance of caesura, the "stylistic device most absent in present curricula."[20] But caesura breaks the links in an argument; it is disconnection, not logical connection. One jumps from concept to concept or from picture to picture without the intermediate steps, as in advertising and Power-Point. Beyond a bullet point on "reflection" being "elaborated and thoughtful," the coauthors never adequately explain how arguing visually could possibly substitute for the sifting of evidence, close reasoning, weighing of objections, rebuttal—the entire "logic and rhetoric of expression."[21]

In *Writing New Media* the first criterion of evaluation is not reasoning but "overall impact." The authors conceive of their techniques as "allowing students an easy entré into composition . . . allowing them to come up with something obscure, perhaps, yet promising illumination. It's difficult to define students' needs, of course." Visual argument is elsewhere praised as "more difficult"; here it is "easy"; they want it both ways. Let it be said, in protest of this application of the principle of least effort, that there is no easy entrée into composition, which is probably the hardest task for undergraduates to master. Moreover, "students' needs" are all too often the very desires implanted by media, advertising, and propaganda, which are continuous with these exercises in visual argument—precisely why the students, products of technicized culture, will find it "easy" to perform them: this is the world they already inhabit. What students should develop are the intellectual skills to question and, if necessary, to resist. One brazen curator "feels his job . . . is to work actively against the museum's role as repository of the culture's finest, positioning the institution instead as a more neutral information-provider for people: art as ideas, data, rather than (overly determined) objects. As curators of academia, then, we can exploit the possibilities of our status, exposing students to a range of culturally valid forms as well as non-mainstream content." So it is better for the museum not to be the "repository for the culture's finest" but to put up the poster boards and send its overly determined Rembrandts into storage. As long ago as 1968, expressing anxiety over charges of elitism, the director of the New York Metropolitan Museum of Art recommended that museums change from being "great treasure house[s]" into "more meaningful and enjoyable playfield[s] of the arts."[22]

Along these lines Web sites are commonly criticized if they are too "text-based," a phrase carrying negative connotations. Courses that mix books and films are offered in the new media-oriented "smart" classrooms (the language of advertising is everywhere). These courses are the first to fill up with students, leading to more courses with mixed media, and half the conversation that results concerns the technological gimmickry of their very production along with inevitable glitches. Mediocre films based on novels often supplement the teaching of those novels, wasting valuable time. Some show films first, hoping to stimulate interest; what really happens is that the student wants to see the film rather than read the book, a far more time-consuming, intellectually challenging assignment. Such courses are "more fun" and "easier" and therefore draw more students, especially where the alternative is *Middlemarch, The Waves, The Ambassadors,* or even Dickens. The technological principle of the least effort applies once again.[23]

An example of this principle shows up in one of the bastions of cultural memory. "Traditional classical grammars were heavily laden with complex grammatical paradigms," notes David Damrosch, "with lots of memorization taking place before students would reach a little reading. Latin and Greek teachers have now chucked this model." Those grammars were "heavily laden" with "complex" patterns, not to torture students but to prepare them for the artistry of Homer, Aeschylus, Virgil, and Horace. But now memorization is out-of-date, and desperate for student enrollments, teachers reduce themselves to the lowest common denominator to lure them back with the salacious: "New grammars are available, and courses offer lively reading early on. Instead of working with disembodied sentences from Plato and Sophocles, students now encounter ribald Hellenistic tales in their entirety." How fortunate those students! As if turning from death to life, they do not have to stumble over "disembodied" abstractions of Sophocles but meet "lively" bodies in action. In an ideologically motivated sally, a late work of the Hellenistic period—something on the level of a sleazy soap opera, something available at every hour of the day and night in Western media—is pushed as more appealing than Greek high culture of the classical age. As for the fragment versus the complete work (but it is only a "tale"), if students can read risqué tales in their entirety, surely their Greek might be good enough to read fragments of Plato ("This plank from the wreck of Paradise," said Coleridge in *Aids to Reflection,* "thrown on the shores of idolatrous Greece"). Even textual ribaldry will not suffice—it must be *seen:* "Classicists have also seized upon multimedia teaching tools, notably with the Perseus Project, an interactive database combining classical text and images that was developed at Harvard."[24] If it came from Harvard, and if it did not just come but was "developed" there, it must be awfully good—such is the language of advertising. Examine Damrosch's verbs: one can "chuck" away the old, a careless flinging away of cultural tradition with its paradigms from Plato and Sophocles; one can "seize upon multimedia teaching tools" as if they were a life preserver: and not just one medium but many media, the "tools" for a utilitarian culture.

If students no longer read for pleasure, do the faculty? In "The Disappearance of Reading," a lament for the loss of the age-old pleasure for its own sake, Robert Alter observes that the great promise of the critical trends in 1960s and '70s "has turned to bitter ashes." The end result of the revival of theory is that "so many among a whole generation of professional students of literature have turned away from reading." Perhaps literature in English suffers from having lacked a world-historical writer in the past fifty years, no one on the level of Joyce or Eliot. It has become an age of criticism and theory. In yet another misapplication of the principle of equality, "In both criticism and in debates over curriculum, one encounters an insistence that daily newspapers, pulp fiction, private diaries, clinical case studies, and imaginative literature belong on one level, that any distinctions among them are dictated chiefly by ideology." Equality trumps quality: everything big or great—social elites, major artists—are lumped together and must be cut down to size, even though the artists earned their way by their own merit, not as mere playthings of the aristocrats or as the mystifying justifications for them. If literature is examined as a symptom of something else, thinks Alter, literature professors would be better teaching in departments of sociology, anthropology, psychology, or political science. "We are now seeing, all of us today," comments George Steiner, "the gradual end of the classical age of reading."[25]

As agent provocateur, Terry Eagleton proposes doing away with literature departments in favor of "discourse studies" whereby the work of art is linked to the "discourse" involved in its social origins and its political orientation. "It is thus quite possible that, given a deep enough transformation of our history," maintains Eagleton, "we may in the future produce a society which was unable to get anything at all out of Shakespeare." One notes the Gulliver-like blandness with which, instead of being appalled, he accepts the inevitable, but what he says is sadly true. "His works might simply seem desperately alien, full of styles of thought and feeling which such a society found limited or irrelevant. In such a situation, Shakespeare would be no more valuable than much present-day graffiti." Marx himself, adds Eagleton, was "troubled by the question of why ancient Greek art retained an 'eternal charm,' even though the social conditions which produced it had long passed." What troubled Marx was that the "eternal charm" of the Greeks had challenged the foundations of his own system. Shakespeare "no more valuable" than graffiti? Such frivolity signifies a cultural decadence. According to Eagleton's misplaced egalitarianism, the great tradition is "a *construct,* fashioned by particular people for particular reasons at a certain time."[26] Art is the high-cultural arm of some dominant power. This "construct" (like *project,* one of the great buzzwords of the times) implies a mechanical manipulation, a committee decision. On the contrary, the Western canon—say, the epic line of Homer, Virgil, Dante, Shakespeare, Milton, Goethe— evolved slowly and organically over many centuries, with contributions from all points along a political spectrum, by many (not all) individuals with no ideological ax to grind and, above all, by Johnson's common reader: "By the common sense of readers uncorrupted with literary prejudices, after all the refinements of subtlety and the dogmatism of learning must be finally decided all claim of poetical honours" *(Life of Gray).*

Notions similar to Eagleton's becloud Clara Hesse's "Books in Time" in which the concept of "temporality" (that is, the present) sabotages the notion of the enduring book. Designers of workstations for the Bibliothèque Nationale de France have redefined the practice of reading: "Gone are the social (learned versus popular), political (public versus private), or economic (fee paying versus nonfee paying) categories that once described the constituencies of literary life." Instead of investigating the qualitative distinctions of "learned versus popular" or "public versus private," however, she embraces their disappearance: "In the future, it seems, there will be no fixed canons of texts and no fixed epistemological boundaries between disciplines, only paths of inquiry, modes of integration, and moments of encounter." Repeating the word *fixed,* Hesse implies that illegitimacy or impropriety attaches to a canon as if the game were "fixed" or a committee in a smoke-filled room conspired to force Great Books down the throats of unwilling students. As for the effacement of epistemological boundaries, one questions whether the well-policed borders between microbiology and cultural studies are about to collapse—and heaven help our health-care systems if they do. "What appears to be emerging from the digital revolutions," she surmises, "is the possibility of a new mode of temporality for public communication, one in which public exchange through the written word can occur without deferral, in a continuously immediate present." In this breathless presentism, the "moment of encounter" is pumped up by the words *continuously immediate,* as if to exclude the intrusion of the past. On the contrary, the present can become so much the product of advertising that only a really important encounter with an author on the order of a Sophocles can crack the mirror. As M. A. Rafey Habib comments on Irving Babbitt, "The world as governed by bourgeois economic and scientific interests is a world of a perpetual present, of historical amnesia." By contrast, Babbitt's approach to humanism was "a means of emancipating humanity from 'this servitude to the present.' "[27]

Countless thinkers have urged a simple truth: human consciousness is such that if one does not know the past, one cannot understand the present or think rationally about the future. "Memory in a personality," argues Jacques Ellul, "is the function that attests to the capacity of acting voluntarily and creatively; personality is built on memory, and conversely memory lends authority to personality." Nor is history to be substituted by current events. The person who lives by the news is a person "without memory": the news that "agitated the deepest corners of his soul simply disappears. He is ready for some other agitation, and what excited him yesterday does not stay with him." Ellul examines the mentality of the person who is au courant, "convinced that the newest thing is the most important. What is more, he is convinced that he lives in freedom precisely *because* he lives in the moment." In an age of video such persons are bound more than ever to the news that may even create or exacerbate the anxieties that it supposedly allays—for example, Rumor Hotline. "We in our time need to recover the past in order to attain fullness," asserts Charles Taylor, "but this is not so much because history has meant decline, as because the fullness of meaning isn't available with the resources of a single age."[28]

Composed of optical tricks in graphics to symbolize the media revolution, *Imagologies: Media Philosophy* is a self-congratulatory exchange of e-mails, faxes, and other electronic communications between Mark C. Taylor in Williams, Massachusetts, and Esa Saarinen in Helsinki. The authors get around the problem of having to use old-fashioned print to trumpet their cause by making the book deliberately hard and unpleasant to read, with dozens of type fonts, breaks in presentation, no pagination, and so on. Temporary problems in transmission, always surmounted by one technique or another, seem only to heighten euphoria. At one point the gaze turns inward: "It is time to stop bemoaning the fact that young people no longer read as we once did," Saarinen states. "If the young are not reading as much as we would like, the problem might be the way we are writing. Perhaps if we were to write televisually, kids would *want* to read more." Imagine thinking that kids would prefer to read the televisual works of Taylor and Saarinen (and others) in contrast to Sophocles, Dante, and Gandhi—or even Agatha Christie or Robert Ludlum. We want kids not to read "us," but to read works of importance in the history of world culture. "Personally, I seldom read books," admits Saarinen. "In the midst of speed, reading a book takes too much time."[29] Although he thinks that he confesses sincerely and spontaneously, he hardly realizes how technicized ("in the midst of speed") he has become; the system speaks through him. He has no time for the very books that might offer resistance to his ideas.

Mark Taylor is ecstatic about the capabilities of the desk computer (e-mail, the Web, and the like): "Recent developments in electronic telecommunications technology have brought us to the brink of an extraordinary social and cultural revolution"; "changes already under way call into question the very foundation upon which the university is built—print culture and everything that goes with it." What is this vague, wishful thinking? *Everything that goes with it?* "Expert language is a prison for knowledge and understanding. A prison for intellectually significant relationships. It is time to move beyond the institutional practices of triviledge [*sic*], toward networks and surfaces, toward the play of superficiality, toward interstanding" [*sic*].[30] What does Taylor mean by "expert" language as a prison? If he means technical language, it is arguable that such language may obscure as much as reveal, and to that extent a prison metaphor is justified (Fredric Jameson had adopted the metaphor along these lines): knowledge and understanding are in a prison house of language. However, not all "expert language" of institutional practice imprisons the reader. Taylor plays at the anti-intellectual intellectual, seeking liberation. Indeed, at the end of the passage, he coins his own "expert language" even more arcane than the one he would supplant. One thinks of Pope's comment on Addison, "And hate for arts that caused himself to rise."

A major reason that less interest attaches to history and languages is that so many current academics have been trained modernistically and not humanistically, and therefore do not feel the need to look for intellectual sustenance much further back than the later nineteenth century. They have no great stake in the past, and what one does not know, one tends to view with suspicion or indifference. Their readings of the past testify to the fact that they never had a deep spiritual encounter with history, even with the history of an Other, and so they do not realize what they are missing. In the course of their education they bypassed Greece and Rome, the Middle Ages, the Renaissance and Baroque periods. The long-standing reduction of literature to method and technique (New Critical, structuralist, deconstructive, new formalist, and the rest) contributed to the dominance of presentism. Though academics may desire otherness and diversity, the emphasis on method over content has the opposite effect, ironing out differences among texts and historical periods, suppressing the much-needed sense of diversity and seeing everything from the prospect of the present. It used to be thought that the past created the present; now it is believed that the present creates the past. Secure in their presentism, academic intellectuals even take credit for the decline of the past, believing that they are victors in the ideological wars, never realizing that the technological agenda drives such forgetfulness. In this respect they reveal their lack of historical sense.

One response to this predicament is to move with the times and acquiesce in the loss of high-cultural literacy. "Perhaps the worst consequence of the spiritually based fixation of university education on reading and writing," proclaims David Marc, "is that it prevents the true functions of literacy in the modern communications market from being determined." We are fixated on the "spiritual" in our basic teaching instead of searching out the market-driven media. Marc wants more education based on audiovisual communications, "vital new vessels of language and imagination," which humanists have ignored.[31] He lambastes Neil Postman for condemning television ("Reading is, by its nature, a serious business [and] a rational activity"; television "promotes incoherence and triviality").[32] On the contrary, Marc defends the visual technologies: "Television, like any transmission medium (including books) can dispense information to those who make the effort to receive it." Is it only information that we want? "To despise the quality of *what* we learn from television is a tacit admission that we are, in fact, learning." The question is *what* we learn. "People who are incapable of writing a grammatical letter and who have never read a whole book can live reasonably prosperous and even relatively informed lives in the United States of America today. Is that a shame or a triumph? As for social maladjustment, it is more likely to be suffered by the intensely literate than by normal people." In other words, people who do not read are more likely to be normal than persons who read long and deeply. Normal according to whose standard? Well adjusted to what? Are we not abandoning an educational mission if we leave students unprotected against the norms of market-based television and other media? It is not a matter of "despising" or "enjoying" a particular program; it is finally a question of judgment. Marc levels down to what he considers a norm, tacitly revealing the technological principle of the least effort. In a now familiar move, he makes the humanities the villain by connecting them with "the desires of a central committee": "If the best hope for the revival of the humanities is authoritarian coercion then perhaps it would be better just to let the whole thing go and focus the diminishing resources of the empire on improving science education by audiovisual means."[33] Coercion is neither the "best hope" nor the only hope.

Cicero may be said to have replied to Marc on morality and learning in his defense of the Syrian-born Greek poet Aulus Licinius Archias in 62 BC. An immigrant, Archias was in court for not having his citizenship papers, the building in Heraclea that had the record of his citizenship having burned down in the Social War. Cicero dispensed with the legal questions quickly—it was not a difficult case—and proceeded to argue by way of digression: we need Archias in Rome because we need the arts for their moral as well as their mental inspiration.

Character is no doubt more important than learning, and learning does not make up for lack of character. But what emerges when character is informed by learning? . . . [T]he number of virtuous and admirable men produced by character without learning exceeds those who are the products of learning without character. Nevertheless I do also maintain that, when noble and elevated natural gifts are supplemented and shaped by the influence of theoretical knowledge, the result is then something truly remarkable and unique.[34]

Cicero gives the examples of Cato the Censor and the Scipionic Circle.

Marc is among those technicized individuals who prefer the image to the text, believing that one can gain any lasting knowledge of World War II or the legal system through television. The time he spent on reading for his World War II college courses does not compare to the "hundreds of hours" he devoted to watching commercial TV series such as *The World at War, Victory at Sea,* and *Prudential's "The Twentieth Century."* What did he learn from these programs? "I can still see the swastikas sweeping out in all directions from the center of the map of Europe after the first commercial." In other words, not much aside from some visual stimuli. The imprint is too weak. The historical sense cannot be supplied by occasional nostalgia or the History Channel. Marc gained little information, not to speak of deeper knowledge. "My imagination of the law and of courtroom procedures was formed by watching television series produced by Steven Bochco, such as *L.A. Law, Civil Wars,* and *NYPD Blue.* Should I have read law books instead?" The choice lies not between television and law books as such (which are technical), but between television and the law in human culture as examined in *Bleak House, Adam Bede, Colonel Chabert, The Oresteia, Billy Budd,* or Ford's *Young Mr. Lincoln.* The television series *Law and Order* "reminds me of literature."[35] What literature? In more than fifty years of broadcasting, with all the immense sums lavished upon productions, television has not produced a single major work of art and lags far behind film itself.

In a survey conducted in 1998 by the American Council on Education and the University of California, 275,811 college students entering 469 institutions were questioned on their "habits and aspirations": 80.4 percent had "occasionally played a video game" in the past year, whereas 18.7 percent had "frequently taken out a book or journal from the school library."[36] Video games impart "undeniable pleasure"—Marc plays them "almost every day." Where reading demands the interpretation of abstract symbols, video games involve simplified thought processes and direct stimulus-response and eye-hand coordination. With video games, as contrasted with reading literature, "it is not the capacity for imaginative identification that is stimulated, but rather the capacity to act quickly and decisively." Speed is one of the main attributes of technology. "The computer," Richard Stivers points out, "turns life into a game." Beyond computer games, this observation "applies to all of the computer functions in which the user participates, e.g. the game of acquiring more information."[37]

Weak remembering is a form of forgetting. So, too, is trivialization, as Pierre Bourdieu has demonstrated. Culture itself can be treated as a kind of show whereby we recognize one another. Yet possession of Arnold's ideal of culture, "the best that is thought and said in the world," is no mere showing off. Contemporary studies of travel writing frequently treat a country as "a text" rather than a living historical reality, thereby relieving scholars of the burden of knowing the country's history. One speaks of "writing France" or "reading France" rather than "writing about" or "reading about" it, as though to indicate that it were all a constructed discourse. The critical effort lies in theory and rhetorical analysis, which can become a self-generating web of terms and procedures. Critics of travel literature posit the Other as a kind of alienated self in projection. Yet it might be profitable to consider that the more one knows the history, politics, and economy of a foreign country, the less its Otherness will seem a projection of one's own hidden obsessions and will become refreshingly Other. The country's historical reality should be the third term against which the scholar's theory and the author's text can be tested.

The past can also be dehistoricized, as in Hayden White's studies, so that history is "a text" to be treated "like any other form of literature." Objecting to this position in his transparently clear fashion, Arnaldo Momigliano argues that in White's view one cannot differentiate between a true and a made-up story, between the historical and the fictional. "Why should I worry if a historian prefers presenting the part for the whole rather than the whole for the part? After all, I never worried if a historian chose to write in epic style or to introduce speeches into his account. I have no reason to prefer synecdochic to ironic historians." The fact that historians employ the arts of language (metaphor, synecdoche, and so on) does not mean that there is nothing true in their accounts. "But I have good reason to distrust any historian who has nothing to say or who produces novelties either in facts or in interpretation, which I discover to be unreliable. Historians are supposed to be discoverers of truth. No doubt they must turn their research into some sort of story before being called historians. But their stories must be true stories." Momigliano points to the resistance that fact and evidence give to the theories and the stories constructed out of them. "Ranke went into the archives because the archives told him facts he did not know before."[38]

Cultural memory can also be frittered away in celebrations, say, of the power of a new machine or the latest Web site. "Cyborgs are not reverent," says Donna Haraway. "They do not re-member the cosmos." "Instead of relating to the past through a shared sense of place or ancestry," argues George Lipsitz in *Time*

*Passages,* "consumers of electronic mass media can experience a common heritage with people they have never seen; they can acquire memories of a past to which they have no geographic or biological connection." Here various pasts are placed on the table like a smorgasbord. We are not readers: we are consumers of two- or three-hour programs or series. Ironically, if the connections with one's own past have been broken and forgotten, if the historical sense has been eclipsed, it is not likely that one will reconnect with another past or other pasts. "This capacity of electronic mass media to transcend time and space creates instability by disconnecting people from past traditions, but it also liberates people by making the past less determinate of experiences in the present."[39] Lipsitz extols the mass media as a universal force of liberation from history. He reduces the vital organicism of the past, most powerfully embodied in a language, to a game of signs. The liberation of which he speaks is a function of the technology's capacity to grind everything together. This is the kind of freedom we have in choosing among five hundred cable channels.

Many intellectuals go beyond indiscriminate forgetfulness to a genuine hatred of the past—that is, the Western past. Analyzing cultural despair and self-hatred in *The Betrayal of the West,* Jacques Ellul tallies up the political, intellectual, and moral balance sheet of Western culture over the past twenty-five hundred years. As a professor of law and one of the foremost critics of unrestrained technologism in the West, he may be credited with a certain degree of detachment and fairness. Yet he finds that Western virtues have outweighed the vices, because the West "attempted to apply in a conscious, methodical way the implications of freedom." The Jews were the first to embrace freedom as "the key to history and to the whole created order"; the Greeks "formulated the rules for a genuinely free kind of thinking, the conditions for human freedom"; the Romans invented "civil and institutional liberty" and made "political freedom the key to their entire politics."[40] An ideal of freedom, the individual, and the rule of law are three major Western contributions to world culture. However, critics look only at the perversions of the West (of which, as he admits, there are many), papering over the glaring inadequacies of their counterideals. "The 'intellectuals'—those in literature, journalism, theology, and some of the arts are singled out—reject everything Western in favor of cultures and ideologies they do not understand but seek only in a foolish way to mimic."[41] Ellul attacks the historians themselves for losing the art of writing history. "From now on, all that is left is a drab, insipid unfolding of implications, an interplay of forces and mechanisms. There will be structures and systems, but we shall no longer be able to speak of 'history.'"[42]

The most Whiggish of Whig historians, J. H. Plumb shows no regrets in *The*

*Death of the Past:* "Few societies have ever had a past in such a galloping dissolution as this. . . . [T]he dissolution is not fast enough." Lowenthal suggests
that this desire to bury the past is class-based. "The past has only served the
few," says Plumb. "Perhaps history may serve the multitude." Grounded in Enlightenment values (he is the distinguished biographer of Sir Robert Walpole),
he associates "the past" with an ideology that is aristocratic, repressive, and
tenacious: "The most remarkable aspect of Western ideology is its leech-like
addiction to the past." Even historical writing "always contains . . . a justification of the authority of the state." What does Plumb mean by "authority"? At
one extreme, it can mean authoritarianism; at the other, a mere holding of the
line against anarchy. If the second, then his statement is a mere truism; if the
first, one questions whether it could "always" be applied, such as in the case of
Tacitus or Josephus. Opposed to "the past" as a bloodsucking disease, Plumb
enshrines the liberating study of "history" that stands for rational analysis,
myth breaking, and progress. The past dissolves because of technological conditions: "Industrial society, unlike the commercial, craft and agrarian societies
which it replaces, does not need the past." If one wants to educate managers for
the commercial-technological system, one cannot deny Plumb's point. De-
ploring the absence of a unifying ideology, however, he wonders why Cato the
Censor's civitas should "haunt the imagination" while secular faith in a sociology of consent "quickly fades," and why no modern myths warm our souls and
give coherence. He seems astonished that an "idealization of analytic understanding" cannot substitute for "creative belief." Plumb's argument for the
demagification of the past extends even to historians: Thucydides, the acknowledged founder of scientific history, is insufficiently *scientific* because he
was concerned with "truths about men's behaviour in war and politics," not
"historical truth." More accurately, Thucydides concerned himself with both
the history of the Peloponnesian War and its political lessons: he said that,
given history's resembling itself, his book was a "possession for all time." Plumb
complains that Job, Odysseus, and Cicero have been "cult objects" to the masses,
whereas "only a few professionals were concerned with their historical context,
or wished to understand their lives by reference to their particular times and
places, conditions which had vanished." Plumb does not appreciate that Job,
Homer, and Cicero are both in history and out of it, that is, they transcend
their times and speak across the ages, as those who teach world literature
courses will attest. The historical context of pastoralism and nomadism is
more or less applicable in understanding the Book of Job (more for Deu-
teronomy, less for Job), yet the human context of Job is more applicable than
the historical one—and universalizes it. Job's historical context has vanished;

its human context has not, and neither has its profundity. But Plumb takes his history lessons from Voltaire, not Gibbon: "The old past is dying . . . and so it should. Indeed the historian should speed it on its way, for it was compounded of bigotry, of national vanity, of class domination. May history step into its shoes, help to sustain man's confidence in his destiny, and create for us a new past as true, as exact, as we can make it."[43]

Only slightly less polemical, Zygmunt Bauman contends that the spirit of the "modern" has meant that "reality should be emancipated from the 'dead hand' of its own history"; what we see is a relentless "profaning of the sacred," for "disavowing and dethroning the past."[44] Since about 1800, he notes, we have witnessed the melting away of those social and political solids, from the last feudal residues and customary obligations to the authority of church, the state, social classes, community, and the family itself. Thus, family albums "have been replaced by camrecorders with videocassettes, and video-tapes differ from photographic paper in being eminently effaceable and meant to be effaced again and again."[45] What is left to be thrown into the melting pot but *the self*? Where formerly the self had been conceived in terms of "harmony, logic, consistency," today, by contrast, individual identity has lost its mass and contour: "The search for identity is the ongoing struggle to arrest or slow down the flow, to solidify the fluid, to give form to the formless"; "identities are more like spots of crust hardening time and again on the top of volcanic lava which melt and dissolve again before they have time to cool and set." In a consumer society, the self becomes what it imitates, shopping the "limitless possibilities." *Master the possibilities,* goes one ad, *with MasterCard.* The will loses itself in the frivolous agony of choice: "The experienced, lived identity could only be held together with the adhesive of fantasy."[46] Bauman holds his cards close to the vest, and one cannot always tell whether he merely reports, or welcomes, or objects. At one point, however, he drops his hand and cites Seneca the Elder's *Brevity of Life:* the present age of frivolity and pleasure seeking is "the lot of people of who have forgotten the past, did not care about the present, and were afraid of the future."[47]

Historical memory is the responsibility of each generation. It takes only two or three generations, less than a century, for memory to be eclipsed. Virgil's Sibyl warns, "Easy is the descent to Avernus"; the doors of the Underworld stand open (*Aeneid* 6.283). It is easy to die, cross Lethe, and forget; it is done all the time, in a thousand ways. "But to return to the air of day—that is the labor, that is the task." Remembering takes mental effort, a willed struggle, and piety. Not many can undertake the journey and return, and none without personal heroism and Jove's love.

## From the Library to the Media Center

In the history of the West, the library has been one of the great symbols of cultural memory. At the present time, however, the American library—on university campuses, at the national level, in small communities—is an institution under siege. One refers not to local censorship and banned books, but to long-term economic and technological challenges. Given the current situation, one might gain perspective by briefly reflecting upon the past mission of libraries in the hope of recovering some of the idealism that they have bestowed upon humanity.

The history of libraries has been described as being nearly as old as history itself, because without libraries we would have very little history indeed. In the valleys of Mesopotamia, around 3000 BC, the Sumerian administrators needed to keep track of housing records, harvests, taxes, court decisions, and trade; they also wanted to save an occasional hymn or poem. So they housed their flat clay cuneiform tablets in deep, dark underground storerooms, the ancient stacks, which they entered by descending a ladder. There, forty-five hundred years later, archaeologists found thousands of wooden boxes, earthen jars, and reed baskets, each labeled as to subject and date, as if waiting to be retrieved.[48] These are the first libraries that we know of. "Each of the few cities recently excavated," points out Edward Savage, "has had its library, in the heart of the community, close by the temple."[49] Incidentally, the archaeologists also found piles of baked and unbaked tablets in untidy corners, along the walls of the corridors, behind the ladders, indicating that the librarians had run out of space. Finding space in a library appears to be an old problem—a very old problem.[50]

One of the great Egyptian libraries was that of Ramses II—Shelley's Ozymandias, the "king of kings," who exclaimed, "Look on my works, ye Mighty, and despair!"—in the thirteenth century BC. The palace library at Thebes formed part of his funerary temple and was built to entertain him on his journey to the afterlife. According to Diodorus Siculus (1.49), over the lintel of the library was inscribed "Healing Place of the Soul."

"By far the most famous" of all libraries in classical antiquity was founded by Alexander's general Ptolemy I Soter at Alexandria in 300 BC.[51] It was located next to the palace and the Lighthouse. Unlike the Lighthouse, the library was not one of the seven wonders of the world, but it should have been. Its legacy has been as durable as the Pyramids of Giza and as beautiful as the Hanging Gardens of Babylon. The Greek librarians kept expanding their collection in an open, Hellenistic spirit, sending emissaries to buy documents across Europe, Africa, and the Near East—eventually accruing some seven hundred thousand rolls. These librarians had a cushy life; to quote one historian, they enjoyed "free meals, high salaries, no taxes, very pleasant surroundings, good lodgings and servants. There was plenty of opportunity for quarrelling with one another."[52] The library was called the Museion, which means "the home of the Muses" and from which we derive *museum* and *amusement*. The sisterhood of the nine Muses stood for a Greek ideal, the interrelation of the arts and sciences; equally important was the name of their mother, Mnemosyne. The Greeks had come up with the best of all names for a library, the House of the Daughters of Memory, though another word, *athenaeum,* is a close second. Frederick Lerner comments that, just as the Lighthouse of Alexandria sent out its guiding beam over thirty miles and "symbolized mastery over night and distance," so the Museion "embodied man's ability to transcend the bounds of time."[53]

Everyone knows how much of the preservation of Western culture is owed to monastic toil, beautifully articulated many years ago by Jean LeClerc in *The Love of Learning and the Desire for God.* "The monastery was generally accepted as a center of learning, and the saying was common that 'a monastery without a library is like a castle without walls.'"[54] The nun Melania had earned a living by transcribing texts before she founded a convent near Carthage in 420. Gertrude, abbess of Nivelle in seventh-century Belgium, is credited with building a library, as is the tenth-century German abbess Saint Hrosvitha who was also a poet and dramatist. To the scriptorium at Fulda, the abbot Sturmi assigned forty monks, thanks to whom many works of Roman history and Old High German literature were copied and survived. Medieval libraries were small: the abbey of Cluny had 570 books in the twelfth century; at this time Bobbio, founded by the Irish abbot Saint Columban in northern Italy, had 650. A ninth-century monk at St. Gall in Switzerland depicted the annual exhibition of all 415 books on a big rug before the abbot. Each member of the community got one book a year to read, and if in the public interview the monk was shown not to have done his homework, he was not "given a new book, but asked to study the old one for another year." If the abbot found that the monk had studied hard yet was simply unable to understand the book, he was given another book "more suited to his abilities."[55]

The monasteries engaged in a European-wide interlibrary loan system, and in the continual process of borrowing and copying, errors slowly crept into the texts, so that one can follow the trail of books across the continent by tracing the patterns of their errors. A manuscript might be so precious as to require leaving another as a security deposit, a Ciceronian oration for a book of Livy. The Roman poet Catullus came through the Middle Ages in a single manuscript, discovered in the fourteenth century in Verona, ironically, his birthplace, and, indeed, it was being reborn. Like Catullus, the manuscript must have traveled widely because a marginal note on it read, "from a far frontier."[56] Let us not forget that in these long centuries, the universities picked up where the monasteries left off, beginning with eleventh-century Bologna. In the words of Edward Levi, the universities and their libraries were and remain "the custodians not only of the many cultures of man, but of the rational process itself."[57]

Such in brief is the ideal history of the library: what has been visited upon the venerable institution in the past decade or two? William Y. Arms is a professor of computing at Cornell, a consultant to the Library of Congress, a member of the National Research Council, and the author of *Digital Libraries* (2001). "Can we envisage a transmogrification of libraries, in which the old structures disappear, but some of the essence remains?" If so, what might disappear? The list contains multitudes: "Library buildings are expensive; they could disappear from university campuses." Then, "Scientific journals are in a period of rapid change." One will download them from one's office. Librarians? "If professional and research information is to be available more widely, either users will have to bypass libraries, or libraries will have to employ fewer people." Information? What "we" need will all be created from this day forth—this is presentism with a vengeance. What about the hitherto recorded works that arrived before digitization? Arms is a short step from wishing away the whole concrete edifice. "Should the Library of Congress celebrate the new millennium with an announcement that it will become purely digital?"[58] If Arms does not need those forty million books and documents that are not online and never will be, he could at least show some sympathetic imagination for the legions of scholars who will. He is also giving aid and comfort to politicians and administrators strapped for funds and looking for an easy way out. And what is more defenseless than a library? For Arms, the model of scholarship is the laboratory and the latest number of an online journal.

Even before the advent of the digital library, librarians had to find ways of removing some books or making them less accessible. Many libraries have had off-site storage for years, though it is only during the past decade that the movement has geared up. "As if to make visible the ending of the era of the book and of reading," laments Alvin B. Kernan, "large numbers of books are literally disappearing before our eyes from the shelves of those monuments of print culture, the great research libraries."[59]

In part this shift to off-site storage came from the sheer number of published books that had filled up the shelves. But the main reason may be traced to those same technological imperatives that have permeated every other aspect of daily life, so that it was only a matter of time before they reached the library, one of the last bastions of the humanities. In the expansion of the online environment, more and more digital services are introduced. Machines take up more and more space, and with space at a premium, machines tend to cannibalize the space of books. Seeking ways of saving money, administrators looked forward to library conventions featuring the latest online equipment, because they believed that such equipment would greatly reduce the need for space and books. The result is that books and "old journals" (though "old" can be as recent as pre-1990) have been hemorrhaging at an alarming rate at many libraries. By last count, 27 percent (roughly six hundred thousand) of the books at my university library were shipped to off-site facilities. The reduced access essentially means more loss of "memory." Furthermore, even in many main libraries, compact shelving cuts down on convenience and makes browsing difficult, if not impossible. One person can shut down as many as eleven bays of compactly shelved books or journals—and this goes for the shelvers as well as readers, so that the bays are effectively shut down twice.

Humanistic scholarship, any genuine scholarship, moves in mysterious ways—browsing, expecting the unexpected, crisscrossing the stacks. One patiently awaits a volume ordered from off-site storage, but it might be the one before or after it on the shelf that contains the clue to one's research. This can be gleaned only through browsing, which suddenly has assumed the aura of some enormously expensive luxury rather than a scholarly necessity. Ross Atkinson, Cornell University's director of libraries, says that "all research and bibliographic searching, no matter how systematic and sophisticated, is a form of browsing. . . . [W]e need, therefore, not only to condone browsing but to improve it."[60] The very book being taken away to storage is the one that good scholars are most likely to need.

Today, the word *library* itself is suspect; many secondary schools prefer the more fashionable *media center*. Library reform is often couched in terms of lounges with Internet connections, workstations, ergonomically designed machine-use desks, networked seminar and teleconferencing rooms, the entire online and video environment, as if books were decidedly obsolescent. One wants the libraries to enjoy these reforms and to be comfortable and efficient places of study. At the same time, one should be aware of the attendant risk of forgetting and the myths attached to the new media centers.

One myth is that the online environment will do away with libraries and librarians since one can do everything at home. But the opposite is true. As Don Schnedeker, business school librarian at Cornell University, has written: "[W]hile information can be moved around the planet at the speed of light, people cannot. People are still in one place and need assistance in the locale." Though William Y. Arms believes that librarians will decrease in number, in fact they will be needed more than ever. One cannot run a library without librarians. Students and scholars require the assistance of trained librarians in gaining access to the increasingly complicated information environment. If anything, the past two decades have shown that the proliferation of machines has not lessened the need for services but the reverse. In their book *Information Ecologies,* Bonnie Nardi and Vicki O'Day consider librarians as the keystone species in the new information ecology. Yet because many people are unaware of how libraries work, there is "a real temptation to assume that the librarian's work is easily automated." The critical guidance and service of librarians are "easily overlooked during planning (and budget cutting)."[61]

Another myth is that libraries of the future will cost less because one can get everything online. The opposite is proving to be true—have you noticed how many of America's four hundred billionaires made their money in the past fifteen years? Technology, once it has taken hold, never relinquishes its grip, and its grip is costly if one wants to compete with one's peers. Books have a way of quietly sitting on shelves, absorbed in their mysterious silence. Aside from a little heat or air-conditioning, they do not cost over and over again. But the digital environment is relentless, ever changing, ever expanding, even self-intoxicating in its prideful usurpations. Computer programs go out of date in a few years, even less, and basic equipment does not last much longer. The machines are expensive and are always in need of being updated: their heavy cost eats into book and journal budgets. To buy EEBO, the online printed books in English before 1700, costs (at present) around two hundred thousand dollars, yet an additional twenty thousand dollars per year is needed just to service and upgrade the system. Arms thinks that "progress is being made" in the reduction of costs: "Open access materials on the Internet are making primary materials available at no cost."[62] But costs crop up elsewhere in equipment obsolescence.

Perhaps the most entrenched myth is that nearly everything past and present will eventually be online. Yet Cornell University did a study that showed it would cost six hundred million dollars to convert their main library and that such a conversion price tag would not take into account ongoing expense of archiving, upgrading hardware and software, legal bills, and more. Although digital resources will sooner or later come to dominate scholarly communication, concludes Atkinson, the "effective management of traditional materials remains essential." These materials will constitute the main library holdings far into the future. They will require the kind of care and financial attention that might well be diverted—indeed, already has been in any number of local and university libraries. Michael Gorman points out that "the vast majority of the [Library of Congress's] collections are not digitized and never will be digitized (for practical and economic reasons)." The upkeep of collections will be costly. "At least 40 percent of the books in major research collections in the United States will soon be too fragile to handle," claims Eric Stange. Yale University conducted a study of its collection and found that, in a sample of 36,500 volumes, 37 percent "had brittle paper (i.e. paper which broke after two double folds) and that 83% had acidic paper (i.e. having a pH of below 5.4)." The report concluded that "all book repositories are self-destructing time bombs."[63]

Today, when one is beginning to hear more of Webliographies than of bibliographies, one asks whether the heritage of the library will be squandered. It is now thought that the Library of Alexandria was not destroyed by the infamous fire set by so-called Islamic militants bent on the destruction of another culture. It was destroyed by two or three centuries of neglect.

## Disfiguring the Past

Readers could no doubt draw from their own fund of illustrative materials on the lapse of cultural memory. "Ours is a forgetful era" opens a recent book on the history of English studies; the premise is stated so casually that the author, Ian Reid, hardly feels required to elaborate. In *The Burden of the Past,* covering the period from 1660 to 1830, Walter Jackson Bate examines mainly neoclassical writers who felt the crushing weight of literary tradition (the Ancients, the Renaissance) yet succeeded in balancing tradition against claims of self, originality, and sincerity. Mark C. Taylor's *Disfiguring: Art, Architecture, Religion* takes up modernist and postmodernist artists who confronted the decline of traditional religion and sought to fill the vacuum. "Where religion has no longer a monopoly on the appeal of the spiritual or the challenge of the unknown," states Bram Kempers, "art has itself acquired a sacred significance that has soared far above the social struggle to achieve status, wealth and power."[64] In agreement, Taylor raises the modern artist to a secular sainthood and the museum to a shrine. His exploration of the interplay between art and religion focuses on the visual arts and architecture where, in his view, the effacement of cultural memory appears radical and ultimate. Perhaps if he had chosen the modernism of Pound, Eliot, and Joyce, with their appeal to the past (if not the near past), he could not have articulated his case in quite the same way. Even with the visual arts and architecture, as Taylor acknowledges, cultural memory is not easily blotted out.

Taylor groups twentieth-century art and architecture into three epochs: modernism, modernist postmodernism, and postmodernism, one following the other (with overlap among all three epochs), each with its own mode of "disfiguring" or negative submission to a deliberate process of aesthetic deformation, which is simultaneously a new formation.

Modernism, the first epoch, is characterized by a process of disfiguring that purges traditional forms, styles, symbols, and ornamentation to clear its own ontological space and create anew. Brancusi, the Bauhaus, the New York School, and the International Style—all search for a pure form that "transcends the vicissitudes of sensual and historical experience." In religious terms, abstract expressionism has an affinity with the ascesis, negation, and severity of transcendence: "The Kingdom is *present* elsewhere." For Taylor, high-modernist artists are "heroic" and "utopian" in their quest for ultimacy exemplified by Barnett Newman's *Vir Heroicus Sublimis* (1950–1951), a vast canvas (roughly eight by eighteen feet) painted in flat red color with five thin vertical bands or "zips." "The value that governs Newman's aesthetic is the *sublime*."[65] One agrees with Taylor on the dominance of the sublime in Newman, but which sublime? Taylor mistakenly ascribes the importance of the Kantian sublime, but Kant's sublime represents an empowerment of the ego, a revival of the noble emotions of Longinus, not the ego's negation. By his own admission, Newman's is much closer to the sublime of Edmund Burke, who identified it with the weakening of the ego, psychological terror, and death. When the viewer stands near *Vir Heroicus Sublimis*, as Newman wanted, the painting engulfs with its size, infinity, power, uniformity, difficulty, privation, and strong color—all features of the Burkean sublime. Burke excluded soft and cheerful colors from the sublime, with the exception of "strong red" (*Enquiry*, 2.15), the color of *Vir Heroicus Sublimis*.[66] Newman's *Stations of the Cross: Lema Sabachthani* consists of fourteen large white and black (in Newman, the color of tragedy) panels: "It was more appropriate for me to be concerned with the Sabachthani ( . . . forsaken me)." Harold Rosenberg calls Newman "a theologian of nothingness" who wanted to "induce nothingness to exclaim its secrets."[67] Even Taylor refers to the "cold austerity" and "agony and despair" of his work.

If the "exclusive logic" of either/or characterizes modernism, the second epoch is marked by the "inclusive logic" of both/and. In their modernist postmodernism, Andy Warhol, Jasper Johns, pop art, the architecture of Robert Venturi, Philip Johnson, James Stirling, and Michael Graves undo their modernist predecessors by "disfiguring" their already nonobjective art and their pure architectural forms with playful decor, mixed materials, quotation, ironic counterpoint, superficial gestures, and satiric reductions. A Philip Johnson skyscraper might resemble a Chippendale or a Dutch gabled house. Charles Moore's *Piazza d'Italia* (1975–1978) in New Orleans recalls classical Rome and medieval Italy with its pastiche of columns, its loggia, elegant marble, Roman lettering, arches, fountain, and graffiti. If modernism removed history by ascesis, postmodernism brings back the flotsam and jetsam of historical memory in parodic form by synecdoche or abridged reference or, to cite Baudelaire on modernity, by "immersion in the ephemeral, fugitive, and contingent." This is the realm of Immanence: "For the pop artist and postmodern architect, the Kingdom is *present* here and now." Taylor forces examples into his categories: as a "modernist postmodern" work, Michael Graves's Plocek Residence in New Jersey (1979–1982) should "counteract modern architecture's insensitivity to nature."[68] If the photograph is any indication, however, this forbidding, block-ish domicile does not fit comfortably within its natural landscape. To take a more recent example, Frank O. Gehry's Stata Center "for computer, informa-tion and intelligence sciences" at MIT (2004) is whimsical, tumbledown, and antirational; take away the colors, add a dense New England cloud cover, and it mimics the movie set of Fritz Lang's expressionist *Metropolis* (1927), set in 2026. Yet to produce this sense of the antirational and play required a large measure of self-conscious architectural rationalism, which quickly shows through and robs the center of its pretense to spontaneity. Moreover, it is fair to point out that modernism itself began the process of dealing with popular art forms and ironic play (early cubism, Dadaism); later forms are reorienta-tions of modernism, not necessarily rejections or oppositions.[69]

Since the second epoch is tied to the "disfiguring" premises of the first, even by irony and rejection, the third epoch, or postmodernism, conceives what has been left "unthought" in the attempt "to figure a disfiguring that struggles to figure the unfigurable in and through the faults, fissures, cracks, and tears of figures." Exemplars of the third epoch with its more radical deformations in-clude Anselm Kiefer and Michelangelo Pistoletto in painting and Bernard Tschumi and Peter Eisenman in architecture. Absence and ascesis yield up mysterious presence: "Torn figures mark the trace of something else, some-thing other that *almost* emerges in the cracks of faulty images. This other nei-ther is nor is not—it is neither being or nonbeing, fullness or void, immanent or transcendent." Such hinted traces, the tragic face of postmodernist quota-tion, are categorized as "altarity," linking "alter" and "altar"; the sacrifice and worship of the different other. Occupying a "middle ground between classical theology and atheism," a/theologians like Taylor search out "interstitial space" and "intermediate time" of third-epoch artists so that they can "refigure the polarities and oppositions that structure traditional religious thought." In his a/theoesthetics, "what neither of these alternatives [belief and atheism] con-fronts is the possibility of the impossibility of the Kingdom—here or else-where, now or then."[70]

This arid, self-made terminology, the language of a decadent criticism, masks an absence of contextualization in the history of religion, art history, biogra-phy, and sociology. It is worth noting that Taylor emphasizes the impact of Madame Blavatsky and theosophy, at the time a new age religion with roots in

Renaissance occultism at the expense of institutional religions. When Taylor investigates Kandinsky and Malevich, mainly their theosophical divagations, not their Russian Orthodox background, come into play; with Mondrian, too, theosophy trumps the iconoclasm of the Dutch Reformed Church; for Ad Reinhardt, it is theosophy, not Lutheranism. Nor does Taylor suggest that Newman's Jewish heritage was a likely source of inspiration for such works as his *Abraham* and *Joshua*. One of the unspoken assumptions in Taylor's a/theology derives from the Enlightenment: in the name of progress and reason, the desire to deliver a historical blank slate.

On the relation between artists and their art-historical contexts, Taylor concedes that he does not deal in strictly historical terms and that the three epochs or styles are "alternative strategies of disfiguring." Yet his language betrays an antipathy to history: "Modern art cannot be forced into the straitjacket of linear development"; a "more responsible approach . . . requires an openness to patterns of change." Though one agrees on the need for responsibility and openness, one questions whether Picasso could have painted before, and not after, Cézanne. Could Frank Lloyd Wright and Mies van der Rohe have come after, and not before, Venturi and Graves? Do not Warhol and company follow, not precede, Marcel Duchamp? If modern art challenges the historian in unexpected ways, one does not need to throw one's hands in the air. When heroic modernists thrust themselves out of history in acts of transcendence, this does not annihilate history; rather, it leads one to ask, what in their historical conditions led them to do so? Where did history fail them? Taylor traces postmodernist artists back to their modernist origins, unwittingly giving evidence for art *history*. It is remarkable that he should take to task the death-of-God theologian Thomas J. J. Altizer for "resist[ing] the careful analysis of contemporary society and culture." Altizer at least appreciates the art-historical approach: "Just as the portraits of the High Renaissance transcend the form established by the human icons of Giotto, modern painting has broken through the forms established by the Renaissance. Yet it is crucial to note that it has broken through them and not simply dissolved them; it has never ceased to embody its Western ground and origin."[71]

As for biography, another potential ground of historical inquiry, Taylor cites Barnett Newman approvingly on the "obsolete props of an outmoded and antiquated legend": "We are freeing ourselves of the impediments of memory, association, nostalgia, legend, myth, or what have you." In the Emersonian tradition, the American artist is "like a barbarian" compared to a "highly civilized" European counterpart. "Free of the ancient paraphernalia," the American artist comes "closer to the sources of tragic emotion."[72]

These comments should, however, be taken within the ironic context of

Newman's work. For him, great artists exist apart from professional institutions and patronage and speak with their art to their own innermost feelings more than to society. This "speech" allows any other great artist to understand them, not on a formal or pictorial level or with some vague spiritualism, as the modernist utopians speculated, but on an emotional level, in direct response to transhistorical factors of human tragedy (war, death, cruelty, and so forth, present in some specific way in every generation). The link of feeling, from artist to artist across time, transcends prevailing political and religious doctrines, which might be useless in the face of the deepest human problems. Though Newman was at one level a "staunch atheist [and] pragmatist," he also had an ecumenical side that enabled him to paint his *Stations of the Cross*.[73] The symbol-laden titles of his paintings—*Ulysses, Prometheus Bound, Death of Euclid, Uriel, Dionysus*—express his desire to communicate "specific and separate embodiments of feeling." He enjoyed claiming that he was in conversation with Michelangelo and Rembrandt. Mrs. Newman insisted her husband had no interest in Nietzsche and did not like anything Nietzschean, but there is a resemblance between Newman's transcendence through feeling and the Nietzschean "untimeliness" of great literary and artistic exemplars standing up and outside of history.[74] Newman does not "forget."

Nor does Taylor come to terms with the relation of art and architecture to social, economic, and political history. He missed an opportunity to explore Andy Warhol's fascination with Ronald Reagan. "For Ronnie, as for Andy, life *is* television." If this insufficient summary were the case, Warhol would never have been an artist, or Reagan a president. Then, approvingly, Taylor finds "not a trace of nostalgia" in Moore's Piazza d'Italia. The hermeneutics of suspicion are at work in placing nostalgia under surveillance—a reactionary attitude, a refuge of paternalism, institutional religion, hierarchy, and the organic community. The minute one states a preference for an earlier period, there is always someone who will level an accusation of *nostalgia*. One would hope for some distinction between superficial notions of nostalgia and deep nostalgia. What is all the imagery of the Piazza *about*? For Taylor, in the footsteps of the Frankfurt School, "myths and rituals can be revived only as theatrical spectacles." On the contrary, it is impossible to look at the Piazza d'Italia without thinking about the past and the ancestors, though one would first have to get over the shabby joke that the place really is. Taylor probably does not know that New Orleans has one of America's largest Little Italies and that many of its inhabitants might well look upon the Piazza with a mixture of pride—and nostalgia. Taylor's promise to clarify a "disturbing complicity" between modernism and fascism never materializes beyond superficial biographical remarks about Le Corbusier's flirtation with Mussolini and Mies van der Rohe's membership in the Reichskulturkammer in the 1930s. Instead of historical analysis, one has portentous clichés that would not survive the seminar room. "What began in the salons of Jena ended on the stage in Bayreuth and on the parade grounds of Nuremberg." "If the twentieth century teaches us anything, it is that our dreams often become nightmares and that utopia can turn into hell. It is an old, perhaps ancient, tale: the repressed does not go away"; "the forgotten never simply disappears but eternally returns to haunt the present and disrupt presence."[75] And so forth.

Above all, attention to the historical setting would have grounded Taylor in the technological determinants in twentieth-century painting, architecture, and religion. At times he seems oblivious to them: post–World War II America was "characterized by growing uncertainty about the benefits of modern technology."[76] Yet apart from a few marginal voices, postwar America was positively ecstatic about technology. Wasn't it the dawn of the television era? Going to the moon? Technological values have more explanatory power than the quasi-religious values in much of the art and architecture that Taylor describes. These values reflect the cultural forgetfulness and indifference to reference—witness the modular International Style skyscrapers; new-brutalist block flats with their inhuman scale, skeletal aridity, and plain surfaces; minimalist art, which is nonrepresentational, "anti-emotional," and "anti-subjective" (the "dominant idea in art of the past forty years").[77] In this respect, Taylor might have consulted Wylie Sypher who long ago explored the connections among Paterian ascesis, modernist aesthetics, and technology: "Artists and scientists submit to the technological canon of parsimony. . . . Pater's style is a technological feat, a version of engineering in art, a manifestation of Taylorism in aesthetics."[78] Finally, postmodernist quotation, play, and ornamentation present an incoherent variety show, and not Immanence, and certainly not History. Within this spectacle the forms and figures of the past return for a final bow.

"Technology's destruction of tradition," argues Ellul, "forces artist to invent a new aesthetic." In summarizing and extending the conclusions of Erich Kahler, Wylie Sypher, Jacques Ellul, and other critics, Richards Stivers enumerates ways in which technology influences artistic production, either directly or indirectly. Modern art mimics technological experimentation by "transitory artistic fashion"; it adopts the technological breakdown of the object and "takes everything out of its cultural, historical, and natural context"; it emphasizes "sheer construction" or making, whose "arbitrariness . . . apes the arbitrariness of technological possibility" ("if it is possible, it will be done"). Also, modern art emphasizes the irrational, protesting the dominance of instrumental reason; it borrows from the techniques of psychology, topology, electronics, and field dynamics; it argues against the "loss of the self" and the rise of the functional "human without qualities." Finally, Stivers cites Josephine Gattuso Hendin's *Vulnerable People* and John Aldridge's *Talents and Technicians* on the "machine-like" characters of postmodern fiction. "The individual," says Aldridge, "has been forced to become obsessed with the technology of all his personal processes, to see them, as he sees himself and other people, as objects to be analyzed and evaluated for their correctness according to various behavioral instruments and sociological surveys." Hendin's recent *Heartbreakers,* a study of women and violence, adds substantially to Stivers's case.[79]

Taylor accuses Philip Johnson of not appreciating the "complexity of his multiple historical quotations" of his "shrine" in the lobby of the AT&T corporate headquarters on Madison Avenue (1979–1984). Yet the lobby displays the large golden statue *Genius of Electricity* that had stood atop the previous headquarters. Why did the *Genius of Electricity* retain pride of place at AT&T? The technological system remains the milieu in which artists, architects, and even a/theologians move and have their being. Even more than a hundred years ago, the genius of electricity drives the system. Taylor's unpalatable neologisms and verbalisms—altarity, imagology, simcult, a/theology, archetexture, anarchetecture, theoesthetics, a/theoesthetics—spread a thin, spiritual veneer over a rather ugly truth regarding the technologization of the inner sanctum. His pages faintly echo the existentialism of the 1950s with vestiges of deconstruction. In his hands, these movements lose their power of protest and critical force. "The word of the call is never truly present; it echoes and re-echoes from the beyond of a terrifyingly ancient that forever approaches as a future that never arrives to disrupt the present that never is."[80] So we live in an echo chamber in which the past is "terrifyingly ancient" and irretrievable. Where Camus imagined Sisyphus as "happy," Taylor's therapeutic a/theology recalls American boosterism; it will never put the fear of God into us.

## Anti–Las Vegas

The Grand Tour was the voyage of education taken by young, mainly British aristocrats and upper bourgeoisie, later by the middle class, to France, Germany, Switzerland, and Italy from the mid-seventeenth to the end of the eighteenth centuries; it then became a generalized name for such a trip in the nineteenth century. Though there were several preferred routes, the tour was not a tour unless it passed through Italy, and it was not grand until it culminated in Rome. Ideally, a high degree of personal cultivation was expected and rewarded; many Grand Tourists knew Greek and Latin. Hester Thrale Piozzi, who traveled through Italy from 1785 to 1787, expressed her sadness on not being able to read a Greek inscription: "I lose infinite pleasure every day, for want of deeper learning."[81] She invokes a classical topos, *utile et dolce,* on the function of the arts to provide instruction and pleasure. Milton, Addison, Thomas Gray, Laurence Sterne, Goethe, De Stael, Byron, Shelley, Stendahl, Margaret Fuller, Ruskin, and thousands of others all made the Grand Tour. They left behind a wealth of journals, memoirs, aesthetic commentaries, guides, travelogues, fiction, and poetry, of which the central, interlinking themes were cultural memory and self-discovery.

One of the best examples of cultural forgetting with the inevitable consequences inflicted upon the self has been happening in Las Vegas, which in the past two decades has become the acknowledged paradigm (architecturally, culturally, semiotically, and so on) of American urbanism. There, in one place, the traveler may embark upon what Giovanna Franci calls "the Virtual Grand Tour" of the themed megaresort hotel-casinos: the Bellagio; the Venetian; the Tuscany; Paris Las Vegas; Caesars Palace; New York, New York; Mandalay; Treasure Island, and more. In 1999, thirty-four million tourists (up 10.5 percent from the previous year) came not only to gamble but also to take in the "phantasmagoria of the latest constructions."[82] Latest, indeed, because in Las Vegas one finds impermanence in the constant destruction and construction of the big casinos, like the Luxor Resort whose thirty-story pyramid will last not three thousand but (at most) thirty years. Virtual Grand Tourists want entertainment and stories to tell, perhaps the reassurance of having enjoyed what advertisers have said they would enjoy. Entertainment is one of the strongest determinants in contemporary society; the sense of a person's very well-being attaches to the word. The sad truth is that, given the intellectual effort involved, more people would rather see the Grand Tour in Las Vegas than in Europe.

A number of the contemporary casinos have an Italian theme, appropriate for a Virtual Grand Tour, when Italy has become an advertising marker for luxury, style, leisure, sexuality, and globalization itself. One might well wonder how Italian Virtual Grand Tourists respond to seeing their old cities and hill towns miniaturized in Las Vegas—as one knows, Italians love gambling, variety shows, and spectacle; *casino* is, after all, an Italian word. What are their impressions on wandering through Caesars Palace (1966), the trailblazer of themed hotel-casinos, and confronting its one thousand–seat "Circus Maximus" resembling a toy Colosseum (but what's in a name?) or its Forum Shops where a statue of Bacchus says, "Come one, come all; and welcome to the mall" beneath a trompe l'oeil sky (but with too many clouds for Italy)?[83] The Tuscany Resort Hotel (1995), re-creating a Tuscan orchard in the middle of the desert, may strike a discordant note in an Italian heart. Cypress trees line the entrance of the costliest resort casino to date ($1.6 billion), the Bellagio (1998), which caters to pampered luxury. It has elegant parterres, a conservatory, and botanical gardens with Mediterranean flora, and it had a $300 million art museum until it was sold off by MGM, its latest owners. Originally, even the slot trays were lined in velvet so that one did not hear the clink of change and be reminded of where one really was, a casino. Enormous fountains spray water 240 feet high, timed to operatic arias and "whimsical music" on an eleven-acre imitation of Lake Como.

The almost equally costly Venetian Resort (1999) has a half-size replica of the Campanile; a small Bridge of Sighs; a Doge's Palace "complete with gold-framed fresco reproductions" of Titian, Tintoretto, and Veronese on a sixty-five-foot-high ceiling; a Ca' d'Oro; and a Rialto, all interspersed with perfumed canals on which tourists ride gondolas through a shopping mall.[84] The Venetian advertises "real" gondoliers. The philosopher Massimo Cacciari, mayor of Venice at the time of the resort's opening, protested the "violent" "architectural rip-off"; the faculty at the Institute of Architecture in Venice spoke of a "monstrosity."[85] Venice needed protection from trivialization, potentially more destructive than the *aqua alta*. The Venetian Resort follows "the logic of a set backdrop" or "pieces of a chess set in a seemingly casual manner," notes Franci. However, the Piazza San Marco lacks the cathedral. "Perhaps in the face of that masterpiece" the designer's "mix and match didn't dare go further."[86] Did they fear imitating the sacred? Did they run out of money, or bad taste?

Furio Colombo, who came in 1988, compared Las Vegas at night to a luxury ocean liner crossing a desert—an apt metaphor given that Bugsy Siegel and the East Coast Mafia developers thought of a Las Vegas resort along the lines of Miami Beach, the Caribbean, and the cruise ships. But on closer inspection, the city lights gave the synthetic impression "not of carnival, but of emergency." In the "intense artificiality" of the place, everything looks "fake," "imitated," "exaggerated," "deformed," "replicated": a momentary feeling of authenticity fades to a sense of falsity that "tranquillizes," a relief that the originals are safe elsewhere, and a negative pleasure in the relaxation of so-called gambler's strain. Artificial, too, is the stratification of the life cycle on the Strip. There are almost no children (at least in the 1980s, before the growth of family tourism, and even at that only in certain specified areas), then people in their twenties and thirties in the service industry. The croupiers are in their forties. Then there is an age gulf beyond which are the gamblers, people in their fifties and sixties, and retirees. The late middle-aged group are the "ideal visitors" because "it takes a certain disappointment, a certain experience of life's limitations, to let themselves be taken in by the lights of Las Vegas."[87] They come seeking therapeutic rehabilitation under the guise of "fun" through gambling and sex. In some ways they resemble many of the entertainers—fading stars trying to make a comeback—with an occasional real star like Sinatra who used to appear for one or two days a year to lend legitimacy.

Casinos are "factories" of "fun" that consume neurasthenia and produce great supplies of energy with the intention of calming and exhausting (or, precisely, tranquilizing) them. In his study of play Roger Caillois also notes that the world of the casino is invaded by modern work.[88] Such energies are needed to last the nights of strenuous gambling, for there is no cessation: casinos operate nonstop twenty-four hours a day in the same artificial lighting and without clocks, adding to the disorientation. Las Vegas is beyond ordinary time. (It is true that the atmosphere of the Forum Shops at Caesars Palace simulates the rise and fall of the sun, but it is on a two-hour timer, so that one gets twelve days in one—a bargain.)[89] Frail, elderly ladies demonstrate the strength of stevedores in front of slot machines whose levers they pull five hundred times a day. In a therapeutic society the gamblers want to win money for their rehabilitation: as Colombo says, "Money is salvation." Even the prostitutes more resemble instructresses at a health clinic or members of the Salvation Army rather than streetwalkers in Montmartre. This is partly because Las Vegas showgirls are not allowed to be even slightly overweight; they must have youthful muscle tone, a high-tech, "ageless smoothness.[90] Everything is "fake joy" and "fake sin," like the nudity that, though real enough, has a certain antiseptic spoofing. Caesars Palace has a touch of the funereal in its ponderous borrowings—is it the death of the past that is being spoofed?

Giovanna Franci sees Las Vegas functioning as a "design lab" for notions of originality and copy, fake, forgery, sign, and plagiarism, and standing for trends in urbanism, entertainment, and globalization. In her view, the city expresses the paradoxical desire for "originality-through-repetition" or "revelation-through-simulation." Where mere copies of buildings or architectural features might elicit nostalgia and correspondent passivity, new aesthetic pleasures are stimulated by the "creative imitation" of the themed casinos, by their "virtuosic and combinatorial game," and by an "amused re-use and conscious retrieval from the warehouses of tradition." Through miniaturization, concentration, synecdoche, and enlargement, products may appear "more real than the real thing," or what Umberto Eco calls the "Absolute Fake." There is currently a proposal on the table for a Casino Las Vegas that will be a scaled-down, three-eighths version of main attractions in Las Vegas itself—the Bellagio, the Venetian, and others. Still, for Franci as opposed to Eco, "a fake can be fun, and in its continual deviation from the imaginary, it can in turn produce a new chain of fakes, each with small differences." Even the ugly as an aesthetic category has its place because it "brings new meaning to the familiar and conventional through the principles of copying and ironic allusion." The whole is original, an "ensemble of copies."[91]

Because history is a mere springboard for fantasy and never deeply engaged, thematic content obsolesces quickly, and the joke wears off. The most well known hotel-casinos are constantly being demolished to make way for new costlier, more spectacular ones, like a product line. "Unlike Honolulu, Miami Beach, Acapulco, and other resort cities," notes Eugene P. Moehring on turnover syndrome, "future-oriented Las Vegas has exhibited no sentimental qualms about destroying its architectural past." In 1972 Robert Venturi published perhaps the most famous book ever written on the city, the bible of postmodernism, *Learning from Las Vegas;* he might be surprised to learn that every major building he discussed has been demolished. Hal Rothman speaks of "a city that implodes its past."[92] The Virtual Grand Tour hardly looks backward or pays homage to a cultural past. It will soon be replaced by some other theme, say, space travel, with casinos named after planets and galaxies. Advertising demands it. No one misses these kitsch casinos and replicas either because their originals are elsewhere or because they are not worth remembering. Without their shock value, they fade soon enough. A fake can be fun but, sad to say, fun can't be faked.

Like Zygmunt Bauman in *Liquid Modernity,* Franci calls attention to the extreme mobility of the current scene in every dimension, a "constant movement" of people, fashions, and ideas across oceans to the point of asking, "Who is imitating whom?" Modern technologies have changed the nature of travel, not only of physical travel but also of the cultural imaginary; direct television and the Internet present events "live and nonstop" from around the world. Where travel once led to knowledge of *the other,* today "either the other has already become like us, or the other is not open to being known." With its leveling, reduction, and simplification, the technological imperatives are busily at work. "Everything seems familiar and partakes of standardization."[93] This is not entirely new—one thinks of World Fairs, dioramas, or London's Crystal Palace. Yet now "it is possible to 'visit' a city without going there," as Henry James thought of Venice. A virtual World Grand Tour can be undertaken in one place, a desert: Rome, the Riviera, Tuscany, Venice, Lake Como, Paris, Luxor, Mandalay, and more.

In the 1970s Umberto Eco bypassed Las Vegas in his travels in hyperreality, believing it to be too much "a 'real' city" rather than a fake one, that is, a theme park like Disney World. Since then, however, the line between theme-park fantasy and urban reality has been blurred. Even Disney World has absorbed or been interpenetrated by its surrounding environment. Bruce Bégout said recently that Las Vegas is "nothing more than our everyday cityscape."[94]

The technological overkill of the casinos, without which these billion-dollar stunts could not exist, has never been given sufficient attention. The connection with technology is crucial because Las Vegas, which receives its water supply and electricity from Hoover Dam (1931–1934), "was possible only with air-conditioning and the other mechanisms of industrial society."[95] One recalls Colombo's luxury liner, sailing on an ocean of sand. Another Italian traveler, Goffredo Parise, sees only death, a "slavery" to consumerism, and the "degeneration of Western man."[96] For him, the dehumanized Las Vegas is spiritually or mythically continuous with the nonhuman desert, both of which are rendered in frenetic, hallucinatory prose. In the desert on the road to Las Vegas he ran out of gas, that is, out of luck, a sign of death. By good fortune, an augury of Las Vegas, a gas station was nearby. Yet the station stood beside an automobile cemetery, which he takes as synecdochic of the city and America at large: deadening technicism. To her credit, Franci can enjoy the game played over Caesars Palace, the Bellagio, and the Venetian without a trace of moral superiority. At the same time the original enters to judge the facsimile. As Franci knows, Las Vegas is a technological, not a Roman, triumph.

Robert Venturi reads Las Vegas in the context of Rome, partly to legitimate his observations. Thus, each city shares in the mixing of high and low culture, of public and private spaces, "the vulgar and the Vitruvian," to their mutual benefit. Venturi embraces sixties-style values, rejecting high modernism as elitist, finding pumped-up similitudes across the world regardless of historical context, downplaying crucial differences, and generally enjoying the postmodern leveling. He remarks upon parallels between the "expansive settings" of Rome and Las Vegas in relation to the Campagna and the desert, "which tend to focus and clarify their images." This could be said of a hundred world cities, and the Campagna was largely populated in the ancient period, as it is increasingly again today. One analogy stretches the imagination to its limits: "Las Vegas is to the Strip what Rome is to the Piazza." The link is the art of strolling, which was lost in American suburbs. But as Herbert Schiller points out, the corporate managers have a palpable design on those strollers from the moment they set foot near their precincts, with all sorts of gimmicks to lure people into the casinos. The Strip is one of those places like malls, theme parks, and corporate "public spaces" that function as "culture industries," that is, as "symbolic sites for the creation, packaging, transmission, and placement of cultural messages—corporate ones especially"—for the sake of promoting buying (and gambling).[97] The Forum in Caesars Palace was the most profitable mall in America in the late 1990s. Besides, the Strip is a wide four-mile-long thoroughfare, hardly with the intimacy of the piazza.

When Venturi argues that in Las Vegas an architecture of signs takes precedence over space and that Rome provides a model for understanding it, he goes seriously wide of the mark. If communication "dominates space" in Las Vegas, one cannot say the same for Rome. According to Siegfried Giedion, the Romans

virtually invented the architecture of internally organized space, and if one believes that architecture is the shaping of space, not just an aggregation of visual
signs in space, this item in the comparison between Rome and Las Vegas is also
questionable.[98]

Venturi's defense of the sign and symbolic content over pared-down modernist architecture ("free from images of past experience") leads him again to
Rome. The Roman triumphal arch is "a prototype of the billboard." Actually,
the triumphal arch tended to announce a spatial demarcation, among other
things—it was either a genuine entrance or a central site. The billboard is stuck
into space that cannot be used for any other purpose and marks nothing, except perhaps, when on the margins of a city, the fact that what is to come is
probably a little more interesting than what has just passed. The Romans did
not top off their temples with billboards on the roof—maybe (later) a cupola,
a spire, or a lantern, not something totally unrelated like a cigarette ad. Venturi's analogy is blown out of all proportion: "Like the complex architectural
accumulations of the Roman Forum, the Strip by day reads as chaos if you perceive only its forms and exclude its symbolic content. The Forum, like the
Strip, was a landscape of symbols, with layers of meaning evident in the loca-
tion of roads and buildings, buildings representing earlier buildings and the
sculpture piled all over. Formally the Forum was an awful mess; symbolically it
was a rich mix." But the symbols of the Romans had depth and density, as they
were founded in religion, legend, and ethos, whereas the accumulation of signs
and symbols in Las Vegas is a flight of mere fancy, corporate logos, ads—thin,
synthetic, replaceable. The whole process of modern desymbolization that
writers from Vico, Schiller, and Carlyle to Jacques Ellul and Lewis Mumford
comment upon and lament makes it impossible for an environment like Las
Vegas to resonate like Rome. Even Venturi admits that "the rate of obsolescence
of a sign seems to be nearer to that on an automobile than that of a building."
Unlike Rome, Venturi adds amusingly, "Las Vegas *was* built in a day."[99] Did the
Romans see fit to dismantle their Forum every thirty years? Although they did
add to it from time to time, they did not regularly recast it because its objects
and forms were cherished as more than mere amusements. Those sites were
richly symbolic even for the Christians afterward; as Rodolfo Lanciani notes,
the Christians preserved many of them. Would Fustel de Colanges confuse
Fremont Street with the Via Lata or the Strip with the Via Sacra? The fact that
the Forum may appear a jumble to Venturi begs the question, what is it a jumble of? The Temple of Romulus, the House of the Vestals, the Temple of Venus
Genetrix, the Arch of Septimus Severus . . .

Assuming the mantle of prophecy, Venturi welcomes the inevitable hour:
"The archetypal Los Angeles will be our Rome and Las Vegas our Florence."[100]

Such is the nauseated wish fulfillment of an architectural formalist who has wandered far beyond his sphere and who, in learning from Las Vegas, took the wrong lesson to heart. If only an appeal to high theory could redeem the unprecedented banality of Las Vegas and its ilk! But the truth is simpler than the simulacrum. Las Vegas, "the place where the twenty-first century begins," is the most extreme version of the tendency leading to a hodgepodge of the flotsam and jetsam of dozens of cultures without respect for their origin or meaning, organized by the technical-managerial state and propelled by Hollywood and advertising.[101] Perhaps Venturi attracts followers because few want to denigrate their times, especially such upbeat ones as ours! Technicism has surely won out when it has produced minds so lacking a sense of historical difference that they mistake the aridities of current experience for the real thing.

On leaving Las Vegas, travelers might notice the advertisement for the restaurant chain Fellini's that reads: "Taking a tour of Italy while visiting Las Vegas." Their sensibilities will receive a final jolt if they pass by Lake Las Vegas. In 1986, Ronald F. Boedekker, a civil engineer and developer, flew over a tract of land fifteen miles southeast of the Strip and found a canyon being used as a conduit for treated sewage: "I saw the potential to remake Lake Como in Italy."[102] Ten years later, at a cost of seven billion dollars, huge pipes had been laid to divert the sewage, the canyon had been excavated to a maximum depth of 150 feet, an eighteen-story dam had been constructed with more earth than the Hoover Dam has concrete, and the lake with a ten-mile circumference was filled with 3.26 billion gallons of water (it took two and a half years to fill up, with about half a billion gallons added every six months). For several years the site remained bare, looking like the stark landscape of an undiscovered planet.

Then new developers stepped in with more money, work was resumed in earnest, and in August 2004 MonteLago opened. The most elaborate of the lake's gated communities is an imitation of an Italian hill town built on a fifty-acre site; streets are named Via Bel Canto, Via Brianza, and the like. In the spirit of the game the marketing directors produced a fake town history: "MonteLago grew organically over the centuries, from a quaint fishing village to an elegant Tuscan estate with its own winery and bell tower." One lake resident who had never been to Italy said that the resort "feels like a European village"; he took pains with the design of his villa, adding a turret of cultured stone: "Now it looks Tuscan." Another resident put the finishing touches on her six million–dollar home with "real" cracked stucco: "This is how they did it in Italy. It's not a faux finish." Certainly not, but it is faux Italy, faux Grand Tour.

One spectacular vista is a lake-spanning wing of the Ritz-Carlton, designed as a colossalized copy of the Ponte Vecchio, the *old* bridge, in Florence. There, in the casino on an upper floor, one imagines that the great forgetters are lounging about. They have no more to forget, not a cloud, not a tree; their work has been done for them. The great forgetting sums itself up in Las Vegas, dehumanized to the point where it becomes the nonhuman and therefore an ironic counterpart to the desert itself.

Las Vegas is approached on all sides from the desert with its mountains, canyons, and petrified forests. Unlike the mountains in Western Europe, with their associations of "millennial wisdom," the Italian novelist and travel writer Guido Piovene maintains that the southwestern Rockies are "inhuman," "abstract," "alienated in themselves," and "refractory to man." The landscape is not "ancient," which would imply a human scale; rather, it is "outside human time," "geological," and "astral." Not anthropomorphic, the divine presence in the landscape is a "sacred horror" of Power and Force. Thick crowds of stars give one the feeling of being inside the Milky Way, not looking up at it; no detachment can be gained. Constellations and mythologies could not possibly organize this night sky that is "without design" and "absolute" ("without ties"). "The profoundest joy that American nature can offer is the sense of grandeur; but not because one feels taken up by the eternal; rather, one feels divided from oneself, never where one is, always elsewhere, projected onto a chance point in the cosmos."[103] Europeans stand before a mountain to feel the eternal within themselves—this is the Kantian sublime with its sense of self-empowerment (as in Caspar David Friedrich). On the contrary, nature in America absorbs the spectator into the aeons of time—this is the Burkean or negative sublime, a disempowerment or destruction of the self. The Grand Canyon—and the other great canyons of the Far West—presents a totally alien world, an "inaccessible kingdom," a "subaqueous vision . . . an ocean seen to the dry bottom." Piovene refers to "our" Alps as if they had long been contained and humanized. But one cannot possess the Grand Canyon, nor does it possess you. It has nothing to do with you. The fiercest Alps are "hospitable" compared to this "necropolis," this "immense nakedness of cruel color." The recurrent image is an ocean without water: the unnatural, terror, death, and the sublime. Las Vegas, the luxury liner, appears on the horizon after crossing "immense basins of stone, almost like a dry sea, with a golden and whitish bottom."[104]

Rugged mountains, deserts, and the wilderness are traditional homes of the sacred: mountains for their grandeur, "freedom," overpoweringness, and "inaccessibility"; deserts in their "sparse simplicity," "constant proximity to death," and "expression of senseless joy amid the brief intensity of life." Writing on the Judeo-Christian and Buddhist traditions, Belden Lane describes the mountain-desert experience as one of renunciation and the *via negativa*, of wastelands, boundary zones, limits, and voids: "Places on the edge, those considered God-forsaken by many, are where his identity as Messiah has to be revealed." Las

Vegas ("the meadows") is an oasis, long known to Native Americans and Spanish missionaries, and once served as a life-giving contrast to the harshness of the general setting. But the first adjective Piovene applies to Las Vegas is *monstrous (mostruosa);* he had already used it twice to depict the desert landscape. Rudolf Otto said that "the monstrous is just the mysterious in gross form"; beyond conception, the *mysterium tremendum* excites terror and fascination, "personal nothingness and abasement" passing into awe before the Wholly Other, and a confrontation with the Void. The numinous is associated with silence, darkness, and emptiness, like the "wide-stretching desert," "a negation that does away with every 'this' and 'here,' in order that the 'wholly other' may become actual."[105]

Like monsters, the astral landscape and Las Vegas—with its technological system on parade, its suppression of clocks, its sense of limitless scale, and above all its great forgetfulness—are "outside human time." Desert and city are strangely interchangeable, and although Las Vegas mimics sacred horror and the negative sublime in the way it mimics everything else, by cheapening and perverting them, the numinous can be present in absence (as it is in the desert) or immanent in the very act of parody and allusion. Otto finds the numinous in wild animals and massive stone forms, like the Sphinx at Giza and the Assyrian lion; there is the Luxor Resort's massive Sphinx who stares not with a sense of withholding secret wisdom but in cartoonish stupefaction at what lies before him, and the giant lion that "swallows" incoming guests at the entrance to the MGM.

Shelley's Ozymandias is a ruined statue whose trunkless legs stand next to the half-buried head and whose pedestal proclaims an empty boast of power. Could this be the same pharaoh who built the library with a very different inscription, "Healing Place of the Soul"?

> Nothing beside remains. Round the decay
> Of that colossal wreck, boundless and bare
> The lone and level sands stretch far away.

# The Circle of Knowledge

## Science and the Humanistic

## Curriculum from Petrarch to Trilling

The words *humanities* and *humanism* have long been applied to things that, if related to them, are not of their essence. One could make a collection of the honorific connotations of *humanistic,* taken to mean "humane" or "kindly" or "sensitive." Although the humanities may promote these qualities, strictly speaking they were for centuries constituted by a curriculum originating in the ancient Greek *paideia,* a special kind of education for shaping individual character. The principle of *paideia* inspired a round of studies, *enkuklios paideia,* the "encyclopedia" or "circle of knowledge." The *circle* implies a full and balanced program as well as a *cycle* in an evolving process, a preparation for a higher level of study, the active life, or both.[1] The circle of knowledge is not only a collection of discrete fields or sciences; it is informed by the Platonic spirit, a "science *of* sciences," "becoming conscious of itself and engaging in a process of self-examination" as it seeks a comprehensive understanding of the subjects, methods, interrelationships, and larger goals.[2] The circle encompasses what Cicero calls "the knowledge of things human and divine" in which knowledge is not only an objective content but a metaphor for the life of the mind itself, and the circle is a symbol of wholeness and perfection of mind and character.[3] The classical ideal of education is one of knowledge, but more essentially of individual character, described in terms of completeness or many-sided wholeness, a sense of proportion, the recognition of universal truths above the self, and the harmonious development of various potentialities, with an end beyond itself, and contributing to the state, the church, or some other worthy ideal or forum.

Renaissance humanists attacked preuniversity and university faculties for neglecting the education of character. If, as we know now, more continuity existed between late medieval educational thought and the humanistic Renaissance, one does an injustice to intellectual history to say there was nothing but continuity. The universities, in some cases only a century or two old, had rapidly become centers of subject specialization and accreditation in philosophy, medicine, law, and theology. With reform in mind, the humanists founded schools and crafted a curriculum whereby they would teach not simply subjects but also persons. "Humanistic learning was known in many parts of Europe as the 'new learning,'" notes John W. O'Malley, "but in fact the universities were what was really new."[4] The humanists took subjects that had been taught for centuries and taught them in a new way or with a new emphasis; in addition to serving as the principal entrance to knowledge in other fields and career advancement, Latin and Greek became a way of thinking about the self, culture, and political society. The Spanish Jesuit Juan Bonifacio wrote in 1576, "Puerilis institutio est renovatio mundi" (The education of youth is the renewal of the world).

The humanists inherited the seven liberal arts from the medieval curriculum: the language-oriented trivium (Latin grammar, rhetoric, and logic) taught in the grammar or "trivial"[5] schools; then the number-oriented quadrivium (mathematics, music, geometry, and astronomy). Overlapping occurred: grammar schools taught some of the quadrivium; universities continued with Latin studies, especially in logic. Thus, the humanistic curriculum covers the stages of present-day primary or grammar school, all of secondary school, and the first years of university education. In Italy, the humanists enjoyed a freer hand in preuniversity training than their northern counterparts. Italian universities were professional schools where "students entered as young men in their late teens or early twenties, usually having already completed or nearly completed their pre-professional study of the liberal arts. By contrast, in northern Europe, boys came to the university considerably younger, at about fourteen," and took up where they left off.[6] The humanist and diplomat Johannes Sturm (1507–1589), who directed the gymnasium at Strasbourg for more than forty years, stipulated two periods in education: from five to fourteen, dedicated to Latin and Greek, with some arithmetic, geometry, astronomy, and geography in the final year; and from fourteen to nineteen, for advanced Greek, philosophy, and one higher field (law, theology, or medicine).[7] Humanism spread more slowly in the North because faculties of arts, conservative by nature and controlling a greater part of preprofessional education, resisted the "new learning."

Long ago Remigio Sabbadini reported on Latin and Greek in the Renaissance classroom. Early humanists exhibited great optimism over the intellectual capacities of their pupils, filling educational programs with long lists of subjects. Yet it is sometimes forgotten (though many of us recall) that Greek alone is a time-consuming addition to a curriculum. Subjects other than Latin and Greek vied for a place in the circle, but the record is far from clear: "Not all the subjects within the *studia humanitatis*," notes David Lines on contemporary scholarship, "have been given sufficient attention"; that pertains to the Renaissance as well as more recent periods.[8]

Such lack of attention pertains to the role of science in the curriculum "from Petrarch to Trilling." Were the sciences considered too specialized, too far removed from the inner life and moral choice to merit much space in the curriculum? And when the sciences were included, how much was required? As the sciences multiplied and grew ever more specialized, did they threaten "round learning" with its ideal of wholeness? Though Thomas Arnold recognized the increasing significance of science in education, he excluded it at Rugby, leaving it for the universities: "It was too big to be treated as a sideshow; yet, if given adequate space, it would crowd out subjects which he held to be of vastly greater importance."[9] Yet how could one attain wholeness without the very subjects that played the greatest role in the making of modernity? The integrity of wholeness—opposing self-division, fragmentation, and specialization—had come first; the circle of studies, contracting and expanding over the centuries, followed "to reproduce that ideal"?[10] Far from being a twentieth-century concern, the role of science in the curriculum was already discussed in the Renaissance, debated in the seventeenth and eighteenth centuries, and fought over in the nineteenth and early twentieth centuries, to the point that now, with roles reversed, it is not so much a question of science in the humanities curriculum but rather, for the average student, a few humanities courses in a predominantly science and social science curriculum. The debates have reflected the larger one over the nature of modernity itself.

Science before the scientific revolution, that is, *before the scientific method,* is more often than not a catchall term for facts, opinions, hearsay, storytelling, invention, tradition, and the like. The borders between disciplines were not well established, let alone well policed. Number theory might inform architectural aesthetics, medicine, and astrology, or serve as the "philosopher's guide to the divine order in the nature of the universe."[11] Further, in modern terms mathematics is more of a constructive method than a science. Historians do not normally speak of science as "a recognised independent branch of learning" until around 1600.[12]

Renaissance humanists who wanted science in the curriculum had precedent on their side. Cicero had transformed *paideia* into *humanitas* and *civitas.* A person is not "perfect" or complete, he says in *De natura deorum,* only "some little part of the perfect" (2.14.37).[13] The claims of the self must be balanced against duties within the greater whole of the family, neighborhood, state, and cosmos. By instructing us in these claims and duties, and offering patterns of perfection, the humanities enlarge our humanity. Given that language serves as the bridge between the private and public spheres, the arts of language, rhetoric, and poetry are central to Cicero's educational program. But science forms part of the larger whole as well. *Studia humanitatis*—the phrase is from the *Pro Archias poeta*—embraces poetry, music, "letters" *(litterarum cognitio)*, and philosophy as well as geometry and "every liberal art and branch of learning," including science. "Letters" means not only the literary arts, but all the productions and communications of the written word: "letters" *(litterae)* "gives us the knowledge of the infinite greatness of nature, and, in this actual world of ours, of the sky, the lands, the seas."[14] In his defense of science the humanist Sassolo da Prato appealed to the authority of Cicero, who "always thought well of mathematics, to the point of saying that those alone who knew mathematics were called learned by the ancients."[15] Cicero's concern for mathematics recalls its role in Plato; over the door of the Academy was written: *Let no one unversed in geometry enter here.*

In like manner Quintilian's ideal orator is not complete without geometry, music, and astronomy, which "supply hidden forces and make their silent presence felt," even when not directly invoked. In particular, geometry "soars still higher" and "demonstrates the fixed and ordained courses of the stars, and thereby we acquire the knowledge that all things are ruled by order and destiny, a consideration which may at times be of value to an orator."[16] Quintilian holds up the pragmatic example of Pericles who by explaining the nature of a solar eclipse calmed the Athenians. The Latin encyclopedists—Martianus Capella, Boethius, Cassiodorus—regularized the classical program, bequeathing it in the form of the seven liberal arts to the Middle Ages.

Petrarch's *renovatio studiorum* raised the status of grammar and rhetoric from the bottom to the top, transforming them from utilitarian studies and formulaic exercises to subjects of continuous, demanding effort. Although Eugenio Garin comments on his "persistently hostile attitude" to the sciences,[17] it is also true that, despite Petrarch's ridicule of abuses, pretensions, and inaccuracies, "at no point did [his] criticism become an attack on natural science" itself.[18] Petrarch found standard works of science to be mixtures of fact and fantasy; not based on observation, they could not be trusted. Mocking outbursts enliven his vast correspondence. "When Petrarch laughed at those of his contemporaries who pretended to know 'about birds and fishes, about how many hairs there are in a lion's mane, how many feathers in the hawk's tail,'" says Eric Cochrane, "he was rejecting the botany and zoology of Vincent of Beauvais and Alexander Neckham, not the botany and zoology as defined by the contemporaries of Francesco Redi." Paul Rose examines Petrarch's friendship with Giovanni de' Dondi, professor of medicine at Padua, who gave him an appreciation of mathematics. In the footsteps of Cicero, Petrarch propounded the myth of Archimedes, "the beginning of a humanist acceptance of mathematics," of which Coluccio Salutati's *De laboribus Herculis* (ca. 1412) was an offspring.[19] Petrarch's rejection of astrology in favor of observation exerted a decisive impact on humanism.

Still, compared with the study of classical authors, scientific knowledge lay somewhat apart from moral discipline and the inner life. "I may well ask myself what the use of knowing the nature of animals, birds, fish and serpents really could be," Petrarch said, "if one has no interest in discovering the nature of man, whence man comes, where he goes." Such cautionary remarks echo throughout the humanistic tradition. Scientific inquiry must be subordinated to human inquiry: Milton's Raphael counseling Adam on scanning the stars, Pope's strictures in the *Essay on Man* on "the proper study of mankind," Samuel Johnson's "We are perpetually moralists, but we are geometricians only by chance." For the Augustan humanists, notes Paul Fussell, "the world of physical nature is morally neutral and thus largely irrelevant to man's actual—that is, his moral—existence." Yet, as Burckhardt said, one of the chief distinguishing features of the Renaissance had been precisely "the discovery of the world and man."[20]

Directly and indirectly, Renaissance humanists played a role in the birth of modern science. Following Petrarch, they spurned blind faith in authority and insisted upon "concrete researches" along two lines: "one in the direction of the moral sciences (ethics, politics, economics, aesthetics, logic, and rhetoric) and one in the direction of the natural sciences."[21] Detachment and objectivity, a historicist perspective, a need for accuracy, a sense of progress, these values accompanied the passionate search for ancient texts. The humanists treated the recovered texts critically, thereby laying the modern foundations for historical method and philology. Ermalao Barbaro, whose early death prevented his editing Greek mathematical texts, claimed to have found "five thousand errors" in Pliny the Elder's *Natural History*, some of which he duly noted in his *Castigationes Plinianae* (1492–1493). "The critical approach that allowed Lorenzo Valla to discredit the *Donation of Constantine* by pointing to its medieval Latin," remarks Pamela O. Long, "was as important to the development of science as it was to classical studies."[22] Less well known is the fact that, "positively receptive to technology," the humanists encouraged studies in perspective, fortifications, mapmaking, and instruments; "handwork, practice, experiment, and observation gained in prestige."[23] For Leonardo, among others, "work, thought, and machines were entering into a relationship that was shortly to change our destiny. . . . Rabelais had not hesitated to include regular visits to technicians and artisans in the educational program of the adolescent Gargantua."[24] In a prespecialized era, some humanists were themselves scientists, like de' Dondi, who designed an astrarium, a "device of consummate mechanical genius," or the polymath physician Girolamo Fracastoro, who wrote a poem on the nature of syphilis and a pioneering treatise on epidemiology.[25]

Above all, from 1400 to 1600 the humanists, or humanist-scientists, or protoscientists, or finally scientists specializing in anatomy, botany, mineralogy, geography, astronomy, and so on, created an intellectual "evolution" in which scientific questioning flourished, and they took care to spread this knowledge to all corners of Europe.[26] The scientists "were ready to adopt the methods of humanism," comments Marie Boas. They "submitted themselves to the rigidity of an intellectual approach which was rooted in the worship of the remote past, and thereby strangely prepared the way of a genuinely novel form of thought about nature in the generation to follow"; with the ideals of humanism they were "in complete sympathy."[27] In *De rebus naturalibus* (1590) Giacomo Zabarella "completed the methodological advances of his predecessors and made them ready for Galileo." The emergence of the scientific spirit in Italy was thus the "natural outcome of a sustained and co-operative criticism."[28] Galileo stands at the end of this transition: "Humanism made him independent of established authority. It provided him with his audience. And it gave him modes of expression."[29] The weight of evidence, then, goes against Robert Proctor's comment: "From the beginning [the humanities] stood in opposition to mathematics and natural science."[30] The real opposition came after the scientific revolution, not before it. "Humanism from the very beginning," maintains Cochrane, "was hostile not to the kind of science later represented by Galileo, but rather to the very kind he did so much to overthrow."[31]

The atmosphere of humanism favored science in the curriculum. Vittorino da Feltre could not afford lessons in mathematics, so he mastered the subject himself, taught it along with Latin, and "maintained a central place" for mathematics and geometry in his program.[32] His boarding school, founded in Mantua in 1424, was the first of its kind and the ancestor of the European and American preparatory schools. It was housed in a villa that had been known as the Casa Giocosa, the joyful house. Vittorino kept the name, for shouldn't a house of learning be a house of joy? He opened his school to both young men and women; he also accepted students from all social classes on the basis of merit and established scholarships for the poor. His ideal was, in his own astonishingly modern words, "equality of opportunity for real ability." There, beginners were taught arithmetic "for its training in accuracy and business-like habits of mind"; older students learned astronomy, natural history, music, geometry and (probably) algebra, drawing, and surveying.[33] According to the Vatican librarian Bartolomeo Platina, a former pupil, Vittorino envisaged a broad educational program because, "just as the body needs a diversity of foods, so the mind needs to be refreshed with varying kinds of study. He praised that which the Greeks call *encyclopaedia,* claiming that learning and erudition result from many and varied studies." Sassolo da Prato, another former pupil, affirmed Vittorino's espousal of mathematics as a "crucial part of the humanist encyclopaedia" in a letter to a "sarcastic correspondent": "Do you know what *humanitas* is?" asks Sassolo, "You who try to overturn and ruin the instruments of *humanitas*? For the ancients sought to imbue the minds of boys with arithmetic, geometry and music, which they thought most suitable for instructing and informing their minds for the reception of the rest of *humanitas.*"[34] In a medallion portrait of Vittorino, commissioned by Ludovico Gonzaga (another pupil), Pisanello engraved the words "Mathematicus et omnis humanitatis pater."

A younger member of Salutati's Florentine circle was Pier Paolo Vergerio, whose *De ingenuis moribus et liberalibus studiis* (ca. 1402) was one of the most influential treatises on education in the fifteenth and sixteenth centuries. Praised by Bartolomeo Fazio as "skilled in law, philosophy and mathematics," Vergerio wanted his students to embrace the "knowledge of Nature—animate and inanimate—the laws and the properties of things in heaven and earth, their causes, mutations and effects, especially the explanation of their wonders"; liberal education meant not only a familiarity with many subjects, but also specialization, since mastery of even one discipline "might fairly be the achievement of a lifetime."[35] This line of thought was taken up by subsequent humanists. Matteo Palmieri in his *Della vita civile* extols "the investigation of the secrets of nature which is sublime and excellent."[36] In *De liberorum educatione* (1450) Aeneas Sylvius Piccolomini, afterward Pius II, includes arithmetic, geometry, and astronomy in his curriculum; in *De ordine docendi ac studendi* (1459) Battista Guarino, the son of Guarino da Verona, assigns Pliny's *Natural History;* and so forth.

Never has European education been so dominated by a single idea as it was by the *studia humanitatis.* In public, private, and religious schools, with only minor variations, the curriculum reigned from Boston to Lima, from Naples, Geneva, and London to Vienna, Kraków, and St. Petersburg. The far-flung Jesuit "colleges" were guided by the *Ratio atque Institutio Studiorum* of 1599, a blueprint for education from elementary school through the university. Its largest section covers secondary education for which are recommended Latin, some Greek, mathematics, and an occasional extra. By 1581 the Jesuits had established 150 colleges; by 1626 there were 441.[37] Protestant academies in Altdorf and Strasbourg, where Calvin had taught, prescribed a program of study that "hardly differed from the one supplied by Jesuit establishments."[38] The English public schools and grammar schools, many of which were founded or refounded in the Reformation, were copies of the ancient grammar school. "Curriculum and methods were not very different from those of the Roman Empire, and an Etonian under Keate [in the 1820s] would have felt quite at home in the schools of the time of Quintilian and Ausonius."[39] In 1864 the Clarendon Commission on public schools reported on average eleven weekly lessons in Latin and Greek, three in mathematics, and two each in modern languages, natural science, and music and drawing. Such in general was the education of Bacon, Voltaire, and Samuel Johnson, of De Staël and the Duke of Wellington, of Disraeli and Max Weber. And Emerson, who wrote in his journal, "And if, in Arkansaw or Texas, I should meet a man reading Horace, I were no stranger." As late as 1944, Patrick Leigh Fermor narrates the crossing of Mount Ida in Crete where the captured German general Karl Kreipe suddenly murmured Horace's "Vides ut alta stet nive candidum / Soracte." Leigh Fermor continued with "nec jam sustineant onus / silvae laborantes"; "for a long moment, the war had ceased to exist. We had both drunk from the same fountains long before; and things were different between us for the rest of our time together."[40]

Emerson and Leigh Fermor represent the best products of the most enduring educational program ever devised in the West. As with any institution over a very long period, however, there were peaks and valleys; the good qualities are always harder to keep. Schedules overloaded with languages, poor textbooks, failure of interest or ability on the part of teachers, cultural letdown when results did not meet expectations—all these factors may be found in the history of the curriculum. The traditional view of the matter is that early Renaissance optimism over a complete curriculum of arts and sciences could not be maintained, that Latin and Greek had ejected other subjects, and that by 1600 "the tyranny of style crept over classical education."[41] In other words, the circle of studies became a semicircle. More recently, this view has undergone some revision. "Late sixteenth- and seventeenth-century announcements of the death of humanism were a considerable exaggeration," comments Anthony Grafton. Humanist enterprises "continued to be carried out, sometimes on a grand scale, throughout the age of science." In the event, adjustments were made in the curriculum; more attention was paid to Cicero's letters, a more appropriate model than the orations for the new administrator. "The curriculum that young men were advised to undertake in the late sixteenth and seventeenth centuries embraced many subjects," notes Grafton, though the distance between advice and actual practice must have been considerable.[42] How far did the new intellectual and social developments change the curriculum?

In the heyday of the humanistic education came the so-called first industrial revolution (roughly 1570–1630) and the scientific revolution, which asserted the power of science and technology to claim truth on a scale and with a certainty hitherto unknown in Western culture. Francis Bacon trumpeted science and technology as a means of making nature more "commodious" to humankind; though he did not design a specific curriculum, works such as *The Advancement of Learning* (1605) and *The New Atlantis* (1624) with its ideal of Salomon's House ("for the finding out of the true nature of all things") inspired generations of educational thinkers across Europe. Baconianism would be congenial in a swiftly changing political and religious situation. Inherent in Protestantism, the "principle of segregation" sundered the realms of transcendent grace and fallen nature, broke the medieval notion of correspondences between realms, and thereby removed a potential barrier to scientific inquiry. In this context, as Charles Webster notes, Bacon's ideas on science and method were "readily assimilated into the social and religious outlook of the reformers during the Puritan revolution" with their "belief in the imminent achievement of a utopian state."[43] Thus, three revolutionary trends had come together: scientific inquiry, nascent industrialism, and Puritanism. Would their total effect return science, at least in England, to an honored place in the circle of knowledge?

Two continental thinkers who had absorbed Bacon's philosophy of education were the Czech Jan Comenius and the Prussian Samuel Hartlib. In 1641 Comenius came to England in the hope of convincing Parliament of the need for radical change in education, beginning with the lower echelons of society; his program was set forth in *The Reformation of Schools* (1637, translation 1642), which encouraged the teaching of languages as the gateway not to classical culture but to universal knowledge. In 1628 Hartlib settled in England where he became a major proponent of educational reform for the next thirty years: his circle included Hezekiah Woodward, Thomas Dury, John Milton, and William Petty. All agreed that if society were to be made anew, then scientific theory and praxis should be two of the foundation stones. Hartlib and Dury proposed common schools for pupils in the lower social classes who, having progressed sufficiently in reading, writing, arithmetic, and geography, would enter a vocational training program (though both wanted educational reform for all social classes, they did not go so far as to advocate a career open to all talents). Petty drew up a plan for "literary work-houses" where science and mechanical arts would be taught to all classes—a forerunner of universal, compulsory education. With such training, as he believed, people in the upper classes "would be less easily cheated by craftsmen" and "could undertake and supervise many practical tasks themselves." In *The Reformed School* (1650)

Thomas Dury advanced the idea of an academy for students from eight to twenty. The standard subjects of the old humanistic curriculum were only one tenth of the entire program. Instead, languages were taught "as a means of conveying information." The schedule was so crammed that two things were left out: the arts and recreation. According to Webster, the idea of extending an education designed for the lower classes to the middle and upper classes shows a fresh approach to curriculum. But the reformers failed because they could not give "the same sense of relevance of a scientifically based education to the higher ranks of society, accustomed to the virtuous or noble education evolved by the Renaissance humanists."[44] (One recalls that college chemistry was commonly called "stinks" in British academic parlance as late as the nineteenth century.) In 1653 Hartlib, Petty, and Dury brought their proposals to the Saints' Parliament, where they languished.

Despite lack of institutional reform, a number of projects went forward on an independent basis. Sir Balthazar Gerbier, an adventurer with an interest in science, ran a gentlemen's academy at Bethnel Green. William Sprigge promoted the idea of colleges nationwide for younger sons, with sciences being taught along with riding, vaulting, and fencing. Abraham Cowley proposed a "Philosophical College near London, lavishly endowed to enable twenty philosophers to research and teach pupils in an adjacent school."[45] The project was never realized, but, like Bacon's Salomon's House from which it descends, the college was a forerunner of the Royal Society.

In the traditional schools, extras like geography were taught on the side and on a fee-for-teaching basis. Long before, in the *Book of the Governor* (1531), Sir Thomas Elyot had urged the study of geography, and in his *New Discovery of the Old Art of Teaching School* (1660) Charles Hoole speaks of an upper floor "wherein to hang maps and set globes, and to lay up such rarities as can be gotten in presses or drawers, that the scholars may know them." Yet in his classic study of the rise of modern school subjects, Foster Watson finds only one reference to the teaching of geography in a public or grammar school: at Westminster, from 1621 to 1628, "after supper (in summer time) they were called to Mr's Chamber (spec. those of the 7th form) and there instructed out of Hunter's *Cosmographie*." Students had more knowledge of ancient geography, which they absorbed from allusions in classical texts, than they did of the age of exploration. The same was true for nature studies, taught as a by-product of Latin: Palingenius's *Zodiacus Vitae* was a standard Latin textbook in "natural knowledge"; it was a "strange mixture of the mythological, zoological, and the ethical, together with the glamour of the marvelous" and including "strong invectives against the Church of Rome."[46] The first history textbook in English schools, Christopher Ocland's *Anglorum Praelia* (1580), was also written in

Latin. In *Of Education* (1644) Milton recommends studying agriculture by way of Varro, Cato the Elder, and Columella. In *Some Thoughts Concerning Education* (1690) Locke recommends some science, which he thought could be presented in Latin (or French) so that one would benefit from learning two things at once.

Equally illustrative is the attitude toward mathematics about which Erasmus had been so cold. In *The Scholemaster* (1570) Roger Ascham says that mathematics produces solitary individuals "unapt to serve the world." Richard Mulcaster, it is true, had proposed a special school for teacher training in mathematics in *Positions* (1581), but his innovative ideas went nowhere. On the whole, mathematics was "mainly outside of the academic system," and the teaching of geometry was "nearly non-existent" through the eighteenth century.[47] In the 1650s the humanist J. F. Gronovius complained that "the age of criticism and philosophy has passed, and one of philosophy and mathematics has taken its place."[48] But it did not affect the curriculum. Samuel Pepys, one of the founders of the modern British navy, who went to St. Paul's and Cambridge, confided to his diary that he was teaching himself elementary multiplication and found it "hard" (he was thirty at the time). He persuaded Charles II to sponsor forty boys with an annuity at Christ's Hospital to study, in addition to Latin, both mathematics and navigation: they were to leave school at sixteen and go to sea for seven years. Hugo Grotius set physics among subjects that future diplomats should study. But for those like Francis Osborn who wanted his son to study "Physic," which would "add to your Welcome where-ever you come," there was nowhere to turn.[49]

In sum, the scientific revolution, Puritanism, and technological developments did not inject more science into the standard curriculum. Reformist influence came outside formal education, as in the eighteenth-century nonconformist academies, "lineal descendents of Dury's 'Reformed School.'" "On the one hand, through the limitation of educational opportunity, the nation's reservoir of scientific talent was not exploited; on the other, the conservatism of traditional education produced an élite unacquainted with science."[50] Even the Protestant demand to study religious texts in the original languages tightened the hold of Latin and Greek (sometimes with Hebrew added) on the schools. Bourgeois parents wanted a classical education for their sons to smooth the way to social advancement. "Latin," said Locke, "I look upon as absolutely necessary to a gentleman." A classical education "not only elevates above the vulgar herd," commented Thomas Gaisford a century later, "but leads not infrequently to positions of considerable emolument."[51] In his *Directions for a Student in the Universitie* (1637–1643) Richard Holdsworth mentions the study of modern history, travel, manners, and ethics, but not a single science. "Mathematics here and there, and a handful of quasi-vocational ventures," remarks Vivian Ogilvie, "this was all that resulted in the grammar school world from the great outburst of scientific enthusiasm and a national genius for commerce, colonisation and industry."[52] If one included history among what would come to be designated the social sciences, only ancient history was normally taught—and it was taught in Latin and Greek.

So matters remained for the following centuries: around 1900 "a boy at a large public boarding school would spend about 40 per cent of his time on classics at age 13, increasing to about 60 per cent at age 15."[53] Yet from time to time the Renaissance spirit behind the circle of knowledge was recaptured, often in the midst of (and as a result of) fierce controversies over the value of the curriculum and the role of the sciences within it.

During the scientific revolution Descartes and his Port-Royal disciples launched the strongest attack on the classical curriculum in more than two hundred years; in the eighteenth century Giambattista Vico conducted its finest defense. Adumbrated in the Plato of the *Phaedo* and the *Republic,* the confrontation between Descartes and Vico presages a debate that has continued down to the present day, though no modern figures have ever plumbed the depths of the issues as profoundly. Though Descartes did not publish a treatise on education, in many works he made his case against a curriculum that he knew firsthand from his training at the Jesuit college of La Flèche. "I compared the works of the ancient pagans which deal with Morals to palaces most superb and magnificent, which are yet built on sand and mud alone," he says in *Discourse on Method* (1637) in which he dismisses humanistic education as mere window dressing. "To know Latin is to know no more than Cicero's servant girl."[54] (Notwithstanding his complaints, La Flèche had taught him something of metaphor and reductionism.) Descartes granted that his studies in history at La Flèche had shown "that values and behavior differed from place to place and age to age. But travel could have taught the same lesson, and probably in a fresher way."[55] Could he? He might have traveled to the Rome of 1630, not the Rome of 30 BC. Such sentiments were echoed by Pierre Nicole, one of the authors of the *Port-Royal Logic,* who sallied he "[took] pleasure in discovering the falsehoods and great delusions" of the ancients: Socrates "is a man full of small ideas and petty reasoning, who looks only on the present life, a man who finds pleasure in discoursing on truths for the most part useless."[56]

For Descartes, mathematics and mechanics that can be studied in terms of axioms and universal laws are far more valuable than languages or history, which are interpreted through inference and probability. Scientific and mechanical experiments can be repeated and their results tested; history cannot. Nor can moral guidance be expected from literary texts when the texts and their interpreters tend to contradict one another. With his rule of doubt and his requirement of the clear and distinct idea, his analytical method supplies the test for truth and absolute knowledge. The clearest and most distinct idea is number: "Most of all was I delighted with Mathematics because of the certainty of its demonstrations and the evidence of its reasoning; I was astonished that, seeing how firm and solid was its basis, no loftier edifice had been reared thereupon" (*Discourse* 1). Language with its variant meanings and ambiguities, the Aristotelian topics or commonplaces, metaphor, and memory are criticized as hazy and misleading; too much depends upon private opinion or mere authority. "There was no more need to know Latin and Greek, [Descartes] thought, than the rustic dialects of Brittany," remarks Anthony Kenny, because logic could be put in any language; the simpler and more economical the language was, the better it would be in conveying scientific argument and results. "He experimented in optics and physiology, grinding his own lenses and purchasing carcasses from the butcher for dissection. When a stranger asked to see his library, he pointed to a half-dissected calf: 'There are my books.'"[57] The scientific method had begun its long, slow rise in education.

Vico had attended the Jesuit Collegio Massimo al Gesù Vecchio in Naples and the University of Naples (Faculty of Jurisprudence). Unlike Descartes who worked outside the academy, Vico was throughout his career a professor of rhetoric at Naples, where, charged with preparing students for the course in law, he grappled with curricular organization. Possibly his involvement with so many mundane details gave him, as with Newman in the next century, a certain realism in his approach to the circle of knowledge. Although his overall achievement has many dimensions, it begins with his recapturing the original spirit of the Renaissance humanists with their concern for language, liberal education, and civic life. As reconceived by Vico, the humanistic curriculum provides the pattern of the soul's progress to wisdom, which is "to know with certainty, to act rightly, and to speak with dignity."[58]

His early work in pedagogy consists of seven Latin orations (1699–1708) delivered at an annual ceremony to welcome new students. The first states that self-knowledge is attainable by seeking beyond the self and completing the "circle of knowledge." The sixth presents a psychological rationale for the humanist education in which Vico reintegrates the sciences, scientific method, and specialization into the program. He argues for a graded, flexible order of studies, dependent upon the normal development from childhood, through adolescence, to adulthood. According to his concept, which anticipates Rousseau, Montessori, and Piaget, Vico treats a child not as a malformed adult, to be reshaped like plastic matter, but as a person with natural qualities and individual talents that flower only at certain stages. (Vico's insight into childhood derives from personal experience: he was the sixth of eight children, tutored four children for nine years, and had eight children of his own.)[59] The seventh oration, *De nostri temporis studiorum ratione* (On the study methods of our time), is almost as long as the previous six combined. Acknowledged by Vico as in the tradition of Bacon, it has been called "the most important pedagogic essay" between Locke and Rousseau (Fausto Nicolini) and "perhaps the most brilliant defense of the humanities ever written" (Elio Gianturco).[60] In it Vico criticizes the Cartesians for imposing their method upon children at a time when they are unprepared for it and for applying it to subject matter for which it is unsuited.

In 1710 Vico published *De antiquissima italorum sapientia* (On the most ancient wisdom of the Italians), in which he attacks Descartes for his imperializing panmathematicism. His last inaugural, *De mente heroica* (On the heroic mind; 1732), is a stirring exhortation: the mind is heroic when, as with the ancient heroes, it recognizes its divine descent; strives with singleness of purpose beyond itself; seeks the "sublime" whether in difficult scientific investigation or mastery of the greatest authors; shuns power, wealth, and accolades for their own sake; and accomplishes its end—or fails in a noble effort—aimed primarily at laying "foundations of learning and wisdom for the blessedness of the human race."[61] Vico welcomes the challenge of the modern—"how many new sciences and arts discovered!" (*HM*, 243)—but cautions on the need for a balanced, inclusive program, the "whole circle of knowledge" (*HM*, 241), which takes in rhetoric, poetics, history, geography, astronomy, geometry, physics, and metaphysics. As Donald Phillip Verene notes, the Vichian *mens heroica* is "never a choice of good against bad, of light over darkness, but rather a surmounting of the two in some way, never actually joining or synthesizing them." Guiding the effort is virtue, which is based in "wisdom" and "piety to the wholeness of the origin in Jove"; wholeness is therefore a pattern from above: "To seek the sublime is to discover for the good of humanity all the marvels within nature."[62] Vico concludes by extolling "sublime" Galileo and "towering" *(ingens)* Descartes (*HM*, 244). The word *ingens* is chosen carefully: the faculty of *ingenium* ("inventiveness") connects what is "diverse" and "disparate" (*AW*, 96), uncovering the secret laws of nature: it is "man's nature inasmuch as our wit can see the symmetry of things" (*AW*, 97). At the end of his career Vico made peace with the philosopher whom he familiarly called "Renato."

The praise of Galileo and Descartes should indicate that Vico did not wage war on science; as he said, his evenhanded purpose was "not to criticize the drawbacks of the study methods of our age or of those of antiquity, but rather to compare the advantages afforded by the study methods of the two epochs"

(*SM*, 5). In his view, the university curriculum lacks balance owing to the "un-contrasted preponderance of our interest in the natural sciences" (*SM*, 33)— *the year is 1708!* Once informed by a "unitary spirit," the arts and sciences are now "unnaturally separated and disjointed" (*SM*, 76). Hans Georg Gadamer's belief that Vico spoke "from a position of opposition to modern science" mistakes his intentions and goals. On the contrary, "with respect to technical advances in the natural sciences," comments Robert C. Miner, "Vico does not hesitate to admit the superiority of the moderns." Noting that Vico was nineteen when Newton's *Principia* appeared, Talcott Parsons remarks upon the choice of *Nuova Scienza* for the title of his magnum opus: "The significance of Vico, from this point of view, consists in the broader setting in which he attempted to place the achievements of physical science which were approaching culmination in his time."[63] Hippolyte Rigault situates Vico within the Battle of the Ancients and Moderns or, in Elio Gianturco's terms, humanism versus scientism: "Vico draws, so the speak, the final balance-sheet of the great controversy; not only that, but transposes it to a ground where the problem posited can receive a solution" (*SM*, xii–xiii). Vico's response to Descartes entailed his rethinking the circle of knowledge on new grounds.

As is well known, Descartes wanted to free the cogito from the traces and delusions of the senses, a deceitful world that may be in the hands of a deceitful demon.[64] He repudiated the classical notion of probability or verisimilitude as leading only to more probability and ultimately to error and confusion. Because he considered childhood to be the kingdom of error and fantasy, "true" education did not commence until the child's reasoning could be trained: "Since we have all been children before being men . . . it is almost impossible that our judgments should be so excellent or solid as they should have been had we complete use of our reason since our birth."[65] No middle period lies between childhood and adulthood, irrationalism and reason, error and truth; no valid substitute exists for the method of doubt and the certainty of the clear and distinct idea. In the ideal detached observer, reason must learn to ignore both memory, which is idiosyncratic individually and collectively, and the "historical reality of the things that are [memory's] province"; to be the subject of a science, the entity in question must become "simple, disconnected, and analyzable into atemporal parts."[66]

Arguing in psychological terms, Vico replies that children should not start with doubt and abstraction because their minds contain insufficient materials to doubt over and to abstract from: "The age of childhood is reasonable but it has no material on which to reason" (*AU*, 145). The Cartesians deny the best part of a child's nature by removing precisely what the child can bring to the process of learning: imagery, metaphor, analogy, probability, feeling. The

Cartesians also treat as false "not only false thinking, but also those secondary verities and ideas which are based on probability alone, and command us to clear our minds of them" (*SM*, 13). This approach produces an inflexibility of mind that sees only along certain sight lines—lines that are clear as far as they go but do not begin to cover reality. "If you were to apply the geometric method to practical life, 'you would no more than spend your labor on going mad rationally,' and you would drive a straight furrow through the vicissitudes of life as if whim, rashness, opportunity, and luck did not dominate the human condition" (*AW*, 99–100). Not long after Vico's critique, Swift satirized the misapplication of scientific concepts in the Laputans' design of Gulliver's new clothes by geometric rules: "In six days [they] brought my clothes very ill made and quite out of shape, by happening to mistake a figure in the calculation." Vico accuses Antoine Arnauld, who coauthored the *Port-Royal Logic*, of bad timing in introducing children to the Cartesian method, "full of rigorous judgments concerning recondite matters of the higher sciences, remote from common sense"; "the result is a blasting of those youthful mental gifts which should be regulated and developed each by a separate art" (*AU*, 123–24). In his autobiography John Stuart Mill describes the drastic effects of such an education upon his character.

Common sense depends upon the piling up of near truths (*verisimilia*) or convergences of opinion, the acceptance of the fact that complete certainty may not always be possible (or even necessary), and a sense of proportion. As Vico notes, one would more likely share common sense with other people rather than one or another theory or method. Common sense resembles Isocrates' "right opinion," which may be improved by a study of the "preserved records of the wisest and most admirable sayings."[67] Vico notes that judges in ancient Rome, "on giving out an opinion, were always wont to say: 'It seems'" (*SM*, 36), as if to acknowledge the hidden connections among custom, common sense, and appearances. Therefore, the Cartesian exclusion of common sense should be seen as "harmful, since training in common sense is essential to the education of adolescents . . . else they break into odd or arrogant behavior when adulthood is reached" (*SM*, 13); they "become arid and dry in expression and without ever doing anything set themselves up in judgment over all things" (*AU*, 124). Applying the Cartesian method at the wrong time is like giving literary theory to students before they have read the primary texts.

With this in mind, the teaching of scientific (or Cartesian and the like) method should be introduced gradually into a child's education, even while the child's common sense and prudence are developing. In this process Vico defends imagination and memory as the necessary preparation for the circle of knowledge as well as a nourisher of common sense. If children are weaker than adults in reason, they surpass them in imagination and memory, gifts of nature that ought not to be suppressed (*OHE*, 135). Their studies should commence with languages, fables, *diversiloquium* (a mixture of image, concept, and story),[68] history, and the *ars topica* or commonplaces, one of the traditional means with which to marshal arguments on the basis of probabilities, hypotheses, apothegms, common sayings, and so on. The topic in Vico is not, as in Aristotle, an element of argument or proof, but rather "a stimulus for promoting, developing and disciplining one's power of invention."[69] With the topics one argues on the basis of probabilities and the evidence of the certain *(certo)* or "the particular and contingent," not on the basis of the true *(vero)* or "the universal and eternal."[70] The practice of the topics stimulates common sense, which is both "the criterion of practical judgement" and "the guiding standard of eloquence" (*SM*, 13). As Norman Douglas asks in *South Wind:* "What is all wisdom save a collection of platitudes? Take fifty of our current proverbial sayings—they are so trite, so threadbare, that we can hardly bring our lips to utter them. None the less they embody the concentrated experience of the race, and the man who orders his life according to their teaching cannot go far wrong."[71]

Arnauld and Nicole wanted the Cartesian method to be applied deductively in every branch of learning.[72] For Vico, however, no single method fits all fields within the circle. Methods should be governed by what he calls their "separate art" or the specificity of their appropriateness and use. "Method must vary and multiply according to the variety and multiplicity of the topics at issue" (*AW*, 180): poetry, history, mathematics, and the like—each has its own method(s). Misapplied, a method would reveal more of itself than its evidence or impose itself and skew the results. In terms of the history of science Vico's warning has a contemporary ring: "The true geometric method works silently. Where it makes a lot of noise, that is a sign that it is not working properly" (*AW*, 180–81).[73]

Vico also objects to the passivity of the Cartesian theory of innate ideas as a basis for knowledge. According to his *verum-factum* principle, we can fully know as true or intelligible *(verum)* only what we have made *(factum)* through mental and physical effort: "verum et factum convertantur" (truth and fact are convertible). Vico first applied his principle to mathematics, a human construction and therefore capable of being known fully as opposed to the world of physical nature. It is a reversal of Descartes, who said one can know the truths only of mathematics and nature but not of history and culture. Vico then extends the principle into human culture: we did not make the world of nature, and so we can know it only approximately; but we did make our own history and culture, and we can know them from within or inside out.[74]

Further, he adds notions of challenge and heroic effort: "As rational metaphysics teaches that man becomes all things by understanding them, this imaginative metaphysics shows that man becomes all things by *not* understanding them; and perhaps the latter proposition is truer than the former, for when man understands he extends his mind and takes in the things, but when he does not understand he makes the things out of himself and becomes them by transforming himself into them" (*NS*, 405).[75] The theme of "great effort" (*OHE*, 40) and "herculean trials" (*HM*, 244) runs throughout the inaugural orations. "The overwhelming shame of those who are indolent—not to be wise!" (*OHE*, 50). Teachers will present "those disciplines that they have mastered during long, sleepless nights by hard work and sweat" (*OHE*, 51). (In his address to Liverpool medical students Matthew Arnold translated Vico's *mens heroica* as "conquering ambition.")[76] Moreover, since we have made our civil history, we can remake it according to higher ideals. In this way Vico's principle buttresses the humanist belief in the social nature of humanity and civic responsibility.

In sum, children should be encouraged to exercise imagination and memory, at their strongest in early years, and crucial for language acquisition and development. Only later, when the mind "begins to emerge from the mire of matter," should one proceed to the new "study methods," mathematics, physics, and the "principles and causes of natural phenomena" (*OHE*, 136–37), then metaphysics and moral theology, thereby rounding out the "complete cycle" (*AU*, 144). The exact organization of the curriculum and its timing "should be left to prudence, which is not governed by any art" (*AW*, 98), a proviso that reveals a practical-minded educator. Still, he enjoins his students, "Cultivate knowledge as a whole" (*HM*, 244). Such cultivation lasts a lifetime, though specialization runs alongside it. For Vico's students this meant jurisprudence and oratory. The final stage of their formal education recalls its origins, which are the same for all, in the arts of language, the golden thread in Vico's pedagogical *renovatio*.

The Cartesians required an instrumental language to convey the results of scientific experiment and research, "a cold expositions of facts and of arguments," where metaphor, figures of speech, and the other arts of language are considered at best ornamental and at worst obfuscating.[77] Although this type of language is absolutely necessary for certain purposes, Vico also requires another kind of language, to be used for different purposes. Language as eloquentia is "wisdom, ornately and copiously delivered in words appropriate to the common opinion of mankind" (*SM*, 78). Such language draws upon the circle of knowledge and the interrelations among disciplines; it summons all the relevant resources of mind and feeling; it makes use of metaphor and the classical figures in such a way that they do not merely adorn, but are intrinsic and help enact a progression of ideas and feelings; it not only informs but also stirs and exhorts, not necessarily for an immediate end, but with the intention of having a long-range effect upon character. Vico's espousal of "copiousness" in eloquence—which, if abused, leads to pompous long-windedness—reveals the desire to leave no stone unturned. "Discretion takes guidance from the countless particularities of events" (SM, 46); to prove a case, one might run through the appropriate topics, apply other mnemonic aids, and review the range of "possible causes, probable causes and their interrelations" (SM, 34).[78]

As in ancient Greece where "a single philosopher synthesized in himself a whole university" (SM, 74) and was the living embodiment of the circle of knowledge, Vico strove in his lectures to be "wisdom speaking" (AU, 199).[79] Hence, the language arts are at the center of his humanistic curriculum. Language as eloquentia has the power of creating and sustaining the common sense among peoples, the agreed-upon values and traditions without which they cannot survive, let alone civilize themselves. "Humanity is the affection of one human being helping another," he comments in Dritto universale (Universal law). "This is done most effectively through speech (oratione)—by counseling, warning, exhorting, consoling, reproving—and this is the reason I think that studies of languages are called 'humanities,' the more so since it is through languages that humanity is most effectively united [conciliata]."[80] When philosophical thought is joined to prudence and conveyed by eloquence, the result is jurisprudence, which is the goal of the law student from earliest education. Cicero's definition of the studia humanitatis is thus at the beginning and the end of the discussion. "The same definition," Vico asserts, "served the Romans for jurisprudence and the Greeks for wisdom: the knowledge of things divine and human" (SM, 49). For this reason, the circle of knowledge is the educational foundation for jurisprudence.[81] Common sense in its ideal form, emerging over time in nations and in great streams of nations coming together, is Vico's way of balancing historicist relativism with a belief in broadly based values (NS, 142).

During Vico's lifetime the sciences with their new methods gained ground in the universities. In 1712 he protested that "today, on the authority of Descartes, the study of languages is considered useless" (AW, 184). In 1729 he complained of the prevalence of "dimostrazioni," "evidenze," and "verità dimostrate": and, "finally, they condemn the lessons of the poets, under the pretext that the poets speak fables." It was symptomatic of trends that he prophesied as the "barbarism of reflection" at the end of the third edition of La Nuova Scienza, which he was proofreading just before his death: "With their ever continuing factions and reckless civil wars, these peoples must turn their cities into forests and the forests into human dens and in this mode, over long centuries of barbarism, rust will blunt the misbegotten sharpness of that malicious wit which has turned them into beasts made ever more appalling by the barbarism of reflection than they had been in the first barbarism of the senses."[82] At the University of Naples, in 1742, two years before his death, new chairs were established in botany, chemistry, anatomy, physics, and astronomy. There, in 1754, his student Antonio Genovesi was awarded the first chair of political economy in Europe. Though a reading knowledge of Latin held its own in the curriculum, spoken and written Latin declined rapidly. In 1765 Genovesi "claimed to be the first professor to teach philosophy in Italian."[83] Meanwhile, the quiet debate over "the humanist values of the ancient world versus the scientific values of the modern world" remained in suspension.[84]

In the heyday of the Victorian period, with the growth of the physical sciences, colleges, public schools, and technical institutes sprouted up all over England and the United States. Philanthropic industrialists endowed their foundations with strings attached and expected them to include new fields. The principle of utility demanded that scientific and vocational subjects find a place in the curriculum. Universities were investigated by royal commissions or subjected themselves to internal reviews with the intention of cleaning house and updating themselves. Parliament, which had established compulsory primary schools, pondered the same for secondary schools (only achieved in 1902). In the 1860s and '70s, explains G. M. Young, the English passed "through the gateway of the Competitive Examination . . . into the Waste Land of Experts, each knowing so much about so little that he can neither be contradicted nor is worth contradicting." Taken together, these events triggered a curricular debate that attracted many of the Victorian sages: Newman, Mill, Ruskin, George Eliot, and Arnold.[85] In 1867, in a three-hour inaugural address as rector of St. Andrews University, Mill referred to the "great controversy of the present day": "the vexed question between ancient languages and modern sciences . . . whether general education should be classical—let me use a wider expression, and say literary—or scientific." He answered "Why not both?" and proceeded to make one of the most enduring statements on the cultural significance of Latin and Greek. Perhaps he believed that sciences needed less defending at the moment. Eighteen years later Walter Hobhouse wrote in a valetudinarian air, "Some voices are still lifted in defence of a classical education."[86] Greek and Latin had lost; "literary" education in modern languages would gradually assume their place, if on a reduced scale.

The Victorian debate on the classical education traces to a series of articles in the *Edinburgh Review* from 1808 to 1811. Harkening back to Locke, Sydney Smith objected to the dominance of classics at Oxford and Cambridge and pressed for the teaching of subjects "useful to human life" such as chemistry, mathematics, experimental science, and political economy: "When a University has been doing *useless* things for a long time, it appears at first degrading to them to be *useful.*" Edward Copleston and John Davison, fellows of Oriel College, defended the classical curriculum with a touchstone from Milton's *On Education:* "Without teaching [the undergraduate] the peculiar business of any one office or calling," wrote Copleston, "[the cultivation of literature] enables him to act his part in each of them with better grace and more elevated carriage; and, if happily planned and conducted, is a main ingredient in that complete and generous education which fits a man 'to perform justly, skilfully and magnanimously, all the offices, both private and public, of peace and war.' "[87] Davison and Copleston strongly influenced John Henry Newman, elected fellow of Oriel in 1822. Though staking out a position of his own, he cites them extensively in *The Idea of a University* (1853), the most famous book on the subject in English.

Appointed rector of the new Catholic University of Ireland in 1851, Newman was confronted with the problems of a university administrator who must do almost everything essential to build an organization from the ground up. He raised funds, located space, appointed a faculty, and attracted students, so that the school could open in 1854. Then, he "strove to promote science as well as arts, to encourage professional education, to provide for research as well as good teaching, and to broaden the curriculum by including more modern subjects than Oxford." His *idea* of a university informed his practice, as he employed the "circle of knowledge" in defense of a liberal education against the proponents of purely professional, utilitarian, or technical training.

His central theme is wholeness: in reality, in the relatedness of fields, in the self. As Vico chose the wide-ranging classical philosopher as a model for the "whole university," so Newman's paradigm is the medieval university where "all subjects of knowledge were viewed as parts of one vast system, each with its own place in it, and from knowing one, another was inferred." He wants a university to expand itself to the point where, though students cannot study every subject, even superficially, "they will be the gainers by living among those and under those who represent the whole circle." He continues, "All knowledge forms one whole, because its subject-matter is one." The subject matter is reality, which is interrelated to a greater or lesser degree. The disciplines are the current "logical records" of our "mental abstractions" of reality; these records "belong to one and the same circle of objects, they are one and all connected together." If theology is left out, the other sciences will be affected, though unequally: "mathematics not at all; chemistry less than politics, politics less than history, ethics, or metaphysics." In an interdisciplinary spirit he argues that the various disciplines "complete, correct, balance" one another. "No one science, no two sciences, no one family of sciences, nay, not even all secular science, is the whole truth," he cautions. "If you drop any science out of the circle of knowledge, you cannot keep its place vacant for it; that science is forgotten; the other sciences close up, or in other words, they exceed their proper bounds, and intrude where they have no right."[89] If ethics were lost, its place would be swallowed up by politics or economics; if experimental science fell out, antiquarianism would fill its place.

The distinction between liberal and useful (or specialized) knowledge that lies at the heart of the book, *Discourses V–VIII,* traces through Cicero and Plutarch back to Aristotle on contemplation and leisure (*Rhetoric* 1.5). Useful knowledge is a *means to an end,* liberal knowledge *an end in itself.* What is this end? Aristotelian leisure (*schole,* from which we get *school*) is not idleness: it is the search after truth; the enjoyment of the arts, literature, philosophical, scientific, or religious thought; serious conversation; and private contemplation.[90] With that end in view, the circle of knowledge is a metaphor for the mind as it absorbs, interrelates, systematizes, and evaluates:

> This enlargement consists in the comparison of the subjects of knowledge one with another. We feel ourselves to be ranging freely, when we not only learn something, but when we also refer it to what we knew before. It is not the mere addition to our knowledge which is the enlargement, but the change of place, the movement onwards, of that moral centre, to which what we know and what we have been acquiring, the whole mass of our knowledge, as it were, gravitates.[91]

In an era of increasing specialization Newman argues that the "general culture of mind is the best aid to professional and scientific study." Knowledge of science is even "necessary" for an educated person, and one of the scientific disciplines studied in depth can be a "real education of the mind." Yet, though he applauds public lectures, scientific societies, literary clubs, and the inexpensive diffusion of ideas in periodical literature, one should "call things by their right names": "recreations are not education"; "do not say, the people must be educated, when, after all, you only mean, amused, refreshed, soothed, put into good spirits, and good humour, or kept from vicious excesses."[92]

A. Dwight Culler comments that in the seventh discourse Newman undercuts what he had said in the fifth: "The knowledge which he had just recommended as 'not useful' was actually, if we considered the matter closely, more useful than 'useful knowledge' itself."[93] For Culler, Newman repaired to the mixed arguments of Davison and Copleston instead of adhering to the clear logic of his own best thinking. Perhaps Newman thought that, with a university to administer, he had to win over his audience, yielding something to the useful without compromising the liberal. If he was forthright about his antipathy to "disciples of a low Utilitarianism," he smuggled in the principle of utility at the higher end. A liberal education "*tends* to good, or is the *instrument* of good"; its products are "not useful in any low mechanical mercantile sense, but as diffusing good, or as a blessing, or a gift, or power, or a treasure, first to the owner, then through him to the world."[94] Even here Newman may be said to contradict himself, because he elsewhere asserts the separation of knowledge and virtue: the gentleman, for example, may only appear to possess "virtue at a distance."[95] One of the great merits of his book is that in whatever direction he pursues his definition he finds a limit acknowledged as a limitation: secular knowledge may produce a gentleman, yet knowledge and refinement are neither virtue nor action; knowledge is useful, though in different senses, which may overlap. In "On Style" Pater said that Newman's book was "the perfect handling of a theory."

The utilitarian principle loomed large in mid-Victorian England and America. In 1867 nine scholars examined British education and paid particular attention to modern subjects, namely, the sciences, and since expansion in one area cannot take place without contraction in another, Greek and Latin were put on the block. The claims of science in the curriculum enter the debate on the grounds of utility. Edited by F. W. Farrar, an assistant master at Harrow and later bishop of London, *Essays on a Liberal Education* has been praised as "one of the earliest works to assert the possibility of a modern humanism, the possibility of extracting from modern literature much which was commonly thought to be derivable from a study of Greek and Latin alone."[96] On close inspection the volume has less to do with humanism, ancient or modern, than with advancing the cause of professional as opposed to liberal education and with abandoning classics in favor of the free-elective system. In the book's most influential essay, the utilitarian philosopher Henry Sidgwick blandly prophesies the death of a cultural tradition that stretched back two millennia. In Christopher Stray's judgment, Sidgwick left the theory of classical education "in tatters."[97] Let us see for ourselves.

With an appeal to utility sixteen times in sixty-two pages, Sidgwick proposes one reason after another for dropping the "system" of Greek and Latin, mocked as "a sort of linguistic Siamese twins," and substituting natural sciences and modern languages. The use of the metallic word *system* to refer to training in Greek and Latin (at its best) betrays narrowness and rigidity. Classical humanism rejects the claim of any single system to explain humanity to itself. Sidgwick delights in demolishing the weaker arguments of his opponents, those of Thring, Wooley, Pillans, and Moberly, and not Arnold or Newman. To defenders of classics who say, for instance, that Greek aids in the understanding of medical terms, he responds that one could learn enough Greek for *that* "in a day"—as if this were the only possible use a physician could gain from reading Homer or Sophocles. "Even [the defenders'] claim to give the best teaching in mental, ethical, and political philosophy, the last relic of their old prestige, is rapidly passing away." Indeed, the classics can be deleterious: Aeschylus teaches "false ornament"; Thucydides shows "ungracefulness"; Lucretius is "unshapely" and Ovid "tinsel." Plato and Thucydides are "exceedingly bad" prose models; reaching for at least something nice to say, he calls the two of them "charming" (the *Edinburgh Review* said Thucydides was "imaginative").[98] *Charming* invokes a theme in nineteenth-century Anglo-American culture; aesthetic values are gendered as feminine and second-class compared with "manly" science, technology, and business. In "Genius, Fame, and Race" (1897), the American sociologist Charles Horton Cooley remarks similarly: "This charm which the Greek spirit has for the northern races is the charm of difference rather than of superiority"—the ancient Greeks are not superior, just different. "It is like the feeling of sex; just as there is something in what is womanly, so that which is Greek delights the modern natures without there being any question of greater or less in the matter at all." One may question using the word *charm* to describe Aeschylus, Aristotle, Thucydides, Sallust, Lucretius, Tacitus, and Demosthenes. Racial bias links to gender bias: "The Teutonic man, one may say, feels toward the spirit of his own race as toward a brother, but toward the Greek spirit as toward a mistress."[99]

Sidgwick bases his argument on an arbitrary and pejorative distinction between "natural" (utilitarian) and "artificial" (classical) education: the former teaches a boy subjects "in which, for any reason whatever, he will be likely to take an interest in after life"; the latter "is one which, in order that man may ultimately know one thing, teaches him another, which gives the rudiments of some learning or accomplishment, that the man in the maturity of his culture will be content to forget." Since one is happy to forget it, why learn it in the first place? Aside from the fact that there is no pedagogical level of the "natural" that does not implicate the "artificial," the argument itself was not new; it descends from romantic sensibility and presentism, and it issues in the twentieth-century movements of Montessori, Dewey, and a philosophy of learning that (among other things) seeks to make the students "feel good" about themselves and "empowered." Rousseau in *Émile* and Johann Gottfried von Herder had questioned the teaching of Latin and Greek because of the "coerciveness" involved and the "neglect of the child's inner capacities, including natural innocence"; Herder campaigned for a curriculum of "living languages" and "knowledge close to the pupil's own immediate experience."[100]

In the end, Sidgwick does pay homage to liberal education with its aim "to impart the highest culture, to lead youths to the most full vigorous and harmonious exercise, according to the best ideal attainable, of their active, cognitive, and aesthetic faculties." But because the precise way to reach this goal "is not easy to determine," natural education at least offers the "rudiments" of what may lead to it. Natural education in physical science "familiarises a boy with the same facts that it will be afterwards important for him to know; makes him imbibe the same ideas that are afterwards to form the furniture of his mind; imparts to him the same accomplishments and dexterities that he will afterwards desire to possess." One seriously questions whether ten year olds can decide what they will desire to possess in twenty or thirty years. Homer or a video game? One could be giving the children the key to their own prison.

Is there any "use" for the classical education? Sidgwick applies satiric reduction: "Boys do acquire some knowledge of two dead languages." For most students, the classical education is a "prolonged nightmare" with its "unmeaning literary exercises" before reaching a genuine appreciation of the texts. Since students know English already, why not teach English literature instead? (In his St. Andrews address Mill recognized the time factor, but advised the adoption of time-saving techniques in the teaching of Greek and Latin.) The opposition between linguistic exercises and literary appreciation is too rigid; one should think of a continuum, with some students learning to appreciate literary qualities almost immediately, especially from a good teacher. As far as mental training is concerned, Sidgwick grants that Latin fosters memory, attention to detail, judgment, and rapid problem solving. But this defense of Latin is a stab in the back since he proposes that science and modern languages are as good as Latin at inculcating mental discipline, while having the added advantage of "preparation for the business of life" and better prospects for getting a job. "The original *studia humanitatis,*" explains Robert Proctor, "began as an explicit attempt to offer something more than training of the mind."[101] This had been Socrates' rebuke to the Sophists. An effective apologia for the humanities must keep in mind the unique substance of what is being defended: not only exercises in logic, precision, and memory but also wisdom, aesthetic value, and historical understanding. Yet Sidgwick states, "In the case of classics the uselessness is by no means admitted."[102]

Against Sidgwick's utilitarianism, one might side with Newman on the study of classics as representing the highest form of uselessness: Aristotelian *schole* or enlightened leisure. The argument from leisure has always been confused with class. Thus, Veblen did not distinguish true from false culture in his disapprobation of the "leisure class," and Pierre Bourdieu in the same spirit mocks the use of literary quotation as a sign of culture, calling it "a quite special use of discourse which is a sort of summons to appear as advocate and witness, addressed to a past author on the basis of a social solidarity disguised as intellectual solidarity." From a Marxist perspective, Christopher Stray decries humanist *paideia* as a kind of aestheticism or obscurantism: "The superiority of the independent gentleman, within the ideological current, is based on a detached wholeness which contrasts with the fragmentation and dependence of the division of labour and those affected by it. The autonomous individual is a work of art transcending division and dependence within an ideological field in which hierarchy and economy are, in the Marxian sense, mystified." It is a strange theory that could render Euripides and Horace as content free: "How, after all, can the exemplary status of a specific source of value be maintained when authority is relativized and rendered relatively content-free?"[103]

A strong response to Veblen, Bourdieu, and Stray on culture as veneer or worse was given by Sebastian De Grazia in his invaluable *Of Time, Work, and Leisure* in which he distinguishes an Aristotelian leisure class from Marx's leisure class caught in the class struggle and from Veblen's class that is rich, consumerist, and aristocratic. "The world is divided into two classes," declares De Grazia, "not three or five or twenty. Just two."

> One is the great majority; the other is the leisure kind, not those of wealth or position or birth, but those who love ideas and the imagination. Of the great mass of mankind there are a few persons who are blessed and tormented with this love. . . . In one century they may be scientists, in another theologians, in some other bards, whatever the category may be that grants them the freedom to let their minds play. They invent the stories, they create the cosmos, they discover what truth it is given man to discover, and give him the best portion of truth and error. It is a select, small world of thinkers, artists and musicians—not necessarily in touch with one another—who find their happiness in what they do, who can't do anything else, their daemon won't let them. The daemon doesn't depend on environment. You have it or have not . . . no matter how much the class is underpaid, it is a luxury class and will always have its select spirits as members. As long as it has leisure.[104]

With regard to a modern humanism—a humanism composed of texts in the modern languages—Sidgwick gave no examples but believed a case could be made. Thinking exactly along the lines of science versus literature, Samuel Johnson had said in his *Preface to Shakespeare* that, with regard to "works not demonstrative and scientific, but appealing wholly to observation and experience, no other test can be applied than length of duration and continuance of esteem." Humanist values can be presented by modern literature and art, but his highest praise is for those works that have stood the test of time—Johnson was writing 150 years after Shakespeare's death. Arnold had also pondered the question of a modern humanism but was skeptical with regard to his own age; modern poetry, he wrote to A. H. Clough, must prove itself by its "contents": "By becoming a complete magister vitae as the poetry of the ancients did: by including, as theirs did, religion with poetry, instead of existing as poetry only, and leaving religious wants to be supplied by the Christian religion, as a power existing independent of the poetical power."[105] Yet modern poetry with one or two exceptions (Goethe or Wordsworth) failed to "interpret the whole of life"; it was too self-absorbed, too concerned with form and style or with manner over matter, too narrow in scope, too fraught with disturbances that found no catharsis, unlike Sophocles, who "saw life steadily and saw it whole." The characteristics of "the great monuments of early Greek genius . . . have disappeared; the calm, the cheerfulness, the disinterested objectivity have disappeared: the dialogue of the mind with itself has commenced."[106] Sometimes those who pushed for modern humanism became entangled in nationalism or ethnocentrism. Thus, Charles Horton Cooley rashly drew up a table of fifth century BC Athenians against Englishmen born between 1550 and 1650, commenting that "few, I imagine, will go so far as to say that the Englishmen are outclassed." Bunyan is opposite Plato.

When Arnold responded to Sidgwick and his coauthors, he had already injected himself into the debate with *The Popular Education of France* (1861) and *A French Eton* (1864) and had completed an extensive journey of the Continent on behalf of the Schools Inquiry Commission. His grassroots understanding of the problem should not be forgotten, as he earned his living for thirty-five years as an inspector for the Education Department, which meant everything from certifying instructors to judging spelling bees. In his commission report, *Schools and Universities on the Continent* (1868), he complains that the humanists and the "realists" (as he labels those in science) unjustly attack one another. Whereas the humanists resist change out of "intellectual insufficiency," the realists want the whole curriculum to themselves—to their own detriment, for "so long as the realists persist in cutting in two the circle of knowledge, so long do they leave for practical purposes the better portion to their rivals, and in the government of human affairs their rivals will beat them." In contrast to English public instruction with its warring parties, he praises a recent report of the Superior Council of Public Instruction in Italy to the effect that "no part of the circle of knowledge is common or unclean, none is to be cried up at the expense of another." Arnold concedes that Latin composition takes time away from the study of Latin literature, and since "vital contact" with the great authors is the goal, exercises in composition might be curtailed. Yet it is not all gain, because Latin composition brings one closer to the models, "which makes us sharers of their spirit and power," and "the power of the Latin classic is in *character*." Concluding with a plea for tolerance and inclusiveness ("the rejection of the humanities by the realists, the rejection of the study of nature by the humanists, are alike ignorant"), he recommends that all students learn Latin, their own language, another modern language, and elementary science before following their aptitude into either the sciences or the humanities—all in the same secondary school so that students will benefit from conversing with one another.[107]

By 1880 the great curricular debate that had opened with Newman was nearing its end. At the inauguration of Joseph Mason's Science College in Birmingham, Thomas Huxley delivered a lecture titled "Science and Culture." He quoted his friend Arnold, "our chief apostle of culture," on the definition of "the best that has been thought and said in the world" and a "criticism of life": the first, establishing the standard of culture; the second, applying the standard. Huxley supported Arnold on the second point, the criticism of life, which he described as the "habit of critically estimating the value of things by comparison with a theoretic standard." With the decline of institutional religion, he agreed, too, on the need for a *magister vitae:* "Perfect culture should supply a complete theory of life, based upon a clear knowledge alike of its possibilities and its limitations." Yet he disputed the first part of Arnold's definition, establishing the standard, and he did not believe that literature by itself (no matter how capacious the definition) should monopolize the curriculum as it could not supply all of "the best that has been thought and said in the world" to prepare a person for modern life. "The distinctive character of our own times lies in the vast and constantly increasing part which is played by natural knowledge." Can there be progress in the intellectual sphere without knowledge of the forces driving the present world? Huxley thought not: the teaching of Latin in the religious Middle Ages and the revival of classical education by the Renaissance humanists were entirely appropriate in their time. However, "the representatives of the Humanists, in the nineteenth century, take their stand upon classical education as the sole avenue to culture, as firmly as if we were still in the age of Renascence." In so doing they have mistaken "the beginning for the end of the work of reformation" and have violated the critical spirit of Renaissance humanism. Furthermore, they "have brought this reproach upon themselves, not because they are too full of the spirit of the ancient Greek, but because they lack it."[108]

Though he might well have ended here, in the spirit of compromise, he went further, in the spirit of hubris, challenging Arnold by stating that "for the purpose of attaining real culture, an exclusively scientific education is at least as effectual as an exclusively literary education." Ideally, one ought to know the major works of English literature, and also French or German, and sociology, but Latin and Greek are too time-consuming for the student who wants to specialize in the sciences. "If an Englishman cannot get literature and culture out of his Bible, his Shakespeare, his Milton, neither, in my belief, will the profoundest study of Homer and Sophocles, Virgil and Horace, give it him."[109]

Arnold answered Huxley in "Literature and Science," one of the lectures given on tour in the United States in 1882–1883. Plato's concept of a priestly and warrior governing elite represented an obsolete ideal; the French Revolution had brought forth a new age; the desire of the enfranchised classes to improve the material basis of life could not be ignored. Because the aim of education is "to know the best" and because the sciences form an indispensable part of it, they belong in the curriculum.[110] Seventeenth-century England and Italy cannot be properly understood without knowing Newton and Galileo. Nor could one advance in social and material well-being without modern science.

The question, as usual, becomes not whether to include the sciences in the preprofessional education, but how much of them. The pressure is to add more and more. "All knowledge is interesting": is it better to understand oxidation or the character of Hamlet? In Arnold's judgment a person was better prepared for the complexity of modern life who grasped oxidation less well than the issues and characters of great literature. In the *Iliad*, Apollo shows his impatience at Achilles' inability to cease mourning the death of his friend Patroclus. Perhaps the eternal gods reveal a limitation: *they* do not know death. So Apollo remarks, half in wonder, half in exasperation: "Yet the Destinies have given to mortals an enduring heart." Holding up such passages before his audience, Arnold confidently asserts that the work of artists who had the most limited scientific knowledge "has not only the power of refreshing and delighting us" but also "a fortifying, and elevating, and quickening, and suggestive power, capable of wonderfully helping us to relate the results of modern science to our need for conduct, our need for beauty." While science would expand its dominion over the curriculum, while other subjects would be "crowded into education . . . far too many," the humanities would retain their "leading place," and "if they lose it for a time, they will get it back again." Arnold also predicted that science would continue to be a "divider and separatist," with the growth of new fields. Yet with his liberal faith in the future, he believed that the disciplines would eventually find their way back to agreement over the "substantial unity of man," elsewhere suggesting that philology might prove fruitful in relating the findings of various scientific fields to a reinvigorated humanities.[111]

Within two generations, however, philology, historicism, and comparative linguistics had triumphed over the humanistic teaching of literature in the universities; instead of relating, they were extinguishing. Unquestionably, the most vocal, persevering defender of the classical curriculum was an assistant professor of French and former student of Charles Eliot Norton at Harvard, Irving Babbitt, whose *Literature and the American College* (1908) was a gauntlet thrown down before the gates of higher education. For Babbitt, the two warring camps in literary studies consisted of the philologists and dilettantes. With their rigorous method, hard work, and better organization, the "philological syndicate" had set the tone and standard and had won control of the academic lines. They borrowed a method from the "narrowest school" of German philology, applied it in a "crude" manner, and, though paying homage to the *litterae humaniores,* succeeded only in "dehumanizing" them and effecting one of the "chief disasters" of modern culture.

> There are persons at present who do not believe that a man is fitted to fill a chair of French literature in an American college simply because he has made a critical study of the text of a dozen medieval beast fables and written a thesis on the Picard dialect, and who deny that a man is necessarily qualified to interpret the humanities to American undergraduates because he has composed a dissertation on the use of the present participle in Ammianus Marcellinus.

Philology presented the "Baconist" side of the problem; the other was the "Rousseauist," one of self-indulgence and pandering to individual tastes ("something of everything for everybody"). The dilettantes gave "evidence of nothing, except perhaps a gentle epicureanism," "temperamental indolence," "impressionism," and "an aversion to accuracy."[112]

Against philologists and dilettantes, Babbitt argues the cause of the humanists. For them, college is the culmination of humanistic training, with some specialization to prepare for graduate or professional school. They encourage a strenuous "effort of reflection" that enables the student "to coordinate the scattered elements of knowledge and relate them not only to the intellect but to the will and character; that subtle alchemy by which mere learning is transmuted into culture." Humanism means knowledge of the difference between one's rational and physical nature, an apprehension of higher reason that can discipline the imagination and emotion, and awareness of the law of the One and the Many, the eternal, unchanging truths and the flux and relativism of everyday life. "Classical literature, at its best . . . appeals rather to our higher reason and imagination—to those faculties which afford us an avenue of escape from ourselves, and enable us to become participants in the universal life. . . . Hence its sentiment of restraint and discipline, its sense of proportion and pervading law." The Greek and Latin classics—and world literature of their caliber—inculcate "a feeling for form and proportion, good taste, measure and restraint, judgment and discriminating selection." When under pressure the philologists tried being "literary," they were merely "dilettantes" who could not tell a good poem from a bad one and whose taste ran from "vaudeville performances" to "light summer fiction." Babbitt's comments on romance philology hardly endeared him to his colleagues: French was "a cheap and nasty substitute for Latin."[113]

In contemporary education the worst resulted when the Baconist and the Rousseauist came together and reinforced each other, when the luxury of choice was funneled into the narrow foci of specialization. On this score Babbitt's bête noire was Charles W. Eliot, one of the principal architects of the modern American university. Eliot began learning Latin and Greek at Boston Latin School and finished doing so in his first years at Harvard, which he entered at fifteen. In its main radicals his education did not differ from Sturm's students at Strasbourg three centuries earlier, even to the age at which he left school for university. He studied chemistry, went to Germany for advanced training, and returned to accept a position at the new Massachusetts Institute of Technology. When at thirty-four he became president of Harvard (1869–1909), three-fourths of the freshman curriculum of twelve subjects (all of which were required) represented the circle of knowledge: two in Greek, two in Latin, two in mathematics, two in rhetoric, and one in philosophy; the other subjects were history, French, and education. (At this time in England the reform-minded Clarendon Commission was recommending that "classics should occupy only [only!] three fifths of the total curriculum.")[114] Eliot asked, "Are our young men being educated for the work of the twentieth century or of the seventeenth?"[115]

Eliot overhauled the curriculum and strengthened the graduate and professional schools, introduced the free-elective system for undergraduates (1872–1885), abolished the admission requirement of Greek (1885), initiated the idea of nationwide college entrance examinations (1877–1900), tried to crowd four years into three so that a student could pass more quickly to graduate or professional school (1908), and much more. His work on entrance examinations, which greatly influenced high school curriculum reform, exemplifies Ellul's self-augmentation of technique: changes in one sphere, for their own benefit, will tend to affect neighboring spheres. For the humanist, Eliot was like one of those Swiftian projectors who built a house by starting with the roof (in this case, graduate education) and worked downward.

As for Eliot's belief that "the well-instructed youth of eighteen can select for himself a better course of study than any college faculty,"[116] Babbitt ridiculed him publicly: "The wisdom of all the ages is to be as naught as compared with the inclination of the sophomore"; "the proper study of mankind is not man, but chemistry." Babbitt deplored Eliot's "department store" approach to education, the metaphor drawing on consumer behavior and university culture in an age of advertising. At a time when the "harmonious rounding out of all the faculties" was more desperately needed than ever, the universities and the secondary schools were going in the opposite direction.[117] Though Arnold's hopes had been dashed and the humanities were not reassuming their "leading place" in education, Babbitt campaigned throughout the rest of his career for a humanistic curriculum with a strong grounding in classics to supply the standard and the "power to relate this knowledge to modern life and literature." Like Arnold, too, he warned the humanist not to "repudiate either sentimental or scientific naturalism; for this would be to attempt an impossible reaction. His aim is not to deny his age, but to complete it."[118] That was Babbitt's answer to Eliot's question on what century one is to be educated for: no particular one, but all centuries.

In the past seventy-five years, the curricular history of Latin and Greek is only the most dramatic example of the general plight of the humanities. Among the well-known reprises of curricular reform, one may point to the Great Books program at Columbia and the University of Chicago in the 1920s and '30s or Harvard's *General Education in a Free Society,* commonly known as the "Red Book," in the 1940s. C. P. Snow triggered the last major controversy over science versus the humanities with his Rede Lecture of 1959, published as *The Two Cultures and the Scientific Revolution.* Lord Snow poured scorn on the literary intellectuals for their ignorance of modern science: *they,* not the scientists, were the ones whose training and predilections rendered them impractical guides in the business of life. But Snow was only making the nineteenth-century case for science that Arnold had answered, while in his reply F. R. Leavis obscured his main points in a fog of vituperation. Lionel Trilling reviewed the controversy in an essay that served as its epitaph.[119] With other preoccupations in the 1960s, the controversy faded from view.

Yet the issues raised by Snow and Leavis as well as the educational agenda of the sixties generation informed Trilling's Charles Eliot Norton Lectures, delivered at Harvard in 1970 and published as *Sincerity and Authenticity,* and his last educational essays. A professor of English at Columbia, Trilling had written a standard study of Arnold and, more than any other figure in his generation, had become the most respected defender of the liberal education.

In 1974 the Aspen Institute for Humanistic Studies in Colorado invited Trilling to discuss the contemporary factors in favor or against "the likelihood that, in the late twentieth century, there would emerge an effectual ideal of education which would be integrally related to the humanistic educational traditions of the past."

Surveying the whole, he found little encouragement. The physical sciences are regarded with "ambivalence" by the humanists. "Not much is expected of what they can do for the moral nature of those who study them." This is an Arnoldian or Weberian stance; science is objective, not value rational (Cicero and Newman had actually granted more to the study of science in relation to humanistic ideals). With regard to the social sciences, the situation appears no better to Trilling: there has been "a marked diminution in the confidence that the social sciences commanded only a few years ago." Here Trilling has been a less accurate prophet: in 1999, that is, "in the late twentieth century," according to statistics available from the National Science Foundation, psychology (third) ranked well ahead of English (eighth) in the number of undergraduate majors at four-year colleges (education was first; health science second, biology fourth, visual and performing arts fifth, engineering sixth, and communications seventh).[120]

In Trilling's view, the only factor in favor of the humanities was that parents of first-generation college students wanted some humanistic training as a social marker—hardly something on which to pin hopes. The students had spurned as unauthentic their parents' wishes for cultural window dressing, thereby mistaking the real thing for the imitation. They wanted subjects that spoke to immediate needs, dealt with current events, or at least exhibited "relevance" to those events (*Antigone* is "about" the individual versus the state, a current issue).[121] The word *relevance* echoed everywhere in the halls of academe, in the way *diversity* would several decades later. In his Jefferson Lecture in 1972 Trilling quotes a recent president of the Modern Language Association to the effect that literature was at best "a diversion and a spectacle."[122] Was literature becoming the game preserve of special interests and the battleground of ideological warriors?

Among the battery of negatives that led Trilling to his pessimistic conclusions, he notes the loss of faith among the professoriate itself: "I can recall no meetings on an educational topic that were so poorly attended and so lacking in vivacity as those in which the report [by Daniel Bell, published as *The Reforming of General Education*] was considered." A more disturbing factor, however, could be seen in the students: "The tendency of our culture to regard mere energy of impulse as being in every mental and moral way equivalent and even superior to defined intention." The "idea of ordeal" was no longer "congenial" in American culture: students resented the "strenuous effort" and "submission" required by a traditional education in language, history, and philosophy (the steep decline of history and foreign-language enrollments had begun). The emphasis on impulse, immediacy, and limitlessness had replaced "defined intention," a cornerstone of humanistic *Bildung,* the concept of "making a life" on the model of a vocation. "[The desire] to shape a self and a life has all but gone from a contemporary culture whose emphasis, paradoxically enough, is so much on self." Secondary schools had abandoned those "substantive subjects" that could initiate the kind of "fashioning, forming, shaping as will prepare [students] for further *Bildung* at the university," and reconstruction at age eighteen is a virtually impossible task for a university faculty. Where students confuse limiting the self with self-denial, *Bildung* sets boundaries and focuses energies; in the choice of a life, a career, one shuts down the possibility of other lives, other careers. Against the dominance of impulse, Trilling opposes "the *mystique* of mind": "its energy, its intentionality, its impulse towards inclusiveness and completeness, its search for coherence with due regard for the integrity of the elements which it brings into relation with each other, its power of looking before and after."[123]

This new attitude toward the self has provoked rebellion in all sectors, but particularly against the past: "Any doctrine, that of the family, religion, the school, that does not sustain this increasingly felt need for a multiplicity of options and instead offers an ideal of a shaped self, a formed life, has the sign on it of a retrograde and depriving authority, which, it is felt, must be resisted." One of Trilling's examples lay close at hand, the *Report on the Fact-Finding Commission Appointed to Investigate the Disturbances at Columbia University in April and May 1968* in which Archibald Cox praises the current student generation as "the best informed, the most intelligent, and the most idealistic this country has ever known." According to Trilling, Cox mistakes genuine intelligence for modish self-awareness, a "congeries of 'advanced' public attitudes" propagandized incessantly by television, journalism, advertising, politics, and the like. "Through the agency of one segment of the culture or another, there is unceasingly being borne in upon us the consciousness that we live in circumstances of an unprecedented sort." These agencies of hyperpresentism supply the information and the panacea, or at least they instill a belief that we can live with our problems, thereby lending a specious "moral distinction" to our lives. Where Vico exhorted, Trilling laments: "Our society will tend increasingly to alienate itself from the humanistic educational ideal." To keep his balance, he points to the history of Columbia in the previous hundred years, as it oscillated between a humanistic education and the free-elective system. Maybe the pendulum would swing back again.[124]

Thirty years later the circle of knowledge has not been restored, nor is it likely to be in the foreseeable future. To be certain, a liberal arts curriculum retains vestiges of the humanistic ideal in its core courses and distribution requirements that diffuse a beneficial effect on some students. Still, year by year requirements are removed, or watered down, or altered beyond recognition by professors who want to teach their specialties or advance private agendas under the auspices of basic humanities courses. As Trilling thought, only a "giant labor" in social history could explain this antihumanistic, antihistorical turn: "The fluidity of the contemporary world demands an analogous limitlessness in our personal perspective" that militates against a solid *Bildung* and its idea of character formation. "For anyone concerned with contemporary education at whatever level, the assimilation that contemporary culture has made between social idealism, even political liberalism, and personal fluidity—a self without the old confinements—is as momentous as it is recalcitrant to correction."[125]

Trilling's prediction has proved generally correct. A participant in that "giant labor" of social history, Zygmunt Bauman chooses the same liquidity metaphor to depict the individual self under the onslaught of postmodern conditions. Where formerly the self had been conceived in terms of "harmony, logic, consistency," today, by contrast, the self has lost its contours and even its center: "The search for identity is the ongoing struggle to arrest or slow down the flow, to solidify the fluid, to give form to the formless." Like avid consumers, we shop in the "supermarket of identities," "a container filled to the brim with a countless multitude of opportunities." In what appears to be a parody of Humean epistemology, the individual will is lost in the agonizing choice among consumer fantasies—fantasies being the "adhesive holding the self together."[126]

What counts today are the requirements for a specific degree in a credentialized world, whether in psychology, education, history, biology, or others. Free electives and humanities courses alike are less of an issue than they were thirty years ago. "'Individualization,'" says Bauman on modern schools, "consists of transforming human 'identity' from a 'given' into a 'task' and charging the actors with the responsibility of performing that task." Fifty years ago, commenting on the transformation of the *enkuklios paideia* into the modern encyclopedia, Freidrich Georg Juenger said that in the concept of "knowledge as power," the Baconian motto, knowledge had been reduced to information, and not reasoning, evaluating, and judging: following the secondary school, the university had become "a technical training center and servant of technical progress."[127] Since techniques are always changing, improving, or being replaced altogether, there is the need for continuous "retooling," and not only in business and industry but also in academe itself, where new methods drive out the old with startling frequency, in an imitation of other kinds of techniques and consumer goods.

Bauman appears to acquiesce at the turn of events; J. H. Plumb welcomes it. "Education at long last is becoming squarely based on the needs and practices of the modern scientific world," remarks Plumb. "It is a movement from education for society, for government, for authority, to education in techniques." For him, classical studies were already outdated in the nineteenth century, when "manufacturer's sons from Manchester or Leeds struggled through their Homer and Virgil and plodded through the arid works of Livy or Xenophon." (Plumb bears no palms to the ancient historians.) Those manufacturers were wasting their money on expensive boarding-school educations, even though what might have been lost in Greek and Latin would have been made up in class solidarity and networking. "Education was classical, backward-looking in the methods, materials and principles it inculcated."[128] Are the materials of Socrates or the principles of universal humanity in the Stoics and Cicero "backward-looking"? Plumb does not appreciate that humanistic education can strengthen one's ability to examine present culture and to hold it to a higher standard, enabling one to resist what is inimical or "bad" in modernity. Nor does he question to what extent an education mainly in empiricism and technique is narrow and limiting. If one were to adopt the kind of education that Plumb wants, one would not be able to diagnose its own deficiencies.

In 2004 Harvard completed its Curricular Review on undergraduate education. The Red Book reforms had been "content-oriented" regarding requirements in humanities, social sciences, and natural sciences. Then, the Core Curriculum review of the 1970s substituted an "approach-oriented" program requiring ten or so courses across the three divisions. As the metaphor implies, the core was still related to the circle of knowledge and a liberal education, but the emphasis on method and technique had pushed its way to the fore. The Curricular Review continues further along the lines of the Core Curriculum. Referring to "fast-changing fields" and "multiple perspectives," the Curricular Review eliminated the core (itself a pale refection of the humanistic curriculum) and proposed a program that "expands the choices open to undergraduates," that allows them to "enhance significantly the opportunities" for "integrative and foundational" courses, that will "enhance curricular choice," "a wide range of courses," "maximize [undergraduate] flexibility," "more freely shape," "move easily among fields," "greater opportunities," "curricular choice," "new questions," "greater freedom of choice," "opportunities," and on and on. "We seek to broaden the scope of a liberal education and to expand choices"—how broad does an education have to be before it loses all sense of definition? President Eliot would have been thrilled with hearing that "multiple disciplines, assumptions, and traditions of knowledge" must be addressed. Plurals are everywhere. The first of the recommendations stipulates that every student "should be educated in the sciences in a manner that is as deep and as broadly shared, as has traditionally been the case in the humanities and the social sciences."[129]

At the same time that curricular reform proceeds in the direction of boundless choice, the loss of faith in the classical humanities is not encouraging. A century of retrenchment has had its effect. The line once drawn before Latin and Greek has been pushed back to the humanities curriculum, and not even that line is holding. Hans Ulrich Gumbrecht points out that "nobody (not even ourselves, the philologists and literary critics), nobody has any use for more of that Sunday morning rhetoric about how wonderful and indispensable, yet underestimated, but ultimately forward-looking the Humanities are." Gumbrecht's glib assumption might be contrasted with Vico and Arnold, if only to underline the contemporary loss of faith in the humanistic curriculum by its very professors; one might think he was playing devil's advocate:

> Nobody needs more debates about whether the task of our disciplines should be "compensation" (i.e. "compensation" for the horrors of technology) or, rather, "orientation" (without knowing who will profit from the blessings of such guidance)—nobody needs more of such empty phrases in order to be finally instructed that the true nature of our disciplines is to be "cross-disciplinary" (something seems to have gone wrong with the logic here), "integrative" and "dialogic." I never want to be exposed again to claims like the one that the Humanities are "enlightening" because it is supposedly their business to resist and, if necessary undo, the "remythologizing effects" of contemporary society; nor do I want to be confronted any further with the distinction between "culture" (=good) and "civilization" (=bad).

Gumbrecht believes that it is "confusion to assume that we can sell, justify, or glorify our work by identifying its 'social functions" and cites with approval Karl Reinhardt's comment that classics might guide its students and readers "to doors through which they will never walk." He also rejects the various uses of classics from Friedrich Nietzsche (aesthetic phenomenon to justify existence), Ulrich von Wilamowitz-Moellendorff (ethical self-governance), Wilhelm Dilthey ("lived experience"), Max Weber (value-free reconstruction of historical circumstance), Stefan George ("integral wholeness"), Friedrich Gundolf ("lived experience as method"), and Werner Jaeger (*paideia* or "metahistorical normative conception of human life"). He suspects the kinds of "integrative" and "dialogic" or interdisciplinary notions that inform, say, the Harvard Curricular Review. For Gumbrecht, the extra virtue of classical study is the confrontation of the individual with "hard-to-tame (and sometimes even artificially maintained) complexity . . . in a situation of low time-pressure." Leisure is thus valued, but what one does with the knowledge gained from wrestling with the angel of complexity is one's own business. Gumbrecht is aware that the notion of truth is being sidestepped and that a university might expect more of itself than providing the "frame conditions that make it *possible* for aesthetic experience to happen."[130]

In the "transitional" period from the early nineteenth to the mid-twentieth centuries, technology did not dominate the social matrix; its imperatives could still be integrated with the rest of life, which retained the upper hand. Now, when we live entirely under technological conditions, and when those conditions have infiltrated every aspect of academic and pedagogical practice, a genuine humanistic education does not take root in students' lives at sufficient depth so that it can survive and sustain them through their careers. Does their inability to grasp, or indifference to, the so-called universal constants of human nature mean that those universals are no longer in force, but that a new, very different humanity is coming of age?

Parents, consumers, politicians, voters, educators—however one names them—demand an education that will outfit the child for living in the technological environment. One may pay lip service to the humanistic ideals of the past, but if an alert, well-meaning parent in a "focus group" inquires what the state or local school board is doing to foster a pupil's inner development, a pupil's understanding of the best that has been thought and known in the world, that parent would be met with quizzical, if not frosty, looks and utter miscomprehension. School boards scramble to find funds for more computers, online services, and "smart" classrooms to replace what are already obsolescent. Yet that parent would have been asking for the essence of the humanistic education that stretches back across the ages to classical antiquity. The circle of knowledge survived in the most diverse educational environments: ancient Greece and Rome, the medieval university, the Renaissance court, the English boarding school, and the bourgeois epoch. Though one cannot say that the circle has entirely disappeared even at the present time, its place in education is more precarious than ever, a smoke ring in the air.

# BELIEF AND SINCERITY

It is bad poetry which proclaims a definite
belief—because it is a sin against sincerity.

—J. B. Yeats to W. B. Yeats, February 27, 1916

"Belief" and "sincerity," relics of the nineteenth century and reflections of historical circumstances earlier still, have not survived the age of criticism intervening between I. A. Richards's major books and the present. Concepts that go naturally together, they entail individual autonomy, intensity of conviction, persuasion, autotransparency, and particular standards of morality and propriety even where those standards are called in question. In *Sincerity and Authenticity,* which chronicles the concept of sincerity beginning with *Hamlet,* Lionel Trilling notes that the word *sincerity* has "lost most of its former high dignity" and makes us "conscious of the anachronism which touches it with quaintness." But for Richards, belief and sincerity were both momentous issues. His studies in belief—chapters in four books and four essays written between 1924 and 1934—take up this exasperatingly vague and potentially arid subject from the most varied perspectives.[1] These topics are raised at or near the end of each book, seeming to indicate a certain ultimacy. Sincerity is the moral climax of *Practical Criticism* (ironically, a book recalled as the foundation of modern formalism), whereas belief remained on his critical agenda through essays on Job and Dante in *Beyond* in his last years.

Richards on belief and sincerity is indebted to philosophical and critical lines of thought going back more than a century and a half: Hume on miracles; James Mill, John Stuart Mill, and Alexander Bain; William James and James Ward; Newman's Christian apologetics; the criticism of Coleridge and Arnold. "Belief" fell under intense scrutiny during the second half of the nineteenth century when the historical sciences and Darwinism were eroding the perceived foundations of religion.[2] Arnold had questioned on what ground one could discover the sanctions for belief and conduct. Such authority should not be left to chance encounters in colleges, reading rooms, museums, and the popular press. In *Literature and Dogma* (1873) he distinguished between "belief" or scientific acceptance (a conviction regarding "what can and should be known to be true") and "extra-belief," taken from Goethe's *Aberglaube* and standing for belief "beyond what is certain and verifiable." "Extra-belief," said Goethe, "is the poetry of life" and, for Arnold, "has the rights of poetry." Poetic beliefs of "high seriousness" felt like religious beliefs in their psychological action. And they too seemed "extra," that is, beyond the complex of ordinary "belief" and capable of serving as a standard, a goal, a sanction.[3] Arnold reformulated the Renaissance educational ideal for modern society and promoted the authority of criticism: in this, as in other ways, he was Richards's chief model. But his religious studies did not encompass the psychology of belief, and many questions were left unanswered; to pursue these, Richards turned to the then neglected terrain of Anglo-American philosophical psychology.

The textbook empiricists had treated belief as either a more intense sensation or, in Hume's words, "a more vivid, lively, forcible, firm, steady conception of an object, than what the imagination alone is ever able to attain." For James Mill belief was an *"inseparable"* association of ideas: the repeated coexistence or succession of two states of consciousness explained both memory and expectation, and there was no "generic distinction, but only a difference in the strength of the association, between a case of belief and a case of mere imagination." In *A System of Logic* (1843), however, J. S. Mill questioned whether belief could be completely defined as ideas joined by association. We can, for example, change our beliefs, an act that would be impossible if the links were "inseparable." Mental association cannot by itself account for the power of belief, the unifying force that presides over the will. In Mill's view the only test sufficiently exacting for this force is what "we are safe in acting on as universal provisionally," or probabilities of a high order.[4] Following Hume, Mill accepted as "ultimate and primordial" the difference between remembering a sensation (memory) and remembering an idea (imagination), and between the expectation of a sensation (belief) and the expectation of having an idea (imagination). This difference led down to the ultimately mysterious "central point" of the mind, "presupposed and built upon in every attempt we make to explain the more recondite phenomena of our mental being."[5] If belief is stronger than imagination, however, it is not stronger than "knowledge." Mill disputed Sir William Hamilton's opinion that beliefs are "ultimate" and that knowledge is "derivative" or contingent upon them, that belief is therefore a "conviction of higher authority" than knowledge. For Mill, knowledge is "complete conviction" based on the most thorough empirical evidence and the application of universal laws, whereas belief is a conviction "somewhat short of complete." Once beyond a certain level of probability the matter is no longer one of belief or disbelief—it is knowledge: "We do not know a truth and believe it besides."[6] Mill's *System of Logic* was one of the fundamental books in Richards's education in moral sciences at Cambridge, and it reopened the case of belief in nearly every area that he would investigate: in affirming the conative as well as the intellectual power of belief, in locating it in the cohesive core of our being, and in giving it the test of action.[7]

Subsequent thinkers examined the psychology of belief in an atmosphere of intense religious controversy: John Venn in *On Some of the Characteristics of Belief Scientific and Religious* (1870), Leslie Stephen in *An Agnostic's Apology* (1876) and "Belief and Conduct" (1888), T. H. Huxley in "The Influence upon Morality of a Decline in Religious Belief" (1877), W. K. Clifford in "The Ethics of Belief" (1877), A. J. Balfour in *A Defense of Philosophic Doubt, Being an Essay on the Foundations of Belief* (1879), and scores of others. Walter Bagehot divided intellectual from emotional belief, which he called "conviction," one of the "intensest" emotions; he emphasized the connections of belief "tendencies" with bodily sensations. In *The Emotions and the Will* (1859), which Richards studied, Alexander Bain defined belief as a "strong primitive manifestation" and the hidden cooperation of "instinctive tendencies," because "delusion, fallacy, and mental perversion could not have obtained so great a sway over mankind, but for the intervention of agencies, operating without any regard to what we find in the world, as the result of actual experiment and observation." Belief is one of the "phases" of the will, the complex that "keeps the energy of the animal alive." From an infant's groping expectantly toward its mother's breast to the routines of mature existence and higher processes of intellection arrived at by trial and error, belief "implicates the order of the world." Put to an extreme test, one might die for beliefs. As Arthur Hugh Clough wrote, "It fortifies my soul to know, / That, though I perish, Truth is so."[8] Although Bain was solidly within the school of associationism and its mechanical or chemical (essentially passive) models, he moved beyond Mill by including a concept of spontaneous brain "activity" within his psychology and transforming belief from an "intellectual" to an "emotional" or volitional issue. William James and Richards alike were indebted to Bain's linking of the progress of higher intelligence to what he called a "sceptical, hesitating, incredulous temper" and to his famous test of action: "preparedness to act" is the "sole, the genuine, the unmistakable *criterion* of belief."[9]

Newman's contribution to the debate extended from "The Tamworth Reading Room" (1841) to *A Grammar of Assent* (1870), which contains the closest introspective analysis of belief in the period. Lord Brougham and Sir Robert Peel had proposed that a knowledge of literature and the sciences obtained through working men's colleges and public reading rooms could maintain religion and conduct. Newman objected to this "dangerous doctrine": not secular knowledge or "literary religion," but personal faith inculcated by private religious training was the principle of "life," and "life is for action." "Instances and patterns, not logical reasonings, are the living conclusions which alone have a hold over the affections, or can form the character."[10] Like these other writers, Newman had his peculiar dualism: *notional* assent to ideas, opinions, and universal laws, and the much more committed *real* assent ("Belief") to persons and things. Between belief and action is the conscience, an "intellectual sentiment" that, on the one side, is "always emotional" and is informed by admiration and disgust, hope and "especially fear," and, on the other, is advised by the illative sense, an intuitive faculty that determines the point at which something not demonstrated by fact may be taken "on faith" as an almost certain probability. Not opposed to discursive reason, the "illative sense" absorbs some of the functions of Aristotelian *phronesis* (judgment) and intuitive or right reason: Newman calls it "right judgment in ratiocination" (which "comes of an acquired habit") and the "ultimate test of truth and error in our inferences." The illative sense operates throughout the entire process of inquiry but takes over when precise formulae or "external rules" give out. Reasoning is the same in chemistry and ethics: "We proceed, as far indeed as we can, by the logic of language, but we are obliged to supplement it by the more subtle and elastic logic of thought; for forms by themselves prove nothing." Thus, in the final judgment of "poetical excellence," "heroic action," or "gentlemanlike conduct," one appeals to a "particular mental sense" (genius, taste, the moral sense) developed by practice, but the guiding faculty at the root of the processes is the illative sense. An informant on truth and probability, this sense contributes to the act of conscience that "vaguely reaches forward to something beyond self, and dimly discerns a sanction higher than self for its decisions."[11]

Richards's first paper, delivered at a meeting of the Moral Sciences Club in Cambridge in 1915, was on Newman's psychology of belief. The close phenomenological approach, the illative sense, the emphasis on imagination and emotion, on discovery of truths of conscience, and on certitude all influenced Richards when he formulated his theories of belief and sincerity. But action, not conscience, was a utilitarian's final test for belief, and it was Bain's definition, not Newman's, that was endorsed by Peirce, James, and eventually Richards. In *The*

*Principles of Psychology* (1890), a frequent point of departure for Richards, James contrasted belief not with disbelief but with "doubt" and "inquiry." Psychologically, both belief and disbelief are characterized by an "inward stability" that ends mental action and leads directly to practical action. But doubt and inquiry are just this "theoretic agitation." James collapsed the categories of "Will" and "Belief" that *are two names for one and the same psychological phenomenon.*[12] In "The Will to Believe" (1896) he set forth two cases for belief, the so-called weak and strong defenses or versions. According to the weak defense, although it was one's duty to collect as much data as possible on every subject concerned with a choice, many decisions had to be made on insufficient evidence. Moreover, we are rarely capable of "weighing evidence in an emotional vacuum." With regard to moral conduct, the possession of objective truth is far more often the exception than the rule, and one cannot wait for absolute certainty before making a decision. Even in science many conclusions are reached through a particular hunch, long before the evidence comes in. Clearly, one has every right to believe in one's religion regardless of certainty or proof. In his strong defense of the will to believe, James asserted that the emotional and volitional components of belief factually played a large role in turning a dimly realized hope into reality: *"Faith in a fact can help create the fact."*[13] This sometimes goes by the name of the "self-fulfilling prophecy."

The last of Richards's precursors, and one of his teachers at Cambridge, James Ward is often linked with James for having overthrown classical associationism. James did so by a radical empiricism, Ward by an idealist metaphysics and a concept of the mind's self-constituting activity. Ward argues that, epistemologically, knowledge is always "impersonal" and belief "personal"; the difference is *"in kind."* Psychologically, however, belief and knowledge "differ only in *degree*"; they are both measured by probability and doubt.[14] Ward did not think that the *ultimate* ground of belief was utilitarian "action," because the prolonged absence of action did not destroy the belief. The basis must be within the "subjective attitude," the "complete 'state of mind'" that requires not only certainty but the conviction and confidence that are fed by certainty as well. If the subject were a logical ego, a mere thinking machine, the emotive and practical effects as they fed back would be meaningless. Ward applies "belief" to the cognitive or objective side of experience. "Faith" lies in the subjective side. "In the one we are constrained, more or less completely, to assent to what is there: in the other we strive to achieve what as yet is not there. In the one, facts convince *us,* the seen and actual hem us in: in the other, we—reaching beyond towards the ideally possible—create *them.*" By and large, belief is a passive response, for one accepts facts and scientific generalizations; faith (applying psychologically to religious faith and "all lesser faiths") is an active one.

With faith, the individual chooses modes of "self-conservation and betterment" that lie "within the possibilities that nature leaves open. . . . It is this open possibility, which Kant effectively disclosed, that leaves 'room for faith.'"[15]

What has mankind done with this open possibility? Although he repudiates "ultra-utopian visions of a final harmony," Ward traces a "tendency to progression," an "upward striving that is the essence of life," from the first tactile response and differentiation of the senses to intellectual perceptions and the romantic "cosmic emotion." It is the duty of "imagination" to explore or to create the "region of the possible."[16] Thus, knowledge, spiritual faith, freedom, and imagination, which constitute the "subjective attitude," lift humanity above mere mechanism and into the "realm of ends." Richards would find congenial the individualist point of view, the cosmic blend of idealism, pluralism, and evolutionism, the interest in science, the notion of infinite possibility, and the vital role given imagination.

The philosophical tradition on belief is not without inconsistences. "Betterment" and "progress" beg the questions: Better for whom? And by what standards? Personal whim can dictate to the illative sense. The utilitarian pragmatist looks to the future and ignores history. The mind's "central point" and "completeness" are, in today's terms, myths of synthesis. None of the belief concepts described above survived the "crisis of reason" in Western metaphysics and science at the turn of the twentieth century: the breakdown of fixed boundaries between reason and emotion, the weight of unconscious factors, and new discourses of rationality in philosophy, literature, and the social sciences. Nor in this crisis did Richards (wisely, as it happened) turn to the work of psychoanalysis. Freudianism entered England in 1913, but the war delayed its progress, and in the early 1920s Richards was much too caught up in mapping out his critical system to entertain seriously anyone else's.[17] In 1924 he noted that psychoanalysis had "touched upon" belief and skepticism, "but not with a very clear understanding of the situation" (*PLC*, 281). In 1929, as a "centrist," he spoke up for the tradition of G. F. Stout and Ward as the "comparatively neglected and unheard-of middle body, the cautious, traditional, academic, semi-philosophical psychologists" as the "main" body of philosophical psychology, with the Freudians on one side and the behaviorists on the other (*PC*, 322). Although in 1934 he said psychoanalysis had "helped us immensely" (*P*, 240) in questions of belief and interest, "us" must be understood in its editorial sense: the influence of psychoanalysis on his thought was negligible.[18] If Richards had been perhaps one or two student generations younger (like William Empson), he might have assimilated a psychoanalytic tradition of thought on the problems he was considering with his Anglo-American concepts of "belief," "purpose," and "sincerity."

By Richards's time everything to be said about belief in Anglo-American philosophy had been said, repeated, and forgotten. His originality consists in lifting a matter out of one context and placing it in another—in this case, at the heart of criticism—and to treat it in a linguistic framework. His path was lit at the outset by a surprising fact: belief had not been a major issue in the history of criticism. It had been handled with ease by the Christian apologetic tradition, whereas with few (mainly Scottish) exceptions Enlightenment thinkers speculated on every conceivable topic surrounding the gods and religion—except belief.[19] In the present age of relativism, "most readers, and nearly all good readers," said Richards, "are very little disturbed by even a direct opposition between their own beliefs and the beliefs of the poet." The *Divine Comedy, Paradise Lost,* and *The Dynasts,* all poems "built upon firm and definite beliefs," are clearly accessible to readers who hold none of the beliefs (*PC,* 271). The belief problem might never have arisen but for the impact of the scientific and historical disciplines in the rapidly changing social context: "science" shifting the burden of belief from religion onto the arts, onto new myths, onto political ideologies, onto itself, or dropping it altogether in bleak skepticism.

Nevertheless, that "belief" was a critical issue was obvious from Richards's classroom experience reported in *Practical Criticism.* Students misread literature either from sharing the writer's beliefs and applauding them or from not sharing them and dismissing them. One praised Phillip James Bailey's *Festus* because it "*sums up my creed* as a Socialist" (*PC,* 27). Another rejected a sonnet by Donne for being "too religious for one who doesn't believe in repenting that way" (*PC,* 46). Retributive justice and the coming millennium are the everlasting nay and yea in Shelley's *Prometheus Unbound,* but, according to Richards, belief in either doctrine could impair one's reading of the poem (*PLC,* 276n). "We need no such beliefs, and indeed we must have none, it we are to read *King Lear*" (*SP,* 62).[20]

To the antiquarian, belief in poetry is not a relevant question; the distance of the past inspires curiosity and fascination. The antiquarian does not need belief, only understanding. Belief may enhance understanding but equally distort it. For Richards, belief is a humanist or hermeneutic concern in an age of unbelief—"humanist" as Arnold understood the term. Richards wants his readers to "translate" the communication of writers whose beliefs, doctrines, or natural systems of thought are foreign. The acid test is the behaviorist reading Dante: "*qua* psychologist he denies the existence of the soul or the self, and stands prepared to translate all statements about the 'spiritual' into terms of visceral reaction systems and yet *qua* imaginative individual he fully undergoes all transformations of feeling and attitude that the poet compels."[21] For the reader to deny the central significance of this *translation* or to aim attention at

formalistic matters merely dodges the issue: "There is something a little ridicu-
lous, at least, in admiring only the rhythms and 'word harmonies' of an author
who is writing about the salvation of his soul" (*C*, 31). Richards therefore dis-
credits as classic "insincerity" a temporary, "pretending" belief in Dante's hell
or Milton's heaven (*PC*, 280).[22] What is covered by the higher claims of belief
in major artists ought to influence and produce "permanent modifications in
the structure of the mind" (*PLC*, 132).

The problem of belief may disturb the experience of virtually any work of
art that "departs, for its own purposes, from the most ordinary universal facts
of common experience or from the most necessary deductions of scientific
theory" (*PC*, 279). It may arise in reading a Blake lyric where the laws of grav-
ity are suspended, but it probably will not. Milton's "dear might of him that
walk'd the waves" in *Lycidas* and Tintoretto's *Christ at the Sea of Galilee* pose
more serious questions. Such religious art presents, in its extreme form, a situation that occurs in "nearly all poetry" (*PC*, 272). In nonreligious art the poetic
fiction may be sustained by a momentary "assumption," an *as if,* for where
one's private beliefs are not fundamentally disturbed by the assumption, it
takes little effort to grant. Even the antics of the Olympian gods in Homer may
not raise the belief problem because of vast cultural differences and an imaginative participation that does not penetrate to the core of our beliefs (*PC*,
272).[23] As assumptions mount up, however, they begin to agitate the reading
process. At last, in a poem by Donne on the resurrection of the body, "it becomes very difficult not to think that *actual belief* in the doctrine that appears
in the poem is required for its full and perfect imaginative realisation" (*PC*,
272–73). Reading Donne correctly does not feel as if we are merely granting an
assumption or even fifty assumptions; it feels like *believing* in something. What
is the nature of this readerly belief?

The fact that most readers tend to solve the problem of belief (if it even
arises) "in minor cases" is heartening, and Richards thinks the same solution
may be applied to the major instances, that is, to Donne, Milton, and Dante. In
keeping with the philosophic tradition and with his division of referential and
emotive language, Richards separates *intellectual* ("verifiable" or "scientific")
*belief* from *emotional belief,* thus inheriting all the problems entailed in the division. Each term is somewhat confusingly allowed to stand for both the emotion of conviction and the object of belief. He compares intellectual belief to
the "weighting" of an idea on a scale; the metaphor embodies impersonality,
judiciousness, and scientific precision. As evidence is loaded, the balance sinks,
and "other, less heavily weighted" ideas *must* "adjust themselves to it." The
loading is either legitimate ("the quantity of evidence, its immediacy, the extent and complexity of the supporting systems of ideas are obvious forms of

legitimate loading") or illegitimate ("our liking for the idea, its brilliance, the trouble that changing it may involve, emotional satisfactions from it"). Richards borrowed *trustworthiness* from James to characterize the feeling associated with intellectual belief. The motive behind holding any intellectual belief is the bringing of it into "as perfect an ordered system as possible." Richards invokes the coherence theory of truth and even paraphrases Spinoza to the effect that we disbelieve only because we believe something else that is incompatible. He presses the point to the extreme: we believe only "because it is necessary to disbelieve whatever is logically contradictory to our belief" (*PC*, 274). Ironically, the mental effort it takes to maintain a long-tested intellectual belief may be slight because it makes no demand on the emotions: "Unless the idea is very original and contrary to received ideas, it needs little loading to hold its own" (*PC*, 275).[24] As in Mill, an "intellectual belief" in its substantive sense is not really a belief at all: it is "knowledge."

According to Richards, then, intellectual belief and disbelief are relatively businesslike affairs, and belief is not aroused *unless the logical context of our ideas is in question* (*PC*, 274–75). The logical connections are crucial to the maintenance of intellectual belief; without them, ideas would simply exist in a free state in the mind, "neither believed nor disbelieved, nor doubted nor questioned . . . just present." In this state of "disconnection" intellectual propositions would resemble most of the ideas that float in the mind of "the child," "primitive man," "the peasant," the "non-intellectual world"—and in "most poetry" (*PC*, 275).

The disconnected ideas may be subject to a second, much older "principle of order" (*C*, 34). In primitive society, "any idea which opens a ready outlet to emotion or points to a line of action in conformity with custom is quickly believed," and this need for the ordering of the whole affective side of our life survives: "Given a need (whether conscious *as a desire* or not), any idea which can be taken as a step on the way to its fulfilment is accepted, unless some other need equally active at the moment bars it out. This acceptance, this use of the idea—by our interests, desires, feelings, attitudes, tendencies to action and what not—is emotional belief" (*PC*, 275).[25] Emotional beliefs may be self-contradictory and also logically incompatible with intellectual beliefs. In analyzing poetry Richards refers to these poetic fictions as "pseudo-statements" (*SP*, 60), "provisional acceptances," and "objectless beliefs" (*PLC*, 278, 280). They are "pseudo" because the statements are not *primarily* asserting a truth in the strict scientific sense, although they seem to be; "provisional" because they may be temporarily held to one organization, then let loose again; "objectless" because they do not refer, like propositions, to objective reality.

An intellectual belief is justified when it finds its logical link to the system, and the system is justified in its turn when it goes down to the "central, most stable, mass of our ideas" whose order is fixed "by the facts of Nature." Here is the bedrock, the confident empiricism of Richards, resorting to the correspondence theory of truth. If intellectual beliefs are not ultimately reconcilable to "Nature," we "promptly perish" (*PC*, 276). (Thus, Hume said that, despite his philosophical skepticism, he always got out of the way of a coach coming down the road.) The difficulty with Richards's position is that it lies at too many leagues' distance from numerous intellectual (social, cultural, historical scientific) "beliefs" in competition with one another. He does not fly up to the general too quickly; rather, he flies to the concrete, which, in its hypostatized state, amounts to the same thing. Emotional belief is justified by providing insight into the whole emotional side of our life and by "meeting our needs—due regard being paid to the relative claims of our many needs one against another" (*PC*, 277). We lend emotional belief to a proposition or a poem in order to understand it. Beyond the advantage of enlarged perceptiveness, emotional beliefs stand or fall on the grounds of pragmatic usefulness, and this subject is best explored under two headings: conflict between emotional and intellectual belief and testing.

How does one prevent such a conflict? Richards argues empirically that the "stable mass" of intellectual belief throws a check on emotional belief, which is always ready to aggrandize itself and reclaim territory lost since the advent of the scientific era, whether one dates that era from three hundred or three thousand years ago. He thinks that poetry has often arisen "through fusion (or confusion)" between emotional and intellectual belief, the "boundary between what is intellectually certified and what is not being much less sharply defined in former centuries and *defined in another manner*" (*PC*, 278–79n). At the same time the ultimate ground of emotional belief is inviolable, and science, no matter how exalted, cannot claim the place of the will. The way to avoid conflict is sheer "prudence," keeping in mind the larger end that the emotional belief subserves. This ethical category traces to the atomic individual in classical liberalism, with his tactful behavior and self-interest, a negative, "cold" virtue without much claim to higher obligation. Coleridge thought of prudence as the bare ethical minimum: "In almost all cases in which there is contemplation to act wrong the first appearances of prudence are in favour of immorality" or crass self-interest.[26] But the spare virtue of prudence cannot sustain a strenuous moral life. This is hardly Richards's last word on the subject.

Intellectual and emotional beliefs may interpenetrate, may mimic one another, may be mutually parasitic, or may have the same "feel" to introspection. According to more recent criticism, one may even be *in* the other. Richards holds that the lines of interest in the two forms of belief must be kept from entanglement, the simplest example of which is being so emotionally attached to a theory that it blinds one to realities. Even physicists, he notes, recognize that what is verifiable is only a fraction of the picture used in framing their problems: many of their "intellectual beliefs" are pictures of their own devising permeated by "illegitimate loading"—for example, the desire for reputation (*PC*, 275–76). Richards seems to have recognized that the complex interrelations between intellectual and emotional belief could be misrepresented by his dualistic terminology. So, instead of cleaving his Gordian knot into halves of belief, he eventually expands upon the harsh division through lexical exercises. For example, he pairs belief with opposing concepts, a procedure that allows him simultaneously to review the philosophical tradition. Belief is contrasted with "knowledge" as in Mill, Arnold, and Ward; with "opinion" as in Newman; with superstition as in Huxley and Clifford; with "doubt" as in Bain and James; and with "imagination" as in Mill and Ward, which is the "most interesting" opposition (*C*, 29–30). He prefers it because "imagination" collects knowledge, doubt, and opinion and adds creative impulse, the power of transformation, an orientation toward the future, and unboundedness. By 1930 Richards was using the phrase "imaginative assent" in place of "emotional belief" (*C*, 33) and stood ready, in the next years and by way of Coleridge on imagination, to rethink his problem in different terms.

But if the terminology changed, Richards's solution to the belief problem in art remained the same: withhold intellectual belief except to probe the "*internal* coherence" of the work of art and grant full emotional belief for the duration. The proviso must not be taken lightly from the author of the "close reading" method. The proper exercise of emotional belief cannot occur without the exacting study of the parts of the poem, both among themselves and in "the relations of its ideas to other ideas of ordinary experience which are *emotionally* relevant to it" (*PC*, 277). Theoretically speaking, the reach of allusion and its emotional relevance can be endless. Practically, Richards would say that where emotional relevance, its feeling in consciousness, approaches zero, one has as good a test as any for the *limit* of the allusion.

Coleridge in *Biographia Literaria* had written that poetry requires the "willing suspension of disbelief." For Richards, Coleridge is right, but not clear enough: intellectual belief never arises when one reads correctly, except in establishing the "*internal* coherence" of the material. And emotional belief is never properly suspended if one is to enter the humanist process of "translation." When intellectual or emotional belief is disturbed, "either through the poet's fault or our own," we are no longer reading poetry; we have become "astronomers, or theologians, or moralists"—or antiquarians (*PC*, 277).[27]

The philosophical tradition had established two tests for belief: the pragmatic test of action and the more elusive test of feeling. They were not in contradiction with each other, and, characteristically, Richards borrows both. His first test measures the "difference in the degree to which success or failure in the action can affect the view which prompts it." Following Bain and James, Richards finds that the "readiness to act as though it were so" is the most satisfactory criterion (C, 32–33). How much belief does one place in a case before committing oneself to action? Commitment depends upon the results of evaluations and the precision of the returns. Exact returns characterize everyday and scientific beliefs and lead to certainty. "Readiness to act" is a factor that should operate "in *all* circumstances and in *all* connections into which it can enter" (*PLC*, 277).

Religious and poetic beliefs, which are placed in the same category, do not have the empirical contact points that scientific and everyday beliefs do; they do not operate in all circumstances. On the one hand, they are very general concepts (for instance, the goodness of the universal deity); on the other, they apply only to restricted spheres of behavior. Their agreement with reality is a matter of the "development of thought, feeling, will, and conduct in accordance with one picture of the world or another" (*C*, 33). The validation of the belief is made against experience and found "true" if it is "rare," "desirable," and "important"; if it "meets deep needs in our nature"; and if it can be "accepted and integrated into the fabric of our personality as a positive determining influence" (*C*, 44) and fosters "the good life."[28] Even at that, Richards was concerned that any emotional belief might rigidify into doctrine and be subsequently confused with intellectual belief, and so he pleaded for delicacy, caution, and perspicacity. In a conversation in 1972 Richards said that he wanted to publish different versions of his three *Beyond* cantos after Dante to show "multiple possibilities." Pursuing him on the question of belief, I said, "Shouldn't one belief finally dominate?" "No," he answered, "only a very strong preference."[29]

The test of action is supplemented by the test of feeling. Beliefs of all kinds normally prompt an initial feeling of "acceptance" or "satisfaction," what James had termed "acquiescence."[30] But Richards identifies a longer-range "backwash effect" peculiar to emotional belief alone (*C*, 32): the "sense of ease, of restfulness, of free, unimpeded activity, and the feeling of acceptance, of something more positive than acquiescence" (*PLC*, 283) to distinguish it from the feeling common to both intellectual and emotional belief. Both feelings *follow* action, in conformity to the James-Lange theory of emotion. Richards is confronted by the odd circumstance that *imaginative assent* is both weaker and stronger than *verifiable belief:* weaker in that it cannot be proved by kicking a stone, stronger in its ultimate claim on the will, for this is the faith that can move mountains. So powerful is this "belief-feeling" that it may lead to confusing the two kinds of belief, and "Revelation Doctrines" do in fact depend upon it. The emotional attitude that accompanies a reading of *Adonais* "feels like belief": "It is only too easy to think that we are believing in immortality or survival, or in something else capable of statement" (*PLC*, 279). But we are not; the attitude is a consequence, not a cause of the experience. Yet, although the sense of revelation fades the morning after, the "shaping influence" of these experiences is not necessarily lost. "The mind has found through them a pattern of response which may remain, and it is this pattern rather than the revelation which is important" (*PC*, 276).

In 1975 Richards acknowledged that his belief theory had been "overly optimistic" considering the world catastrophe that lay ahead. The theory gave individuals too much credit for making rational choices and extremely fine distinctions. Still, he stood by its refusal of "insulted revulsion" (*épater le bourgeois,* modernist spleen) and its "call to action" (*C,* 24).[31] The last phrase may surprise readers of his restrained pages on belief. He called for "humility," honesty to experience, and a return to the "arduous discipline" of poetry that would clarify limitations and extend capacities. But he specified no line of action; he made no rousing calls; society was addressed only in the most general terms. Surely this is why in the turbulent 1930s his voice was drowned by the more exigent Leavisites and Marxists in England, while in the "end of ideology" era of the late 1940s and 1950s, the New Critics could simply brush aside his theory of "belief" and concentrate on his formalism.[32]

For Richards, however, a principle of continuity informed the belief theory, and no gap separated the experience of poetry from life. There must be harmony between the inner and outer persons. He restated *his* belief in terms of the Renaissance ideal of *litterae humaniores:* the "verbal expression of this life, at its finest, is forced to use the technique of poetry." The struggle between good and bad life is conceived in terms of good and bad art: "If we do not live in consonance with good poetry, we must live in consonance with bad poetry." Even so, behind his hope was a realistic assessment of human waste, of the "idle hours of most lives . . . filled with reveries that are simply bad private poetry" (*PC*, 319–20).

The belief theory settled a mysterious obligation upon individual character; upon the *act* that summoned will, emotion, and intellect in a single moment of choice leading to action; upon both a particular faculty and the quality that the faculty discovers; upon a reader's "sincerity." Realizing that sincerity could be invoked to prove anything and to justify anything, Richards exerted an enormous effort to define his ideal rigorously and then to safeguard it, as much as possible, from unbridled relativism and self-deceit. Sincerity is as central to his writings as intuition is to G. E. Moore or the sublime to Longinus: a signal virtue, a matter not only of intellectual or aesthetic import but of moral and social character. "Whatever it is," sincerity is "the quality we most insistently require in poetry" and "most need as critics" (*PC*, 282–83).

As Trilling has shown, *sincerity* entered English in the sixteenth century from the Latin *sincerus,* meaning "genuine," "whole," "natural." One drank a sincere or unmixed wine, heard a sincere or harmonious bell, and led a sincere or genuine life, "consistent in its virtuousness" and without "feigning or pretence," a meaning that occurs a dozen times in Shakespeare.

In *Practical Criticism,* Richards hoped that his twofold theory of belief would protect intellectual and emotional beliefs from encroaching on each other's territory. In advocating emotional belief detached from intellectual belief, however, he realized that a split response might be felt—quite unjustifiably—as "insincerity" and hence as damaging to the aesthetic experience. A full investigation of sincerity itself was needed to clarify the question, and he began by surveying what sincerity could *not* be: an artist's premeditated attempt to deceive a reader. Nothing could be more insincere. Neither should artists confuse their motives, professing one thing while being motivated by another. Both cases obtain when a gap exists between the "*shaping* impulses in the poet's mind" and the poem's "claim upon our response" (*PC*, 280), when there is a dichotomy between the motives that created the art and "nonartistic" motives such as ambition, greed, or pique—a point equally insisted upon by R. G. Collingwood.[33] Following the classical motto "Art is to conceal art," Swift hides behind layers of irony, and the modernists encrypt their truth deep within. But Richards's belief in the artists' basic desire to speak what they think and feel is not incompatible with either Swift's irony or modernist hermeticism: there is a "sincere" Swift, a "sincere" Eliot, and a "sincere" Whitman.

Numerous student protocols cited in *Practical Criticism* invoked "sincerity" as a touchstone for appreciating "genuine" or "authentic" as opposed to "spurious" emotion. Again, Richards demurred. Seldom can one disengage a "genuine" emotion, derived solely "from the prompting situation *plus* all the relevant experience of that mind" yet "free from impurities and from all interferences." Only the greatest poets in their greatest moments approached such an ideal, a worthy one but "nowhere obtainable in this obstructive world" (*PC*, 281). An additional difficulty with this standard of sincerity is that its opposite requires the stupid person or the mental case, the mind crippled by interferences. If the great poet is the most sincere, the mental case could hardly be called insincere. Therefore, to make a standard of one "sincere" emotion is impractical, and, along these lines, Richards moved to reject subcategorical definitions of sincerity such as the "simple," the "spontaneous," and the "artless." None of these standards could be applied as a test to most art. The "spontaneous" or "natural" feeling, as opposed to the "sophisticated" or "self-reflecting," pertains to a relatively small portion of literature and is in any event a romantic fiction. As Richards notes, proponents of "spontaneous" emotion remain notoriously blind to ugly examples of the case, and the expression of even the most simple emotions often results from extreme training and cultivation (*PC*, 281–82).

Arnold had spoken of Jesus' "method" of "inwardness and sincerity in the conscience of each individual man" as the essence of Protestantism, placing "sincerity" among the critical virtues.[34] Yet it was Tolstoy who declared "sincerity" the "most important" of all artistic and critical premises, and, at a time when it was hardly fashionable, Richards gave a chapter and a half to Tolstoy in *Principles of Literary Criticism*. For Tolstoy, sincerity meant an honest response to an honest feeling:

> As soon as the spectator, auditor, or reader feels that the artist himself is affected contagiously by his production, and is writing, singing, or playing for himself, and not only to produce an effect on others, this mental condition in the artist affects the perceiver contagiously, and, on the other hand, as soon as the spectator, reader, or auditor feels that the artist is not writing, singing, or playing for his own satisfaction, and does not himself feel what he expresses, a resistance is felt.[35]

Sincerity stood higher in Tolstoy's estimation than his other criteria, the "individuality" of the communicated feeling and the "clarity" of transmission. Richards disapproved of the manner in which Tolstoy then proceeded with "sincerity," condemning all but the simplest and most directly communicable art, and he also believed that Tolstoy had left the issue "obscure" (*PLC*, 188–89). Nonetheless, he acknowledged Tolstoy's psychological clue of "kinship" or "bonding," which he rephrased tactfully as the "absence of any apparent attempt on the part of the artist to work effects upon the reader which do not work for himself" (*PLC*, 271).[36]

The statement receives support from several remarks in Richards's early books. In *The Foundations of Aesthetics* (cowritten with C. K. Ogden and James Wood), "contact with the personality of the artist" was number 15 in the "multiple definition" of beauty and stood in the middle of the preferred grouping of synaesthesis (nos. 14–16). In *Principles*, Richards found an analogue to sincerity in Wordsworth's "emotion recollected in tranquillity," an emotion "kindred" to the emotion that had been the "subject of contemplation" in the poet's mind and that is again "gradually produced" until it exists in the reader's mind.[37] Richards's examples of the contrast between sincerity and insincerity were

Burns's "Ae Fond Kiss" and Byron's "When We Two Parted," two poems in which a parting lover addresses his mistress. Burns fails to convince us of "his probity and sincerity as an artist": it is "well known" that Burns was "only too anxious to escape Nancy's (Mrs. Maclehose's) attentions" (Richards gives "Nancy's" real name). There is, in other words, a divided response. Byron's poem, in contrast, has "no flaw" in its "creating impulse" (*PLC*, 271). Note that, despite his stated position against biographical interpretation. Richards reached into Burns's biography to help decide the case. Without doing so, one could argue that Burns was "sincere" in his deception: he was on the whole glad to be through with the unwilling lady.[38] At this point in his career (1924) Richards's position on sincerity may be summarized as "wholeness" in the imaginative moment, a condition that entails "free participation" of all relevant impulses and attitudes, "conscious or unconscious" and "without suppressions or restrictions"—admittedly, "the rarest and the most difficult condition required for supreme communicative ability" (*PLC*, 189).

Richards's visit to China in 1927 rekindled his interest in the *Chung Yung*, the ancient *Doctrine of the Mean; or, Equilibrium and Harmony.* Two years later, in *Practical Criticism,* he called it "the most interesting and the most puzzling" of the Confucian books and dwelt at length on its concept of sincerity. In the nineteenth-century translation (by James Legge) that Richards used, *sincerity* alternates with *singleness* to describe the felt convergence of three "virtues": knowledge, magnanimity, and energy. Unified by sincerity, the practice of the virtues enables the individual to "obey" or "complete" familial, social, and political duties and thereby "complete" the self and proceed upon the Way: "Sincerity is the way of Heaven." Legge and Richards interpret the Way as both a mean between extremes and the "principle of reciprocity": the Confucian text reads, "What you do not like when done to yourself, do not do to others."[39] When Confucius or Tsze-sze calls the Way a means of self-completion, he does not advocate that the self should freely fashion itself into a Nietzschean Superman. The authoritarian manuals, the repetitive maxims, the various rites, and the vague religious aura all point to the deeply embedded social system and serve to reinforce it. The Confucian texts aim at instilling "singleness," obedience, unity, and closure—altogether strange territory for a liberal pluralist like Richards. Yet he needed a text against which to parry on so vague a subject—preferably one beyond his tradition and his epoch—an ancient and authoritative text that had been "tested" over the centuries.

Richards does not distinguish Confucius's contribution in the *Chung Yung* from that of his grandson Tsze-sze (to whom Legge grants authorship), but he surely read Legge on Tsze-sze's individualist expansion away from Confucian rigor to a warmer emotional tone. "The sincere, or perfect man of Confucius,"

Legge comments, "is he who satisfies completely all the requirements of duty in the various relations of society, and in the exercise of government; but the sincere man of Tsze-sze is a potency in the universe."[40] Possessing "complete sincerity," the individual may progress toward self-realization, urges Tsze-sze, and become a moral exemplar: "Able to give its full development to his own nature, he can do the same to the nature of other men" and thence to "the natures of animals and things"; he then can "assist the transforming and nourishing powers of Heaven and Earth" and with them "form a ternion."[41] In the end, however, Tsze-sze comes around to fusing his self-realizing instincts with the imitation of the universal Sage and so effects a Confucian closure. Richards inclines to Tsze-sze's "romantic" side. Although he had no wish to turn Tsze-sze into a modern liberal, Richards still read more of himself into these maxims than they would seem to allow. Rather, the maxims *as maxims* are lifted from their historical context—they hide that context with a lightninglike "truth" that both reveals and blinds.[42] Nor are they logically connected to an argument—a quality typical of maxims, and the reason Bacon referred to them as "broken knowledge." In this respect we note the varied tasks to which Confucian maxims are applied—by Richards, by Irving Babbitt, by Ezra Pound. How clear can the original concept be if three such different writers all "follow" it? It was incidentally T. S. Eliot who first pointed out the shared interest of these writers in the Confucian books and suggested as its basis their "deracination from the Christian tradition." He also recommended that Richards's "long and important" analysis of Confucian sincerity be read "attentively."[43]

The ten passages on sincerity that Richards cites from the *Chung Yung* may be grouped under three broad headings: intuition, self-completion, and the union of internal and external. On intuition Confucius says that the possessor of sincerity "without an effort, hits what is right, and apprehends, without the exercise of thought;—he is the sage who naturally and easily embodies the right way." Confucius probably meant that the external standard (the target, the Way) controls the intuitive decision. On the contrary, with his radical Protestant inwardness, Richards wants the intuitive judgment to remain free, so far as it can, from any scientific, religious, or psychological system that imposes its external standard. An additional consideration is that any fool or knave will testify "without an effort" to the clarity of his intuitive reason. This faculty can be misinterpreted, or inaccurate, or partial, or wrong; it is no oracle.[44] Hence, following Confucius, Richards requires "unremitting research and reflection" (*PC*, 287), which aim at improving the analytic reason and preparing for acts of intuitive reason. He thinks it highly probable that such exercise, by method and criticism, strengthens by unconscious pathways the intuitive reason. The Confucian texts stipulate that one reaches the point of trusting intuition only after "extensive study of what is good, accurate inquiry about it, careful reflection on it, the clear discrimination of it, and the earnest practice of it."[45] They make it clear, notes Richards, that intuition is not an alternative to reflection: it is a last resort.

As such, intuition is the "prerogative only of those who have attained to sincerity" (*PC*, 287). Richards obviously cannot mean that one must never practice intuition until perfection is achieved. Sincerity is both the vehicle and the goal. This may remove an apparent contradiction: the preliminary reflection demands "unremitting research," whereas the final intuition happens "without an effort" and "without the exercise of thought." Sincerity thus restores to the self its natural state, natural according to that romantic estimate of the goodness of human feeling that is one of the deep presuppositions of Richards's thought. Confucius himself indicates that some are "born with the knowledge of those duties" and often resorts to nature metaphor, but he also notes shrewdly that others acquire knowledge only by study or "after a painful feeling of their ignorance." Using a nature metaphor, Tsze-sze says that the sincere person "cultivates to the utmost the shoots of goodness in him." Richards also believes that "superior persons" will perceive the insufficiency of their sincerity through intellectual "effort," a concept that is as difficult to understand in theory as it is easy to recognize in practice. Again, Richards gives a liberal reading of the conservative Confucian doctrine. Confucian sincerity comes to rest in acceptance and observation of some propriety or rule, of finding that the preestablished form is indeed right for oneself. Confucius, Tsze-sze, and Richards, for their own separate aims, are each at pains to demonstrate with regard to "effort" that "if another man succeed by one effort, [the superior man] will use a hundred efforts. If another man succeed by ten efforts, he will use a thousand."[46] Self-restraint—prudence, tact, the observance of the proprieties— acts as a further protection. If superior persons cannot continue to do the right thing, they at least refrain from doing the wrong thing.

Self-completion is the centerpiece of sincerity. Tsze-sze's texts are sparse and vague. We are to understand that sincerity is "that whereby self-completion is effected"; "its way is that by which man must direct himself."[47] Read in the light of earlier sections of the *Chung Yung*, self-completion requires the fulfillment of duties (filial piety, submission of the younger to the elder brother, knowledge of the ceremonies, loyalty to the state) and the consequent loss of individuality in the imitation of the Sage, the ideal of humanity, and the Way. The Confucian program offers the spectator an inherent harmony that society (not to mention history) continually falls short of. The system is corporate, hierarchical, patriarchal, ritualistic, and repressive—Pound saluted it in 1938 as "totalitarian" and "whole" (closure) and a welcome change from Greek critical thought or "splitting" (anticlosure).[48] However, read in light of Tsze-sze's expansion, self-completion speaks for individual potentiality, whose Western analogue is romantic self-realization (and the accompanying "cosmic emotion"). Tsze-sze asserts that to his ideal of sincerity "belongs ceaselessness": "Continuing long, [sincerity] evidences itself. Evidencing itself, it reaches far. Reaching far, it becomes large and substantial. Large and substantial, it becomes high and brilliant . . . it overspreads all things . . . it perfects all things."[49]

Confucian doctrine holds imitation in high esteem because it can be used to imprint deeply the social ideology. Richards's concept of self-completion faces back toward imitation and ahead toward the emergence of what is uniquely genuine or "perfect" in the self. Unlike the romantics who associate sincerity exclusively with originality, Richards finds sincerity at least compatible with imitation. But unlike Tsze-sze's instances of imitation (such as the Sage's wisdom or the canonical books), Richards's example of imitation is not single but multiple: the greatest poets in their greatest moments, a far more open—and undefined—model for shaping human character. Richards was always cautious about imitation, either in art or in conduct. Bad models outnumber the good. Yet imitation was undeniably primordial in human nature; Aristotle had rightly said that imitation is an instinct lying deep in our nature and that by imitation one learns (*Poetics* 4.1448b). Richards's favorite citation from the *Chung Yung,* occurring many times in his writings, shows his attempt to award imitation its place while preventing it from cramping originality: "In the Book of Poetry," says Confucius, "it is said, 'In hewing an axe-handle, in hewing an axe-handle, the pattern is not far off.'"[50] One imitates a pattern, but the tool is still in the hands of the shaping agent. The tool is a shaping tool; what is being made is an instrument, not a finished product: the shaper should be subtler than the tools (or the terms). The repetition of the clauses emphasizes the sense of identity and difference. The craftsman analogy presupposes the integrity of the craftsman.

Richards's "forward" example of self-completion is anticlosure, an "open possibility," and is directed toward change in the individual and the social milieu. Suppose, he muses, that "in the irremediable default of this perfection"—a mind without interference or disorder, the great poet in his moment of creative synthesis—"default due to man's innate constitution and to the accidents to which he is exposed, there exists a tendency towards increased order" (*PC,* 285). The language deserves close scrutiny, standing as it does at the climactic moment of *Practical Criticism.* The terms *tendency* and *increased order* trace to the main nineteenth-century metaphor of organicism and its leading representations: evolution, both natural and social, and self-realization. In Wordsworth's *Excursion,* the Wanderer, "venerable Sage" (9.2), discourses on

the "active Principle" (9.3), and the "mighty stream of tendency" (9.87) immanent in Nature. Defining *godhead* from the standpoint of science, Arnold spoke
of the "central moral tendency" and "the stream of tendency by which all things
seek to fulfil the law of their being."[51] The words *tend, tended,* and *tendency* figure in the death speech in book 5 of *Paracelsus* where Browning describes the
"long triumphant march" of life:

>          all tended to mankind,
> And, man produced, all has its end thus far:
> But in completed man begins anew
> A tendency to God.[52]

Browning shared with his contemporaries the intellectual presupposition that
was analyzed by Arthur O. Lovejoy as the static and vertically hierarchical great
chain of being become a horizontal dynamic progression.[53]

The metaphysics of progress shows Richards's nineteenth-century roots,
and the writings of Ward may serve as an example of the vast literature on this
subject on which he obviously drew heavily. In *The Realm of Ends,* Ward embedded an idealist principle within biological evolution. If the "tendency of
science" had been "to diminish the seeming variety of the world and ultimately
to eliminate it," human agency was not thereby threatened (*RE,* 65). Rather, it
had an empirical sign of an intelligible, intelligent universe. Ward wanted to
explain and to justify the contribution of thinking and striving subjects: "As a
necessary consequence of the interaction of a plurality of individuals, intent
on self-betterment as well as self-conservation, there should be a general tendency to diminish the mere contingency of the world and to replace it by a definite progression" (*RE,* 97). If human effort, trial and error, does not count in
steering evolution, if quantity alone, and not quantity and quality, is the determining factor, what then becomes of human initiative, belief, and moral conduct? To enlarge the role of conative behavior, Ward rejected the Leibnitzian
evolutionary concept of "preformation," by which the adult is contained in
miniature in the embryo, and he adopted "the very different theory of epigenesis or new formation," whereby the parts are not present in miniature but are
"gradually organized . . . in due order" (*RE,* 98). Preformation favors the absolutist, the "singularistic," or what James called the "block universe," where the
end is prefigured in the beginning (*RE,* 99). Epigenesis favors a continuous os-
cillation between disequilibrium and "integration and equilibration" (*RE,* 101),
an idea that Ward took from Herbert Spencer's synthetic philosophy. Compounds have synthetic properties that differ from the properties of their separate parts; something new is added to the universe. Such is the case with

matter; so too with mind. Creative synthesis produces not "new entities" but "new values" that make "higher unities and worthier ideals possible" (*RE*, 434). For Ward, no sharp discontinuity separates the material from the moral world. According to his "pluralistic" (as opposed to "atomistic") spiritualism, social organization presupposes cooperation and consensus at every level; the "pluralistic goal" is that reconciliation of the many in the one that preserves individuality and human freedom in "final harmony or equilibration" (*RE*, 114). Ward saw (in 1911) the "tendency to progression" in many areas of human life, though he acknowledged that what had been accomplished was only a fraction of what was possible (*RE*, 113). "We begin by trying and end by knowing"; faith and knowledge accompany man's progress from chaos to an order ever more about to be (*RE*, 106).

Ward was a theist, Richards an "a-theist." But this placed only a heavier burden on human effort that had to operate without any help from above. The epigenetic version of evolution would give Richards the "long view" congenial to his conception of human history. It supplements by way of science and biology the poetic, religious, and philosophical texts on self-completion. Like Ward, Richards thinks primarily in terms of development and potentiality, of self-realization in a pluralist universe. Although he does not go so far as Ward as to think matter spiritualized to a greater or lesser degree, he too wants to save a measure of freedom. He conceives of mental "wholeness" as something greater than its parts (greater than a formal or mathematical whole); the difference between the parts and the whole (the creative synthesis, the artwork, the equilibrium) is a kind of rescuing from waste. Like Ward, too, he juggles with evolutionary theories seeking confirmation of his beliefs.

Thus, defining the "tendency towards increased order," Richards states that the "need" derives from "*the* fundamental imbalance to which biological development may be supposed to be due." Some imbalances trace to the "defaults" in the "innate constitution," some to "accidents," "disease," "frivolousness," habit, disorganized emotion, lower-order demands dictating higher-order ones—the entire tribe of enemies to the perfectibility of man (*PC*, 285–86). The stress on "the" indicates that the "fundamental" condition is one of striving against, of trying to (re)gain equilibrium and "advance," an equilibrium that can at best be temporary and is quickly felt to be disequilibrium within a larger system. Sincerity as "partial" self-completion entails this perception. But here this line of analysis, already conjectural in the extreme, ends. Parodying Spencer, Richards derives only "amusement value" in treating evolution as a pendulum swinging back and forth between need and satisfaction, a zigzag from a "primal imbalance" to "increasingly complex forms right up to Shakespeare."[54] Curiously enough, his dissatisfaction at not finding an explanation expresses itself in a comment on the barrier between genotype and phenotype, Weismann's inviolable "germ plasm." The "great difficulty" in evolutionary theory, Richards notes, is how to "get around" the separation of the "reproductive functions" (with the immutable genotype) from other behavioral functions, "but that is a difficulty for any cosmologist" (*PC*, 286n1).[55]

What Richards means, in current terms, is that if evolutionary progress is based on natural selection (an article of neo-Darwinist faith), there can be little advance from generation to generation, only from eon to eon, and individual effort in the phenotype toward organization and equilibrium does not influence the interaction of genotypes. Richards has an almost instinctive Lamarckian side, and he is trying to come to terms with Darwinian orthodoxy. It is conceivable that, in searching for his "tendency towards increased order," he came to realize that natural selection was not quite adequate to it. Darwin had the same problem himself.[56] This is truly the "great difficulty" and continues to be for any evolutionary theory that is better than Procrustean, especially today when the barrier between genotype and phenotype has been shown to be permeable (artificially, as in gene splicing and in other ways). The human species, for the time being, is the end of evolution, and what is next is social evolution (unless the species itself is artificially interfered with). Within this process, Richards's "tendency towards increased order" would fit.

Sincerity as self-completion is the "obedience to that tendency which 'seeks' a more perfect order within the mind," in the "direction of greater complexity and finer differentiation" of responses (*PC*, 288, 286). The quotation marks around *seeks* show that Richards does not give a soul-animating principle to these tendencies; some tendencies, if obeyed, yield positive results and, if resisted, negative results. Tendencies are natural forces; reasoning and conscience decide whether to obey or dissent. He would agree with Ward that, "but for this power of directing it, the progress of development would be, to say the least, immeasurably slower than it is" (*RE*, 111). Richards's words—*obedience, seeks, perfect*—are the common coin of Arnold's religious writing. Yet Richards does not rewage the battle of literature versus dogma. He fills out the ethical background of his picture by repairing to Cambridge humanism (J. M. E. McTaggart, G. L. Dickinson, G. E. Moore) at the turn of the century. Sincerity depends on "health," on the "quality of our recent companions," on "responsibility," on "our nearness to the object." "And when we doubt our own sincerity and ask ourselves, 'Do I really think so; do I really feel so?' an honest answer is not easily come by" (*PC*, 283). Thus, the questions to be asked of responses and tendencies are: Do they further the growth and responsiveness of mental life? Do they heighten levels of discrimination and widen the basis of wholeness? Do they foster "sanity or integrity or sincerity of the mind?"[57]

Self-completion leads to the final phase of sincerity, the "union of internal and external," self and world, subject and object, which gives Richards the opportunity to sketch social dimensions of the virtue. We have seen that the evolutionary process brings about an increase of "mind," which is a "differentiation" and complexity of response to the environment. Internalization reduces "interferences" and relieves "internal strains" placed upon the individual from living in a "partly uncongenial environment." Individuals "change" through internalizing conflict or, if the environment is too uncongenial (how else may one read "partly"?), presumably they change the environment, and Richards labels the compromise as "partial self-completion" (*PC*, 286–87). In the *Chung Yung* conflict is suppressed through the imitation of the Sage, the highest social and moral representative, thus reinforcing the traditional order. The cultural traits associated with this order greatly appealed to Richards: the decorum, restraint, emphasis on language, nonviolent streak (it of course concealed a massive violence on another plane) that would have supported Richards's pacifist beliefs.[58] But, again, it is Tsze-sze's passages that expressed his ideal the best. Tsze-sze, though no revolutionary, elaborated upon the element of personal achievement, on the connection between sincerity and the other virtues, and on the individual himself becoming an ideal of imitation, one who "may with Heaven and Earth form a ternion": "The possessor of sincerity does not merely accomplish the self-completion of himself. With this quality he completes other men and things also. . . . [T]his is the way by which a union is effected of the external and internal."[59] The individual has become a sage and therefore worthy of imitation.

Persons with sincerity have "singleness" or "wholeness" and are thus at peace with themselves and can, in Richards's words, be "more appropriately responsive to the outer world." Richards even thinks it possible to read the text to the effect that "freedom calls out freedom; that those who are 'most themselves' [for example, artists in their creative moments, readers in theirs] cause others about them to become also 'more themselves'" (*PC*, 287). Richards here speaks solely for himself; one cannot wring this interpretation out of Confucius or Tsze-sze. For Richards, however, becoming, and not being, defines sincerity in all three divisions of the Platonic soul: "to act, feel and think in accordance with [what Confucius calls] 'one's true nature.'" Then he breaks off discussion with a reference to the pragmatic test: "In practice we often seem to grasp it [sincerity] very clearly." The sense of equilibrium *(Chung)* and harmony *(Yung)* gives one the sense that one is already "on the Way"; "sometimes we can be certain that we have left it" (*PC*, 289).

Opportunities are far greater for insincerity than for sincerity. Richards's discussion of the *Chung Yung* was meant only to help reduce to the slimmest margin the possibility of mistaking one or the other. If these guidelines fail, however, one further "technique or ritual" remains for developing sincerity in the moment of choice. "Technique" and "ritual" have scientific and religious associations; Richards's attempt in sincerity is to find the meeting point beyond them. His version of sincerity develops both from Oriental mysticism and meditation and from G. E. Moore's method of "absolute isolation" whereby a proposition is separated from extraneous elements and intuitively evaluated:

> When our response to a poem after our best efforts remains uncertain, when we are unsure whether the feelings it excites come from a deep source in our experience, whether our liking or disliking is genuine, is *ours,* or an accident of fashion, a response to surface detail or to essentials, we may perhaps help ourselves by considering it in a frame of feelings whose sincerity is beyond questioning. Sit by the fire (with eyes shut and fingers pressed firmly upon the eyeballs) and consider with as full "realisation" as possible: i. Man's loneliness (the isolation of the human situation); ii. The facts of birth, and of death, in their inexplicable oddity; iii. The inconceivable immensity of the Universe; iv. Man's place in the perspective of time; v. The enormity of his ignorance. (*PC*, 290–91)

Detached from the schedule of "research and reflection" that precedes them, the five topics appear like airy nothings. Richards did not mean that one should hear them going off like bells when considering the value of a poem; their presence or absence constituted no criterion of value; obviously, great literature was not confined to them. Not for the expert so much as for the student entering upon the "arduous discipline" of poetry, the list was a temporary aid, something to lend distance and objectivity (note the generality and remoteness of the topics, yet they could be a dangerous invitation to plunge more deeply into subjectivity). In *The Use of Poetry and the Use of Criticism,* Eliot, who praised the "intense religious seriousness" in Richards's concept of poetry, mocked this "recipe," this "regimen of Spiritual Exercises," this "modern emotional attitude" whose "most sentimental expression" was Russell's *Free Man's Worship,* and he subjected each of Richards's topics to merciless ridicule. For instance: "I cannot see why the facts of birth and death should appear odd in themselves, unless we have a conception of some other way of coming into the world and of leaving it, which strikes us as more natural."[60] Richards replied with a long footnote to the topics in later editions of *Practical Criticism.* He chided Eliot's "perhaps not unintentional obliquity" and cited passages from Yeats, Pascal, and Eliot himself to illustrate that his topics were the universal themes of literature (*PC* [1956], 291). Sitting by the fire and shutting one's eyes—these could be eliminated (Richards did so in later editions). The topics themselves have lost none of their force.

Any reappraisal of Richards on belief and sincerity might take into account Theodor Adorno's Hegelian-Marxist critique of authenticity or the "genuine." The historical limits of this category extend from the *honnête homme,* the Enlightenment man of sense, and romantic "originals" down to the "existential man." Adorno connects bourgeois morality to what purports to be an "autonomous norm" of the "genuine" that anchors itself in the unitary, solitary self and equates itself with truth and freedom. The *principium individuationis*[61] is enshrined as a source of value and is further enhanced by eighteenth-century empiricism: "The desire, through submergence in one's own individuality, instead of social insight into it, to touch something utterly solid, ultimate being, leads to precisely the false infinity which since Kierkegaard the concept of authenticity has been supposed to exorcise" (*MM,* 153). Truth and freedom are subjectivized and distanced from the social context. Authenticity trades on Protestant notions of selfhood and "religious-authoritarian pathos without the least religious content" (*MM,* 152). Moreover, the language of authenticity suggests "something higher," an "aura," the sublime. In Adorno's words, "Expressions and situations . . . are forever being blown up as if they were empowered and guaranteed by some absolute which is kept silent out of reverence." "Heroic striving," "engagement," "commitment," "self-transcendence," "self-realization," "being in the world": such "jargon" only dazzles, makes "phantasmagoric," and reifies its subjective emanations, hiding rather than analyzing the hard social realities that it proposes to transcend.[62]

Adorno finds the premise of authenticity throughout the bourgeois period: in the quest for the original over the derivative ("always linked with social legitimism" [*MM,* 155]); for the true and sincere over the artificial; for the autochthonous over the alien. Only by dialectical analysis, which reconstructs the social process, does he believe that relations between the subject (extreme inwardness) and object (historical and social conditions) can be understood and the real origins of the distorting notions of authenticity can be uncovered. Adorno employs concepts of imitation and "tact." The *honnête homme* thinks of himself as an independent agent, true to himself and avoiding falsehood. However, though he professes genuineness, he is thoroughly mediated by his "sincere" attachment to social norms, to ideals of moral rectitude (Molière's *raisonneur*), and to etiquette; the eighteenth century heavily emphasized social manners, the most artificial of human conventions. There is, incidentally, a strong parallel to the Confucian stress on ceremony, rules of behavior, and aphorisms; the eighteenth century deeply admired Confucius and Chinese so-

ciety. Goethe, Adorno continues, established "tact" as the "saving accommoda-
tion between alienated human beings." Tact ("and humanity—for him the
same thing") was Goethe's form of renunciation, occurring at the historical
moment when the individual had rid himself of royal absolutism yet had not
accustomed himself to the "threatening impossibility of all human relationships in emergent industrial society" (*MM*, 35–36). The forms of hierarchical
respect were thus turned on their side and were used to define boundaries between "equals."

Imitation is another trenchant weapon in the critique of authenticity. In
Diderot's dialogue *Rameau's Nephew,* the conventional man of sense converses
with a wildly eccentric and "unreasonable" nephew of the musician Rameau.
The nephew's self-abasement, role playing, and loss of self in virtual delirium
render untenable any notion of a fixed and reliable self. The nephew in effect
renders the *honnête homme* time bound and strips him of his pretensions to
utter genuineness. But what of the nephew? Is he the forerunner of the romantic "original" and its new pretensions to genuineness? Romanticism applauds
originality that is freedom from imitation: of models, of outworn social codes.
Is the nephew somehow more "sincere" and "authentic" than his antagonist,
or is he an altogether different type?[63] Goethe translated *Rameau's Nephew*
and described the nephew as the "self-estranged spirit." Hegel analyzed the two
characters in terms of the "honest soul" versus the "disintegrated consciousness." In a Hegelian mediation, however, what has "disintegrated" has not therefore yielded up the ground of "authenticity" but has only engendered the next
movement of dialectical spirit—for which the image of role playing provides
the clue. As Adorno asserts, we live on our "mimetic heritage." No matter how
many layers one peels away, there can be no ultimately genuine self. From one's
first experiences one is imitating, "playing," establishing gradations of likeness
and difference. The individual may suppose that "what is biologically one must
logically precede the social whole," but this is mere illusion. Societal values permeate the self that "owes society its existence in the most literal sense." (The
nephew is identified by his famous uncle's name.) In Adorno's somewhat cyn-
ical conclusion: "Anything that does not wish to wither should rather take on
itself the stigma of the inauthentic" (*MM*, 53–54).[64] In his terms, the genuine is
"fraud" when it *poses* as the genuine.

However dated Adorno's Marxist critique, the analysis of the genuine has
the virtue of rooting Richards's topics in their social and historical context. Let
us collapse belief and sincerity into a single category: one's beliefs, after all,
penetrate the self's core—Mill certainly thought so, and the pragmatists made
belief (what one could safely act upon) the fulcrum of their system. The three
components of Richardsian sincerity are intuition, self-completion, and the

union of internal and external. In Adorno's critique, Richards fares poorly on all three counts. Adorno would frown upon intuition even as (especially as) a last resort. He inveighs against the "phantom" inwardness that he considers a religious remnant, a methodological escape hatch, or a justification for "naked self-interest." Richards's language of belief and sincerity carries religious overtones; its texts are the canonical books of Confucius; its "ritual" of sincerity resembles prayer; even his "equilibrium" can be understood as the mystic's point of rest. More damaging still, by an Adornian analysis, would be Richards's abrupt halt at Confucius's "one's true nature." Nor would Adorno approve of the borrowing of the Confucian moral universals, which dehistoricize the situation. Most important, the moment in which authenticity thinks it touches bottom and declares itself genuine should be not an end but the beginning of the second or negative movement in dialectical procedure. This is one of the most instructive examples of the difference between the two methods: Adorno's allows him, through a countercategory, to decompose sincerity and proceed onto new paths—analysis is theoretically interminable; Richards's comes to full stop at the unique essence of the individual. Richards believes that in moments of sincerity, within a religious aura of late Protestantism, the self is responsible to itself. It fully discloses itself, and it stands on its own ground.

How contrary is this Richards! Adorno might respond. Genuineness, he maintains, is "a defiant and obstinate insistence on the monadological form which social oppression imposes on man" (*MM,* 154). That form is the self; its "defiant and obstinate insistence" is Richards's striving to maintain equilibrium within "the fundamental imbalance" of the biological environment. Richards's evolutionary category would fall under Adorno's interdict against assuming that what is "biologically one must logically precede the social whole." Blind instincts and tendencies may go back to nature or ahead to increased order, but always in and through the social and economic setting. Self-completion and its synonyms (equilibrium, order, creative synthesis, unity) are representations of the myths of autonomy and wholeness. At the same time Richards's biological metaphor of imbalance, the striving against "developments imposed from without," the repression of "internal strains," and the "uncongenial environment" point to the social disharmony: he is being true, at one remove, to the facts of the case.

With respect to wholeness, an Adornian critique must reject the final component of sincerity, the union of internal and external, as romantic and utopian. With his long vistas and abstractions, Richards keeps his individuals and society too far apart. John Fekete argues that Richards suppresses too many mediating social circumstances, and this suppression confirms the individual in his alienation and society in its role of crude manipulator and wasteful exploiter of human value. At the same time Richards never pretended to be a sociologist or historian.[65] The social and historical resistance to "union" helps explain Richards's admiration for the sense of tact, propriety, and nonviolence in the Chinese texts; detached from the hierarchical order, the qualities are easily assimilable within the social code of the *honnête homme*. Furthermore, the idea of self-limitation or renunciation may lie at the root of Richards's (moderate) inclination to pacifism, as expressed in his short book *Nations and Peace*. Here he proposes that one of the smaller nations give up its national defense to one of the superpowers as a first example; ultimately, the United Nations would be responsible for world law and order. The pacifist tendency is expressed not only with reference to the Chinese but also to the Socratic principle of never doing a wrong in return for a wrong done to oneself. In these instances Richards is pulling back as much as possible.

One final example must suffice to show Richards's acknowledgment of the separation between the internal and the external in absolute terms: the ritual of sincerity. He lists the "isolation of the human situation," but isolated from what? The "facts" of birth and death are "inexplicable," but what is between the biological termini? The "immensity of the Universe" (capital *U*) and the "perspective of time." But we live in local space and real time. The absent term in every instance is the social world that Richards frankly assumes in a common-sense way. Moreover, one cannot underestimate Richards's own distaste for history and biography. Unlike Adorno, he is not primarily a social theorist attempting to construct a cogent logic of explanation.

Adorno's analysis of authenticity not only tests Richards's limitations on sincerity and the individual but should also confer a certain respect on what passes its critique. Richards lacked the systematic method by which to connect the individual with society. Nonetheless, he showed a deep insight into the social matrix in which habits and beliefs are formed and creative drives stifled. He was under no illusions about the union of internal and external in the present circumstances and articulated his ideas on belief and sincerity within an intensified social critique. In *The Meaning of Meaning* and *Principles* he lambasted the "Wills of Gods, the Conscience, the Catechism, Taboos, Immediate Intuitions, Penal Laws, Public Opinion, Good Form, . . . Custom, Convention, and Superstition" as causes of "great difficulties and many disasters." He complained of society's intolerance of innovation and the hypocrisy of its teachers. Involving "waste and misery of appalling extent," society was "cruder and more costly" in its organization of human resources than the standard of its best members (*PLC,* 56).[66] In *Practical Criticism,* Richards commented on the manacles of stock responses and doctrines; on failure in communication between the artist and the public; on the inimical influence of the press, cinema, and other "mechanical inventions" aimed at "communication"; on the displacement of knowledge by information; in sum, on the enormous obstacles to the attainment of equilibrium and sincerity in modern society (320). All of his social theory presupposes the continued existence of the autonomous subject capable of self-realization and "sincerity," but much of his research gave evidence only of the subject's erosion at the hands of the social order, mass culture, and dehumanized technologism. In fact, his findings provide abundant evidence for sociological critics, and his formalist, micrological methodology became one of the sharpest instruments for detecting textual—and therefore other—nonsynthesis.

# The Tranquilized Poem

## The Crisis of the New Criticism

the tranquillized *Fifties* . . .

—Robert Lowell, "Memories of West Street and Lepke"

The New Critics invented the tranquilized poem; they performed surgery upon a poem as if it were a patient etherized upon a table. In the event, the poem was not tranquil, only tranquilized; artificially drugged and immobilized were the political, social, and historical implications of the text that still bore all the suppressed and conflictual problems. This fact was noticed and partly tolerated almost from the rise of New Criticism. But only in the 1950s did the overwhelming success of the movement provoke repeated attacks by a formidable array of scholars and critics. What were the origins of this ideological crisis in New Criticism?

American New Criticism surpassed most modern critical movements in longevity. John Crowe Ransom's *World's Body* appeared in 1938, the same year as Allen Tate's "Tension in Poetry" and Cleanth Brooks and Robert Penn Warren's influential college anthology, *Understanding Poetry.* By 1956–1957, in the Hegelian twilight, historical consciousness of the movement emerged in Murray Krieger's *New Apologists for Poetry* (1956) and William K. Wimsatt and Brooks's *Literary Criticism: A Short History* (1957). A major recent work of critical history, Frank Lentricchia's *After the New Criticism,* begins with Northrop Frye's mythical approach in *Anatomy of Criticism,* published in 1957. For a variety of reasons the New Criticism declined slowly (it reigned in the academy well into the 1960s), and New Critical method was never really ousted from the classroom until the 1980s. In 1978 Evan Watkins observed that "while critical theory has achieved a much greater degree of sophistication in the last three decades, in practice, when we talk about individual poems, we still sound like New Critics."[1] Why then in the early 1950s did the New Critics meet a series of blocks that were not overcome? Why did their method continue to dominate classroom teaching? Ransom's "excruciating impasse" (1950) was patent: the theory was churning out dull, mechanical proofs and exercises that had provoked intense attacks. More seriously, *"impasses"* in the theory (1955; again Ransom)[2] left an unbridgeable chasm between the universal and the concrete, value and fact, determinism and indeterminacy.

Despite the fact that the New Criticism was "no monolith" but an "inconsistent and sometimes confused movement,"[3] and that differences among its exponents were possibly greater than the similarities, several generalizations hold. The high-modernist aesthetics of Hulme, Eliot, and the early Pound[4] furnished its poetic canon and elements of its basic theory: the poem as object, craft and technique, economy, precision, complexity, antipersonality, antiromanticism. Then I. A. Richards gave many of these ideas their exact theoretical shape. He "academicized" them; added topics of his own (contextualism, emotive and referential language, attitude, "belief," tenor and vehicle of metaphor, "tone," the "speaker"); and in later chapters of *Principles of Literary Criticism* (1924) and *Practical Criticism* (1929), he inaugurated the famous "close reading" method. Ransom said the "New Criticism very nearly began with [Richards]" and "in the right way": Richards attempted to "found it on a more thorough and comprehensive basis than other critics did."[5] And, indeed, in the "right way" New Criticism quickly proved an invaluable corrective to misapplied historical, biographical, and philological criticism.

A strong "unifying effort" also characterized the New Critics, a cohesiveness and sense of mission that new humanists and Marxists might well have envied.[6] It is true that even in its heyday of the late 1940s and 1950s New Criticism did not too seriously affect the predominance of historical criticism. But it did win the ideological high ground of the academy. This concentrated unity was maintained through exclusivity. The New Critics did not encourage dialogue, nor did they incorporate the findings of the flourishing schools of European criticism: Freudian psychoanalysis, Jungian mythography, the Prague Linguistic Circle, the Frankfurt School (in residence at Columbia during the war).[7] Nevertheless, as Grant Webster pronounced, "Formalism conquer[ed] universities" between 1938 and 1948, and by 1950 most of the major universities had at least one exponent of New Criticism. The Chicago Aristotelians and the "history of ideas" critics at Johns Hopkins were notable centers of opposition.[8] Columbia, too, lacked a New Critic.

The fact that politics was considered outside the boundaries of criticism had the effect of further uniting the New Critics. One reason for their success and longevity was that the doctrine did not threaten anyone's basic political assumptions. The New Critics represented most shades of political opinion from reactionary conservatism to liberalism and progressivism. "Before the New Criticism" its future leaders, it may be recalled, were the Fugitives and the Agrarians. As Fugitives at Vanderbilt University in the 1920s, these conservative southern intellectuals (Ransom, Warren, Tate, and Donald Davidson) fashioned an image of the "outcast seeking a refuge in an ideal realm." The Agrarian phase in the 1930s was militant: Ransom denounced northern industrialism, utilitarianism, the capitalist state, commercialism, urban society, modern science, and technology. But John Fekete notes that the Agrarians fought with a sense of an already "lost cause" and did not come close to developing a political structure capable of putting their ideas into action. With the collapse of Agrarianism, "all possibilities of reshaping the exterior world are renounced to gain social sanction for the perfection of the interior world, the sensibility, through the strictly literary experience of life."[9]

Such a sanction consorted neatly with the political liberal's sense of pluralism, "negative liberty," and perspectivism. If the conservative ideologue viewed the poem as a verbal mirror flashing light from a transcendent reality, the postwar liberal might find in it a storehouse of recorded values, a pragmatic source of inspiration, an ideal surrogate for the autonomous unity of the self, or an exemplum of the Arnoldian "best self." In one debate in 1952 Douglas Bush kept referring to Brooks's position on Marvell's "Horatian Ode" as that of a "good modern liberal"; Brooks, a student of Ransom's, retorted that he was "more often called a reactionary."[10] The point is that there was simply no way of telling from the critical analysis.

The American New Critics were not great theorists—there was no Croce or Richards or Lukács among them. Yet they did not need to be great theorists; they barred so much from their chosen excellence, which was practice. In *Theory of Literature* (1949) René Wellek and Austin Warren, two New Critical allies, asserted a strong preference for "intrinsic" criticism anchored in Kantian-symbolist aesthetics. Biography, psychology, sociology, the history of ideas, the relation of literature to the other arts—all were considered "extrinsic" approaches. In practice, as everyone knows, the New Critics focused on the poem as object. It was not fully appreciated—or noticed by only a few—that the unquestioned empiricism, the naive epistemology, the Cartesian separation of "subject" and "object" and of fact and value all concealed the very power relationships between subject and object that only a strong historical, sociological, or dialectical model could adequately expose. However, after the ideological wars—the Moscow trials, the Nazi-Soviet pact, the socialist and Marxist collapse at the end of the 1930s, the postwar anticommunist paranoia, the Wallace campaign of 1948, McCarthyism—a strong reaction against ideological criticism swept through the literary academy. So New Critical dominance after the war fitted in with what Daniel Bell called the "end of ideology" spirit, the "disconcerting caesura" that lasted through the 1950s. "Few serious minds believe any longer that one can set down 'blueprints' and through 'social engineering' bring about a new utopia of social harmony," wrote Bell. "At the same time, the older 'counter-beliefs' have lost their intellectual force as well." The "overwhelming experience," wrote Robert Weimann, "was one of the worthlessness of theory, ideology and utopia."[11] The time of "truth" was over; it was the time of *techne*.

Was there an "end of ideology"? Or was it only the rhetoric that was being changed? The evidence may be read convincingly both ways. One can argue that there is never *an end* of ideology, but only an exchange of one for another, or a different covering for the same underlying principles. In this sense there was no "end of ideology" because there was little in the political and social principles or governing coalitions in the postwar United States that differed from the prewar United States of the New Deal. Extremes on the Left and the Right did move closer to the center, but the Roosevelt coalition had not broken down; the welfare state was accepted; "big business" had recuperated; the Supreme Court continued to broaden individual rights. As Fekete says, "Ransom's values as such have not had to change" from his Fugitive to his New Critical period—and neither, for that matter, would the values of the New Deal liberal. The rhetoric of liberalism with its latent antihistoricism, like Ransom's ahistoricism, was perfectly suited to cover ideological differences. In one of the major studies of American politics to emerge in the postwar period, *The Liberal Tradition in America,* Louis Hartz characterizes liberal language (and the "natural liberal mind") as having a "quiet matter of fact quality": "It does not understand the meaning of sovereign power, the bourgeois class passion is scarcely present, the sense of the past is altered, and there is about it all, as compared with the European pattern, a vast and almost charming innocence of mind."[12] Such consensual theorizing—David Riesman's *Individualism Reconsidered* (1954) is another example—was typical of the period.

Before looking at the case *for* the "end of ideology" and the place of New Criticism within it, we should introduce two of its most perplexing contradictions: its Kantian goal of aesthetic nonpurposiveness against its technical ideal of instrumental purposefulness and its desire for synthesis and closure as opposed to an equally strong demand for the open, the unexpected, and the undetermined (to be discussed at the end of the chapter). The nonpurposiveness of art was always high in New Critical tables on goals: Brooks's idea of the autotelic poem; Wimsatt's insistence on the mystical iconicity of art; Ransom's appeal to Kantian resistance to utilitarianism in art; Earl Wasserman's "autonomousness" and "interinanimation"; Archibald MacLeish's "A poem should not mean / But be." In 1955 Ransom interpreted Hegel's historicist Concrete Universal in Kantian terms. The Universal is "any idea in the mind which proposes a little universe"; the Concrete is the "objective element" to embody it. (In Richards's terms, according to Ransom, the Universal is the "tenor," the Concrete is the "vehicle." In Brooks's terms, the Concrete is "metaphor.") The "play" between "understanding" with its free, moral Universal and "imagination" with the purposive Concrete brings forth the poem. How can freedom and mechanism unite? How can we "locate the common moral impulse in the animal perspective of human nature"? Kant and "many humanists" must resort to God or the Moral Law Within, grasped in a moment of intuition, an example of extreme Protestant inwardness. Or else we may recognize through experience the "hospitality" that the Universal finds in nature: the moral Universal "goes out into nature not as a predatory conqueror and despoiler but as an inquirer, to look at nature as nature naturally is, and see what its own reception there may be."[13] One notes the inherent dualism in the position with its isolated observer ("to look at") and the objective world ("nature as nature naturally is," where redundancy emphasizes the reification).

Ransom contrasts Kant and Hegel to explore "freedom" in nature and poetry. The Kantian Universal does not exhaust nature in its search for examples of freedom; it does not "use" nature instrumentally, but does use it as an end—like a person. We perceive these moments of freedom when we "find" the presence of beauty *in* nature or *in* a poem; freedom is this "moment of illumination" when the "soul" of poetry is "caught briefly," like Eliot's moment "in and out of time." With Kant, the artist still has the power of discovering one of the inexhaustible relations between freedom and necessity, the Universal and the Concrete, in an infinitely abundant, open nature. On the contrary, in Hegel nature is all used up *or about to be used up*. It is only a matter of time, the march of Historical Reason toward the Absolute. Where Categories of Reason and the Universals predominate, Ransom finds "no unused remainder" of Concreteness, nothing left to chance or "play," no "residue" of freedom, no casual "differentia," no "tissue of irrelevance" in nature or in the experience of the poem. As Hegel declared, art and aesthetic consciousness were headed on a downward path in the modern age. Kant gave us "nature and poetry" and was associated with "old agrarian life" *(Gemeinschaft)*; Hegel, who offered us "society and politics," looked ahead to a natural world that had "become mechanized," that is, "modern urban life" *(Gesellschaft)* and closure—what Max Weber called the "iron cage of modernity."[14] Ransom's Kant must, however, be understood in light of his purposes. The historical Kant was a cosmopolitan thinker and no champion of old agrarian life; he was an advocate of the mature Enlightenment and modern science, admired Rousseau, and sympathized with the French Revolution (though not the Terror).

Now we can understand why refuge from the law of historical determinism lies in nostalgic withdrawal, imagination, poetry—and the pre-1960s university. Espousing Kant, Ransom reaffirms local freedom, *Gemeinschaft*, and the semifeudal, conservative, antitechnological premises upon which his entire criticism rests. His own verse, with its often stubbly surface texture, roughened meters, and *Dinglichkeit* (thingness) is meant to capture this freedom. He specifically invokes "piety," from the classical *pietas*, a religious love for the *genius loci*, the traditions of the locale and of those who lived and died there. Ransom's Kant has a "more poetic soul" and "greater piety" than his Hegel. Ultimately, poem and land reflect each other as Ransom compounds land, poem, imagination, and freedom: "In the poem we have here or there, and in some confused sense all together, nearly everything we can possibly desire." The poem is utopia, the "best of all possible worlds," yet inefficacious, "not really possible"; "when we settle down into that grim realization, we are beyond the help of any poems at all." The poem is memory, the world "we think we remember to have come from," an imitation of "our Earthly Paradise."[15] But between the imagined past and the impossible ideal lies the historical moment of the present, to which Ransom stoically resigns himself.

At the same time the New Critics were attempting to define a verbal object that was free from the pressures of historical necessity and "mere utility," their method was a direct reflection of these pressures. In this sense, one may legitimately speak of an "end of ideology," and New Critical tenets conform to the premises of "nonideological" technology, with what Jacques Ellul has termed "*technique*," the guiding principle of the technological society. The essence of technique is rationalization; its operative assumptions are efficiency, speed, scheduling, punctuality, measurement, parsimoniousness, standardization, segmentation, and totalization. All procedures are fully articulated to attain specific ends. Rather, technique subordinates ends to means to such an extent that ends are lost, swallowed up by means. Human values are filtered out except where they facilitate the technical means. Technique permeates every aspect of business administration, state bureaucracy, and industrial planning. The technical-experimental state of mind, the product of technique, dominates contemporary education from the earliest grades through the university. Ellul concludes that capitalism did not create the modern world; machinelike "autonomous" technique did. Antihistorical and nonideological, technique is a unifying practice stronger by far than the ideologies that divide nations.[16]

In important ways New Criticism can be seen to have accommodated itself to technological society. First, it has *its own* business to do within the system, and *no other* business. As Mario Corona notes, New Criticism occupied a small part of a total picture of set structures: university-level education, literature departments, theory sector, analysis of poetry, and classroom method.[17] Cut off from other parts of the system except by innumerable mediators, the oppositional element in New Criticism is neutralized; it cannot stand outside the system and make critical judgments upon it. (*Inside* the system its chief opposition was, significantly, historical studies.) There is a loss of "ends" and a concentration on "means."

Second, New Criticism is not only "a part" of the technological system but also a synecdochic condensation of it. One can point to its antihistoricism, its emphasis on specialization and technique, its scientific objectivity, its meager and mostly inconsequential theorizing, its myths of synthesis, its many metaphors for poetic "organization," its extreme ideal of poetic autonomousness and stylistic anonymity. For the New Critics, the poem is a complete system in itself and discontinuous with the materials out of which it is constructed, including historical materials, poetic traditions, and the artist's psychology. All the values and norms by which the poem is judged must be drawn formally from the poem itself, which is thus isolated historically. A poem does not imitate reality; it is a reality itself, a "little world" (Ransom) unified by the poet; a "simulacrum of reality," "*being* an experience rather than any mere statement about experience" (Brooks). A poem does not mean to "*designate*" its particulars but means to "*contain*" them (MacLeish). The words of a poem, then, do not refer in the same way as words in the outside world. Here the New Critics were indebted to Richards and C. K. Ogden's distinction between emotive and referential language: the emotive use of language is self-referential, expressive of an individual psychology; a referential or "scientific" use asserts a proposition about the world. "It is never what a poem *says* which matters," argues Richards, "but what it *is*."[18] The New Critics generally adopted Richards's distinction and, with their antipathy to science, made it more deeply ingrained in their aesthetics. Brooks and Wimsatt added another distinction: emotive language referred not "inward" to the poet's or reader's mind but only to itself. Both distinctions are formulas for reification.

Finally, New Critics fostered the straightforward, roll-up-your-sleeves attitude to criticism that mirrored technocratic expertise, objective neutrality, teamwork, bureaucratized efficiency, and anonymity. Most movements have their terms and strategies, yet no British or American literary movement ever had such a procedures manual of methodological strategies, terminology, common texts, and objectives. Paraphrasing Le Corbusier's "a house is a machine to think with," Richards said "a book is a machine to think with." One approaches poetry with the same seriousness, objectivity, and austerity with which one approaches higher mathematics. Ransom urged an aesthetic attitude that is "tough," "scientific," and "aloof" from the "literary 'illusion' which it examines." He wanted criticism to be "precise" and "systematic": "It must be developed by the collective and sustained effort of learned persons—which means its proper seat is in the universities."[19] The extinction of personality that Eliot had advocated for artists reaches its logical culmination among these critics. "There is remarkable adaptability in Brooks's style," comments John Hardy, "an apparent capacity of his mind for anonymity"; Brooks has been "able to collaborate with several people of vastly different interests and training and bent of thought."[20] William R. Elton's glossary lists more than a hundred New Critical terms—a formidable tool kit.

The hegemonic aims of what Ransom called "Criticism, Inc."[21]—and this was the decade of *The Organization Man*—were twofold. The first was the immense practical task of reanalyzing English and American literature and criticism. To be certain, each New Critic had invented his signature vocabulary: Brooks, *paradox* and *wit;* Ransom, *structure* and *texture;* Tate, *extension* and *intension;* Wasserman, *syntax;* Brower, *allusion;* everyone shared *context, irony, ambiguity, attitude, response, unity,* and what Richards called *free imagery.* As time passed, however, New Critical differences were ironed out and conformed to a pattern. All the cards were marked in advance. Even Ransom lamented (his "excruciating impasse") that the very repetitiveness and predictability of the exercises made for easy targets. The decade of the 1950s was a period of themes and variations, and, as someone quipped, the academy was strewn with New Critical books that were never written.

In retrospect, a second concern was more pressing. The New Critics had defended their key notion of poetic autonomy against "paraphrase," "intention," "affect"; against "communication"; against mimesis, didacticism, neoclassicism, and all other forms of "impurity." Exceptions were numerous. With his concern for southern "memory and history," Tate also practiced historical criticism.[22] Greco-Roman literature and philosophy informed the work of Brower and Wasserman. In "Pure and Impure Poetry" (1942) Robert Penn Warren actually argued on behalf of "impurity" ("ideas," "truths," "generalizations," "intellectual images," "situation, "narrative," "logical transition," "meter," "subjective or personal elements") and worried that the "new" theory of "purity" would banish "complexities," "ironies," and "self-criticism"; "If all of these items were excluded, we might not have any poem at all."[23]

Nevertheless, these were exceptions: the rule was a narrowed version of Richards's theory of emotive language. Although Richards had lowered the importance of a poem's strictly referential meaning, the poem was still exposed to the poet and reader. The effort of the New Critics, remarks Edward Wasiolek, went toward "making the defense more complete: to cut off poetry not only from the world of meanings outside it but also from the inner world of the poet and reader. The practical consequence of this was to establish poetry's independence by cutting it off from the world, the poet, the reader, other poems, and theoretically even from acts of interpretation." Thus, for Eliseo Vivas, the reader of the poem is transfixed in a moment of "intransitive attention." The poem is "literally impervious to thought," says Watkins. "One enters it by a kind of miracle."[24]

"Miracle" is a well-chosen metaphor for the New Critical poem: Krieger employed it in *A Window to Criticism*, defining "the conversion of tension to a catharsis which keeps its tension still." Ransom spoke of an ideal compromise between "physical" and "Platonic" poetry that is the "miraculism" of "metaphysical" poetry; Warren praised poetry's "miraculous" power and said the theory of purity was the "enemy of all faith." As Christopher Norris comments, "What the orthodox New Critics sought in the language of poetry was a structure somehow transcending human reason and ultimately pointing to the religious sense of values." The absolute division between poetic and referential language served the additional purpose of preserving the "authentic 'mystery' of poetic truth." Norris cites Walter Ong's essay on "Wit and Mystery (1962): "At the point to which the trail of wit leads, the very texture of poetry itself . . . is seen to come into functional contact with the heart of Christian doctrine."[25] Many New Critical titles have mystical connotation: Brooks's *Well Wrought Urn* (1947) (a vessel containing the ashes of the dead); Brower's *Fields of Light* (1951) (Virgil on the Elysian Fields [*Aeneid* 6.640]); Wasserman's *Finer Tone* (1953) (Keats's "mystic blending"); Wimsatt's *Verbal Icon* (1954) (religious transcendence); and Philip Wheelwright's *Burning Fountain* (Shelleyan Platonism) (1954). One approached the poem on bended knees, empty in oneself, ready to be filled with the spiritual substance of the poem. Moreover, although all critical theories have their oppositions, the New Critics anathematized them as "heresies" and "fallacies."

The religious motive does not necessarily entail the suppression of the historical factor. However, coupled with other elements of New Critical theory, the motive takes on a definite Augustinian coloring with its antithesis between the fallen world of sin and error and the poem as the image of the ancient Paradise. Though Ransom attempted to maintain a bridge between the noumenal realm of value and the phenomenal realm of nature, he acknowledged that the whole drift of modern society was toward collapsing the realms with the inevitable loss of individual freedom. Ontologically, poetry for Ransom is outside time and "interrupts" history. In 1950 Allen Tate converted to Roman

Catholicism and argued shortly afterward that "the possibility of human life presupposes, with us, a prior order, the order of a unified Christendom." Wimsatt, a Roman Catholic, said that the Christian doctrine of creative Logos could be used to illustrate the "various levels of verbal meaning," thereby forging a relation between "modern critical polysemous" reading and the Patristic and Stoic view of language. R. P. Blackmur argued in 1956 that only in poetic analogy "are the oppositions identical. . . . [I]t was a similar perception which led Saint Augustine to say that in every poem there is some of the substance of God." The religious motive further tightens the connection between New Criticism and the "end of ideology"; as Bell points out, antirationalism, Freudianism, Jungianism, and the "neo-orthodox theology (i.e. Reinhold Niebuhr and Paul Tillich)" with its "anti-rational stoicism" were among the dominant intellectual trends in the 1950s.[26] One should also note the neo-Christian movement (C. S. Lewis, Charles Williams) taking place in England at this time.

Brooks's success, wrote William Empson in 1947, "seems so great that one begins to fear a new orthodoxy."[27] Yet New Critical defenses had shortly to withstand repeated attack. Lionel Trilling's *Liberal Imagination* appeared in 1950; its wide-ranging sociological, psychological, and historical method, as well as its topical breadth (Freud, Tacitus, Wordsworth, Kipling, Henry James, the *Kinsey Report*), was an open rebuke to New Critical scope and method. In one essay, "The Sense of the Past," Trilling mocks New Critical studies in irony and ambiguity as an "intellectual calisthenic ritual" and points out that in their antihistoricism they had forgotten that a literary work remains a "historical *fact*." Recalling Eliot's "Tradition and the Individual Talent," Trilling argues that each work of art stands in a relation to its past tradition and "change[s] that tradition," that "we are creatures of the historical sense," that even the New Critics repair to the seventeenth century for poetic virtues and to the romantics for poetic vices. Most important, "*pastness*" itself imparts an "extra-aesthetic authority" that becomes an inherent element of the work's "aesthetic power."[28] Trilling plays on the self-reflexivity of the New Critical phrase "the poem itself" and Brook's "simulacrum" and repairs to Arnold's goal of seeing the object "as in itself it really is": "A poem does not always exist only in itself: sometimes it has a very lively existence in its false or partial appearances . . . and sometimes in its effort to come at the poem as it really is, criticism does well to allow the simulacra to dictate at least its opening moves." Conceding Freud's theory of art to be "inadequate," Trilling nonetheless argues that the "elements of art are not limited to the world of art. . . . [W]hatever extraneous knowledge of them we gain . . . may quicken our feelings for the work itself and even enter *legitimately* into those feelings." Anticipating later trends in reader-response criticism, Trilling connects the experience of tragedy to the "repetition-compulsion" that develops the sense of fear and control of difficult situations and that overrides the pleasure principle. Tragedy is a "homeopathic administration of pain to inure ourselves to the greater pain which life will force upon us."[29]

First articulated in 1942, William Wimsatt and Monroe Beardsley's intentional fallacy was one of the main premises of the New Criticism, the bulwark against expressionist literary theories, Freudianism, and Jungian criticism but also "authenticity," "spontaneity," "originality," "sincerity," and romantic and Victorian concepts of genetic criticism. To fall victim to this "fallacy" meant to treat an author's recoverable or inferred design or intention as the standard for judging the poem. Although the "designing intellect" provides the *cause,* contend Wimsatt and Beardsley, too many problems arise in making it the *standard* of judgment as well. Not only is it impossible to probe into the deepest unconscious workings of genius (where creative intentions are to be found), but also the relevant materials for even beginning such a search in many writers is either unavailable or available in the most uneven ways. Then, if an author succeeds in achieving his or her intention, the literary work provides all the proof and makes redundant any search for prior intention. If the work does not succeed, the poem lacks the proper evidence for determining intention, and the "critic must go outside the poem—for evidence of an intention that did not become effective in the poem." Alluding to Richards's distinction between emotive and referential language, Wimsatt and Beardsley insist that a poem cannot be judged like "practical messages" that succeed "only if we correctly infer the intention." They also adopt Richards's notion that poems—even lyric poems—are "dramatic" and contain a "speaker" or narrator responding to a situation. In other words, there is no need to cross-examine the biographical poet. If an author revises his or her work, then the new work results from the correct intention, and the previous intention was not the author's intention after all. They cite Hardy's rustic constable: "He's not the man we were in search of, that's true. For the man we were in search of was not the man we wanted." Brooks reviewed the case on intention in 1951: "Speculation on the mental processes of the author takes the critic away from the work into biography and psychology . . . which should not be confused with an account of the work."[30]

The critique of the intentional fallacy came from an unexpected quarter. In *The Structure of Complex Words* (1951) William Empson argued that an "emotion" attached to a word, like one of the "senses" or meanings of a word, is an "extremely public object," and we implicitly presume that "anybody would feel it under the circumstances." Although many words do not convey emotion, in poetry they tend to, and these emotions are frequently moral in intention, that is, they assert judgments and ask for approval or disapproval. Whether these feelings are akin to the consciousness of a bodily reaction like "sweating" or the Richardsian "tendencies to action" is, for Empson, not strictly relevant. The important point is that moral feelings claim *not* to be private ones—"If nobody knows what is right except me they still ought to know."[31] Poems build themselves up out of these emotions, feelings, and senses, which leave themselves open to the same kind of questionings made of any other public utterances. The critic must measure the poem's total meaning against standards of "open-minded reasonableness" and an equally generous-minded skepticism.[32]

Yet it was not Empson's briefly sketched theory of public utterance or "other minds" that undermined the intentional fallacy so much as the cumulative force and brilliance of his exegeses, as if the only means of destroying the orthodoxy were on grounds that it had made exclusively its own: analytic practice. As with the New Critics, Empson's chief evidence is mainly the sifting of words and meanings; he introduces relatively little in the way of conventional biography or social history (at least through this point in his career). Still, he finds authors accountable and explores their motives in analyses lexically grounded in history and common experience. Against Brooks, who argues for extreme irony, he asserts that the third stanza of the "Ode on a Grecian Urn" is concerned "directly about the feelings of Keats. He is extremely *un*-happy, we find, especially about his love affair." The words *honest* in *Othello, dog* in *Timon of Athens,* and *fool* in *King Lear* evoke a wide range of meanings; a lexical knowledge of the words within a changing social pattern, from late Elizabethan England to the *honnête homme* of the Restoration, enormously enhances an understanding of Shakespeare's intentions. The same is true for *sense* in *The Prelude,* which extends from meaning ordinary perception to supreme imaginative vision. Wordsworth unites these two meanings of *sense* by a jump, "the same kind of jump as that in the sentence about crossing the Alps, which identifies the horror caused by the immediate sensations with the exultation that developed from them."[33] In both instances, Wordsworth jumps over "common sense," which lies in the middle range of meanings for *sense* that might have uncovered the mediation between the two outer meanings. "This 'mediating process,' lacking in Wordsworth, is the locus of wit and self-possessed intelligence in Marvell's more tempered mysticism," says Norris. "It warrants the appeal to poetic 'intention,' in the fullest sense; that reserved and articulate play of meanings which, according to Husserl, leads us back to the *intentionality* of experience itself."[34] Intentionality is no fallacy.

In 1953 Empson published lengthy "character" studies of Hamlet and Falstaff, something not done by a major critic since A. C. Bradley. Again, he pressed beyond what New Critics considered the formal confines of the plays. Because the issue remained "fundamental," Empson took aim at the intentional fallacy in his review of Wimsatt's *Verbal Icon* in 1955. He recalled his qualms of 1946: "(and if just a lively paradox nothing to grumble about)." However, despite the fact that Wimsatt had since introduced crucial qualifications (for example, allowing lexicography, which, notes Empson, "might give one a lot of freedom"), matters had gotten out of hand. Thus, Wimsatt believed that it did not matter what Shakespeare the author *wanted* to mean. Empson worried about the pedagogical effect of "slogans which take effect from the way they are misunderstood rather than from the qualifications of them." Authorial intention should be one of the main issues to be determined by criticism. "Among the first things a baby has to learn, and if it can't it's mad, is that other people really exist." Experience requires that we continually gauge other people's intentions. Legal fictions (the greatest being the "reasonable man") are based on the ability to determine intentions: "Only in the criticism of imaginative literature, a thing delicately concerned with human intimacy, are we told that we must give up all idea of knowing his intention." It is "petulant" to demand that one *only* read the words on the page, "like saying 'of course I won't visit him unless he has first-class plumbing.' If you cared enough you would." Without assessing intention, no reader can tell whether the writer is "sincere" or striking a conventional pose: Rochester, for instance, "does not seem impressive unless you decide that he really meant it." Empson challenges Wimsatt on his intentionalist question begging with regard to Coleridge's *Ancient Mariner*. Wimsatt had written that Coleridge drew on the history of the maritime empires "then passing into the very stuff of our language." This, Empson retorts, "is much better than pretending you can't know anything."[35]

Empson also questions Wimsatt's "inconsistency" with regard to his religious criticism, a highly charged issue for Empson, who at the time was ensnarled in a controversy with the neo-Christian movement. In "Poetry and Christian Thinking," Wimsatt had drawn a comparison between patristic criticism and "modern polysemous reading," noting that the latter had emerged historically from the former. Modern critiques are, however, somehow "fully concrete"; one reads a poet's words "not within his limits as intender," and one deals with a "symbolism of words, or if of things, of things only as refracted through words, and the limits of such a pursuit are set only by verbal contexts." Scriptural exegesis, on the contrary, has been "implicitly intentional" because it concerns "inspirations." The paradoxes of religious language must be unraveled, and the meanings must be made "sharp" and "definable" to determine God's intention. In other words, the intentionalist fallacy applies to modern, not patristic, analysis because the latter deals with "revealed messages," the former with an "aesthetic medium."[36]

Empson was aware of Richards and Ogden's observations on religious language in *The Meaning of Meaning,* where they had shown that paradoxes and "tricks of verbal logic" were often the "source of religious and theosophical doctrines."[37] Empson's prose, so often oblique and head-on at the same time, is especially dense in his ironic reply to Wimsatt: "Surely the obvious, as well as the ancient, opinion is that there can indeed be occasions when the author is hardly *answerable* for his intention—when he is inspired."[38] The modern and the ancient critic do not differ in assessing the nature of "intention"; the critic may temporarily excuse an author on grounds of "inspiration" or "divine madness," knowing all the time that an author must be, in some sense, finally "answerable." (Much depends on how one interprets *hardly.*) All judged both divine and human agency. Any language excluded from the test of intention allows an author—or an author's gods—to escape moral responsibility, and thus the terms are set for Empson's critique of the Christian divinity in *Milton's God* (1961).

In 1973, long after the intentional fallacy had collapsed, Empson ridiculed New Critics and their epigones, the "high priests" who were now qualifying their belief in the "dogma": "They explain (with tender humour and so forth) that nobody ever intended the crude interpretation evidently held by outsiders and students. . . . We have heard this kind of thing before. The crude doctrine is what does all the harm, whatever the intention may have been; and whether or not the high priests imagine they are above it makes no difference."[39]

When the intentional fallacy went down, the way was cleared for historical, biographical, and psychoanalytic critics to cross the barricades. Historical critics had taken stands against New Criticism in the 1940s, but Douglas Bush, Walter Jackson Bate, and Perry Miller made their central contributions to the debate in the early 1950s. In 1952 Bush wrote a response to Brooks's close reading of Marvell's "Horatian Ode." Declaring himself "in entire sympathy" with the intentional fallacy and disparaging the "coarse" method of historical criticism, Brooks was nonetheless adept at introducing the historical evidence surrounding Marvell's tilt from royalism to republicanism around 1650. Brooks accepted editor H. M. Margoliouth's judgment that "royalist principles and admiration for Cromwell the Great Man exist side by side" in the poem and biographer Emile Legouis's opinion that Marvell shows "complete impartiality." However, we shortly realize that Brooks's elaborate layout is rhetorically designed to come to naught. The insufficiency of the historical evidence, the inconclusiveness of the scholarship, and the very evenness of the political positions in the ode demand a close reading of the poem's "organization" that might resolve the riddles and lead to a triumphant vindication of New Critical method. We cannot know Marvell's mind; we can determine the "speaker's attitude" to Cromwell. The various positions of the poem are "somehow unified," and, in accord with the Richardsian precept, the judgment over these positions may be appealed to the "total unified attitude" of the poem.[40]

In his rejoinder Bush gives numerous instances where Brooks distributes ambiguities unevenly, imposes irony where none exists, and is guilty of special pleading. Brooks transforms the historical Cromwell into a "Puritan Stalin" and forces his evidence to fit his "unspoken assumption," that is, "a sensitive, penetrating, and well-balanced mind like Marvell could not really have admired a crude, single-minded, and ruthless man of action like Cromwell." In the poem's opening simile, the "restless" Cromwell who "Urged his active Star" is like the "forward Youth" who forsakes the Muses for war. Brooks states: "'Restless' is as ambiguous in its meanings as 'forward' and in its darker connotations even more damning." *Urged* shows a "compulsive" desire for glory. Bush replies that, though Brooks may be right here, his glosses shut down options and prejudice the total case too early in the reading.

Marvell likens Cromwell to "three-fork'd Lightning," which for Brooks makes him "an elemental force—with as little will as the lightning bolt, and with as little conscience." Again, Bush asks, does Marvell's language warrant this interpretation, or is it Brooks's "prejudiced addition"? The metaphor becomes one of the key points at issue: "'Tis madness to resist or blame / The force of angry Heavens flame." Brooks questions whether Charles has angered heaven, commenting that there is "no suggestion" that Cromwell is the "thunderbolt hurled by an angry Jehovah." According to Bush, where Brooks has dredged so much ambiguity in other lines, there exists at least the suggestion that Cromwell could be a providential agent. For Bush, this is the primary meaning of the lines: Cromwell is the "traditional 'Scourge of God.'" Going outside the poem, Bush finds similar metaphors in other poems by Marvell, "The First Anniversary of the Government under O. C." and "Poem upon the Death of O. C." In the latter one finds "angry Heaven": "And he whom Nature all for Peace had made, / But angry Heaven unto War had sway'd." "In these later poems," concludes Bush, "Cromwell is unquestionably the instrument of God, and if in the earlier one the lines about 'angry Heavens flame' do not say the same thing, one does not know what they say." Further, Brooks does not discuss the passage on Cromwell's peacefully tending his garden until pressed to war that, as Bush indicates, connects him with Cincinnatus and other "simple, frugal heroes of Roman tradition." The allusion raises Cromwell too high for Brooks's reading.

One more example brings up the political quietism implied in the New Critical method. Marvell wrote: "Though Justice against Fate complain, / And plead the antient Rights in vain." For Brooks, this unequivocally favors the Royalist position: "The poem does not debate which of the two (Cromwell or Charles) was right, for that is not even in question." If "right" is not at issue,

Bush questions, why is Brooks so concerned in his analysis with distinguishing right from power and with adjudicating moral praise and blame? "Although elsewhere Brooks is on the watch for sinister ambiguities, even in words that appear innocent," comments Bush, "here words of at least equal ambiguity have become moral absolutes that condemn Cromwell." *Right* has several meanings, from abstract right to the traditional (yet by no means unquestionable) claims. Marvell's "great Work of Time," now overthrown, is "not necessarily or wholly the good work of time: a great nation may have nourished wrongs that must, at whatever cost, be righted." What Bush does not determine, however, is whether Brooks's need for moral absolutes (royalism, Anglicanism) derives from Brooks's political and religious position: reactionary Agrarianism, religious orthodoxy, contempt for bourgeois capitalism. The battle of Royalists and Roundheads is revived in this debate under the guise of delicate ironies, disinterestedness, and technique. Yet Bush himself was a political centrist and an Anglo-Catholic: one wonders, is this why he puts down Brooks's position (against a "Puritan Stalin") as "liberal"?

Another critique from the historicist position, less direct than Bush's but more powerful in the event, came from one of Bush's former students at Harvard, Walter Jackson Bate. Although he was never considered a New Critical ally like Empson (who published regularly in their journals), in *The Stylistic Development of John Keats* (1945) Bate had demonstrated a mastery of "intrinsic" criticism (metrics, musicality, metaphor, and line break) and had earned the praise of New Critics; therefore, his critique of their practice was, like Empson's, made from a perspective high enough to give a view of both sides. In 1952 Bate published *Criticism: The Major Texts,* which contained long introductions to the major critics and amounted to a miniature history of criticism. (These introductions were published separately in 1959;[41] the anthology itself was enormously successful and remains in print after fifty-three years.) Bate's last "major text" was Richards, not one of the "official" New Critics, but Bate took the opportunity to applaud the "brilliant and searching thoroughness" of their treatment of individual poems. However, the long historical perspective had a sobering effect and revealed more shortcomings than virtues. By Aristotle's standard, New Critics concern themselves with only one of the two fundamental "instincts" to which poetry is traced, *harmonia* or the "unifying principle of experience"; they lack the balancing emphasis on the "instinct" for mimesis or the "massiveness and significance of the context of experience." Like an extreme wing of the high-neoclassic mode, New Critical formalism is ahistorical. Unlike the neoclassicals, New Critics leave no assurance that its goals are "capacious and humane." Like the romantic poet-critics, New Critics appeal to the integrity and organicity of a work of art. Unlike them, the New Critics restrict their organicism almost exclusively to form and style and omit the vitalist aspects of German and British romantic criticism with its interests in history, society, and "Nature." "The question," concludes Bate, "is whether such an organic approach [of the New Critics] is sufficiently organic."[42]

Bate also protests the confined scope of New Critical interests by powerfully reasserting the claims of biographical criticism, one that is deeply informed by close textual readings, the history of ideas, sociology, and psychology. His *Achievement of Samuel Johnson* (1955) was the first in a series of major biographical studies: Keats (1963), Coleridge (1967), and Johnson (1976). It is appropriate that Johnson should have been the locus of reaffirmation, since he wrote fifty-two literary biographies, established the interplay of life and work as the ideal of literary biography, and was himself the subject of the greatest biography in world literature. Of all literary figures he is the one in whom the separation of "life" and "work" is the most arbitrary and leads to the most disastrous consequences in interpretation. *The Achievement of Samuel Johnson* focuses on that part of his writings—chiefly, the moral essays—dealing with "human experience in the broadest sense" and on the relation between his writings and the "immediately personal" side of his life. Among genres, the moral essay most resists New Critical method, since it is neither poetry nor imaginative prose and it is didactic. Bate also describes the "organic character" of Johnson's mind, his "personal struggle," his "psychiatric problems," the nature of the "strangely infectious humour." He wants to see Johnson the man "as a whole" and at the same time assess his work in light of what Johnson found "most interesting," his fundamental intention: "the possibility of human achievement." Bate's crossing back and forth between literature and life, his psychological and moral insight, his awareness of the social and political background all argue for Johnson as the moral exemplum, one of William James's "twice-born" souls who "attain fulfilment only precariously, after prolonged self-struggle and despair."[43] Yet Bate's historical and psychological approach does not escape its own history. In his dramatic portrayal of lonely, heroic, ultimately tragic figures against a vast and impenetrable darkness, one may deduce an implicit, existentialist critique of bourgeois individualism in the latest phase of its epoch.

One of the most provocative attacks on the New Critics came from an entirely different quarter: the emerging "myth and symbol" criticism of Leslie Fiedler and Northrop Frye. In "Archetype and Signature: A Study of the Relationship between Biography and Poetry" (1952) Fiedler urges a new commitment to exploring the artist's life and *other* writings in interpreting the work of art. The "antibiographist tendency," which he traces to Eliot's concept of the "objective correlative" and Richards's formalism, was a reaction of "pre-Freudian" critics that is now "hopelessly outdated." According to Fiedler, the older biographical and historical critics submerged the work of art in a sea of facts, leaving readers to draw their own critical conclusions. The New Critics turned against the facts. Both positions are wrong, as both fail properly "to connect." Philosophically, New Critical method depends upon an "extreme nominalist definition" of a work of art whereby the poem is "*nothing but* 'words' "; the reductiveness of this argument is "metaphysically reprehensible." Fiedler lambastes the New Critics' "internal contradictions," how they order their students to "stay *inside*" the poem while they meanwhile are "bootlegging from 'outside' all kinds of rich relevancies." Many poems obviously lose in meaning without recourse to the author's biography. One of Fiedler's best examples is Donne's line "When thou has done, thou hast not done"; without knowing the author's name, one misses the pun and, more important, the significance of a pun in a religious poem. Although the New Critics in their "excess of anti-Romanticism" no longer reject Shelley and Swinburne outright, their commitment to the intentional fallacy has not been relaxed. Fiedler wonders how this "central dogma" (an "immortal platitude") could have won so many adherents; the obvious disorganization of the opposition must have played a hand.[44]

A poem is not just its words; by "rather ridiculously over-emphasizing *medium* as the differentiating factor," notes Fiedler, the New Critics have denied *symbolic* values, what a life and a poem share in common: "A pattern of social behavior can be as much a symbol as a word, chanted or spoken or printed." This is a promising start. Fiedler wants to tear down the barriers between a poem and a poet's life. The essence of his system is that a poet creates a personality "in a profounder sense" than does a nonartist. The "total meaning" of an artist's work contains the life as well as the work. Sometimes, the biographical materials are minimal or nonexistent; where available, however, "a sense of the life of the writer will raise that meaning to a still higher power." Merely by placing two works by the same author side by side a critic has effectively come into contact with and begun to interpret this personality. Rather, "this interconnectedness is fully explicable only in terms of a personality." For Fiedler, the work of art is the sum of two kinds of meaning that he labels archetype and signature. Archetypes, synonymous with "myths," are held by the community: they may be domiciled within the Freudian id, the Jungian collective unconscious, the Platonic world of ideas, or elsewhere—depending upon one's persuasion. They are the "immemorial patterns" of response to the "human situation" in its "most permanent" aspects: "death," "love," the "biological family." Signature is the artist's individual stamp on these materials. In Freudian terms, it is the ego and superego divided between author and community: "The Signature is the joint product of 'rules' and 'conventions,' of the expectations of the community, and the idiosyncratic responses of the individual poet." "Baldur the Beautiful" and Shakespeare's *Tempest* draw upon the immersion and resurrection myth. Whereas *The Tempest* has a specific diction and patterns of imagery, and so on, the Baldur story can be retold many ways so long as the basic plot line is held: "It is pure myth."[45]

Fiedler's practical investigations of the artist's biography are much subtler than his model implies. But like the New Critics, his model is essentially antihistorical. For all his pleas on behalf of biography and "community," myth replaces history as explanatory cause. Fiedler wants to study the "patterns" of social behavior, which he identifies in terms of "myths" and the "human situation" in its "most permanent" aspects.[46] His schematic reduction of Freud takes the psychoanalytic case out of its social and historical setting. No can one "connect" the id with the community as Fiedler suggests; according to Freud in *The Ego and the Id* (1923), the id is "the great reservoir of libido," the source of the psychic energies needed to form the ego and the superego. The superego psychically represents the community. Finally, the relation between the Jungian collective unconscious and Plato's world of forms is outlandish. Plato's forms are perceived by the intuitive and discursive reason; they constitute the eternal presence of the true, the good, and the beautiful; with them Plato denies the power of (Homeric) myth. Jung's collective unconscious is a generalized and nonrational id; it serves as the core of a highly personal "secular religion" with an elaborate mythography based on the late-nineteenth-century reaction to science.

Although myth criticism was for a time seen as a possible alternative to New Criticism, as Gerald Graff has shown, it turns out to resemble it in basic ways, thereby perpetuating its influence. Fiedler's system shares key themes with New Criticism: antihistoricism, formalism, the resolution of opposites, the quasireligious motive, and the quest for totality. Yet the continuity between New Criticism and myth criticism is better illustrated by Northrop Frye. Unlike Fiedler, Frye did not attack New Critics; he recognized the strong resemblance between his premises and theirs. He participated in the *Kenyon Review* symposium of 1950–1951, contributing his essay "The Archetypes of Literature," which was widely anthologized. Here the similarity of assumptions stands out clearly. As is well known, Frye extended the New Critical limits of the autotelic poem to take in all products of the imagination: "Literature is a body of hypothetical thought and action: it makes, as literature, no statements or assertions."[47] A gap exists between this "imaginary universe" and reality, a gap that is protected by the "representational fallacy"—yet another fallacy, an "antimimetic" subcategory of antihistoricism. Like the New Critics, Frye makes a distinction between literature and criticism, but it is not the traditional division of value and fact. Frye banishes "causal value-judgments" and other examples of "meaningless" criticism to the history of taste. Pragmatic concepts such as "belief" and "sincerity," by which Richards intended to bridge the gap between literature and conduct, find no place in Frye's criticism. But he does follow Richards in one important respect: the positivist program. Criticism must be "scientific" and "systematic," for "systematic study can only progress." In his classification, criticism is a form of "literary anthropology," a field in which Frye begins by postulating a closure, "total coherence," in which individual works produce a "total structure of significance" and form a part of a "total literary history."[48]

This totalizing attitude, which reflects the postwar technological urge to expansion, informs Frye's system; he pushes New Critical concepts to their logical conclusion. His practical criticism is founded on an "order of words corresponding to an order of nature in the natural sciences." This "order" is encrypted within the text by means of certain fixed formulas, the interlocking myths or archetypes, primordial in human nature and subsisting through all the vicissitudes of culture, convention, and "progress." This antihistoricism enables Frye to repair frequently to "nature" for his governing myth: "In the solar cycle of the day, the seasonal cycle of the year, and the organic cycle of human life, there is a single pattern of significance, out of which myth constructs a central narrative around a figure who is partly the sun, partly vegetative fertility and partly a god or archetypal human being." The recurrent metaphor of the sphere or circle stands for the fullness and totality of the system. The myth unites human and natural energies and forms the infrastructure of the narrative: this in turn is seen to connect with religious ritual. Certain image patterns themselves are "oracular in origin," issuing from an "epiphanic moment" in the subconscious. Waking and dreaming, light and darkness, the human and the natural, these are the antitheses that art *as its final cause* claims to resolve. In this resolution the utopian imagination creates "a world in which the inner desire and the outward circumstance coincide. . . . [S]o in terms of significance, the central myth of art must be the vision of the end of social effort, the innocent world of fulfilled desires, the free human society."[49] Frye has taken the New Critical poem and raised it to the status of all literature; he has resolved oppositions in terms of a utopian vision at once primitive and futuristic; closure is effected by a cycle of nature and its parallels in religious ritual (Frazer and Jung are credited with discovering the importance of the solar myth). Frye's original division of fact and value will therefore be overcome in the romantic synthesis, a religious "vision" of an "innocent world" won through toil and suffering (and resembling Schiller's concept of the "idyll" and the fourth and highest stage of Blake's "vision," "organized innocence").

In sum, although Frye's catholicity of judgment and taste finds a place for the various trends in modern criticism, his own system represents the culmination of New Critical tendencies. As such, it did not effectively challenge its governing principles, and it is subject to the same critique.

The strength of New Criticism, as I have said, was founded in practice, not theory, and that helps explain why it was relatively easy to pick apart New Critics' concepts and why in a few years their theoretical edifice was reduced to a shambles. Yet the truly remarkable fact is how little effect all these attacks had on the New Critical movement itself. It is as if the movement were determined to die a natural death no matter how many mortal blows were dealt to it from the outside. Why did New Criticism continue to dominate the academy through the 1950s and beyond? Was it merely faute de mieux?

Again one points first to external circumstances, the shake-up of the traditional academy and curriculum owing to World War II and the immense expansion of higher education following it, both of which favored the fortunes of the New Critics. Timed perfectly, the movement rode the crest of an enormous wave. Then, they had constructed a theory that exalted method, and so they fit in with the nonideological mood and technologism of postwar culture. The New Critical antipathy toward literary history bore a close resemblance to a prevalent attitude in postwar American historical studies with their shift away from Enlightenment ideas of progress and liberalism, with their revisionary approach to key events in American history (Daniel Boorstin on Jefferson and the Revolution, Richard Hofstadter on Lincoln), and with the tendency to base themselves "on antiliberal points of reference" and "on mythological and anthropological concepts or on Freudian and Jungian psychology."[50] Such historiography reflected the larger crisis in the American sense of history, portrayed in 1960 by Robert L. Heilbroner: "At bottom our troubled state of mind reflects an inability to see the future in an *historic* context."[51] Antihistoricism coupled with mythological and anthropological models culminate in a flight from reason. New Criticism itself opened a special wing for myth-and-symbol criticism (Frye, Charles Feidelson, R. W. B. Lewis). Above all, the New Critics prized impersonality and ambiguity, qualities that gave New Criticism a long lease on life and prepared the ground for deconstruction.

Indeed, as Gerald Graff has noted, deconstruction is "in many respects old ambiguity writ large." In a new Hegelian twilight, numerous commentators (Frank Lentricchia, Remo Ceserani, Paul Bové, Christopher Norris, Henry Staten, Barbara Foley, Stephen Melville) have uncovered continuities between New Criticism and deconstruction, and an essay remains to be written on *The Pupils of Reuben Brower*.[52] Using the optic of Charles Feidelson's *Symbolism and American Literature* and arguing from a Marxist epistemology, Foley contends that New Criticism's formal autonomousness valorizes "linguistic self-reflexivity," which

deconstruction extends "to its logical limits in the openly antimimetic poetics": "Where [Feidelson] envisioned symbolism as a mode of bridging the epistemological gap between subject and object, his descendents propose that
subject and object are themselves fictions, and that the goal of criticism is to
reveal the implication of writer and reader alike in an infinite regress of texts
that do not reflect and mediate historical reality, but instead constitute that
reality." Besides self-reflexivity, the two movements share other affinities:
(1) New Critical ambiguity, paradox, and irony and deconstructionist illogicality; (2) the symbol that "creates its own meaning" (a remnant of logocentrism)
and Kenneth Dauber's claim that "meaning is not embodied in the written but
is a function of writing"; and (3) the New Critical rejection of scientific language with its empiricist claims and the more thoroughgoing poststructuralist
collapse of the distinction between poetic and scientific language into the single category of textuality.[53] Both movements also espouse a strong version of
antihistoricism, either the New Critical "concern with the isolated, autonomous monad" or the deconstructionist "tendency to dissolve literary history
into a repetitious synchronic rhetoric of the *aporia*."[54] Finally, the antihuman-
ist theme in both movements emerges in the approach to the self. The modernist–New Critical claim of impersonality argues for the detached, scientific
point of view, the gaining of perspective, a "confidence in locating a 'point of
presence,' a 'fixed origin' outside the labyrinth." But, as Wyndham Lewis points
out with regard to Eliot and Richards, this only masks radical depersonaliza-
tion.[55] The total effacement of the self is accomplished in deconstruction with
its decentering, its view of fluid transsubjective desire, and the "end of Man."

Sharing key assumptions, New Criticism and deconstruction leave themselves open to similar attacks. Both theoretical approaches, though engaged in
oppositional strategies, may be accused of reifying their oppositions instead of
dialectically overcoming them in historical analysis. Both formalize and fetish-
ize ambiguity or the more radical undecidability and the playful signifiers.
Technical analyses lose their radical oppositional force in an idealist metaphysics. Deconstruction "desires to freeze in time (or, better, to hold in suspended animation) its act of epistemological transgression and actively to
block the possibility of resolution." Foley concludes, "Marxism has been finally
banished from the scene, this time with a vengeance."[56]

It remains to be seen why New Criticism should have been so disposed to
take the direction toward radical undecidability instead of pursuing ever more
strident attempts at formal closure. The New Critics plotted wide swings of
opposition within a text, yet they expected the "total unified attitude" to
emerge; to the extent that it did not emerge, the poem failed—Richards had
called it "badness in poetry." Only by a forced emphasis, however, could one

read their version of synthesis in many of the masterpieces of modernism: Eliot, Joyce, Pound, Kafka, Pirandello, Céline. The principal modernist themes are alienation, cultural anarchy, the grotesque, fright, despair, and nothingness—not balance, wholeness, and synthesis. New Critics would equivocate, but, as Paul de Man points out, their criticism was primarily a "criticism of ambiguity," an "ironic reflection of the absence of the unity it postulated."[57] In this respect, New Critics belong wholly to their age; fidelity to their method, wherever it led, proved stronger than their desire for closure as stated in their theory. They were willing to take the cure of history as mediated by the great texts of modernism.

The issues can best be analyzed in the dialectical relationship between the concept of the "tranquilized poem," where all political, social, and historical implications are suppressed, and the concept of "tension," which was equally essential to New Critical poetics. *Tension,* introduced by Richards in 1924, is one of those ambiguous New Critical terms: it does triple duty, sliding between the ideological (various positions), the psychological (the reader's and the speaker's equilibrium), and the formal (balance of components, strained relations between cognitive and poetic linguistic functions, points of maximum stress). The question of how much tension a poem can take remains open because, ideally, the poem wins its unity on the strength of its inclusions, not on the force of its exclusions. Richards even located a tensional element in the metaphoric process of tenor and vehicle, the process that is the "omnipresent principle of language," a "borrowing between the intercourse of thoughts," a "transaction between contexts" in which what is expelled is even more important than what is included. Nor is tension merely a formal device: for Brooks, "to widen the context of the poem—to challenge its ability to mesh with other contexts—tests the fidelity of its language to the language of human experience."[58] For the New Critic the poem is the "working out of the various tensions," resulting in a "pattern of resolutions and balances and harmonizations." Yet it would have to be a fine balance between the "tendency of science" to "stabilize" terms and the "poet's tendency," which is "disruptive," the terms "violating" their dictionary meanings.[59] At some point the pressure of expansion, splitting, and violence overcomes the forces of closure and synthesis. In Richards's terms, is "badness" always a "failure to unify"? Are not completeness and fidelity to experience more important critical values?

It is precisely the forces of expansion that are awakened by practice so that, dialectically speaking, the New Critics' greatest strength is also the most formidable enemy of their ideal of synthesis.

Some New Critics, it is true, resisted the pull toward nonsynthesis. Wimsatt's difficulty with religious inspiration and intentionality has been mentioned. If

Brooks criticized the poetry of exclusion, he was not above omitting an obvious meaning of "tease" in Keats's "Thou, silent form, dost tease us out of thought" in order to unify a reading. Likewise, Tate thought that the last stanza of Keats's "Ode on a Grecian Urn" added nothing to the poem; he also objected to the seventh stanza of the "Ode to a Nightingale," where in "Thou wast not born for death, immortal Bird!" Keats "merely *asserts.*" Wimsatt and Brooks comment that although the semantic analysis of Richards and Empson "does seem to imply a value in complexity itself," the "great poems reveal an organic structure of parts intricately related." These critics point to an ideal of "simplicity" by way of Plotinus on the "simple" that "may describe either *absence* of *internal differentiation* (as with the simplicity or unity of a pebble) or precisely the opposite, a high degree of *internal differentiation*—in other words, organic unity (as with unity of a living body)." At the same time Richards had initiated the critical movement toward complexification and the play of signification.[60] In *The Structure of Complex Words,* Empson devotes so much attention to the ambiguities of single words that he sometimes loses sense of the whole; Lee T. Lemon compares his method to stopping a film and reading single frames. Warren prefers that poetry not "be purged of all 'impurities' or, as Richards might put it, draw upon too narrow a context."[61] The New Critical tilt toward open form is also apparent for Ransom for whom a poem's structure is "determinate," "logical," "abstract," "universal," and linked to "scientific bondage," "prose," and even *death* ("something is continually being killed by prose"), but structure is opposed by the poem's "totality of connotation," "texture," "irrelevancies," "tissues," and "differentia," all of which he subsumes under the category of "indeterminacy." This is the "residue," the critical remainder and "miraculism," that could not be contained by structure and that "the poet wants to preserve"—a living principle. The character of the poem resides "in its way of exhibiting the residuary quality." Following the poet, the "ontological critic" must unearth the "denser and more refractory original world" known to "perceptions" and "memories"—a releasing from repression—and confront the "ontological density which proves itself by logical obscurity."[62] The New Critical practitioner is torn between the instrumental and the mystical, the determined and indeterminate, the abstracted and the repressed, the universal and the concrete. "Tranquilizing" the poem only intensifies the oppositions, yet it is tension that tunes the poetic experience.

The entire dialectical series of oppositions should be placed in a larger historical and cultural context. For their ideal of synthesis, the New Critics looked backward. It was a vestige of the cultural ideal that traces through European romanticism to the seventeenth century, where it is already a nostalgic recollection of the Renaissance paradigm: the individual, self-realization, unity, freedom, and organicity. Giuseppe Sertoli comments that "resolved ('closed') in the perfection of its own form, the work of art is already a completed totality, the realized conciliation, the utopia present in the here and now."[63] In Mac-Leish's "Ars Poetica,"

> A poem should be palpable and mute
> As a globed fruit,
>
> Dumb
> As old medallions to the thumb

The poem closes in upon itself: it is "globed"; a circle of perfection contains the life-giving nature ("fruit") within the bounds and artifice of geometric form. The "old medallions," themselves circles, connote value, fame, immortality; imagistic compression, economy, and chiselled perfection; the circle of the globe (Pope's "narrow orb" in "To Mr. Addison"); and qualities associated with Ransom's *Dinglichkeit,* impressions felt with pleasure. Yet this myth of synthesis imposes itself on ultimately recalcitrant materials whose cultural contradictions have not been overcome. Rather, those contradictions have been "intensified" in the modern period; organicist critical theory, argues Sertoli, treats the work of art as a "fiction of a totality," a "pretence of an impossible reconciliation." Thus, *palpable, mute,* and *Dumb* refer to the poem's "thingness," to its otherness and silence, to its illogicality, to that which cannot "speak" in modes of rationality as currently construed; *mute* and *Dumb* imply the repressed, the emarginated, that which is beyond the limit of the "meaningful": "Leaving, as the moon behind the winter leaves, / Memory by memory the mind."[64]

The New Criticism had installed the much needed corrective to historical studies, which by themselves were incapable of mastering the linguistic challenge of modernist texts. It had ridden the upsurge of national unity during and after World War II, and this unity survived into the cold war period, a synthesis prolonged by the "tranquillized *Fifties.*" But the claims of antihistoricism, ambiguity, and nonsynthesis were also satisfied by its methodology, and these proved to be what the New Criticism bequeathed, allowing it to endure in the academy for years after its myth of synthesis had collapsed.

# The Disappearance of the Self

## Contemporary Theories of Autobiography

I will rouse up my mind and fix my attention.
I will stand collected within myself and think upon
what I read and what I see.

—John Adams, *Diary* (1756)

Older historical studies in autobiography compared an author's narrative against the hard biographical facts. Generically, autobiography was a branch of biography. Though valuable in themselves, these studies tended to resolve problems on the plane of truth and reliability, or at least sincerity. They neither disentangled the authorial consciousness from its antecedent causes, treated it as the form-giving presence, discovered the fictional elements in the narrative, nor distinguished among autobiography, chronicle, memoir, and the like. "In the autobiography," explains Roy Pascal, "attention is focused on the self, in the memoir or reminiscence on others." Moreover, since earlier studies did not expatiate on the theory of autobiography, relying instead upon positivist historicism, and since New Criticism with its antihistorical bias had quarantined biography and autobiography, theorizing was more honored in the breach than the observance. René Wellek and Austin Warren denied full literary status to autobiography in *Theory of Literature,* widely used by graduate students in the 1940s and '50s. In 1968 Stephen A. Shapiro protested its virtual exclusion from literary studies in "The Dark Continent of Literature: Autobiography."[1]

Even then, if one looked far enough afield, the matter was not entirely dark.

Georg Misch, Wilhelm Dilthey's son-in-law and intellectual disciple, devoted his career to the history of autobiography, starting with Babylon and Egyptian tomb inscriptions. He rejected any but the broadest of definitions: "the description (graphia) of a life (bio) of an individual by himself (auto): prayer, factual account, lyric, confession, family chronicle, novel."[2] By his death at eighty-seven in 1965, he had published six volumes of his *Geschichte der Autobiographie* (3,885 pages) without completing the Middle Ages. Loyal disciples carried on with his manuscripts and brought the story forward to the nineteenth century.

Meanwhile, in 1956, the Belgian critic Georges Gusdorf had published his pioneering essay "Conditions and Limits of Autobiography" in which he downplayed the factual history on which the life was based and concentrated on the "art" of autobiography, the "lived unity of attitude," and the moral struggle of an autonomous individual to find meaning in life's "mythic tale": autobiography is "a second reading of experience, and it is truer than the first because it adds to experience itself consciousness of it." Because critics had spent so much effort on background evidence, they neglected questions of identity, intention, fictionality, and formal design. Gusdorf probed into the Enlightenment origins of modern narrative autobiography that bespoke a "new spiritual revolution."[3] His work anticipated developments elsewhere.

The 1960s are crucial to the history of theoretical studies in autobiography. New Criticism had waned, though its impact on formal analysis persisted. Roy Pascal's *Design and Truth in Autobiography* (1960), David Levin's "*Autobiography of Benjamin Franklin:* The Puritan Experimenter in Life and Art" (1964) (with his New Critical distinction between author and central character portrayed), and Francis R. Hart's "Notes for an Anatomy of Modern Autobiography" (1970) raised questions regarding fact, fiction, and types of truth.[4] Poetry of the 1950s and '60s—the Beats, Robert Lowell's *Life Studies,* the confessional poets—involved private life, "performance," and aesthetic form. Nor can we forget the revival of biography in the bold, synthesizing vein of Richard Ellmann's *James Joyce* (1959) and Walter Jackson Bate's *John Keats* (1963). The civil rights movement and Vietnam War brought history and politics to the forefront of consciousness; works like Hemingway's *Moveable Feast* (1964), Lowell's *For the Union Dead* (1964) and *History* (1973), and Norman Mailer's *Armies of the Night: History as the Novel, the Novel as History* (1967) blurred the lines between history and self-portrait, and between politics and fiction.[5] At Johns Hopkins University in 1966, a symposium on the "structuralist controversy" inaugurated deconstruction in the United States. Ironically, just at the time when the theory of autobiography was beginning to be taken seriously, the very concept of the self—"the Enlightenment or liberal-humanist notion of selfhood as the universal, transcendent marker of 'man' "[6]—was coming under fire. Rather, *renewed* fire. Wylie Sypher noted in *Loss of the Self in Modern Literature and Art* that twentieth-century concepts of the self had long since grown tenuous and fragile, succumbing to collectivism, bureaucratism, conformism, or anomic atomism: "The individual is vanishing behind the functionary throughout the technological world."[7]

Canonical autobiographers from Augustine, Cellini, Saint Teresa, and Rousseau to Mill, Newman, and Ruskin had affirmed the core self as primordial, however much they recognized the various roles that they were called upon to play. Cellini was artist and artisan, courtier, friend, thief, soldier, and sinner, but an essentially independent subject, Cellini, seems to subsist in and through them all, shaping his destiny according to his own chosen ends. Jacob Burckhardt traced the concept of the "complete," "free-standing" individual back to the close of the thirteenth century when Italy began to "swarm with individuality." In his analysis an individual "casts off the authority of the State," "retains the feeling of his own sovereignty," "forms his decisions independently," knows "inward resources," enjoys a "developed private life," and seeks an "inward equilibrium" and a "harmonious development" of "spiritual and material existence." The aesthetic category with which Burckhardt conceived of state formation, seen as the product of reflection and calculation on the part of the ruler, and not tradition or divine right, he applied to persons; individuality is something that they must fashion for themselves: "In itself it is neither good nor bad." This concept was bequeathed by the Renaissance to modern Europe, undergoing various permutations and ideological alterations. In his study of one of these ideologies, "individualism," which relies on Burckhardt, Steven Lukes summarizes four germinal ideas of selfhood: "the supreme intrinsic value, or dignity, of the individual human being"; "autonomy, or self-direction"; privacy, "an area within which the individual is or should be left alone by others and able to do and think whatever he chooses"; and self-cultivation or self-realization, the pursuit of one's own "genius."[8] In the romantic version of the theory, the self remains an unfathomable mystery, a cone of darkness at best affording brief glimpses of insight. The "individuality model" or "subjectivity ideal" is a basic assumption in criticism through the 1960s and well into the '70s, and when it breaks apart, so too will autobiographical theory.

Appearing in 1964, Robert F. Sayre's *Examined Self: Benjamin Franklin, Henry Adams, Henry James* outlines two major traditions in American autobiography, both founded upon the individuality model: the religious ("more formal and self-conscious") and the secular ("looser" and "more inclusive"). Saint Augustine is the model for the first (Puritan apologies and confessions; Jonathan Edwards); Franklin for the second, with its far more numerous offspring.

Franklin expresses the difficulty of writing without the "ordering beliefs" of religion but also the possibility of structuring a narrative around the events of one's life.[9] He overcame the tendencies toward psychological disorder with the help of the stable realm of eighteenth-century cultural ideals and the secularized concept of selfhood inherited from New England Puritanism. Sayre does not stretch his notion of the two traditions, which is more of a heuristic device than a rigid paradigm; they do not organize his entire argument; Edwards is treated only briefly. Moreover, the two traditions do not run parallel through American literature; the Augustinian tradition fades in the eighteenth century, though it returns from time to time. Sayre's best efforts go toward exploring the two great problems posed by Franklin and given different solutions by Adams and James: how to construct and educate the self to be a coherent, flexible, active force in a rapidly changing social context, and how to unite knowledge with (mainly civic) power.

Franklin's notions on selfhood are nowhere stated and everywhere implied as he discloses the role-playing, "pluralism," and "unending versatility" in his quintessential success story. Contextualizing each of the four parts of Franklin's book, Sayre examines Franklin's multiple "poses," "games," "masks," "props," and "pretenses," from penniless Boston boy to the newly adopted Quaker naif, the printer and journalist, American patriot, civic projector, scientist, diplomat, retired gentleman, and renowned, cosmopolitan, rustic philosopher, each part highlighting one or another pose before the reader. Franklin's genial self-concept was sufficiently large and elastic to embrace all of them, give life to them, and exploit them, partly due to the fact that he was looking back from the perspective of a crystallized self, on his view, an *honnête homme*. He prefigures the Emerson of "Experience" and the pragmatism of C. S. Peirce and William James. His religious, humanitarian, and social philosophy is the combined result of "experimentation" and "intelligence."[10]

Instead of pursuing the matter sociologically Sayre concentrates on self-construction, taking a cue from Carl Becker. "Franklin was never submerged in anything he undertook," Becker had observed. "Behind the gestures and routines of his participation was always a reserve, a certain ironic sense." Franklin was an eighteenth-century satirist and ironist, but irony does not undermine his selfhood any more than it did Swift's; on the contrary, it strengthens it. For Sayre, the "actor" Franklin "recognized his freedom and realized that whatever actions he took were in a dramatic sense, 'acts,' roles to some degree thrust upon him but also consciously selected and therefore open to whatever interpretations he wished to make of them." Worthy of note is how New Critical concepts and strategies—the "free" artist, the persona, drama, and multiple interpretation—inform Sayre's historical analysis, or rather dehistoricize it at the moment when his categories might have yielded quite different conclusions of selfhood, less self-fashioned, more socially determined. Sayre might have noted, for example, that puritan antitheatricality had cooled down sufficiently in nascent capitalist culture to enable a man like Franklin to talk freely about his self-constructions without feeling that he was duplicitous or dishonest, the ultimate sin of the *honnête homme.* In diagramming Franklin's multiple "selves," Sayre has set the elusive self, the primordial Franklin, beyond the margins of analysis. The text was Franklin's principal means of self-construction and experimentation: "The fact that [he] conducted such a large amount of his business by writing—letters, reports, scientific papers, pamphlets, proposals, propaganda pieces—is interesting in this respect because the printed page was obviously the medium through which he learned many of the gestures and postures of his multiple lives."[11] Stressing language, Sayre also reveals New Critical influence.

The autobiographies of both Henry Adams and Henry James derive from Franklin's model, even though Adams "in effect chose to try to unite [the Augustinian and Franklin models]." *The Education of Henry Adams* has strong affinities with the third part of Franklin's *Autobiography,* composed in Philadelphia in 1788, in which Franklin draws the lines of his life together from the perspective of the national hero. On the other side, James's *Small Boy and Others* (1913) and *Notes of a Son and Brother* (1914) resemble the first part, the so-called Twyford section, written in 1771 in the form of a letter to his son, in which Franklin explicates the formation of his adult self, the "established gentleman at the writing desk." The Adams and the third-part Franklin are "epic," "ironic epic" (or in Adams's case antiepic), and "objective" autobiography; the James and first-part Franklin are "subjective" and "lyrical," with a "lyricist's or elegist's response to immediate feeling." Adams focuses on the historical destiny that rides over him, putting him out of joint with his time. In this regard, he said ironically, he wished to "complete" Augustine who "alone has an idea of literary form": the form of the book and the concept of selfhood coincide. Reinvigorating autobiography with the Augustinian model, Adams's drama arises from the tension between education, which is form giving, and the many conflictual forces of modernity, in which "chaos is the law of nature."[12]

James's subjective approach to autobiography leads him to dwell on past events and relationships that have spontaneity, yield up their own inviolate meanings, and interrelate seemingly organically with one another. Where Adams finds that the pieces of his education are "discontinuous" and cannot be made to fit into a historical pattern, James's education was "continuous," "more rounded," "interconnected," and "compressed," approaching the organicity he sought in his fiction. Adams moves from unity of concept to multiplicity of

event; James from multiplicity of event to unity of form. Without equivoca-
tion, Sayre counsels that "the usual, more desirable kind of education, that is,
of personal growth and experience, is definitely James."[13] This is not entirely
fair to Adams, who faced up to his fragmenting social and cultural environment and refused to impose a premature aesthetic unity on recalcitrant materials. Adams saw modernity for what it was and, in this sense, adumbrates
Spengler, Mumford, and Ellul. James may be said to have achieved organic
unity at least partly from what, quite knowingly, he omitted to tell. Adams's
failure represents the greater autobiographical achievement, the finished product (to borrow Leslie Stephen's phrase) showing enormous tension between
the forces of symmetry and completeness.

Selfhood remains the central problem. In contrast to James, Adams was "born
a public figure," an "heir apparent"; this set him immediately apart. "What
Franklin could not do until his eighties when he really was a national hero,
what Whitman had to do by song and celebration, fate granted Adams to do by
the merest reference." However, that same fate did not grant Adams a world in
which his inherited eighteenth-century values applied. Whereas Augustine
could search out his own interior time and suppress historical time in order to
glorify God's eternity, in which all times are copresent, the historian Adams
must contend with rapid historical change and with "chaos" in the godless
nineteenth and twentieth centuries.[14] In terms of sheer labor power, things destroyed and constructed, and people moving and being drawn into the activity
of civilization, Mill's age of transition, the nineteenth century far outstripped
the traditionalist cultures. Adams's faith in history forced him to accept a "discontinuous" education and thus "discontinuous" self-formation: the only way
the events of his life could fit into the pattern was by comprehending their degree of unfitness.

Adams's life unfolds as a series of lost illusions: "How to tell a story of what
was not a story?" is Sayre's description of the psychological and aesthetic predicament. The conflict between order and chaos in nature, in history, in the
individual, is the "subject" of *The Education of Henry Adams* and also a "technique of its own internal structure." Even the dynamic theory of history and
law of acceleration (historical change will tend to occur exponentially) is an effort, however incorrect as theory, to "make order of life in the modern age," "to
'fix'" the position of that multiplicity and reckon its future course. In this respect Adams's education is an Augustinian exemplum. "Chaos" in personal
terms is "created by dressing the journalist, the teacher, and the man in all the
old illusions he ever wore," then mercilessly stripping them away. "Beneath all
the misfitting toilets—all meant to be instructive to later young men—is the
manikin, the effaced Ego, who was inevitably growing into the tailor, the author."

As impersonal artist, the ego creates order in the third person, braving historical time and erecting a monument in its midst. The self is swept up by history, unable to tame it, yet able to exploit and to teach it: "Man needed to understand history the way he needed to understand magnetism: not to know why, but how; not to control, but to use, like the compass, in steering his way."[15] Looking into America's future at the conclusion of his autobiography, Adams mixes pessimism and optimism, and keeps his balance. The Augustinian Adams had schooled himself in the "prophetic mode."[16]

What had taken Adams a lifetime to realize appears to have been James's birthright. But whereas Adams's book was long in preparation, James decided to write strict autobiography only in his later years when, pierced by grief over the loss of his brothers in 1910, he began telling stories of his childhood to William James's widow. Then he wrote quickly; his storytelling was an elegiac act of *pietas,* though the results are better described as idyllic, and centered on a sensibility, revivified, strengthened, and unified by an excursus into lost time. Sayre focuses on *A Small Boy and Others* and *Notes of a Son and Brother,* both of which had been sadly neglected (and remain so). He also gives a few pages to *William Wetmore Story and His Friends,* which Adams himself thought "pure autobiography." Sayre might also have included *The Middle Years* (1917), the third part of James's autobiography (to the 1870s), and his semiautobiographical travel narrative *The American Scene* (1907), which Gordon O. Taylor refers to as "a methodical rather than incidental autobiography."[17] And what of the abundant autobiographical materials in the prefaces to the New York edition? James's autobiographical writings are many and diverse.

Sayre's two main themes are observation and interrelation. James's odd word for the first was *gaping,* and his "method of consciousness" is founded on his rich capacity for seeing. The reminiscent James watches "the small boy dawdle and gape" through a fence at barnyard animals: they were the "others"— this was one of his primal memories. Then, his autobiography of childhood devotes an extraordinary quarter of its pages to the theater, to old actors and actresses, whom he recalled with great affection and accuracy: "What James longed for in his education . . . were more impressions, more 'vistas,' more 'scenes,' and more luxurious gaping." The method of consciousness sets him at variance with Adams's dialectical and ironic design. Adams's attitude toward Boston and Newport had the intended effect of satiric distance and reductionism; and the past dwindles. "Poor Henry James," wrote Adams on reading *Notes of a Son and Brother.* "[He] thinks it all real, I believe, and actually still lives in that dreamy, stuffy Newport and Cambridge, with papa James and Charles Norton—and me!" Adams never escaped his own irony ("and me!"). But irony applied to one's whole upbringing inevitably has a withering effect, which Adams escapes by the brilliance of his art. On the contrary, James did not "judge": he virtually let the stories of "rediscovery" tell themselves, "flower" (to use one of the James's favorite metaphors in his autobiographical narratives), and reveal the child as father of the man. The theme of interrelation follows closely upon the method of consciousness. Oddly enough, whereas James's anecdotes seem to stand alone like pearls without a string by comparison to Adams's tight organization, the anecdotes ramify and overlap, interconnect, and give a deeper sense of developing consciousness, a "history of an imagination." James himself defined the problem: "To recover anything like the full treasure of scattered, wasted circumstance was at the same time to live over the spent experience itself . . . and the effect of this in turn was to find discrimination among the pasts of my subject again and again difficult—so inseparably and beautifully they seemed to hang together."[18] As Sayre notes, even the titles of James's books, so seemingly casual, place the child in context: Small Boy *and others,* the Son, the Brother.

While remaining sensitive to historical and economic matters Sayre successfully establishes the *autos* at the center of his study and sets versions of selfhood in comparison and contrast. A domesticated New Critical vocabulary enables him to explore masks, ambiguity, and self-irony. In concluding remarks he even broaches the relation of autobiography to fiction, as in Hemingway's Nick Adams stories, James Baldwin, and Ralph Ellison. Perhaps, in the end, the preferred Jamesian attitude distorted, however slightly, Sayre's readings of Adams and Franklin. In the balance, form weighs more heavily than biography and history, another New Critical value.

In *Metaphors of Self: The Meaning of Autobiography* (1972) James Olney presents the case for the Gusdorfian *autos* in the strongest possible terms. For him, the subject of autobiography is best understood not as a formal or historical problem, "which would be to separate it from the writer's life and personality," but as a "vital impulse to order that has always caused man to create." Olney posits a "creative impulse," a "yearning for order" in man, a passion "greater than his desire for knowledge." If, however, the desire for knowledge were not greater than the yearning for order, it is doubtful whether the critical attitude could have developed, the attitude that fights against settling for the first order of the day. "The order that men seek," comments Olney, "is never static and out there but always going on, and going on within them." Olney rings the changes of the precedence of faith over reason: Blake's attacking science, Newman's belief that "Reason . . . is subservient to faith," Rabindranath Tagore, Jung. "Creative vitality" is general in the species; particular is the autobiographical form to which the individual's "private spirit impelled him."[19] Individual initiative is valorized over history, economic necessity, and cultural forms. On Olney's agenda is nothing less than a secularized religion of the self.

In all autobiography, Olney argues, the individual standpoint emerges from

a core at once "unitary" (showing the desire for "coherency"), "specifically human" (as opposed to what is shared with animals), and "personally unique"
(the one-of-a-kind in the history of the universe). Likewise unitary, human,
and unique are the metaphors that the autobiographers employ to express
themselves. These metaphors of self mediate between internal and external; if
the use of metaphor says "very little about what the world is, or is like," it says a
"great deal about what I am, or am like, and about what I am becoming." (Actually, Homeric metaphor says a great deal about what the world is like.) Thus,
anything is potentially expressive of the totality of the self: Heraclitus on the
logos, Einstein's theory of relativity, Keynes's *General Theory of Employment,
Interest, and Money:* "The final work, whether it be history or poetry, psychology or theology, political economy or natural science, whether it takes the form
of personal essay or controversial tract, of lyric poem of scientific treatise, will
express and reflect its maker and will do so at every stage of his development in
articulating the whole work." The tendency of such a romantic *Weltanshauung*
is to absorb the Not-I into an all-encompassing category of I. In making these
claims, Olney misreads Heraclitus, who based his philosophy on the sharp distinction between the public and private worlds, not their collapse into each
other. In a fundamental breakthrough in the history of science Heraclitus
states that "although the logos is common, the many live as though they had a
private understanding"; the logos "always existed." In W. K. C. Guthrie's gloss,
the logos is "something with an existence independent of him who gives it verbal expression." But Olney comments: "What the Logos demands of the individual is that he should realize his logos, which is also more than his own or
private logos—it is the Logos." It is not a question of my logos or your logos,
the logos is not unique to the individual; it is the general truths of reality, the
universal laws, the measure of things, and the logical capacity to discover them.
For Olney, who foists a romantic reading on Heraclitus, not to recognize the
triumphant power of the self-realizing ego voyaging through space and time
amounts to bad faith. "Perhaps the greatest mystery is that men so often refuse
credit for what they have achieved, disclaiming their accomplishment as something objective or scientific or impersonal or divine instead of proclaiming it as
their own and emotionally satisfying."[20] James Olney is a hedgehog, not a fox.

Most moralists have not found men and women so modest before their
achievements. Augustine and Boethius thought it more "emotionally satisfying" to worship the godhead (the "impersonal," the "divine") beyond themselves; by their counsel, it was when one arrogated the impersonal and the
divine to oneself that one's grief began. Whereas the phenomenological self
needed its explicators in autobiography, Olney does not allow his empowered
subject to share the palm with the object. Everything is based on a premise of

radical inwardness; he throws up his hands at attempting to analyze such inwardness beyond vague, Jungian philosophizing, most of which leads to final
unknowability. The self's essence that he tries to fathom is "infinitely difficult
to get at," "to encompass," "to know how to deal with"; "it squirts like mercury
away from observation"; "it is not to be known except privately and intuitively." The self "is, for each of us, only itself" (which is tautological). The self
is prior even to "soul," which is an "aspect of self." Olney festoons his text with
the humanistic catchwords—"man," "private spirit," "internal harmony," "oneness of self," the "balance," the "poise," the "cooperation of opposites" (no un-
canny doubles or irreconcilable clashes, of course, but peaceful coexistence),
and metaphors of wholeness—what Theodor Adorno calls the "jargon of authenticity." In place of history and sociology, Olney substitutes the humanistic
universals, which he strains to assimilate to Jungian archetypes: "Like the elements, individual man never is but is always becoming: his self, as C. J. Jung
will say some twenty-five hundred years after Heraclitus—nor did man change
much in the interim—is a process rather than a settled state of being."[21] It is
hard to reconcile the two sides of this sentence: man is "always becoming";
man has not changed "much" in twenty-five hundred years. It is easier to argue
that "man" has undergone considerable change on account of, say, the Greeks,
or the Church, or the Renaissance, or technological society.

The fact is, we do not need to approach the individuality model with such
reverence to appreciate its value. Olney disparages scientific and philosophical
efforts to pin down the self lest it be robbed of its mystery. But science and philosophy can enhance its mystery, too. Reference to any number of schools and
thinkers—Nietzsche, Anglo-American cognitive psychology, sociobiologists,
French and German phenomenologists, deconstruction—would have shown
that the self is not unequivocally "unitary" or even "specifically human." Stephen
Jay Gould has called attention to behavioral patterns that humans share with
animals, for example, altruism: "We seek a criterion for our uniqueness," asserts Gould, "settle (naturally) upon our minds, and define the noble results of
human consciousness as something intrinsically apart from biology."[22]

Olney is as antiscientific as he is antihistorical, citing Blake on Swedenborg:
"Man can have no idea of anything greater than Man, as a cup cannot contain
more than its capaciousness." This serves as Olney's text for something that resembles a self-help television lecture:

Yet philosophy, in disregard of this human truth and imagining its metaphysics to be objective and verifiable, is forever filling its cup to overflowing
in the delusion that for once its capacity might surpass its capaciousness; and
psychology, calling itself an exact science, perpetually chases its own tail,

sending its naked intellect after its back end in the vain hope that this time it may prove a little faster than last time, or may surprise the tail and come upon it unawares.[23]

If bad psychology assuredly exists, one does not judge a field from its worst examples, and because psychology cannot be as exact as chemistry, all its findings are not rendered null and void. Olney cites William James on the "will to believe"; James is also the author of *Principles of Psychology*.

Years ago Karl Popper proposed the test of falsifiability for distinguishing scientific from religious and other questions. If a specific proposition is susceptible to methodologically objective testing and could at least be proved wrong (leaving what might be *right* open to further debate), one was acting scientifically. If the proposition is not falsifiable, it is a matter of belief and dogma. The creation of the universe is a case where it is not possible to have a valid test. In this instance the question is whether one may at least approach the problem in a scientific manner, say, by analogy to the birth of planets and galaxies, or whether it is simply beyond the bounds of all possible discussion.

At moments Olney seems aware of Popper's falsifiability principle, as when he argues that "the billion phenomena that bombard us can at best advance our understanding negatively by proving a particular theory invalid or insufficient." Olney is fond of cosmic romantic metaphors that empower the self. Yet, ultimately, this will not suffice: "On their own, however, [the phenomena] will never fall together into a pattern, nor formulate a law." Olney wants the self to create order rather than read the signs of possible order from the outside: science, theology, and art are all "based on acts of faith." Surely, he must recognize that many phenomena fall into patterns "on their own," like seashells and snowflakes. Kepler did not invent the laws of planetary motion out of thin air; he needed Tycho Brahe's data, for science is a collective enterprise. Galileo did not create the fact that "light" and "heavy" bodies fall at the same rate of thirty-two feet per second. Olney's epistemological remarks on the self lead in circles: "One goes to Shakespeare, to Marvell or Keats or Eliot and finds there, time after time, new and inexhaustible access of being." What is this mysterious being? "Their works, like the archetypes, are the efforts and the achieved meanings of humanity precipitated into objective forms that remain there for us as perpetual possibilities for realization, but not as experience to grasp per se." Yet one experiences them in some sense when one reads them, as he himself proves in his sensitive reading of Eliot's *Four Quartets*. Olney transforms the reference to Mill on matter as the "perpetual possibility of sensation" into the possibility of self-realization. But if the literary works "there" can be realized, they must form experiences grasped "per se," that is, in their objective otherness. If not, we would have no idea of the difference among Shakespeare, Marvell, Keats, and Eliot. As G. E. Moore remarks, only the fact that "they" are "outside the circle" of our subjectivity guarantees one's own separate existence.[24] One cannot quarrel with Olney for centering his discourse on the autobiographer's uniqueness, but it has to be judged on the grounds of all the evidence, objective and subjective, and not exclusively on its own terms.

A final representative of the individuality model, Karl J. Weintraub's *Value of the Individual* is one of the most penetrating studies in autobiography in the past three decades. He writes within the Swiss-German tradition: Dilthey, Weber, Misch, Lamprecht, Meinecke, and, above all, Burckhardt. Planted on this solid theoretical ground, Weintraub surveys with sweeping gesture the ancient world to the romantic period, with chapters on Augustine; Abelard; Petrarch; Cellini; Cardano; Montaigne; the mystics Seuse, Saint Teresa, and Madame Guyon; the Puritans Bunyan and Baxter; Franklin; Vico and Gibbon; Rousseau; and Goethe. The absence of Dante's *Vita Nuova* is regrettable in light of Weintraub's comment that it is "the medieval autobiography possessing the greatest artistic unity"—which should indicate that he is not primarily concerned with artistic unity.[25] His book reaches its climax with Goethe's *Dichtung und Wahrheit,* beyond which his thesis would have to contend with how the individual self has been challenged and undermined by industrial and technological society. In a larger sense, his defense of "the value of the individual" protests its so-called disappearance in postmodernity.

At the heart of Weintraub's theory is a polarity of, or tension between, the model personality (or "personality ideal") and individuality. Working with Max Weber's notion of ideal types, he argues that particular societies present their members with a finite number of "personality ideals" that simultaneously open up and limit the possibilities for a given life. The history of the West before the eighteenth century encompasses such "personality ideals" as the Homeric hero, the *polis*-minded man, the Roman matron, the ideal schoolmaster, the saintly nun, the crusading knight, and the *honnête homme.* The ideal types dictate "certain substantive personality traits, certain values, virtues, and attitudes"; in Weintraub's metaphor, they are like a script where "only in the unprescribed interstitial spaces is there room for idiosyncrasy." Thus, for the earlier autobiographers, concentration on difference would distract from what is essential to the ideal type. Anecdote, which matters much in later autobiography, is consequently thin; too much detail might confuse or distort the personality ideal. The biographical facts are chosen and assembled according to the configuration and fulfillment of the type, and not too many are needed. Details do not fall casually from an author's pen; most often they have a symbolic aim. The young Augustine's stealing pears from an orchard symbolizes theft and the brotherhood of thieves; it is not a mechanism of retrieving private childhood memories and stimulating others. No other memories like it are mentioned: Augustine would have found them repetitious. Thus, in earlier autobiography the balance shifts toward the ideal, with attendant consequences: "The more the mind's eye is fascinated by the ideal model before it, the more a man will strive to attain *it,* and the less he will ask about the fit between the model and his own specific reality." The Ciceronian tradition of emulation in art and education plays a crucial role: an individual is not likely "to suffer from a sense of 'falsifying himself' by fitting into the norms demanded by his model, to feel 'hemmed in' if the ideal expresses the values of the society, or to lament the lost opportunities of his previous individuality."[26] In other words, the individual has little or no possibility of succumbing to existential bad faith.

At the other pole of individuality, genuineness resides in and through particulars, and "no general model can contain the specificity of the true self"; "the great fecundity of nature and of the human potential specifies each separate existence as a unique being of irreplaceable value," a unique event or rather process of development in the history of the universe.[27] Against Augustine, contrast the young Wordsworth's theft of bird's eggs in book 1 of *The Prelude:* the scenes portray the subjective life of the character, not the generality of the type. Or Rousseau on the first page of the *Confessions:* "I am unlike anyone I have ever known; I may not be better; but at least I am different." Despite the claims of difference and uniqueness, models obviously persist, new ones for old—for instance, the Organization Man. "Models still provide for those aspects of the personality where the self subjects itself to externally defined roles."[28] Weintraub realizes the self must compromise between the general model and uniqueness, but he refuses to treat the model as bad faith. After all, it can be through or with the help of the model that individuals discover what their individuality consists of and how to realize it. The relation between the socially approved model and individuality is not necessarily oppositional but dialectical. Weintraub's polarities resemble the distinction between classic and romantic premises of taste in the second half of the eighteenth century, where the breakthrough to modern narrative autobiography has its origins.

Weintraub cites the Latin epigram *individuum est ineffabile,* where *individuum* has its original meaning of indivisible and *ineffabile* means unsayable or indescribable. This motto, which Friedrich Meinecke attributes to Johann Gottfried Herder, can mean that the particular cannot be contained by a generalization, whether one studies an individual, a historical period, or a work of art. Historicism, asserts Meinecke, is "the application to the historical world of the new life-giving principles achieved by the great German movement ex-

tending from Leibniz to the death of Goethe." Chief among the principles is
"the substitution of a process of *individualising* observation for a *generalising*
view of human forces in history." *Individualizing* is the investigation of the particular, a direct consequence of Renaissance naturalism and historical writing[29]
and the scientific revolution with its systematic study of natural phenomena.
Meinecke links *individualizing* to the dissolution of natural law in the Enlightenment, though he cautions that natural law was never entirely abandoned—
witness "self-evident" rights in the American Declaration of Independence and
the French Rights of Man. Moreover, the Enlightenment did not fully break
ranks with natural law on the nature of the individual. The fixed, abstract individual of natural law makes an almost smooth transition to the Enlightenment, with its general laws and types, and with its timeless, ahistorical,
immutable reason buttressed by Stoicism, Christianity, and Newtonian law.
The real break comes with the newly discovered sense of self-formation or self-
cultivation *(Bildung)* that recognizes dynamic social and cultural forces, especially the "deepest moving forces of history, the human mind and soul."
*Individualizing* takes into account the feelings, the irrational, "spontaneity,"
"plastic flexibility," and "incalculability," in flux and influencing one another:
"It belongs to the essence of individuality (that of the single man no less than
the collective structures of the ideal and the practical world) that it is revealed
only by a process of development."[30] The duty of the individual is to release the
potential for being true to that which makes him or her unlike anyone else. The
autobiographer should record that process, giving it artistic shape from a point
of view in time: "The dominant autobiographic truth," Weintraub concludes,
is "the vision of the pattern and meaning of life which the autobiographer has
at the moment of writing his biography."[31]

From *individuum est ineffabile*, Goethe said in 1780, "I derive a whole world."[32]
He brought the scattered ideas that constitute historicism to their synthesis
with his notion of organic process, applying it in both his autobiography,
*Dichtung und Wahrheit*, and his bildungsroman, *Wilhelm Meisters Lehrjahre*.
The individual contains a totality—in the making. Self-realization forms the
basis of the great nineteenth- and twentieth-century British and American
autobiographies, from Carlyle, Mill, and Ruskin to Adams, Yeats, and Edwin
Muir:

> I held it truth, with him who sings
> To one clear harp in divers tones,
> That men may rise on stepping-stones
> Of their dead selves to higher things.
> (Tennyson, *In Memoriam*)

Weintraub's book reaches its official climax in romanticism, the heyday of individuality; it has a happy ending. But these autobiographers remind us that the story is not over, and not to test it in the latter half of modernity robs the drama of its peripeteia, if not, catastrophe. Only the inwardness of the stauncher souls can resist the conformist pressures of contemporary social models or "lifestyles" that hold out the illusion of individuality and freedom in everything from choosing a career to buying a car.

Weintraub defends Jacob Burckhardt on the historical origins of selfhood against Etienne Gilson and Johan Huizinga, both of whom placed the origins of the modern European personality in the High Middle Ages, not the Renaissance. "The insecurities and the instability peculiar to many lives in northern and central Italy during the fourteenth and fifteenth centuries necessitated a stronger reliance on one's own resources," contends Weintraub, summarizing Burckhardt's thesis. Those instabilities and insecurities continue to characterize modernity, as Weintraub, who fled the Nazis in World War II, was painfully aware, and so the story of autobiography is carried forward obliquely to the present: "An 'objective' view of the surrounding realities becomes forced upon the personality; a sober statistical inventory of controllable resources helps one to cope more than the best formula for what 'should' be or how a man 'ought' to act." Also in light of Burckhardtian self-reliance, Weintraub distinguishes individuality from the more common, sociopolitical notion of individualism that flourished in the nineteenth and twentieth centuries. Individualism is defined by the *Oxford English Dictionary* as the "social theory which advocates the free and independent action of the individual." Social control is at a minimum in standard nineteenth-century liberalism. Weintraub notes that individualism implies a *relationship*, whereas "individuality," being "the form of self that an individual may seek," implies no such relationship. A society dedicated to rugged individualism might produce nothing but individuals who are copies of one another, effectively suppressing individuality. Yet Weintraub concedes that his ideal society of individualities "seems to demand the freedoms of a society devoted to individuals," even possibly an economic theory that centers on them.[33] For this reason, critics in the Frankfurt School argue that this concept of the self is a microcosm of an ideal totality projected at a utopian moment of class consciousness and within the bourgeois-humanist worldview; the bourgeois self-concept requires a bourgeois power base. It was Karl Weintraub's achievement to have argued the case for individuality in its best light, even as the self was about to come under attack.

If the 1960s saw the shift "from *bios* to *autos*—from the life to the self,"[34] the primordial self had a short run in autobiographical theory. By the 1980s attention had shifted from the *autos* to other literary questions, fanning out to matters concerning the text and intertextuality,[35] myth,[36] genre and typology,[37] techniques or "technologies" of fictionality,[38] the "structuralism of subjectivity" and the "ideology of the self,"[39] the Other,[40] even the rejection of writing itself.[41] Whereas Heidi Stull laments the "now all but meaningless category of autobiography," Sidonie Smith and Julia Watson list four new journals devoted to autobiography and fifty-two subgenres, from "apology" ("self-defense against the allegations or attacks of others") and "ethnic life narrative" to travel writing and trauma narrative ("writing the unspeakable")—a classic example of field formation.[42] In the era of cultural studies, with loose connections to a dozen fields, one is more likely to encounter general notions of "the autobiographical" or "the autobiographical imaginary" rather than "autobiography" as a formal text. Moreover, any life narrative that is circumscribed and tightly unified arouses the suspicion of exclusion and repression, a complaint lodged against Gusdorf.[43] The general definition has reverted to Misch's, that is, virtually any first-person, self-revelatory writing (diary, drama, bildungsroman, poetry, letter, novel). From the margins, autobiography had come to the center of interest, "a battlefield on which competing ideas about literature (and for that matter history) are fought out."[44]

The reigning paradigms claim that traditional concepts of the self—particularly the individuality model, enshrined in the bourgeois epoch—can no longer provide the formal solutions that are expected of them. The autobiographical self cannot shape or control all the evidence of the self; it can only pretend to. The materials that make up a life are too deceitful, self-blinding; many magnets, not just one, lie in the arena of the iron filings. One exaggerates to say that the empirical self completely dissolves under analysis, yet, taking leave of deconstruction and trends in philosophy, psychology, medicine, poststructuralist theory, and postmodernist fiction, drama, and poetry, recent critics of autobiography propose that the self, in Petrarch's words, is "not whole, not complete."[45] The self or (in recent theory) the "subject" is a historically conditioned fiction, a "shifter" that lacks an essence and so assumes meaning only within a discourse or in relation to others. These theories are grounded on the demise of the metanarrative of absolute autonomy (authenticity, wholeness) and the absence of the "objective" world of reference or empirical reality.[46] The self deconstructed is an illusion, a *mise en abîme.* "Man is an invention of a recent date," says Foucault, "and one perhaps nearing to its end." For Paul de Man, autobiography must be "unmasked or 'defaced' as the most suspect of genres because of its claim to write the essence of a self." Jeffrey Mehlman argues that autobiography "proclaims the impossible dream of being alive to oneself in the scriptural"; in doing so, he "joins in a broader tendency to see representation and other displacements as a kind of death." Michael Sprinker comments that "concepts of the subject, self, and author collapse into the act of producing a text"; no "I" means "the end of autobiography." Linking Jürgen Habermas to the critics of modernity from Nietzsche to Adorno, Stephen K. White declares: "Habermas argues that the paradigm of a 'subject-centered' 'philosophy of consciousness' is 'exhausted.'" Genaro M. Padilla describes the complex genealogy of the "discursive formation" or "construction of the immigrant subject," criticizing Robert Redfield for condescension in his discussion of "concrete materials" for "scientific study."[47]

The sovereign self—the subjectivity ideal—has become impoverished and sickly; for some, it has died. Encyclopedia entries appear on "the death of the self," and books and articles are published with titles like *The "Death of the Subject" Explained, Who Comes after the Subject?* and *Feeling in Theory: Emotion after the "Death of the Subject."* This latter reaches an almost hallucinatory conclusion: "If we really were subjects, we would have no emotions at all."[48] The nineteenth century witnessed the so-called disappearance of God, the twentieth century the disappearance of the self.[49]

What has disappeared is the subjectivity ideal. In its place is an assertive self with an ideal of feeling good. With an abundance of evidence the psychologists Roy F. Baumeister and Jean M. Twenge observe that "over the last 30 years, the self has become increasingly individualized and autonomous." They instance the number of self-help books, the "Me" generation, the self-esteem movement (where everyone is a winner and lovable), and the focus upon the self over the other (with the soaring divorce rate and the declining birth rate) diagnosed by Christopher Lasch in *The Culture of Narcissism.* No article on self-esteem or related subjects appeared in the *Reader's Guide to Periodical Literature* in 1965; in 1995 there were twenty-seven. "A search of the Lexis-Nexus database for 1995 articles mentioning self-esteem exceeded the search limit of 1,000 articles; the 1,000-article limit was still exceeded even when the search was limited to a single month (June 1995)."[50] In academic psychology there has been a "virtual explosion of theory and research in recent decades" on the nature of the self.[51]

The rise of autobiographical theory is itself a manifestation of the zeitgeist. The Carlylean captains of industry, whom even Marx admired, have given place to an army of therapists, consultants, mediators, gurus, spokespersons, career specialists, and facilitators. One notes the surprisingly large number of new personality disorders and their therapies. In February 1999 the association Counselling, Advice, Psychotherapy, Advocacy, and Guidance calculated there were in Great Britain 540,000 advice workers, 5,000 advocates, 632,000 counselors, 44,000 guidance workers, 5,500 psychotherapists, and 4,500 mediation workers: a total of 1,231,000 counselors, or ten times the number of police officers in a country of 60 million. As Michael Fitzpatrick comments, "We now inhabit a culture of complaint and victimhood, in which everybody blames somebody or something—their genes, their hormones, their childhood, their parents, their education, their dysfunctional relationships, their adverse experiences—for whatever difficulties they face."[52]

How do all this high and popular theorizing and practice square with the death of the subject? They may best be read as symptoms of the disease, the general feeling of low aspiration, disengagement, and helplessness. Low self-esteem drives the self-esteem movement.

One of the most prominent theorists to analyze the "death of the subject" is the British critic James Heartfield who points to many underlying factors: the diminution of organized labor; the collapse of the French left wing (Foucault, Baudrillard, Althusser), following the steep decline of the French Communist Party in the 1950s; the failure of the student revolts in 1968; and the breakdown of both right and left agendas in the West at the end of the cold war. These and other examples of cultural despair were internalized, engendering cynicism, self-hatred, and misanthropy; one questioned "whether Man was indeed the central figure of the human story, and whether he deserved to be." The Subject (white, male, European) is deconstructed, replaced by the excluded Other. Meanwhile, progressive energies are siphoned off into New Social Movements such as environmentalism, educational reform, no-globalism, animal rights, Slow Food, Third Way, counterculture, health struggles, communitarianism—a fragmentation of the Left (and Right), or what Heartfield calls the "the boundless etcetera of difference." He deplores the oddly conservative nature of these purportedly liberal movements that "recoiled from universalism into particularism" and shunned the rough-and-tumble business of mass politics. "Where early on the talk was of revolutionising sexual relations, race and society, in more recent times the preoccupation is with negotiating power, managing change and maintaining equilibrium." The general failure of nerve has its counterpart in death-of-the-self theorizing: "Without an ideal of subjectivity to live up to, or to challenge, subjectivity itself is degraded."[53]

Heartfield envisions the "retreat of the elite" from its own subjectivity. This retreat or "collapse" has taken many forms: the elite's loss of "confidence in its own achievements," self-flagellation among liberals and conservatives alike, mediocre ideals, fear of solitude and love of aggregation, and the sense that everything is out of one's hands, a reaction to the technical-managerial state and globalization. Walled-in suburbs, a frequent target of postmodern satire, conceal a ruling class that has withdrawn not only from society but also "from the purpose of its own existence," to provide leadership and "act as an elite." Excellence itself is considered a "questionable virtue"; requirements multiply while exams are simplified so that they can be passed easily: "The entire culture is reluctant to demand high standards." The greater number of people entering higher education is offset by the decline in literacy; as one British educator observed, "Improbable as it may seem, it appears that we have rising standards and falling standards at the same time." The distinction between high and popular culture has been lost. Even when avant-gardism attacked the traditional order, it did so to replace it, not to give up on standards: "What the avant-garde shared with the high culture it attacked was a desire to raise itself about the everyday." In the 1960s the avant-garde ceased opposing bourgeois Establishment culture and vice versa, when both met in agreement on the plane of popular culture (film, jazz, television, rock and roll, pop art); the avant-garde soon died. "Today's elites . . . have prostrated themselves before the judgment of the wider public. . . . [T]he city fathers have opened up the gates and surrendered to the imaginary horde." Heartfield's conclusions apply across the West:

> Without an ideal of excellence to strive for, society loses its incentive to progress. Where the values of competitiveness and enterprise are held in low esteem, the motivation to achieve becomes flattened. Cultural achievements are held lightly and the very ability to judge is compromised. The resistance to elite culture carries the appearance of a plebeian revolt from below. Of course the reduction of Western civilization into a badge of superiority was itself a vulgarization. But without any higher ideals to strive for, it is not possible to challenge elitism, only to dumb down.[54]

Since, as a Marxist, Heartfield rarely implicates technology in the erosion of the subjectivity ideal, one may amend his argument: there is no core self powerful enough to resist the germs of decline because it has abandoned its cultural past, opting for smooth efficiency and untroubled consumption.

From the primordial self to the nonself stretches a vast distance, and there is something to be said for wandering back to a middle ground for a workable hypothesis that may help explore current autobiographical theories. Commenting on the wealth of research as yet untapped by cultural-studies scholars, Seyla Benhabib cautions that "the thesis of the Death of the Subject presupposes a remarkably crude version of individuation and socialization processes when compared with currently social scientific reflections on the subject." To glean from these reflections, a relational model of the self has installed itself in the social sciences in the past twenty years, though its origins lie in the chapter on interpersonality in William James's *Principles of Psychology* and its genealogy runs through Charles Horton Cooley, George Herbert Mead, David Riesman, B. F. Skinner, and Jerome Bruner, among many others. In 1971 Skinner wrote that "the great individualists so often cited to show the value of personal freedom have owed their successes to earlier social environments."[55] At the present time Ulric Neisser, Ian Burkitt, Susan M. Andersen, Charles Carver, Serena Chen, M. R. Leary, Roy F. Baumeister, and Jean M. Twenge (again, among many others) have contributed significantly to the social-cognitive theory of the self.

Neisser enumerates five interacting aspects of the self, "so distinct that they are essentially different *selves,*" commencing at different points in the life cycle, though all present by the age of five or so: the ecological self ("certainly by 3 months of age and probably from birth") is "the self as perceived with respect to the physical environment"; the interpersonal self (in place by two months) is "specified by species-specific signals of emotional rapport and communication"; the extended self (by three years) is "based primarily on our personal memories and anticipations"; often taken in Western philosophy as "the only self worth knowing," the private self (by four years) "appears when we discover that our conscious experiences are exclusively our own" (following Isaiah Berlin, Neisser credits Vico as the first to theorize about this form of knowledge in developmental terms); the conceptual self or "self-concept" (unspecified but "very early" in the life cycle) "draws its meaning from a network of socially-based assumptions and theories about human nature in general and ourselves in particular."[56]

Just as Plato's tripartite soul (reason, will, desire) was an image of the state (guardians, soldiers, people), so Neisser's selves mirror contemporary society, with its complexification, functionalism, pluralism, antihierarchism, power sharing, and above all its relationalism. In Plato, reason is the charioteer of the soul. Which self in Neisser's model is responsible? Who is in charge? His model has been praised because "it does not posit a unified self, identifying instead prominent modes of self-information while privileging none of them." Actually, Neisser argues that although the selves "are held together by specific forms of stimulus information," the conceptual self "helps to hold all the others together": "It does so by providing a roughly coherent account of ourselves as persons *in interaction with our neighbors*" (my italics). Such an abstraction is not a lot of glue; worthy of note, the private self has been demoted from its traditional hegemony in favor of conceptualism, about as far from the sense of a unitary self as a rich organic process as one can go. Given the potential for splintering and centrifugality, Neisser asks then, "Why [do] we (usually) experience ourselves as unitary and coherent individuals?" His answer is in terms of information sharing among the selves and with other individuals' selves; when it comes down to responsibility for distortions of memory or irresponsible acts, the answer is "I am"—presumably the conceptual self.[57]

Andersen and Chen base their theory on the "human motivation for belonging and connection" and propose that "the self is relational—even entangled—with significant others and that this has implications for self-definition, self-regulation, and . . . personality functioning." They do not mean that the self is exclusively interpersonal; on the contrary, they point to abundant evidence indicating "that private, internal states are important in self-perception and self-judgment." Nor do they deny the importance of cultural difference in tracking personality development. They want to determine the extent to which mental representation (memory linkages) of a significant other is "activated in an encounter with a new person, leading the perceiver to interpret the person in ways derived from the representation and to respond emotionally, motivationally, and behaviorally to the person in ways that reflect the self-other relationship." Their evidence leads them to conclude that "one's sense of self, including thoughts, feelings, motives, and self-regulatory strategies, may thus vary as a function of relations with significant others"; indeed, one's self is shaped by these experiences: the self and personality are "fundamentally interpersonal."[58]

These findings are seconded by Baumeister and Twenge who also ground their theory on the need to belong: "Although the very concept of the self seems to denote individualism, the self is nevertheless incomplete without acknowledging our interactions with others." No one could deny the balanced truth of this statement, but then the authors move on: "The self is constructed, used, altered, and maintained as a way of connecting the individual organism to other members of the species"; "relating to others is part of what the self is *for*." The emphasis falls on relationalism and adjustment, which dilutes attention to the core; the authors do not explore what one is relating *to*. They observe that the self-esteem movement seems to have enjoyed success since children's scores in the Coopersmith Self-Esteem Inventory rose from the early 1980s to '90s, while there have been corresponding increases in assertiveness and extroversion. But what is the self that is so esteemed? What are its values? What has it accomplished? Their categories (belongingness, ostracism, prosocial behavior, self-defeating behavior, self-presentation, embarrassment, shame, guilt) and their evidence of interest in the self cited above might well lead one to question their conclusion that "over the last 30 years, the self has become increasingly individualized and autonomous." Without a study of the surrounding social ambience, one might as well say that such autonomy is superficial—in Weintraub's terms, it is individualism, and not individuality—and that conformism, the retreat of the elite, and the death of the subject are the more prevalent. "Selves," they rightly state, "do not develop and flourish in isolation."[59] At present it may be more instructive to be reminded of Pascal's *pensée:* "All men's miseries derive from not being able to sit alone in a room."

The relational model should be viewed in tandem with two of the more important theorists of the self in contemporary moral philosophy. In *After Virtue,*

Alasdair MacIntyre proposes a narrative concept of the self: "Man is in his actions and practice, as well as in his fictions, essentially a story-telling animal."
MacIntyre believes in seeing each self as a narrative whole, and like most narratives the self involves *actions* that necessarily entail others in a moral context.
"Narrative history of a certain kind turns out to be the basic and essential genre
for the characterization of human actions." His premise is Aristotelian (neoclassical, Arnoldian): "Character determines men's qualities, but it is by their
actions that they are happy or the reverse"; character is fully realized only in a
plot that is "serious, complete, and of a certain magnitude" (*Poetics,* chap. 6).
For MacIntyre, a life should not be arbitrarily separated from its social context,
as in existentialism, where society is seen as the realm of the conventional, absurd, or unauthentic as opposed to the potentially authentic self; or, on the
other hand, the self should not be dissolved into so many exercises in role-
playing without a central governing self informed by "intentions, beliefs, settings." Since we put together our own lives as narratives, with intentions, a
causal and temporal order, a setting, we tend to make narratives of others too,
and study history and even fiction for similar selves. "The notion of intelligi-
bility is the conceptual connecting link between the notion of action and that
of narrative." The self, as in Cicero's *narratio,* should be intelligible, plausible,
and accountable. What is the unity of a human life? MacIntyre's answer is
that it is the "unity of a narrative quest," where the word *quest* contains quasi-
religious associations. Such a view does not guarantee success in attaining
one's goal, but, in the event, character is proved in action. Quests sometimes
succeed, and sometimes fail.[60]

Charles Taylor's approach to the relational self (though he does not use the
term) is through moral philosophy and history. Like MacIntyre, he is linked to
the neo-Aristotelian revival in his attempt to ground values in a nonnaturalis-
tic realm and espouses an ideal of community. Taylor presents a richly detailed
picture of the historical development of "highly independent individualism"
that "many people consider the finest achievement of modern civilization" and
is "peculiarly powerful in American culture." This ideal of self-authenticity entails
the right to choose one's life, to act on conscience and make one's own decisions, to be true to one's self, to find "*my* way." It has its knockers and boosters,
both on the right and on the left. Its knockers complain that authenticity has
led to moral relativism, deviancy, anticommunalism, a loss of higher values,
and a caving in to "pitiable comfort" (Nietzsche): "The dark side of individualism is a centring on the self, which both flattens and narrows our lives, makes
them poorer in meaning, and less concerned with others or society." Its boosters
want still more individualism, more freedom, "more of more." Taylor awards
points to both sides. Unlike other critics of modernity, such as Allan Bloom,

Daniel Bell, Christopher Lasch, and Robert Bellah, he does not disparage the ideal of authenticity in itself, yet he deplores its degraded contemporary manifestations. "Modes that opt for self-fulfilment without regard (a) to the demands of our ties with others or (b) to demands of any kind of emanating from something more or other than human desires or aspirations are self-defeating, they destroy the conditions for realizing authenticity itself." In the romantic period, Taylor thinks, we came closer to an ideal balance between the self and others, and between the human community and nature, as in Goethe and Wordsworth. He criticizes late modernity for its "rejecting our past as irrelevant, or denying the demands of citizenship, or the duties of solidarity, or the needs of the natural environment."[61] In sum, the ideal is not at fault; rather, it suffers malaise, and it can grow healthy by returning to its sources and by retrieving a broader moral perspective, as suggested by the titles of Taylor's books: *Sources of the Self* and *The Ethics of Authenticity* (originally, *The Malaise of Authenticity*).

How can we repair the damage to the ideal of authenticity? The nub of Taylor's argument concerns what he calls the manner versus the matter of authenticity. He accepts the manner that stipulates that the clearinghouse of history, ideals, and values must be referred to the individual self because there are no longer shared assumptions like the great chain of being, Christian sacramentalism, or a public vision of a cosmic order. But this should not mean that the matter or content needs to be exclusively self-referential "*as against* something that stands beyond these": God, a political cause, the environment, the community, tradition, and what he calls "epiphanies of modernism" (readings of such writers as Rilke, Eliot, and Pound that reveal transcendent worlds of value). The matter of authenticity is unnecessarily restricted to "subjective goods" and "values." Liberal neutrality and Mill's negative liberty have meant a moral relativism in light of the ideal of authenticity, with a failure to acknowledge that "some forms of life are indeed *higher* than others." Above all, Taylor sees the good life in terms of a community. Even where the self draws "its purposes, goals, and life-plans out of itself . . . one cannot be a self on one's own"; that is, even where the manner remains the self, the self must realize that the matter and moral goal must be referred to a point beyond the self. In this respect, as with MacIntyre, a "basic condition" for understanding ourselves is that "we grasp our lives in a *narrative*," which will reveal the connectives between ourselves and others and the ends beyond them: the self is "something which can exist only in a space of moral issues." He appropriates George Herbert Mead's concept of "significant others" and M. M. Bakhtin's notion of "inner dialogicality."[62] Some will question whether Taylor's approach is too idealistic. Can one expect people to reexamine the sources of the romantic harmony of the self and others or to yield an inch on their individualism and give up on their comforts?

In an interesting aside Taylor turns his attention to contemporary academe. There is not just one "slide" in the culture of authenticity, but two, and both lead to decadent forms of individualism. The first is in popular culture with its material appetitiveness and low aspirations. The second is high cultural nihilism as expressed in, say, deconstruction: descending also from romantic self-expression via Nietzsche, it is now a "shallow" "prolongation of the least impressive side of modernism." The odd thing about this "subjectivism of self-celebration" is that it manages to preach the death of the subject while asserting the most tremendous power of the self toward independence, free play, conscious self-fashioning, and aesthetic representation. "Nothing emerges from this flux worth affirming, and so what in fact comes to be celebrated is the deconstructing power itself, the prodigious power of subjectivity to undo all the potential allegiances which might bind it: pure untrammelled freedom."[63] Taylor saves his harshest criticism for this school; filtering down, their ideas corrupt (even further) popular culture, leaving it without direction to remedy its miseries.

In one way or another, relationalism and community inform much of autobiographical theory since the 1970s. One of the trailblazers was Elizabeth W. Bruss. Her well-argued *Autobiographical Acts: The Changing Situation of a Literary Genre* (1976) draws on the speech-act philosophy of Austin, Strawson, and Searle; the reception criticism of Hans Jauss; as well as Saussurean linguistics, and proposes a "functional" theory of autobiography. Like speech-acts, autobiographical "acts" perform and fulfil a variety of functions through language, though the material form of the language may differ widely (letters, interviews, confessions, and the like).

To seize upon what is special to the genre of the autobiographical, Bruss establishes a working definition of genre itself, based on the notion of the illocutionary nature of utterance: its capacity to assert, command, promise, question, and so on. Each genre is not merely an action but an "interaction"; a text depends upon "implicit contextual conditions, participants involved in transmitting and receiving it." Theoretically, these conditions are infinite; practicality requires that one draw the line: "Just as speaking is made up of different types of action carried out by means of language, the system of actions carried out through literature consists of its various genres. An illocutionary act is an association between a piece of language and certain contexts, conditions and intentions." How can a genre retain its identity while allowing for significant variation? Although Bruss does not explain the rise of a genre, she elaborates four ways in which an individual work may vary from the type: (1) variation of textual features denoting the generic function of the text, (2) degree of integration between the generic function and other functional features, (3) variability in the literary value attached to the genre, and (4) variability in the illocutionary value of the genre at a given historical moment. For instance, with regard to the first, the changes that a genre undergoes depend upon its relation to other genres: the decline of letter writing gave the autobiography the chance to absorb functions of intimacy and spontaneity. The creation of the first-person bourgeois novel of realism relieved autobiography of the necessary acts of direct observation, eyewitness testimony, and "density of domestic detail," enabling autobiography to take a more subjective nineteenth-century turn.[64] These other acts were not eliminated entirely, but they were, in Jurij Tynjanov's term, "effaced." As for the second, a work like John Bunyan's autobiography, written early in the English history of the genre, was barely distinguishable from conversion narratives. It was difficult to pick up on the illocutionary markers that signal "autobiography." As the genre became established, however, the signals become so obvious that they were taken for granted. Even a title page might suffice, such as a magazine titled *True Confessions*. These markers became so embedded that they could be subverted only radically, as in Gertrude Stein's *Autobiography of Alice B. Toklas* and *Everybody's Autobiography*.

Having established these generic parameters, Bruss focuses on the constitutive order of rules, which apply to the making of autobiography and to the reading of it, because the rules map out the expectations of the audience. If the rules are violated, there are consequences—accusations of insincerity or even fraud, as when Clifford Irving was sentenced to jail for publishing the autobiography of Howard Hughes without authorization:

Rule 1. An autobiographer undertakes a dual role. He is the source of the subject matter and the source for the structure to be found in the text. (a) The author claims individual responsibility for the creation and arrangement of his text. (b) The individual who is exemplified in the organization of the text is purported to share the identity of an individual to whom reference is made via the subject matter of the text. (c) The existence of this individual, independent of the text itself, is assumed to be susceptible to appropriate public verification procedures.

Rule 2. Information and events reported in connection with the autobiographer are asserted to have been, to be, or to have potential for being case. (a) Under existing conventions, a claim is made for the truth-value of what the autobiography reports—no matter how difficult that truth—value might be to ascertain, whether the report treats of private experiences or publicly observable occasions. (b) The audience is expected to accept these reports as true, and is free to "check up" on them or attempt to discredit them.

    Rule 3. . . . [T]he autobiographer purports to believe in what he asserts.[65]

These rules are meant to allow for the dynamically "changing situation" of the genre. They persist, as Bruss points out, even as autobiography has draped itself in various guises, as when it adopted the style of the seventeenth-century sermon, when it incorporated eighteenth-century representationalism and nineteenth-century psychological realism, and when it acquired the habits of modernist prose and underwent restructuring from the experiments with postmodernist fiction. (A separate chapter presents stylistic and thematic features indicating how the "act" is transferred to the "text".) Bruss maintains a middle position; her definition overcomes the division between memoir and autobiography and so is broader than Roy Pascal's. She criticizes Pascal for his privileging the individuality model when he blamed the "greatest number of autobiographies" for a "certain falling short in respect of the whole personality," "a lack of moral responsibility towards their task, a lack of awareness and insight."[66] On the other side, Bruss's concern for information, events, and truth value make her definition narrower than Olney's. Indeed, she is among the few critics in recent memory to invoke sincerity as a value.

    Bruss is not only interested in this (for her) fundamental distinction between fact and fiction. She recognizes in, say, a writer like Boswell the opposition between new kinds of subjective fact, and then, in the nineteenth century, in the opposition between the transcendental subject and the psychological creature, as in Kant's *Anthropologie.* Her study proceeds by comparison and contrast through strong readings of Bunyan, Boswell's *Journals,* De Quincey, and Nabokov. Significant biographical facts enter into a context where they become autobiography or fiction. Both De Quincey's *Autobiographical Sketches* and his *Suspiria de Profundis* (the little-known forty-page sequel to the *Confessions of an English Opium-Eater*) begin with the same focus on personal history, even with the same arresting chapter title, "The Affliction of Childhood." Yet the first is succeeded by fourteen other autobiographical episodes leading toward a sense of the narrator's "egocentricity," "sentimentality," and "whimsy." The second moves beyond autobiographical event and transforms experience into "universal dream language": the work issues in "tragic resolution." The Dark Interpreter of *Suspiria de Profundis* has no formal counterpart in the *Sketches.* Even their readers differ: the *Sketches* are directed toward an audience "indifferently singular or plural"; with its lyrical "communion" of author and reader, *Suspiria de Profundis* seems written for a very private audience, the kind about which Brahms (thinking of his late intermezzi) said, "One listener is almost too many."[67]

Autobiography and biography have remained among the most popular nonfiction genres for the past three centuries (surpassed only by travel writing). "The autobiographical endeavour has endured," points out Bruss, "and variety, human variety, may be the secret of its endurance." Like an institution, it has absorbed change by changing, "first toward individualism and representational realism, psychological density, and sociological particularity, and then toward expressionistic form." Toward the end of her study Bruss cites from Claude Lévi-Strauss's *Tristes Tropiques* on the death of the subject: "Not merely is the first person singular detestable; there is no room for it between 'ourselves' and 'nothing.'" Are we prepared to drop the "I" for the generic "we"? Bruss seems frankly puzzled: "With so much of life and even identity beyond our personal control, we perhaps cling all the more fiercely to an institution which offers us at least one remaining area of symbolic power over our destiny as individuals." That institution, autobiography, may appear to be a frail raft in such a storm. Bruss simply acknowledges the forces (conformism, technological society, culture industry, and the like) that have brought us back to the "one remaining area of symbolic power," that is, the autobiographic page, the reflex of the individual soul. "Despite attacks upon the notion of individuality," she asserts bravely, "it is still at the center of the way we organize and imagine life in our society and in our literature." Four years later, in 1980, she is concerned that film and video are displacing literature as the preferred system of representation. These media do not provide the conditions allowing for the peculiar subjective depth and analytic reflection required of the autobiographical act; "if . . . there is no real cinematic equivalent for autobiography, then the autobiographical act as we have known it for the past four hundred years could indeed become more and more recondite, and eventually extinct."[68]

In a 1984 interview J. Hillis Miller said he was inclined to agree that the self is a sociological necessity in present culture—how else could we be held accountable for a promissory note or a mortgage payment? However, deconstructive practice constrained him to accept provisionally that language is "prior to selfhood," that the self is "generated by language." The biological and anthropological evidence support language as one constituent, but hardly the only one; the most recent theories stress interrelationship, not priority. Nietzsche's belief that the self is constituted by a "congeries of warring selves" has textual analogies in nineteenth-century fiction where the self, taken to be primordial, is also made problematic. In George Meredith's *Egoist,* Clara Middleton comes to realize that her decision to marry Willoughby has presupposed a "fixed and unified self on the basis of which promises can be made," whereas she knows that she does not possess such a self. In Meredith's words, she is "a multitude of flitting wishes." Without intending to weaken his position, Miller thinks that questions of selfhood "should be raised in a relatively safe area like novels rather than in other areas" (one thinks of criminal responsibility in a trial). The interviewer, recalling Miller's essay "The Function of Rhetorical Study at the Present Time," asked whether deconstruction only affirmed the self in the very process of calling it into question. Miller agreed that it had, again repairing to Nietzsche. It should be noted, however, that this questioning and affirming of self had been a hallmark of bourgeois selfhood going back to the seventeenth century. According to Sacvan Bercovitch, the Puritans struggled dialectically with selfhood: one denies the self in order to imitate Christ. Yet every effort to repress the self only seemed to energize it the more. He speaks of the Puritans' ambivalence and "horror at the 'very name of *Own,*' their determination 'to *Hate* our *selves* and *ours,*' their opposing views of *soul* and *self*. . . . We cannot help but feel that the Puritans' urge for self-denial stems from the very subjectivism of their outlook, that their humility is coextensive with personal assertion."[69] To continue this line of reasoning, assertions of moral superiority may mask self-interest. Nevertheless, after deconstruction, the notion of the "fixed and unified" self was no longer the starting point in autobiography studies.

In *The Changing Nature of the Self: A Critical Study of the Autobiographic Discourse* (1987), arguing from perspectives within poststructuralism and Marxism, Robert Elbaz proposes a historically and culturally determined approach to the self, a conclusion of the story begun by Weintraub, that is, what happened to autobiography after Goethe. Unlike Weintraub, Elbaz traces the "centralised, territorialised, rational, methodic, self-sufficient, free, responsible and contractual selfhood" back to Augustine and Abelard; its dominant exponents are Descartes and Rousseau, and the model was overthrown in the twentieth century by writers like Malraux for whom "the self is not and cannot be defined. . . . It constitutes an ongoing process of redefinition dependent upon the transcendental-historical phenomena which shape it." Elbaz disapproves of the typological approach to autobiography (Shumaker and Lejeune) because it reifies the concept of an ahistorical genre, and "generic classification has to do with institutionalisation—canonisation, and therefore fetishisation—of literature." Genre criticism (Shapiro and Pascal) tends to circularity, hypostatizing a typical text that embodies formal characteristics previously synthesized. The "dynamic" approach to autobiography (Bruss and Renza) is rejected since it bases itself on a transcendent structure with historical mutation—better than the typological, but still too much extratextual reification. Elbaz spurns autobiographical theories that rest on the division of fiction and factuality as they are founded upon naive empiricism. Stephen A. Shapiro and Roy Pascal are faulted for their empirical ideology and mimetic theories. Louis A. Renza fares better: he at least focuses on "writing" and on autobiography as the "interpretation of the present," not on the "recreation of the past" that would valorize the historical moment. But Renza does not escape the problem of fact and fiction.

His "split intentionality" between the persona of the autobiographer and the real author regurgitates the ideology of the self, "although this self is not what the autobiography is about since it is limited to the writing performance." Renza even reintroduces the problem of classification by proposing a new genre: autobiography "is neither fictive nor non-fictive, not even a mixture of the two"; it is a "unique, self-defining mode of self-referential expression, one that allows, then inhibits, the projection of self-presentation, of converting oneself into the present promised by language,"[70] that is, a "text."

Unlike these critics, Elbaz makes his work a good deal easier by his dismissal of a referential component of autobiography; his critique of Louis Renza on historical re-creation is an instance of the great forgetting. "Autobiography, it is held, purports to represent a 'truth' about a given reality (through its duplication), while fiction does not. It will be argued, however, that through the processes of mediation (by linguistic reality) and suspension (due to the text's lack of finality and completion), autobiography can only be a fiction." Yet does not Elbaz himself introduce lords, vassals, and the Magna Carta into his discussion of medieval subjectivity? Are they mere wandering ghosts? By reducing everything to language, Elbaz has only shifted the problems onto another plane. "The text can no longer be classified due to its ceaseless beginning, its endless process of productivity: it exists only to the extent that it produces meaning. Textuality, in opposition to the specific work, the specific genre, is a field of play for an endless process of transformation and metamorphosis." The typological and dynamic models had postulated a particular ideology of the self, according to which the self has a "pre-given structure" (like a "finished product"), is "free" (an attribute of exchange relations in the free market), and becomes a saleable commodity in the form of an autobiography. Elbaz cannot fail to notice the concentration on the self or at least self-promotion in  celebrity autobiographies and the self-promotion in self-orientation industry, examined by Edwin M. Schur in *The Awareness Trap: Self-Absorption Instead of Social Change* (1977).[71]

To say that "everybody has a self" or that "the self exhibits continuity in change" is only common sense, but Elbaz wants attention focused on autobiography as both a process of the production of meaning and as a construction of the self. For this reason he resists any method that imposes its ideology on the "ceaseless flow" of structuration. The division of fact from fiction, the separation of person from persona, the valorization of the self (as in R. D. Laing's "good" madness), the insistence upon closure (the form of the life isomorphic with the form of the work): each breaks the flow of historical change and gives an impression of fixity. Elbaz reminds one of Heraclitus's disciple Cratylus, who interpreted Heraclitus's "all things flow" so strictly that he refused to speak, believing that by the time his observation had escaped his lips, the universe would have changed and so proved him wrong. So he only wagged his finger.

Two writers who create a postmodern concept of autobiography are Gertrude Stein and André Malraux. Stein exemplifies the crisis in modern autobiographical practice and therefore of the self. Elbaz cites approvingly a passage from *The Autobiography of Alice B. Toklas:* "About six weeks ago Gertrude Stein said it does not look to me as if you were ever going to write that autobiography. You know what I am going to do. I am going to write it for you. I am going to write it simply as Defoe did the autobiography of Robinson Crusoe and she has and there is it." Elbaz admires the passage for three reasons: it stands at the conclusion of the book instead of (where one might expect it) at the beginning in order to show that the life story "cannot be laid out in full detail from beginning to end; the significance of that life cannot be exhausted in a single narrative." Then, Stein "speaks" in the voice of a mediator, Toklas, aware that the "consistency and the continuity of the 'I' are mystifications."[72] Last, the reference to Crusoe as model for autobiography calls attention to the sheer fictionality of the process.

If Stein's work expresses the crisis in autobiography, Malraux's *Antimémoires* (1965) is the achieved masterpiece of a new form. Its definition of selfhood "negates concepts of truth and veracity by abolishing the distinction between reality and falsehood," thereby fostering the fictional self. Quite consciously, the book presents considerable readerly difficulties: it presupposes knowledge of all Malraux's novels and other writings—and only then, initially, will it resemble nothing more than a vast jigsaw puzzle where many pieces do not seem to fit. Elbaz's model of autobiography can justly be said to account for its organization. For him, Malraux "seems to have forgotten himself with a vengeance" and emarginates most of the biographical part. Times and voices overlap, and, by means of simultaneity and juxtaposition, chronology is baffled beyond recognition; repetitions destroy expectations of development; characters from fictional works enter and tell stories about other characters and events in real life; there is "negation of closure"; imaginary conversations take place between world-historical figures. Through it all, Malraux tells the story of a life immersed in twentieth-century history; he is not (like Adams) the sole proprietor of his relations with history, and his book shows all the complexities of these relations. His "meaning" lies somewhere between the story he tells and history itself, and, as Elbaz cautions, only retroactive interpretation—after the fact of history—can solve the problem of meaning, but *that* interpretation in turn is subject to its own immersion in history, and so on. "Meaning is the metaphorisation of history by the story," and autobiography in particular is the "story of the phenomena which continually give birth to that self."

Even memory (and individual time), the last bastion of selfhood, is now a "secondary process" in that creation; memory is no longer the "primary organising principle of experience."[73] What is that principle? Each autobiographer must discover that "cluster of experiences" around which the biographical details are organized. It was God's time for Augustine, individual time for James, and historical time for Malraux. The achievement of Malraux is that he has forged both a "new form" of the autobiographical and, in so doing, has transcended the "world view in which the world is reduced to the self." The liberal humanist or existentialist view of the "tragic" Malraux gives way before the historical figure uniting art and revolution.

The career of Paul John Eakin is instructive in plotting the shifting fortunes of autobiography studies, given that his stated goals have been "redefining autobiography, recasting its canon, and rewriting its history." In 1976, solidly Gusdorfian, he wrote that an "uncompromising commitment to the truth of one's own nature . . . will yield at the last . . . a final and irreducible selfhood." Nevertheless, even then doubts nagged as he questioned if an autobiographer could "keep pace with the biographical fact of 'a ceaselessly evolving identity.'" In 1985, at a time when selves, cities, and nations were becoming "texts," and with his Pyrrhonism on the rise, Eakin wondered "whether the self . . . is literally discovered, made 'visible' in autobiography, or is only invented by it as a signature, a kind of writing, is beyond our knowing." By 1997 he is reluctant to speak of "the self" at all because the definite article might imply "something too fixed and unified": "Now I prefer to think of 'self' less as an entity and more as a kind of awareness in process." His theorizing recalls Proust on the gap between experience and memory: "We never catch ourselves in the act of becoming selves," comments Eakin. "There is always a gap or rupture that divides us from the knowledge that we seek." True enough, yet just because one lacks absolute knowledge does not mean that one has to go to the opposite extreme of the death of the subject: "the myth of autonomy dies hard"; autobiography promotes an "illusion of self-determination"; "our sense of continuous identity is a fiction"; "the reign of the Gusdorfian model will surely end." No self can determine 100 percent of its fate—this is a truism—but to say that it has no control over it is absurd. Machiavelli gave it 30 percent to 50 percent if one used all one's power of reflection and calculation. Eakin turns away from the inner being to the outside, to others, in an emotional flutter: "Why . . . did it take me so long to respond to the relational dimension of identity experience if it is indeed as fundamental as I now claim?"[74]

To borrow Samuel Johnson's rebuke to critics for attacking Shakespeare on the unities, Eakin "assumes, as an unquestionable principle, a position, which, while his breath is forming it into words, his understanding pronounces to be false." Despite his pronouncements on the death of the self, his report of his intellectual career conveys all the marks of a classical autobiography: the first-person singular, self-reflection, personal emotion, memory and the differentiation of time periods, progressive development, and self-discovery or epiphany. Small wonder he elsewhere calls the self "indispensable." Though Eakin may decry the "referential aesthetic" or the "referential pretensions" of the genre, he includes dates and facts and expects us (as Bruss would want) to believe in them; his book has 154 footnote references and a 15-page bibliography that must contain thousands of other references. As with so much else dealing with the self, it is a matter of nuance. "Why do we so easily forget that the first person of autobiography is truly plural in its origins and subsequent formation?" Rhetorically, his intensifiers *easily* and *truly* de-tensify by protesting too much; one could as easily reply that the self is truly singular in its origins—and be as inaccurate. One of Eakin's sentences begins glibly: "While commendably repudiating 'the whole Western tradition of binary thinking . . .'" How commendable, to repudiate not just a part, but the *whole* Western tradition "of binary thinking," one of enormous scientific and humanistic achievement. This is a caricature of Western science, a swipe at the West. But if Eakin rejects dualisms such as subject-object and male-female, he must know that dialectical reasoning is also a part of the Western tradition going back to Plato. In all likelihood binarism in literary criticism did not come from the "whole Western tradition" so much as from New Critical practice, where it served to stack oppositions and bring out ironies. "The selves we display are doubly constructed, not only in the act of writing a life story but also in the lifelong process of identity formation." Words like *construction* and *text* (and his *discursive* and *discourse*) imply that the most fugitive social and psychological processes can be premeditated, which again gives the lie to self-determination as illusory.[75]

Eakin will not abandon the self because his wide readings in cognitive science, neurology, biomedical technology, developmental psychology, and feminist theory have given him a deep appreciation for what he calls "relational" or "interactive" autobiography. His central thesis is that "the self is defined by—and lives in terms of—its relations with others," a far more sensible position than to say that the self is "plural." Following studies of psychologists such as Ian Burkitt, John Shotter, and Daniel N. Stern, he objects to the false oppositions between models of autonomy (male, autonomous, individualistic, narrative, and unified self) and models of relationalism (female, relational, collectivist, and nonnarrative) that marked earlier theories of autobiography. Autobiographies written by men may be as relational as any by women, and autobiographies by women can be as individualist as any man's. Carolyn Kay Stedman's *Landscape for a Good Woman: A Story of Two Lives* (1986) is both individualist and relational. Where earlier feminist theory, having focused upon the conventional oppositions, had the unintended effect of reinforcing instead of overcoming them, Eakin finds multiple modes of crossing (race and ethnicity, class, gender, the body, and so on), steering a middle ground between the autonomy and relationalism with strong supportive evidence. The self is deeply implicated by a "proximate other": father-son—Philip Roth's *Patrimony* (1991) and Blake Morison's *And When Did You Last See Your Father? A Son's Memoir of Love and Loss* (1993); mother-daughter—Vivian Gornick's *Fierce Attachments: A Memoir* (1987) and Janet Campbell's *Bloodlines: Odyssey of a Native Daughter* (1993); father-daughter—Mary Gordon's *The Shadow Man* (1996); mother-son—Robert Dessaix's *A Mother's Disgrace* (1994) and James McBride's *The Color of Water: A Black Man's Tribute to His White Mother* (1996). Collaboration is no mere "as told to" autobiography. In Kim Chernin's *In My Mother's House: A Daughter's Story* (1983) the mother, Rose Chernin, the Russian immigrant and social activist, asks her daughter to write her life story. In the long process of composition, the autobiography covers four generations of Chernin women, making it the autobiography of not only a mother-daughter relationship but also a family. John Edgar Wideman in *Brothers and Keepers* (1984) tells how he became a college professor and novelist while his brother was sentenced to life imprisonment. The narrative draws on the brothers' mutual search for the reasons behind their current lives, "uncovering within the walls of the prison that paradoxically brings them together the walls that kept them apart when they were growing up in a black ghetto of Pittsburgh." Beyond these examples of "relational autobiography," straightforward ones can be read in this light: James's *Small Boy and Others* and *Notes of a Son and Brother, The Autobiography of Malcolm X*, Alfred Kazin's *Walker in the City*.[76]

Dickens put the matter of relationalism in the balance: "David Copperfield" writes the first sentence of the novel that will become *David Copperfield*: "Whether I shall turn out to be the hero of my own life, or whether that station will belong to someone else, these pages will show."

Continuing in the line of the "death of the subject" studies, Julia Watson deconstructs the self of canonical autobiography, which is white, male, and European oriented, in favor of a relational model that expands on contemporary feminist theory. In Western biography and autobiography—Plutarch's *Lives* is a prominent example—the expectation is that "the significant, usually public, events of the life of a 'great' person will be recounted." To this component of "monumental Western selfhood" Watson gives the term *bios*, distinguishing it from identity or the self; the *bios* "signals the significance of a life within authorized traditions of representing lives in Western culture." How exactly this fits into Augustine's or Dante's autobiographies, which are canonical, but hardly "public" or official, she does not say. Until recently, and as a result of the enduring "*bios*-bias," the emarginated groups—women, the poor, those discriminated against for reasons of race or ethnicity—have fallen outside the pale of the autobiographically worthy. Although she applauds the "new model" attempts to destabilize the subject, the "*bios*-bias" holds on, with some adjustments—for instance, in treating noncanonical autobiographies of canonical writers. She questions canonical models derived from Mary McCarthy ("her proximity to the world of New York publishing, the Great Tradition, and the *New York Review of Books* hardly makes her typical of the great majority of women"), Lillian Hellman, Malcolm X, James Baldwin, and what she calls "sanitized" treatments of Gertrude Stein or Maxine Hong Kingston. As she demonstrates persuasively, however, even canonical writers like Montaigne, Rilke, and De Quincey can be shown to have written "trangressive boundary texts that disrupt the genre's *bios*-based self-definition." In this respect she has been influenced by Nancy Chodorow, Mary G. Mason, and Susan Stanford Friedman, who explores "the notion of fluid or permeable ego boundaries to describe the sense of collective identification and yearning for maternal nurturance and community" in contemporary autobiographies by women. Friedman's alternative canon would include Charlotte Perkins Gilman, Anaïs Nin, Isabella Leitner, Ntozake Shange, HD, and Audre Lorde.[77]

Like Eakin, Watson gives a reading of the German socialist novelist Christa Wolf's *Patterns of Childhood*. Wolf, who grew up in Nazi Germany and was a member of the Hitler youth movement, wrote about three phases of her life, suppressing the "I" as unreliable and employing the second and third persons as well as a fictitious name for the central character. "All characters" in her book are "the invention of the narrator," though (or because) they are based upon the most painstaking investigation into actual experiences. Eakin, using his own terms, understands Wolf as writing an "*intra*relational life" in order "to reforge the link between selves past and present." Watson associates these and other rhetorical strategies with the larger social and historical forces that shape her life and narrative: "To see the self as an 'individual,' that is, outside of and 'transcending' the circumstantial context—the emphasis of traditional autobiography that the *bios*-bias insists on—is for Wolf a willed delusion that, on a national level, may create culture but also permits atrocities against those whose subject status has been denied or revoked." At the same time, neither Eakin nor Watson can account for Wolf's Goethean observation regarding a "strange lack of individuality in the behaviour of many contemporaries."[78] It would seem that only good individuality can drive out the bad.

Cyber-age critics show no letup on theorizing on autobiography. If Elizabeth Bruss wrote an epitaph for the genre, Michael Renov argues that it has been "reborn" in a way that responds to our need for "speed" and "accessibility"; as so often, the technological values are assumed as a "need." Film and video are taking over from writing as the "chief means of recording, informing and entertaining," and new forms of autobiography have emerged alongside them. He focuses upon the personal Web page, running from mere information to elaborate showcases and photo albums. Currently available on the Internet are various how-to sites: *"Memories & Reflections" Autobiography Kit* is produced by a company that advertises itself as an "expert in preserving the memories of a lifetime"; it will make family history taking "fun, easy and affordable," at $49.95. (The site trades apparently on the title of C. G. Jung's *Memories, Dreams, Reflections,* truncated for lack of space.) *Cyberscribes 1: The New Journalists* has a section on "Writing the Story of Your Life" that does not pull any punches: "Define and design yourself as if you are a product to be sold." MY BIO and MY STORY are online products; the latter, "easy to use," lures customers with formulaic software: "Describe who you really are in your own words"; "No one like you has ever been; you and your life are unique." When advertisers get buyers to believe that a product can help empower the self, it flies off the shelves.

In all these developments Renov finds signs that autobiography, "far from being extinguished, has in fact proliferated, percolating down to the level of popular, commercial culture." What he fails to consider is that the individuals poured into these software dummies will in all likelihood come out looking roughly similar, and whatever individuality they have will be flattened en route: the software is a perfect example of an Ellulian technique applied across the board. Yet Renov welcomes the personal Web site as "one manifestation of that 'tremendous shattering of tradition' of which Benjamin wrote." Renov takes comfort in these "small victories," the fact that personal Web sites have sidestepped some of the worst aspects of commodity capitalism and situated themselves in "small, alternative spaces," as "artisanal sites squatting within the precincts of high-powered corporate culture." One sentence captures his autobiographical philosophy of freedom and feel-good populism: "Whether garage bands, amateur pornography or zines [fanzines, fan magazines], these cultural forms, peripheral though they may be, can achieve a measure of autonomy and relatively free circulation, mobilising values other than those current in mainstream culture." Although personal Web sites go "from the homespun to the whimsical, from the lyrical to the mordant," they share "ephemerality" in contrast to the solid "fetishised" book. Joining ephemerality to Walter Benjamin's notion of the loss of artistic aura in an age of mechanical reproduction, he argues that the personal Web page is a type of autobiography that "has sacrificed its object status."[79] Does not the ephemeral imply, too, a lack of significance?

The sacrificial selves assume the immateriality of cyberspace. So much for the memories of a lifetime.

But what of the individual of the future? In "Kin or Clone: Contemporary Biotechnologies of the Self," Sarah Kember reviews a growing literature on the "challenges posed by the Internet, cloning, transgenesis and artificial life to the unitary, authentic, well-defined self—and to (natural) life itself." Sherry Turkle is perhaps the most widely known investigator of the impact the computer screen has in our daily lives. "When we step through the screen into virtual communities," explains Turkle, "we reconstruct our identities on the other side of the looking glass. This reconstruction is our cultural work in progress." Fifty years ago, the same lofty claims were made for television. As she wonders in "Cyborg Dreams": "We are encouraged to think of ourselves as fluid, emergent, decentralized, multiplicitous, flexible, and ever in process. The metaphors travel freely among computer science, psychology, children's games, cultural studies, artificial intelligence, literary criticism, advertising, molecular biology, self-help and artificial life."[80]

In her "Cyborg Manifesto," Donna Haraway welcomes the possibilities of identity transformation in a general breakdown between humans and machines (in fact, as Kember notes, "between all apparently discrete disciplines, objects and entities"). Since in her view nature is not so much discovered as constructed, it can be reinvented. In relational terms the subject, the object, and the onlooker are "kin"; the FemaleMan and the Onco-Mouse (a commodity used in cancer research) "have a common circulatory system." Relationalism has turned into something else: "Who are my kin in this odd world of promising monsters . . . ?" How does such a monster write a memoir? What history could it possibly have?[81]

On the subject of human cloning Gunther S. Stent argues that one Einstein or Monroe is fine, but "the idea of having hundreds or thousands of their replicas in town is a nightmare." For him the problem is "the generally shared belief in the uniqueness of the soul. Even though the soul is incorporeal, it is supposed to fit the body, hence it is not conceivable that a unique soul should inhabit each of thousands of identical bodies. Self-replication through cloning threatens to destroy the notion of the self in as far as it is tied to the concept of a unique, authentic soul."[82] But it is entirely possible that by the advent of human cloning, diversity will already have been so reduced by other means of the technological system that there will be a relatively smooth transition.

Future society will extend human life by interchangeable, manufactured parts. Although many of these developments are sold for their genuine medical benefit, this is really the side benefit of the disturbing main thrust. With sperm sorting, cloning, and other interventions, breakthroughs in consumer or designer genetics will enable us to fashion offspring on a genetic template, to determine gender and all sorts of qualities. But the choice is really an illusion because one will be ordering on the basis of advertising in reference to set patterns of social engineering and a limited set of cultural stereotypes. A universe of things presents itself in the ever increasing ascendancy of nominal over verbal style;[83] the norm will be the passive voice.

# Don DeLillo

## Ethnicity, Religion, and the Critique of Technology

There is "no widely recognized body of work" in American literature by Italian Americans about "the Italian experience in America," wrote Gay Talese in 1993. Why, given a population of some twenty million, were they "so *under-represented* in the ranks of well-known creative American writers?" Talese's question provoked the ire of Italian American scholars and critics, not to mention writers. Some protested by publishing lists of significant Italian American novels, while others presented claims for neglected writers such as John Fante, Pietro di Donato, and John Ciardi. *Italian Americana* published a symposium presenting various responses to Talese's question. As Dana Gioia observed in his contribution, Talese had not suggested that Italian American fiction is negligible or unworthy, but that it had not been "widely recognized" on the national scene. "Whatever disagreements I have with Talese's thesis," his article is a "valuable, levelheaded, and engaging discussion of an issue that is usually ignored by mainstream American *literati* and distorted with partisan rhetoric among Italians."[1]

A weakness that went unnoticed in Talese's article is its unduly narrow concept of the ethnic writer. To infer from his examples, the (a) novelist or dramatist (Talese excluded poets) should be (b) a person of Italian American descent (c) writing about Italian American subject matter (d) in an open idiom. This strict-constructionist definition is grounded in literary realism and reportage (Talese's forte), which favor realist fiction and slice-of-life drama—for example, di Donato's *Christ in Concrete,* Fante's *Wait Until Spring, Baldini,* Mario Puzo's *Fortunate Pilgrim,* or Helen Barolini's *Umbertina.* Such a standard marginalizes or eliminates writers in the self-effacing high-modernist and post-modernist modes (Gilbert Sorrentino, Mary Caponegro, Albert Innaurato,

Michael Palmer, Carole Maso) or writers focusing on non–Italian American themes and characters (Bernard DeVoto, Hamilton Basso, Frances Winwar, Paul Gallico). Talese's razor cut too much meat away from the bone.

The absence of manifestly ethnic subject matter in a book or film does not preclude the informing presence of ethnic themes and cultural values. Sicilian-born Frank Capra, who said he was "10–90 Italian-American,"[2] did not direct a major film with Italian American protagonists until the end of his career, yet a reading of his entire work shows a preoccupation with such typical Italian American themes as home, family, the child, endurance, and individualism. On the other hand, writers of a given ethnicity are not necessarily in denial if they ignore ethnic subject matter. To paraphrase Coleridge, let us not introduce an Act of Uniformity against ethnic American writers.

The most serious casualty of Talese's razor was Don DeLillo who, more than any other Italian American writer in the past half century, has made the strongest claim for inclusion among mainstream novelists in the American canon. He was being regularly anthologized; his novels appeared in college courses; his career went from strength to strength. Surely, he was the exception to Talese's critique. Since he had not written directly about Italian America in his ten novels, however, Talese did not refer to him. For the record, there are two early stories about New York ethnics, "Take the 'A' Train" (1962) and "Spaghetti and Meatballs" (1965), though one cannot fault Talese for overlooking them or even for failing to examine the many minor characters with Italian names in the novels. Others, too, overlooked the ethnic component in DeLillo's fiction, and the Catholic one as well.

In "How to Read Don DeLillo," Daniel Aaron comments that "nothing in his novels suggests a suppressed 'Italian foundation'; hardly a vibration betrays an ethnic consciousness. His name could just as well be Don Smith or Don Brown." Similarly, Aaron's treatment of DeLillo's religion displays the superiority of inattention: "DeLillo's presumably Roman Catholic upbringing rarely surfaces in his books although his accounts of the spiritual and carnal excesses of his seekers, prodigies, terrorists, spies, academicians, gangsters, entrepreneurs can be read as the musings of a crypto-Christian and profane moralist." One does not have to employ explicitly Christian symbolism and subject matter (for instance, rituals, crucifixes, festivals, processions, prayers, curses, or hellfire) to express the experience or the effect of a Catholic education. In "musings of a crypto-Christian" Aaron misperceives the writer's convictions. DeLillo's world is permeated by spiritual values and an incarnationist mode, sometimes in parodic form, with an Italian Catholic emphasis on immanence rather than transcendence, though often mediated, indirect, and always rendered artistically. Aaron mentions DeLillo's attending Jesuit-run Fordham University—

nothing presumable about it—and further investigation would have shown that he went to Catholic primary and secondary schools. No one who had not been to a Catholic grammar school could have created *Underworld*'s Sister Alma Edgar; she resembles the fanatic protagonist of *Sister Mary Ignatius Explains It All for You* (1979) by Christopher Durang, who had "twelve years of Catholic schooling" (DeLillo had sixteen). Like Aaron, Pearl K. Bell connects the religion and the ethnicity, both of which she dispatches in a peremptory manner: "His ethnic background and Catholic upbringing are entirely absent from his work."[3] If Bell and Aaron had not been so eager to see DeLillo one-sidedly as a postmodernist, and if they had appreciated his Italian Catholicism and ethnicity, they might have excavated their foundations in his work, even before he himself brought them nearer to the surface in *Underworld*.

Tom LeClair, Thomas DePietro, and Fred Gardaphé have identified motifs and values that demonstrate, from the outset of DeLillo's career, the ethnic presence in his fiction. For LeClair, "The social distance of his upbringing contributed . . . to his double view of American life." DeLillo's background is implicated in not only his choice of literary terrain but also his stance within it. His fascination with the "seductions of American leisure and privacy" oppose the fact of his having been "raised in a world of work and family." His "early social distance" triggered contradictory attitudes and the desire "to insert himself into yet remain alien from American life." Rather than giving an account of ethnic assimilation, which one might have expected from the "son of Italian immigrants," DeLillo's first novel *Americana* (1971) is a "narrative of mainline 'desimilation.'"[4] These unresolved oppositions argue for the pressures upon a second-generation ethnic sensibility.

In a similar vein, conceding that DeLillo has "written nothing" about Italian Americans, Thomas DePietro welcomes "something uniquely Italian and American" about his "fictional project"—for example, "mysteries of identity." *Mao II* (1991), DeLillo's tenth novel, is "in the Italian American grain" because of its central preoccupation with *omertà*, "that silence which Talese himself argues is at the core of Italian culture."[5] Joseph Tabbi and Andrew Jude Price have examined silence and withdrawal in DeLillo on other than ethnic grounds and add weight to DePietro's conclusion. Fred Gardaphé meets Aaron's assertion head-on: DeLillo's work has an "Italian foundation" that forms a "vital basis of the philosophy on which he constructs his narratives." Though no Italian American is a central character in his fiction—Gardaphé was writing in the year before the publication of *Underworld*—nonetheless, his ethnic values provide underpinning and structure, while sundry minor characters with Italian American names and characteristics inhabit the house. In a detailed, convincing analysis of the ethnic stories and the novels, Gardaphé locates themes such as alienation, the relationship to family and history, superstition, violence, the artistic impulse, sensuousness, and the "sensual other." Still, DeLillo's literary odyssey expresses the "abandonment" of Italian America, "suggest[ing] the decline of a distinct *italianità*, which has assimilated into the larger American culture."[6]

DeLillo discloses few clues about his biography, or rather (because the facts are known) his attitude to his biography. Since his grandparents spoke to him in English, and not in the Italian in which they spoke to each other, DeLillo has said, "I do not feel, in the narrow sense, an Italian American writer."[7] Such is his principle of exclusion, "in the narrow sense": he did not grow up in an Italian-speaking household or was not bilingual from childhood. Consequently, he is still not an Italian American writer "in the narrow sense" when he writes about Italian American themes and characters, directly in *Underworld* or indirectly in his other novels. His explanation is as peculiar or arbitrary in its way as was Frank Capra's, and no sociologist would accept either at face value. *Italian American* signifies two components in the identity: the second necessarily influences the first, most strongly at the outset in language (the first thing to go in the transition), so that one can be "Italian American" without growing up in an Italian-speaking household or being bilingual. DeLillo's statement exhibits some of the conflict of second-generation ethnics, who according to Hansen's Law tend to distance themselves from their parents' background, confirming ethnicity in the very attempt to suppress it. In one of his profiles of second-generation ethnics in *Italian or American?* Irvin Long Child calls attention to rebelliousness toward the clan and the desire for rapid assimilation.[8] If this is the case, it might help explain why DeLillo showed extreme reticence with regard to his biography and cultivated impersonality in his fiction.

If not "in the narrow sense," however, does DeLillo imply he is an Italian American writer *in the broad sense*? Take, for example, his preoccupation with the theme of death: "There is a sense of last things in my work that probably comes from a Catholic childhood. For a Catholic, nothing is too important to discuss or think about, because he's raised with the idea that he will die any minute now and that if he doesn't live his life in a certain way this death is simply an introduction to an eternity of pain."[9] Not only this statement, but *Underworld* and, indeed, all DeLillo's work argue strongly for his being an Italian American writer in the broad sense, with the presence of central themes and values of his ethnicity: tradition, family, the "religion of the home," hard work ("which sustains the home"),[10] the child, mutual aid, realism, nostalgia, a sense of limit and a residual fatalism, anarchic individualism, violence, sports, spectacle, and leisure (not to be confused with comfort). In *Underworld*, DeLillo chronicles the half-century trajectory of the Italian Americans from Little Italy to the suburbs, their move from one part of the country to a distant region, the dispersion of the family, the culture clash between the Italians and the WASP mainstream, *Gemeinschaft* versus *Gesellschaft*. He also portrays the third and fourth generations, those now in their twenties and thirties, in what Richard Alba terms "the twilight of ethnicity."[11] Essentially, though, the novel belongs to DeLillo's generation, between the immigrant grandparents (and, in his case, parent) and the suburbanized grandchildren. It is, moreover, significant that America's greatest Italian American writer of the past half century would choose the Underworld for the subject of his major work, build it on the moral foundations of Aquinas, and plan it on an epic scale, thereby testifying to the influence of, and paying homage to, Dante.

If, with a few important exceptions, DeLillo's ethnicity has been largely neglected, his religious background has been almost entirely so. Here it appears that everything except his Catholicism has been given its due. His novels are informed by the kabbalah and the occult (Little); mysticism (Annesley and Maltby); sacrifice and the sacred (Born); miracle, "tabloid spirituality," and astrology (McLure); and glossolalia and Pentecostalism (Osteen). Some of these religious themes may overlap with Catholicism: "Mystery in general rather than the occult is something that weaves in and out of my work," said DeLillo. "Possibly it is the natural product of a Catholic upbringing."[12]

In his exploration of diverse religious paths or his own religious origins, DeLillo does not differ from other postmodern writers who, antagonistic to bourgeois material culture and the absence of spirituality, have reflectively engaged, if not embraced, the religious revival of the past half century.[13] John A. McClure refers to contemporary "re-sacralization" of life through "ecological sensitivity" and "poststructural respect for difference" where DeLillo's Americans are "driven by homeless spiritual impulses and mesmerized by new religious movements." Suzi Gablik applauds the "re-enchantment" of nature in "reconstructive" postmodernism that "implicates art in this awakening sense of responsibility for the fate of the earth and of the high levels of psychic and physical toxicity in our environment," a statement that well applies to DeLillo's *White Noise*.[14] Although such critical approaches sometimes result from the postmodernist, antifoundationalist attack on the West, including its religious institutions, DeLillo's fascination with many varied forms of spiritual experience as well as his self-effacement on biography have also covered his tracks.

The main feature of DeLillo's Italian Catholicism upon which, together with his ethnicity, he will draw in his critique of global technological culture is its immanent particularism. Italian Catholicism combines the concept of a single transcendent deity with the belief in the local presence or immanence of the divine within everyday life.[15] Although God is the *mysterium tremendum,* he reveals himself in the sacraments, rituals and the Church, the saints and holy people, works of mercy, prayer, the quotidian, and nature (God-in-nature). This blend of transcendence and immanence may be contrasted with Calvinist Protestantism, a "religion of the 'either-or,'" which holds that God, the Wholly Other or the God-out-of-nature, "participates in the universe he created and controls it but is in no way incorporated in it."[16] Nor is there room for intercessors, elaborate ritualism, or most sacraments. On the contrary, Italian Catholics have traditionally involved themselves in devotional practices "with a strong emphasis upon the concrete and the visible":[17] pictures, statues of local saints (some not officially recognized), crosses, crèches, rosaries, ex-votos, front-yard and roadside shrines, decorative frescoes, and street festivals and colorful processions (festa). Boston's North End and West End Italians stood amazed at the iconic spareness, plain glass windows, and plentiful white paint in the Protestant churches in their midst—Old North Church, New North Church (now St. Stephen's), West Church—where an austere aesthetics of transcendence prevails decidedly over that of immanence. The clear light that streams into these churches contrasts with the light refracted through stained-glass images of saints interceding between God and his worshipers in Catholic churches.

The sharp difference between transcendence and immanence in theological terms stems from the fact that, generally speaking, Protestantism divides the realm of transcendent grace from fallen nature.[18] This principle of division differs from Catholic analogical thinking whereby theologians and artists posit a web of correspondences between God and his creation or similarities-in-difference, bridging the broad gulf between grace and nature and arranging a series of "ordered relationships" on the divine pattern—for instance, "the relationships within the self, the relationships of the self to other selves, to society, history, the cosmos."[19]

Backed by what Catholics regard as an objective hierarchical order of being, Catholic analogizing differs from metaphor and simile that require no such dependence. Analogically, any object in the natural order of things (with "its scandalous particularity, its concreteness, its opaqueness, its temporality") may potentially illuminate some other thing: "It is known—and loved—not only in itself and for itself but also in its degree—its degree of participation in the vast hierarchy of being which reaches to God."[20] In artistic practice, analogy may work by parallelism, as in Dante where the journey through the afterlife is like a pilgrimage of the soul, or by the so-called contraries in analogy where spirit may reveal itself in and through that which stands against it, or by reference to the most mundane object.[21] The Anglican George Herbert likens Christ's spear wound to a mailbag in which one puts letters to the Lord. The physical and moral universe is crisscrossed by innumerable correspondences, linking the otherworldly Absolute and the God of generativeness or pantheistic participation.

The immanental doctrine was perfectly suited to incorporate southern Italian peasant beliefs and practices from the world of magic and witchcraft (amulets, *malocchio* [evil eye], *corno* [horns]) to saints' cults, *festa,* and the religion of the home and family. *Festa* entails a procession with a raised saint of the Redeemer, the Madonna, or a patron saint, and a rich plenum of sensation involving a bazaar, food, tournaments, prizes, music and dancing, fireworks and entertainment, reinforcing "sacred membership" in the community, marking its boundaries, even defending it from other groups.[22] Could there be a better example of religious immanence in its joyful, epiphanic moment than a saint's procession? "Quando passa il santo, la festa è finita" (When the saint passes by, the *festa* is over).

The most important example of immanence is "the religion of the home."[23] Though the phrase describes Giovanni Verga's *I Malavoglia* (1881), the concept traces to the Romans for whom religion began in the home. In the *Aeneid,* an epic that seems written for immigrants, Aeneas carries his household gods from Troy to Italy: images of illustrious ancestors (Lares) and other gods (Penates) protecting the home and the food supply. Aeneas, who has lost one home and has yet to find another, exemplifies a higher *pietas,* the foremost value in the epic: wherever one's household gods are, there one's home is. Founded in familial relations and the "domus,"[24] the religion of the family extends in concentric circles outward from the home to the neighborhood, city, and country, and ultimately to the natural universe.

Building upon this tradition, the Christian ideal of the Holy Family was one of the most familiar subjects in Italian art, high and popular. As for the food supply, Simone Cinotto does not hesitate to use the word *rituals* in his comprehensive examination of Italian American family relations centered upon food. For the sacred hearth of the Romans, the Italians substituted the kitchen table: "Siamo fratelli e sorelle quando tutti i piedi stanno sotto una tavola" (We are brothers and sisters when all our feet are under a table).[25] Richard Gambino notes that family gatherings at Sunday dinner are a "communion" of the family; food is "sacred" because it is the "tangible medium of that communion."[26] *Pietas,* the religion of the home and family, and the "sacred community" are the foundation of Little Italy, which became a byword for a safe, cohesive neighborhood in American culture.

The Italian immigrant attitude toward death and the afterlife, which looms importantly in DeLillo's critique of American culture, differs markedly from that of nineteenth- and early-twentieth-century American notions. According to Philippe Ariès the classical Mediterranean attitude is a condition of familiar, natural acceptance of a universal fate, "half-way between passive resignation and mystical trust"; he calls it Tame Death. In life, people want to be near the dead; their cemeteries are close to their churches, in town centers, or within a short walking distance, symbolizing the "coexistence" of the "unbroken family" of the living and the dead, the one true community. Physical death is a kind of sleep, an intermediary state between this present life and the Last Judgment. Other attitudes depart from Tame Death in increasing degrees of neurosis, terror, or suppression, which Ariès labels Untamed: the romantic cult of the dead linking death and the beautiful (death is rarely considered "beautiful" in the classical world), Victorian mourning taken to grotesque lengths (contrast the gods on Achilles' grief), or—wildest of all—the contemporary view in which death is shameful, a nonsubject that is what happens in hospitals, the furthest thing from natural acceptance of the biological fact (80 percent of Americans die alone in hospitals surrounded by machines).[27]

Without an appreciation of Tame Death among the southern Italians one can easily misconstrue their behavior. In *Human Organization,* Leonard W. Moss and Walter H. Thomson argue that "while there is a heavy emphasis on death in Catholicism generally, this body of religious belief is not sufficient in itself to explain the preponderant death-orientation found in the rural family." Is there a "heavy" emphasis? Or is the emphasis exactly right for a family member's death? Moss and Thomson are condescending: "Even the pin money jar will be raided to provide for the pocket of the deceased." Heirs to the classical tradition, one of our last direct links to it, the family members are performing a pre-Christian rite of great dignity. "Raided" implies panicky, superstitious behavior. Objectively speaking, Moss and Thomson err in taking as absolute their own position on such a complex question. A dry secularism has driven death "out the world of familiar things," notes Ariès, where it becomes virtually "unnameable." Searching for a reason for the "preponderant death-orientation" of the "superstitious" southern Italians (as if they were clinically death obsessed), Moss and Thomson fail to comprehend the immanent supernaturalism of the preindustrial, rural world where "death was both familiar and near," "a simple thing."[28]

Cleaving to their Catholicism and "strange" cults and practices, Italian immigrants clashed with a hostile Church hierarchy. Irish American Catholicism, which from the 1850s imposed its distinctive doctrinal and "green" orientation on the official Church in America, shared certain features with northern European and American Protestantism: an emphasis on transcendence, juridical formalism, neo-puritanism, a concentration on instruction. Thus, whereas the Church in Italy not only tolerated but even encouraged cultism and *festa,* the

American Church frowned on the popular Catholicism of the Italians well into the twentieth century (at least until Vatican II).[29] The *feste* were outdoors (as opposed to the church's dark interior), too noisy (as opposed to solemn), too random and spontaneous (as opposed to ritualized, though processions follow specific routes), and assuredly too much fun for such a serious matter as religion. It was the "Italian Problem": how to make Italian immigrants into American Catholics. As it happened, becoming an American Catholic entailed becoming a modern American, which had its measures of pain, testing, and doubt. Some anger and frustration must have been wrongly directed at the official Church, which, to be fair, was only hastening the general process of modernization with its rules, rationalized procedures, nonemotionalism, method, and instruction—indeed, the pattern of technology.[30]

In 1997, at sixty-one, DeLillo published *Underworld,* his longest and most ambitious work, which explores the enormous expansion of technological society in the second half of the twentieth century.[31] Not that the theme of technology was new to his work. It had figured in nearly all his fiction, whether he treated television *(Americana)*, sports *(End Zone)*, celebrity *(Great Jones Street)*, artificial intelligence *(Ratner's Star)*, surveillance *(Running Dog)*, ecodisaster *(White Noise)*, or mass events *(Mao II)*. Yet the difference between these novels and *Underworld*, with its chronological sweep, global journeys, and multiple intersecting plotlines, is still very considerable. The novel depicts a technological environment that has become so intrinsic and normative that, to cite Jacques Ellul, it "shapes the total way of life."[32] The novel's special focus is upon waste, its containment, storage, elimination, and recycling, in landfills and nuclear dumps, in garbage bags and computer banks. Reaching back to *The Waste Land,* one of the archetypal works of modernism, DeLillo treats waste as the end result of consumerist materialism and massification, which go in tandem with the decline of community and the loss of historical memory. Through its analogical relation to damaged human souls, waste pertains to the fear of death, loss of transcendence, and despair over the future of civilization. Having followed him across fifty years, we last see the novel's central character, Nick Shay, a semiretired managing director of a waste-containment company, living in a pseudopastoral suburb of Phoenix, Arizona. As he gazes on the computer screen, seeking intimations of immortality, the novel shifts perspective and ends in cyberspace.

In an entirely new way, however, *Underworld* marked a departure in DeLillo's career. It was the first of his eleven novels with an Italian American Catholic protagonist and narrator, his first directly to treat ethnic themes, and his first with scenes—central to plot and symbolic structure—set in a Little Italy with its innumerable Mediterranean ties. These scenes take place in the post–World War II period and again around 1990, that is, from a still-bustling neighborhood to its fragile survival amid urban decay. He contrasts technological society with one of New York's ethnic neighborhoods, the Belmont section of the Bronx, where he, his protagonist, and other leading characters grew up. As if to personalize his themes, DeLillo dedicated the novel *to the memory of my mother and father.*[33] The oppositions between the technological milieu and the ethnic neighborhood include such features as speed and efficiency versus natural rhythms, *festa*, and religious ritual; overconsumption versus scarcity; suburban solitude versus community; demagification versus sacramentalism; silence versus sound; surface and screen values versus a plenum of sensation; and an obsession for security and physical health versus danger and violence. Not all the plotlines in *Underworld* cross through Little Italy and Phoenix, but with his Mediterranean theme as a running thread DeLillo explores the loss of individuality, spirituality, and communal values amid the technologization and flattening of global culture. His concern with immanence and the analogical image, often in the portrayal of consumerism, the media, and techniques, in *Underworld* and his other novels, ranks at the highest level of his artistic achievement and probably will mark his main contribution to American literature.

Like his protagonist, Nick Shay, DeLillo was born in the Bronx in 1936. DeLillo's family is southern Italian on both sides, his father having emigrated in 1916 from Montagano in the southern Abruzzi (in 1963 the town was included administratively in the province of Molise).[34] A knife grinder in *Underworld* comes from the region of Nick's father's people, "near a town called Campobasso, in the mountains, where boys were raised to sharpen knives."[35] Montagano lies five miles north of Campobasso. Italian Americans had the reputation of fighting with knives, not with fists. DeLillo attended St. Martin de Tours grammar school, Cardinal Hayes High School (Christian Brothers, Xavierian Brothers), and Fordham University (Jesuit), graduating in 1958 with a major in "communication arts."[36] His training culminated in a Jesuit program with a core of theology and philosophy and with a "humanistic ideal" according to which "formation of character is the first goal of education."[37]

In *Underworld,* Nick says he went to a Catholic grammar school and public high school, omitting two facts to conceal his past. Albert Bronzini, his high school science teacher, fills in the blanks with academic accuracy: Nick remained at his high school for "one semester only" (671) before going to reform school in upstate New York. The high school is across the street from Fordham; Theodore Roosevelt High School, unnamed in the novel, is across the street from Fordham (619; cf. 701). Bronzini wants Nick to attend college, and when he asks his friend Father Paulus, a philosophy professor with degrees from

Louvain and Yale, to talk up Fordham, Paulus instead recommends "Voyageur College," an offshoot of Fordham in northern Minnesota. Thus, Nick goes to a Catholic grammar school (eight years), a public high school (one-half of a year), reform school (three years), and then Paulus's "little experimental college" (543) (four years). Like DeLillo, Nick has an essentially Catholic education (twelve years).

These novelistic and biographical details bind DeLillo to his protagonist, substantiating his admission that "I do not identify with Bronzini, though he is a character whom I like: I feel nearer to Nick Shay."[38] One might question why DeLillo attaches himself to Nick in sundry ways when he could have chosen different dates, towns, and education to distance himself. Whereas the mix of life and art could be ascribed to a parody of modernist impersonality making for a postmodernist autobiographical novel, DeLillo would probably not endorse such a formula. More likely, the correspondences may have stimulated memory and imagination, opening the deepest sources of inspiration. In this way DeLillo leans closer to the mirror.

His earlier novels with their nonlinear, open forms had contextualized his point of view so that, as Paul Civello notes, the author became "part of the event itself," entangled by an "all-encompassing system of mutually interacting systems"—scientific, political, social, cultural.[39] The frustrated protagonists of these novels are typically "caught up in the mesh of activity of overlapping systems."[40] But in *Underworld*, DeLillo moves beyond the so-called "systems novel"[41] to what may be termed the "system novel," because there is only one main system to which all others are subordinate: a universalizing, technological monism whose varied elements are united to one another and recombine easily since they do not vary in their essentials. "We have created a closed system," comments Richard Stivers on technological hegemony.[42] Formally and structurally, *Underworld* is only superficially "open."

Yet DeLillo's point of view in this novel is not absorbed by the system, however much it is affected by it. By the 1990s he had so fully studied the technological environment that he stood apart from it. Strong awareness is a kind of liberation; his religious training, his weapons of satire, and his cultural and ethnic past all contribute to his act of selective resistance. In *Underworld*, DeLillo is both more involved and more detached than he was in his earlier novels: more involved because he endows his protagonist with some his own biographical and ethnic "facts," as if to pursue parallel mysteries, so much so that DeLillo allows to Nick alone the privilege of acting as narrator for his sections of the novel, and more detached because DeLillo's grasp of the totalizing aspects of the technological system enable him, as author, to achieve moments of epiphanic clarity of the kind Charles Taylor associated with the great modernist writers.

DeLillo decontextualizes himself as far as possible from his work, approaching an epic impersonality, a distance finally not of rejection but of inclusiveness. Like Dante, he is both pilgrim and narrator of his journey into the Underworld. Where Dante's pilgrim and narrator are ultimately saved in unison, however, DeLillo's pilgrim has only flickering hope in a psychological limbo, while DeLillo as narrator triumphs through his art and spirituality.

*Underworld* tells the life story of Nick Shay, the son of James ("Jimmy") Nicholas Costanza, a small-time bookie, and Rosemary Shay who is Irish. He bears his father's middle name, but because the father left the family shortly before his birth, his mother retaliated by having Nick's last name changed legally to her own. Nick will thus be able to hide his ethnic background, essential in the waste-management business with its supposed connections to the Mob. When a coworker finds out that Nick is half Italian, he asks, "When did this happen?" (165), as if it were a traffic accident.[43] Jimmy Costanza returned to the family shortly after Nick's birth; there was another son, Matt, also given Shay as his last name, perhaps with the father's acquiescence. Jimmy remained with the family until Nick was eleven and Matt six, then disappeared for good. This event, which took place in 1947, is the novel's point zero. Fifty years later, Nick thinks, "The failure it brought down on us does not diminish" (809). He both looks and feels like his father: "olive-skinned" and "dark as my father was" (64; cf. 120), with "a graveness that was European in a way" (416); there is "a certain distance in my make-up, a measured separation like my old man's" (275). By contrast, Matt, younger by five years, is a redhead, possibly resembling the Irish side of his family. The mother's name, Rosemary, shortened by the Italian women in her tenement to the more familiar Italian "Rose," links to redness, though she has brown hair.[44]

The father's abandonment leaves deep, permanent scars on the family. Whenever Rosemary tells a story about him, her boys listen "with a shared intensity that no other subject could remotely provoke": "It was the thing that made them a family, still" (199). From an early age the brothers have fought over the reasons for their father's disappearance, projecting their own needs to come up with a livable history.[45] "He did the unthinkable Italian crime," says Matt. "He walked out on his family. They don't even have a name for this" (204). It is the chief sacrilege in the religion of the home and family, which DeLillo encrypts by displaying the force of its breakdown (*costanza* is Italian for "constancy" or "loyalty"). For Matt, Jimmy could not bear the stress and burden of a growing family, and he may have been pushed over the edge to run away by failing to cover a large bet. In any case, Matt persists in believing his father is alive and living under an assumed name in southern California. But Nick, who was eleven and much closer to his father when he walked out, is far more troubled: "We are the ones with assumed names" (Shay) (276). Rejecting his brother's psychologizing, Nick speculates that his father was executed by the Mob after failing to cover the bet, or that his mother's coldness drove him away, or perhaps both. Rosemary withdraws into her private world; she "could not bear to think Nick might be right" (204); it would "make her Jimmy innocent" (208), that is, make him not guilty of betraying the family and therefore make her at least partly guilty of driving him away. Matt reacts by finding a surrogate father in Bronzini, of "Calabrian heritage" (472), and cleaving to a secure, more or less conventional, path.

From boyhood Nick has acted out "vibrant dramas of crime and bounding heroes" (211). His response to the abandonment is to imitate his father by pursuing what he thinks his father pursued, a wild life: car theft, small errands for the wise guys, then the accidental shooting of a drug dealer, George Manza, who tried to lure him into drugs. In reform school for "criminally negligent homicide" (502) the psychologist "tried to work my soul" (511) and recommended psychotherapy as the "way to my salvation" (502, 511). Streetwise and suspicious of her preposterous theories, Nick refuses to tell her anything—his *omertà*. Instead, this "lazy and unmotivated" (671) delinquent sees his only escape by identifying with the strict system of rules and lets his life be organized by its draconian code. Released at nineteen, he is ready for Father Paulus and the Jesuit college that wants a "special kind of boy" (675) for an education "better suited to a fifty-year-old who feels he missed the point the first time around" (540). The "jebbies worked him over," "minting intellect and shiny soul" (450). The life of pretense has begun.

With the exception of a prologue (1951) and epilogue (mid-1990s), chronologically the novel moves (mostly) backward in time, from the 1990s to Nick's reckless youth in the '40s and '50s, as he retrieves layer upon layer of the past. Young Nick participates in the life of the Bronx Little Italy, even then entering its decline as urban dwellers began their exodus to the suburbs. Though he entertained the idea of teaching Latin ("I studied Latin" [281]; "I want to teach Latin" [619]), representative of tradition and the past, he turned to a modern subject, "behavioral research" on education that he applied to "ghettos and marginal parts of town" (619), which he already knew well; then he switched to business speech writing and public relations (282; another tie to DeLillo's early career in advertising), before moving into waste management and working his way up the corporate ladder. In late middle age, Nick's perspective is Janus-faced: he can look back fondly on the immigrant grandparent generation among whom he was raised, and he can ponder the fate of his thoroughly assimilated grandchildren to whom he can impart nothing.

The prologue ("The Triumph of Death,"[46] consisting of 49 pages), a tour de force originally published separately, describes the legendary Dodgers-Giants playoff game in Brooklyn's Polo Grounds on October 3, 1951, also the date of the Soviet Union's testing of an atomic bomb and thus an escalation of the cold war. Part 1 of the novel ("Long Tall Sally," 74 pages) jumps forward to 1992: Nick's life in Phoenix; a second game between the same teams in Los Angeles, long since transferred to the West Coast; and a visit to New Mexico to see the large-scale artwork by Bronzini's ex-wife, Klara Sax. Thus, a Southwest section of the novel balances the prologue in the Northeast. Part 2, "Elegy for the Left Hand Alone: Mid-1980s–Early 1990s," depicts a decayed Little Italy in the Bronx. Then the narrative moves backward in time, in discrete stages, over 424 pages to a long (120 pages) penultimate section, part 6, "Arrangement in Gray and Black: Fall 1951–Summer 1952," set in the same thriving Little Italy of the early 1950s, with the events leading up to and including the killing of Manza. The epilogue (42 pages) returns to the mid-1990s, synchronous with the time the novel was being written.

The playoff game of the prologue—baseball was at the time without a rival as America's pastime—enables DeLillo to assemble different ethnicities, religions, races, and classes in a grand panorama of America at midcentury. With an operatic flair, DeLillo excels at such choric, carnival scenes. Streaming into the stadium are wealthy stockbrokers from Wall Street, ethnics from Brooklyn, suburbanites from New Jersey, and truants from all over the city. The focus soon falls on a quartet of celebrities seated together: singer Frank Sinatra, comedian Jackie Gleason, New York restaurateur Toots Shor, and FBI director J. Edgar Hoover: Italian, Irish, Jewish, WASP, each acting and speaking in his own person yet representative of his ethnic background. They sit in a choice section, but it is not separated from the crowd in a glassed-in club box such as that from which Nick and the waste managers will be "pretending to watch a game" (91) in 1992. Hoover receives word that the Russians have tested an atomic bomb and escalated the cold war—the international reality of the next thirty-eight years, coterminous with the novel's chronology. The playoff game was won sensationally by the Giants in the ninth inning when Bobby Thomson hit a home run off Ralph Branca. Instantly become an object of monetary value, the baseball that Thomson hit is retrieved by an African American in the stands (DeLillo introduces another ethnicity), the first in a chain of owners ending with Nick, who buys it for $34,500. Ownership of this prize baseball is one of the novel's many rhizomic, strandlike linkages.

For Nick (who did not actually attend the game), the baseball is talismanic not only of an earlier, simpler America, but also of his own lost world. While time moves on, Nick's desire (and the objective narrator's collusion with it) drives him inexorably backward to his youth, giving formal shape to the novel.

Joseph Dewey describes it as DeLillo's "most intimate record of his own child-hood in the Bronx"; Jesse Kavaldo comments that, unlike F. Scott Fitzgerald, DeLillo is "not fighting against the waves of the past but embracing its joy while mourning its loss."[47] Memory works against the grain of historical chronology to culminate in "Arrangement in Gray and Black" (the last pre-epilogue part). Thus, the novel contains two journeys: Nick's external story, outward from the Bronx to the larger American world, from the lower or lower-middle to the upper-middle class; and the internal story, moving in the opposite direction, from the American world back to the Bronx. DeLillo has commented upon the contrast between Little Italy and the wider American scene: "There are two sets of language in this book. The difference between them isn't very stark but in fact a sort of journey is detectable, solely in sentences and pacing and word choice, between the Bronx in Part Six and the larger environment that surrounds it."[48]

What activates the polar tensions between present and past are the contrasts between corporate, technologized America and certain domains within it, or slightly separated from it, including Little Italy. The two narrators, "DeLillo" as author and Nick, share an Aquinian vocabulary and a strong emphasis on immanent particularism over dualistic transcendence to carry out the task. "The Jesuits," Nick says, "taught me to examine things for second meanings and deeper connections" (88). One lesson of immanentism is that "everything is connected" (131, 289, 408, 776, 825, 826). Matt, too, believes that "everything connects in the end" (465). The family takes to naming Nick "the Jesuit" (450): he is jesuitical, a crafty debater on every side of an issue of right and wrong. Perhaps Nick "missed the point" of his education "the first time around" (540); he took the letter, not the spirit. Over fifty, however, it enables him to see beyond facile linkages of the parts to the larger whole and his place (albeit self-condemned) within it. Although the technological system denies the grounds of the incarnationist mode, the reverse is not the case. The Christian universe contains the technological system so that one may analogize every form of technique and man-made apparatus. As Romano Guardini comments, "God is greater than all historic processes . . . and can at any time influence a world that was created, not to function like a machine, but likewise to create, in the living spirit."[49]

Naming, to begin with, connects the disparate worlds of the novel for the purpose of comparison and contrast, for ironic undercutting or satiric reversal. After reform school, where Nick is sent for committing an accidental homicide, he attends "Voyageur College" in "northern" (harsher, more ascetic) Minnesota, honoring the French Jesuit missionaries like Father Marquette who explored the interior of the continent and introduced Christianity: the college name signifies spiritual daring. But in a novel in which the satellite *Sputnik* figures, Voyageur may also recall the two *unmanned* spacecraft named *Voyager*, triumphs of cold war technology, which explored the outer planets of the solar system. At this college, Father Paulus tells Nick that he does not know "how to look because you don't know the names" (540). And thereafter he is fascinated with names. The opening sentence of part 1, Nick's first as narrator, is an excellent example: "I was driving a Lexus through a rustling wind" (63). Caught up in the world of style and consumption, he refers casually not to a car, but to the brand name of the car, a high-priced one favored by the upper middle class. He is driving through the desert of New Mexico, an extreme setting, where the biblical divinity manifests himself; the wind or spirit is "rustling." *Lexus* is a pun on *lexis* or reading, and, by synecdoche, the novel. The Lexus is "assembled in a work area that's completely free of human presence" (63)—like the desert. The absence of the human, the presence of the divine; the narrator catches himself: "except for me, of course, and I was barely there" (63); his mind was elsewhere: the novel will show where his thoughts might be, but for now he participates in the analogy of presence and absence, "barely" applying to both himself and the desert. Two characters from opposing lives share a name with Edgar Allan Poe. Sister Alma Edgar, the grammar school teacher, and J. Edgar Hoover thrive on fear and secrecy, and both suffer from a germ phobia connected with their obsessive anticommunism (communists = germs). She strikes terror in her pupils by reading Poe's "Raven"; he "parleyed a pathological fear of invasion into a public policy."[50] They appear in a number of scenes, without of course meeting, until the end of the novel when, summoned by a few keystrokes, they are hyperlinked in cyberspace.

Beyond naming, if "everything is connected," one world or underworld informs upon another. At it most referential, *underworld* refers to Nick's mainstream position as a waste analyst and international consultant. On the ethnic side, the underworld is the *malavita* of Nick's father in Little Italy; Nick himself flirted with the Mafia in his teens. Maybe the Mafia was responsible for the father's disappearance into that other underworld, the classical land of the dead, through which Nick (someone who loves Latin) searches for him, like Aeneas for Anchises, though Nick searches in vain. The father "went under" (809), in every sense of the term, punning on the novel's title. Then, on a business trip to Milan Nick finds himself on the Via della Spiga, in the fashionable Montenapoleone district, the kind of place where a well-heeled American might stop over. Suddenly, an Italian seen from the back—that is, faceless, mysterious for the absence of the chief mark of identity—recalls the person he accidentally killed when he was sixteen: "Half a second in Milan . . . reminded me of a thousand things at once, long ago" (88). *Via* is "the way," and *spiga,* or "ear of corn," is sacred to Ceres, goddess of the natural cycle of life, death, and rebirth: Ceres' way. The dead man returns "alive" from the underworld to Nick's guilt-ridden conscience. Other underworlds include Sergi Eisenstein's "lost" film *Unterwelt*—a pure invention on DeLillo's part. Lenny Bruce's antibomb refrain that punctuates his comic monologues is *"We're all gonna die"* (547). Finally, underworld is Nick's death-in-life existence in the "unspeakable hanging heat" (86) and self-imposed "silence" ("the judgment on your crimes" [345]) of suburban Arizona, DeLillo's version of hell. Running through these underworlds are the themes of loss, waste, and death.

Connectedness, which can serve the actions of immanence, is the essence of the technological environment, from waste containment and recycling down to the tightest meshes of electronic communication: "fax machines," "voice mail" and "e-mail" (806), redial buttons, "the web, the net" (825). Light imagery and the false sublimity of the language convey the aura of the infinite and the magical: "oceanic logic stored in computers" (89); "lustrous rushing force" (825); "contact points that shimmer in the air somewhere" (806). In Nick's office the "caress of linked grids" "lap around you" (89, 806), imparting a sense of "order," "command," and pseudointimacy but also enclosure or entrapment; this contrasts with the spontaneity and joy associated with the chalk "painted grids" (234) of the children's street game. "How can you tell the difference between orange juice and agent orange if the same massive system connects them at levels outside your comprehension?" ponders the insomniac Matt. "And how can you tell if this is true when you're already systemed under, prepared to half believe everything because this is the only intelligent response?" (465). The "cell" (806) in *cell phone* links on one side to the vitally organic and on the other to the inorganic communications system, with its fantasy of human connectedness celebrated in American advertising. Nick, like DeLillo, had written advertising copy: one repeated phrase could be an ad: "Everybody is everywhere at once" (805, 808). Such disorientation in human terms is in perfect accord with the technological system. As Ithiel de Sola Pool notes, "The communications distance between all points within [a satellite's] beam has become essentially equal."[51]

By contraries of analogy, the spirit in its highest exaltation links to the crudest matter: waste in all its forms, from nuclear waste to human excrement ("The deeper into communist country, the more foul his BMs" [313], connecting waste, death, and communism), to the Swiftian "synthetic feces" (805) for the product testing of diapers. Since everything is linked to everything else on the scale of hierarchy, Nick can say that, though it is at the bottom, still "waste is a religious thing" (88). His colleagues are "Church Fathers of waste in all its transmutations" (102), the parodic inversion of the fathers who consecrate the bread and wine in transubstantiation and perform the rites of burial. "Waste must also suggest its metonym, burial."[52] Nick's company "entomb[s] contaminated waste with a sense of reverence and dread" (88); it builds "pyramids of waste above and below the earth" (106), the sacred tomb monuments of consumer society, the final destination of those staggering displays of expendable goods, as in the supermarket scene at the end of *White Noise*. Waste management is his "faith to embrace" (282); he apparently lost his other faith. "Waste has a solemn aura," an "aspect of untouchability" (88): the solemnity of the dead, the distance of the sacred, the hidden God.

The strong emphasis on immanence over dualistic transcendence is fully realized in the connections among waste, death, and the spirit. When the elderly Sister Alma Edgar and her young assistant, Sister Gracie, drive into the South Bronx to deliver food and medicine, they meet with sickness, drugs, hunger, cocaine babies and child abandonment, blindness, epilepsy, and AIDS. Among the "hardest cases" in tenement corridors, Sister Gracie "believed the proof of God's creativity eddied from the fact that you could not surmise the life, even remotely, of his humblest shut-in" (246). Extreme abjection challenges her imaginative empathy beyond the human limit, bordering on the immensity of the sacred: in this instance, the contraries of analogy are near/remote, humble/exalted, shut-in/boundless, death/creation. God bestows "grace" upon the nun, true to her name, in her attempt to "surmise," the recognition of its impossibility, and the willingness to close the distance between herself and the abject. The eddy, a contrary and interrupting motion within a current, implies the whirling of the spirit against the nonspirit, as in Coleridge's "eddying of her living soul" ("Ode: To Dejection").[53] Sister Gracie's action on behalf of the "humblest shut-in" recalls the Book of Matthew. At the Last Judgment the Lord addresses the righteous, "I was a stranger and you welcomed me, I was naked and you gave me clothing, I was sick and you took care of me." When the righteous do not recollect seeing the Lord, he responds: "Truly I tell you, just as you did it to one of the least of these who are members of my family, you did it to me" (24:35–40).

DeLillo's espousal of Tame Death in relation to technology is best exemplified by *White Noise*, which exhibits all forms of socially imposed, media-driven attitudes toward death from paranoia and panic to morbid curiosity and outright suppression. A chemical spill or, in sanitized technical language, an "airborne toxic event," obsesses Jack Gladney, professor of "Hitler Studies" at a small midwestern college.[54] Fearing deadly contamination, he undergoes exhaustive medical tests that only make him feel "televised so to speak," separated from his body, and "a stranger to your own dying" (142). One test called SIMU-VAC makes a computer–calculated probability of one's death; according to the computer results, he is already dead. From time to time, like Nick, Gladney has moments of awareness: "I could easily imagine a perfectly healthy person being made ill just taking these tests" (277). His doctor, a cold technician who, like the other doctors, brims with health, is "eager to see how my death is progressing"; he wants to "insert" Gladney into the "imaging block." Gladney fears "what it knows about me" (325). Yet, in keeping with the principle that the problems of technology can be solved only by more technology, the new drug "Dylar" takes away the fear of death—this is Ariès's Death Untamed, in which an excessive preoccupation with death betrays a fear of life. In a Catholic hospital Gladney gazes at a picture of John F. Kennedy and John XXIII holding hands "in heaven," which is "partly cloudy" (a hilarious sign of an imperfect understanding); "sentimentally refreshed" by this view of an afterlife, he thinks of his childhood (316–17). In Ariès's analysis of the Untamed romantic cult of the dead, popular throughout the nineteenth and early twentieth centuries, friends and lovers tend to meet again in death exactly as if on earth. Looking at the picture, he asks Sister Hermann Marie who is dressing his wound: "What does the Church say about heaven today? Is it still the old heaven, like that, in the sky? She turned to glance at the picture. 'Do you think we are stupid?'" (317). Repudiating Gladney in the bluntest terms, she urges patience and duty in this world: "Only this" (318). She believes in her ethical vows of poverty, chastity, and obedience, but not in "the old heaven and hell," and unleashes a ferocious, well-deserved browbeating in German, which the professor of Hitler studies does not even know, that is, it all passes over him. In sum, the nun's conduct illustrates Tame Death, the simple acceptance of the eternal fact.

In *Underworld* the analogy of waste unfolds in "scandalous particularity" from international consulting on nuclear waste landfills to the "lowest household trash" (88): scandal (from the Greek *skandalon* or "stumbling block") attracts and repels; it offends as it fascinates. True to the exacting formalism of his training, Nick separates waste "according to the guidelines" (803). He wants "clean safe healthy garbage" (119): "We separated our waste into glass and cans and paper products. Then we did clear glass versus colored glass. Then we did tin versus aluminum . . . Then we did newspapers including glossy inserts but were careful not to tie the bundles in twine, which is always the temptation" (89; cf. 804, 807). Concern with technique and ritualistic precision, a mock Last Judgment of garbage expressed in a dry tone and paratactic mode, the danger of "temptation"—all suggest a parallel spiritual world (cf. 84). It is like "preparing a pharaoh for his death and burial" (119). Nick's point of view shifts in the process: "People look at their garbage differently now, seeing every bottle and crushed carton in a planetary context" (88). Not only do these passages on proper bagging satirize American habits, but also, as in Herbert's

"Bag," they analogize the containment and preservation of spirit within a hierarchical ("planetary") context, in Nick's words, the "whisper of mystical contemplation that seems totally appropriate to the subject of waste" (282). In a liminal moment the talk of bagging intersects with the apprehension of the sacred in the negative sublime (darkness, emptiness, silence, stillness): "We remove the wax paper from cereal boxes before we put the boxes out for collection. The streets are dark and empty. We do clear glass versus colored glass and it is remarkable really how quiet it is, a stillness that feels old and settled, with landmark status, the yard waste, the paper bags pressed flat, the hour after sunset when a pause obtains in the world and you forget for a second where you are" (807–8).[55] Clear versus colored glass marks the distinction between transcendence and immanence. The arc of apprehension leads to the loss of self, "for a second," a kind of death.

One does not proceed far into *Underworld* without realizing that connectedness as achieved by the technological system is associated with increasing disconnectedness on the human level. That is, everything is connected in a bitterly ironic sense: our human weakness, our fear, in Mark Osteen's apt words, the "shared sense of *un*connectedness—of loss, alienation, dread, and confusion."[56] Nick suspects his wife of having an affair; she is, and he is too. In a pun she calls him "laconic Nick" (86). The language of feeling fails him all around. He communicates poorly with his mother, whom he dislodges against her will from her crumbling neighborhood to live virtually a prisoner in the back room of his house in Arizona. Neither can he fathom the reason for his father's abandonment, live amicably with his brother, nor find comfort in his old Bronx neighborhood, which he visits only rarely. But he is furthest from his own "distant mystery" (810).

*Distance* is perhaps the key word. What best characterizes him, as he tells his wife, is "an Italian word, or a Latin word . . . *lontananza*" (275) (distance), which for him is a detachment from the self that is not objectivity but affectlessness. He is "a country of one" with "a certain distance in my make-up, a measured separation like my old man's" (275), thereby strengthening his identification with the lost father. Toward his work he maintains a "shifting distance" (103), a self-alienation for which he cannot find a cure. Indeed, his work within the well-oiled machine of his headquarters only exacerbates the problem. Business corporations, he says, "shape you in nearly nothing flat, twist and swivel you. . . . [T]hey do it with smiles and nods, a collective inflection of the voice. You stand at the head of a corridor and by the time you walk to the far end you have adopted the comprehensive philosophy of the firm" (282). Thoroughly technicized and absorbed by the corporate life, saved only by his awareness of his condition, Nick suffers the almost total suppression of his identity: "It's not that you're pretending to be someone else. You're pretending to be exactly who you are" (103).

Nick's quasi-disembodied narration with its dry, depressed, mechanical tone betrays disconnectedness, a drab parataxis: "I live a quiet life in an unassuming house in a suburb of Phoenix. Pause. Like someone in the Witness Protection Program" (66, 80, 209). The self-referential stage direction "Pause" indicates someone "seeing himself live" at one remove, a form of paralysis (as in Pirandello); the "quiet life" on the surface seethes with hidden contradiction.[57] The past has been publicly wiped out, as if for his own protection, but the protection is self-imposed, and he needs most what he protects himself from, his "animating entity" (804): ironically, he is left defenseless. Witness protection relates to the Mob. In Nick's eyes, gangsters possess a "hard-edged," "fine-grained," and "perfected distance" of a "made man" (275), where *perfected* has the Latin sense of "completed," like the divine, but also like dread waste with its "aspect of untouchability" (88). His unsuspecting colleagues at waste management marvel at his impersonation of a Mafia boss with a "scraped-raw voice" threatening: "I'm telling you once and for all that I, me, Mario Badalato, I'll sever your fucking family's head off" (104). Even joking, with a stage Mafia name, he expresses his fear that the Mafia killed off his own "head" of the "family." Funny as they are, his *Godfather* gags express his contradictory desires for the father and the absolute (*absolutus*, having been freed from) that is, for proximity and for distance.

*Underworld* also protests the general loss of social memory, the relentlessly aggressive ahistoricism or antihistoricism that reduces the continuities of the past to isolated bits of information in a society dominated by presentism. The representative of Western memory, and DeLillo's strongest contrast to corporate America, is the ethnic neighborhood in its prime. Its sympathetic oral historian is "sweet-natured" (211) Albert Bronzini, who, unlike Nick, never left home. A science teacher with a love of empirical detail, Bronzini makes a trustworthy guide to his "compact neighborhood," with its "complex deposits" (661), its "little histories hidden in a gesture or word" (673). Also unlike Nick, who insulated himself from his environment whether he drives a Lexus through the desert or jogs with a "wireless headphone" (89), Bronzini refuses to own a car, preferring to walk and connect with his community: "The voices fall and the aromas deploy in ways that varied, but not too much, from day to day" (661).

In DeLillo's prose Little Italy comes vibrantly alive. One hears those "men with sledgehammers," "Sicilians busting up a sidewalk" (670), "voices from Italian radio drifting faintly out the open door" (674). One tastes the "autumnal pink Parma ham, sliced transparently thin" (672). One smells the "rolled beef, meatballs, basil" (699) in the hallways. One sees, as in a quiet cameo, "a waiter having a smoke during a lull, one of those fast-aging men who are tired all the time" (661). Unlike Nick's office, where the managers imitate one another in a terrifying self-parody, the locals seem both individual and uniquely at one with their work, and so are named George the Waiter, Joe the Butcher. With his "burly grace" the butcher "belongs to the cutting block. . . . [H]is aptitude and ease, the sense that he was born to the task restored a certain meaning to these eviscerated beasts"; his "own heart and lungs ought to hang outside his body, stationed like a saint's, to demonstrate his intimate link to the suffering world" (668). Bronzini chats with members of his social club: "Loud, crude, funny, often powerfully opinionated, all speechmakers these men, actors, declaimers, masters of insult" (766)—genuine Mediterranean types. The men speak "mostly English"; dialect came into play "when an idea needed a push or shove into a more familiar place." These earthy voices take Bronzini back to childhood: English is "the sound of the present," Italian "took him backwards, the merest intonation, a language marked inexhaustibly by the past" (767–68). Such linguistic endowment, "inexhaustibly" rich in implication, lies at the furthest remove from Nick's mechanical tone. After the death of his grandparents, whenever DeLillo heard particular Italian words, he said that he would reconstruct "the phrases of that forgotten but still familiar lexicon."[58]

All ages are represented in Little Italy, from children playing in the streets to the old men in Mussolini Park, nicknamed prejudicially for its being a meeting place of Italians. Divorced and raising his daughter, Bronzini enjoys watching children play in the streets, one of the novel's recurrent life symbols: the games have Italian or Italian-sounding names: *ringolievio* and *salugo* (possibly from *saluto*). Observing the increased traffic since the war, he worries about the "status hunger" for "cars, more cars" and predicts that the children will be forced from the streets, a "dying practice" (662) in 1951 that completely disappears by the 1990s. He sympathizes with them in their plenitude ("fullness of the moment" [668]). They invent games with found objects, using brick walls, lampposts, curbstones, stoops, manhole covers, and fire hydrants, testifying to the imaginative ingenuity of a childhood that, however poor in one sense, has not yet succumbed to the consumer technology of play. "We turned junk into games," recalls Bronzini, "gouging cork out of bottle caps . . . cork, rubber bands, tin cans, half a skate, old linoleum that we used in carpet guns" (663). The children redeem waste by their imaginative play; in this, the child is father of the artist.[59]

Father Paulus, whom Bronzini introduces to the local scene, responds to the "European texture of the street, things done in the old slow faithful way, things carried over, suffused with rules of usage" (672). *Slow* contrasts with the speed and pressure of modern time, but the entire passage on the lore and unwritten tradition (from the Latin *traditio*, a giving or carrying over) is rich with implication: European, texture, street, faithful, suffused or integral customs that grow together, the organic nature of community life on which Jane Jacobs has written so perceptively. Bronzini gives the history of the almond biscotti even as they are tasting them: "direct descendents of honey and almond cakes that were baked in leaves and eaten at Roman fertility rites" (672). The lines connect history, food, pleasure, sexuality, and the sacred.

Not immune from the larger history, as the reference to Mussolini implies, with its mean streets, "the street fights, the alley sex, the petty theft" (86), and broken families, the old community even in its prime is not presented as a golden age. Drug abuse lies in the chain of causes leading to George Manza's murder. Buying a pignoli cookie, Bronzini asks after the shopowner's son, an artillery-man in Korea. The day before the novel opens, the Russians have exploded a nuclear test bomb (October 3, 1951). It is the headline in the newspaper that a boy picks up from a pile and waves as he wraps a fish in the open market. DeLillo emplots the core idea of his novel—the redemption of waste—in scrap newspaper recycled to wrap fish, symbolic of Christ. "Bronzino" is a type of fish (dialect for *branzino*, white sea bass), a sign of Bronzini's own redemption.

The darker side of the ethnic neighborhood is not neglected, even in *festa*. From his earlier years Bronzini recalls an unnamed saint's day every summer when the members of the church band played "heart-heavy pieces that brought women's faces to the open windows of the tenements" (736). In this anecdote from the first decades of the century, women are associated with the home. Playing a dirgelike song, the male musicians "slow-step along a certain resident street and stop at a particular private house, a frame structure with a front porch and rose trellis, the home of the olive oil importer" (736–37). The Mafia boss lives in a frame house, not a tenement, and fronts as an olive oil importer, a "shady" (737) house appropriate for an underworld lord. Bloodred, the rose is a flower of death. Turning aside from their true mission, the band members in their white shirts and black pants (the dress of priests and altar boys) enter this house of death and, in a satanic inversion of epiphany, pay homage to a hidden godfather by taking a sacrificial "glass of red wine" (737), also the color of blood, which profanes the saint's mass. Perhaps the reason the saint is unnamed is that the sacred has been inverted. The unnameable is associated with awe, fear, and transgression, as in Manzoni's l'Innominabile. This scene is flanked by a visit to a cemetery and a funeral home.

With regard to *festa*, DeLillo said, "I'm interested in religion as a discipline and a spectacle."[60] The artist Klara Sax visits Sabato Rodia's Watts Towers in Los Angeles, an enormous work of bricolage made from crushed glass, bottle

tops, shells, and other debris. Transforming waste into art on the analogy of redemption, Rodia "rucked in the vernacular" to build the towers, but how to define them? "An amusement park, a temple complex and she didn't know what
else. A Delhi bazaar and Italian street feast maybe. A place riddled with epiphanies, that's what it was" (492). Sax, who is Jewish, had been married to Bronzini
and lived in the same Bronx Little Italy as Nick (with whom she has had an affair). Her allusion to *festa* is not adventitious—she must have seen many of
them. She knows too that Rodia was an Italian "immigrant" (492); Rodia
might even have prompted the *festa* association. In free indirect discourse, the
arc of associations builds from the amusement park and the blocked "she didn't
know what else" to the bazaar and *festa,* to "that's what it was," the climax indicating that her attempt to find a spiritual context in which to place the Watts
Towers has been successful. She employs epiphany in the Joycean sense of a
"sudden spiritual illumination." Though Tony Tanner objects that "simply asserting that something is 'riddled with epiphanies' does not, of itself, bring the
precious glow," he misses the key point that Sax has already had the epiphany
in standing before the towers.[61] The passage cited above shows her coming to
understand the surprising nature of this epiphany by having to reach for contrary examples (cheerful amusement park, arcane temple complex), then universalizing this form of religious experience by passing from West (Italian
*feste*) to East (Delhi bazaar).

Even after the old neighborhood declines into a stark, ravaged scene with its
empty lots enclosed by barbed wire, a saving grace surrounds its elderly sur-
vivors who "sat on the stoop with paper fans and orangeades" (207). They cannot afford air-conditioning, as people can in the suburbs of the Southwest, so
they use fans; their inexpensive orange drink contrasts with the advertised
Minute Maid Orange Juice: "The Italians . . . They made their world. They
said, Who's better than me?" (207) The word *world* reverberates with its many
uses, including underworld; in spite of their poverty, these people make their
world rather than having it made for them. "Who's better than me?" is a way of
cheering themselves up, of showing pride even in the little they have; but there
is also blindness, too. Nearing eighty and walking with a cane ("stop walking
and you die" [232]), Bronzini makes the rounds, to cut a friend's hair, to sit in
a café, to play cards in his social club, to stop in on Nick's aged mother. Visiting
his old mentor, Matt stands by the entrance of his "sad building" and notices
"specimens of urban spoor—spray paint, piss, saliva, dapples of dark stuff that
was probably blood" (211). The elevator is broken, so he walks up five flights; a
child's sandal points to the disarray. As he looks into the peephole of Bronzini's
apartment he reflects upon his own pampered life in southern New Mexico
(like Nick, he lives in the Southwest): "the life of the computer suburb, those

huddled enclaves off the turnpike, situated to discourage entry"; the corner store sells "eleven kinds of croissants" and "twenty-seven coffees . . . somehow never enough" (211)—one recalls Bronzini and Father Paulus's conversation in a Little Italy café, dipping biscotti in coffee and discussing the future of the young Shay boys. What could Bronzini be thinking now? By his own admission, Matt's life is "completely unconnected to root reality," yet by contrast Bronzini watches "the ruin build round him [Bronzini] on the actual planet where he was born" (211).

One of Matt's visits to his mother coincides with Nick's, and they argue (as usual) over whether their mother should live with one of them or remain in the Bronx. (Unlike Matt or Nick, Bronzini had cared for his widowed mother at home, as he is now caring for his invalid sister.) Nick wants her to leave: the neighborhood is repellant. His mother's apartment is on a sufficiently high story for him to look down on the half-abandoned slum; he wonders why anyone would build a new motel in the area: drugs, sex, crime. The people who relax on the motel roof, "extracting pleasure from the grudging streets," make him nervous, "another local sign of instability and risk" (196). His mother lives on "the longest, saddest, scariest, most depressing" (202) hallway he ever saw. But Matt defends it as filled "with little kids most of the time" (202). If the children play in the hallways, and not the streets, they still humanize the otherwise depressing locale. The older kids are in the streets, and potentially dangerous; still, Bronzini says, "they leave us alone, the kids" (211).

Bronzini protests on behalf of the neighborhood and Mrs. Shay's remaining there in a series of life metaphors: "We want nothing to do with this business of mourning the old streets." He rejects nostalgia, invoking a model from his distant cultural past to do so. "We've made our choice. We complain but we don't mourn. . . . I don't want to adjust. I'm an old Roman stoic" (214). These people demonstrate what Wordsworth in "The Old Cumberland Beggar" called a "vital anxiousness," asserting their independence and humanity. Rosemary Shay should remain because she has "her church," "her stores," "all the familiar things, "the friends that are still alive" (197): "She lives a free life. . . . The neighborhood's still a living thing" (202), recurrent life references. Portraying their world with harshest realism and Tame Death, DeLillo admires these holdouts, as if to say, the old neighborhood is dying, yet it is "a living thing" that is dying, and not a dead thing that is given artificial life.

For this reason Osteen is wrong to claim that the "squalor" of the decimated Little Italy of the 1990s is a "different form of the same disease that plagues Nick Shay."[62] This mistakes DeLillo's intention, according to which the opposite of life is not death, which is a part of life; the real opposite of life is death-in-life. The externalization of Nick's condition is not his dying Little Italy but his comfortable, antiseptic life in Arizona. Instead of the crowded, noisy Bronx streets in the "compact" (661) neighborhood, Phoenix has a "downtown hush" and "open space" (85) between office buildings as well as in its sprawling suburbs. Instead of the "varied" richness, "disorder" (819), and "tabloid atrocity" though with a "matching redemption" (86), there is a rigid, "self-replicating" (85) order in Phoenix with which Nick identifies. Instead of the "complex deposits" and "little histories" that Bronzini as oral historian carries within him, history in Arizona "did not run loose": "They caged history, funded and bronzed it, they enshrined it carefully in museums and memorial parks" (86). The pun on *Bronzini* ("bronzed") reinforces the antithesis between the living and the dead. Protesting too much, Nick says, "I told myself how much I liked this place" (85); he would not need to keep reminding himself if his life were truly satisfying. Though the name of the city is Phoenix, with a temperature of "maybe a hundred and eight degrees out on the street" (85), one wonders if the fire bird of the spirit will rise from its own ashes.

Nick works in a "shimmering bronze tower" within a "fairy ring of hills" (85), as unreal as the imprisoned princess in a Grimm tale or a Disney cartoon. Like "bronzed" history, references to the bronze tower (85, 86, 87, 104, 119, 803) recall Bronzini in his fifth-story walk-up, its moral antithesis. Nick prides himself on feeling "assured and well defended, safe in my office box . . . connected to the things that made me stronger" (119). Not himself, "the things" are stronger from having sapped his strength. "Bemoan technology all you want," he pleads, as if to disarm criticism, "it expands your self-esteem and connects you in your well-pressed suit to the things that slip through the world otherwise unperceived" (89). The stiff, "well-pressed" suit of the Organization Man, like the illusionary "shimmering" bronze tower, exhibits surface values; the adjectives imply a robotic unnaturalness. Nick has used *connect* twice in these passages. Secure in corporate command, Nick literally "towers" over the landscape, an endless stretch of "squat box structures" (85); product stores for hearing-aid repairs and pool supplies come to mind, two items of interest to retirement communities: health care and leisure. He gazes at the "umber hills and ridges that defined the northeast view" (85), that is, toward New York and home.

Without a spiritual center, Nick focuses obsessively on ways to control his body, which he treats like a robot and which exerts its control over him. Paranoid and hypochondriacal, he rejects the food with the "old deep tomato taste," archetypal of his southern Italian roots (198); "I drank soy milk" (86), not even regular milk.[63] Everything is quantified in the technological environment: the hyperbolic "absolute maximum" of sunblock protection, "fifteen to thirty to sixty" (120; cf. 84); jogging the "metric mile," not the old-fashioned

American mile (86); a device on the waistband of his running trunks, "only three and a half ounces" (86), with its readout showing distance traveled, calories burned, and length of stride; the heat of Arizona, "a hundred and ten, a hundred and twelve" (808). He has become the mocking sum of his needs that seem endless and so can never be satisfied: "I carried my house keys in an ankle wallet that fastened with a velcro closure. I didn't like to run with house keys jiggling in my pocket. The ankle wallet answered a need. . . . It made me feel there were people out there in the world of product development and merchandising and gift cataloguing who understood the nature of my little nagging needs" (86). He buys Turkish prayer rugs and jogs listening to Sufi chanting on his Walkman, a sign of dabbling in Eastern mysticism (89). Ethnicity (East or West) has become a commodity. Nick's daughter, Lainie, and her husband, Dex, "made ethnic jewelry and sold it over a shopping channel, bracelets, chains, the works" (90). The last vestige of ethnicity is a trinket for sale on cable television. Names like Lainie and Dex have no clear referent to an ethnic past, only to the vaguely Americanized world.

Of these dangers Nick had been apprised, years before, at Voyageur by Father Paulus in a "confession" (539) of his own weakness to his pupil: "Too much irony, too much vanity, too little what—I don't know, a lot of things. And no rage." Paulus, it would appear, has not lived up to his name, has had no Damascene moment. But in his sixties he did challenge himself by organizing the college for troublemakers and misfits (as well as a few rich Catholic boys to help pay the bills). He hopes in Nick to have found a student whose very real "rage," if controlled, might lead to something of value.[64] Without essential desire directed toward a worthy object, warns Paulus, there is no possibility of self-completion: "Rage and violence can be elements of productive tension in a soul" and "can serve the fullness of one's identity. One way a man untrivializes himself is to punch another man in the mouth" (538).[65] By no means justifying Nick's accidental homicide, Paulus defends the passionately lived life. *Velleity,* with its "nice Thomistic ring" (539), is volition at its lowest ebb; "if you're low-willed, you see, you end up living in the shallowest turns and bends of your own preoccupations" (539). He paraphrases Aquinas's *Summa Theologica* (1–2, q. 52, aa.1–3) to the effect that "only intense actions will strengthen a habit. Not mere repetition. Intensity makes for moral accomplishment. An intense and persevering will" (539).[66] Intensity implies moral challenge, deciding, action, and consequences; only such actions, not mere inculcation and drill, improve an individual over the long term; the emphasis falls on the will to act and to change, both the self and the world, for the better. Paulus also teaches Jesuit lessons of naming, connections, and immanence, with a delight in linguistic precision. "Everyday things represent the most overlooked knowledge":

"Quotidian things. If they weren't important, we wouldn't use such a gorgeous Latinate word. . . . [It] suggests the depth and reach of the commonplace" (542)—and of the immanent.

Sage counsel, given to him at twenty. Yet Nick never learns to guide his rage—he simply loses it in becoming the Organization Man. He identifies with that which is apart from any "animating" presence in himself: reform school rules, Jesuit discipline without its spirituality, the corporate world, the technological system. And why not? Has he not been rewarded in conventionally societal terms? It is ironic that Nick works with hazardous waste because his life risks nothing. He does not, however, forget the lesson of the quotidian, "second meanings and deeper connections," even when putting out the rubbish.

In the epilogue Nick often thinks back to his youth, when his life and world had been continuous in their energy, passion, spontaneity, risk (not risk management), danger, and authenticity, and when life was all potential and, to that extent, free. "I long for the days of disorder. I want them back, the days when I was alive on the earth, rippling in the quick of my skin, heedless and real" (810). Since Nick recalls a time when he was "alive," he confesses that, by contrast, he is now suffering death-in-life. "I was dumb-muscled and angry and real. This is what I long for, the breach of peace, the days of disarray when I walked the streets and did things slap-bang and felt angry and ready all the time, a danger to others and a distant mystery to myself" (810).[67] He felt "real"; now it is implied that he is unreal, despite living "responsibly in the real" (82). As Father Paulus had feared, his rage went for naught; he was swept up and "systemed under" (465) as to the underworld of the technological system.

Nick's mother is moved from the Bronx to Phoenix where, alone much of the time, she watches television reruns to while away the hours—most popular is Jackie Gleason's *Honeymooners,* the title making an ironic comment on her own marriage. "Irish like her" and from a poor background, Gleason "alone can make her laugh" (106). Their own lives have the quality of reruns: "We felt better with Jackie in the room, transparent in his pain, alive and dead in Arizona" (106). And "sometimes" he accompanies her to mass, regretting that it is conducted no longer in Latin but in English: "What a stark thing it was, without murmur or reverberation" (196). For him, English robs the mass of some of its sacral quality and tradition; its Englishness is a synecdochic condensation of a technological, not a religious, universalism. "We may teach Latin as a spoken language" (675) at Voyageur, Father Paulus had told Bronzini in 1951, when it was as yet unthinkable that a church council in little more than a decade would entirely alter Latin's nearly two thousand–year role in church services. The lingua franca of the Mediterranean world has yielded to the lingua franca of technological society: "*Nostra aetate,* as the popes liked to say. In our time" (805). Yet attending mass with his mother is the "best part of my week" (106), answering his need for spirituality, linking him to his past.

At climactic moments in the epilogue, "with the years blowing by" (803), Nick wins moments of clarity and an enlarged sense of humanity. After thirty years of marriage he and his wife are "more intimate than we've ever been" (803), an achievement he rightly thinks worthy of calling attention to, at least to himself. The family is intact: they visit their daughter, son-in-law, and grand-daughter in Tucson; their son, Jeff, is living with them. At his mother's death, "I felt expanded, slowly, durably over time. I felt suffused with her truth, spread through, as with water, color or light. I thought she'd entered the deepest place I could provide, the animating entity, the thing, if anything, that will survive my own last breath, and she makes me larger, she amplifies my sense of what it is to be human" (804). This expansion of soul, rendered in images of utmost simplicity (water, color, light), opposes the analogically correspondent deple-tion of his soulless life amid corporate trappings, consumer amenities, and technological gadgetry—which, he said earlier, "expands" (89) self-esteem. The "animating . . . thing" is his skeptical presentation of the soul ("if anything"). At the funeral Matt "fell against me and wept" (806). Quietly, Nick affirms the religion of the family ("a family, still" [199]).

Drawn to esoterica, Jeff comes upon a Web site, http://blk.www/dd.com/ miraculum on which "the miracles come scrolling down" (807, 810). The word *scrolling* puns on medieval religious literature, analogizing the computer to the reception of the sacred. A twelve-year-old homeless girl named Esmeralda was found raped and murdered in the South Bronx and has become a cult figure. Jeff shies away from discussing miracles with his father; for this suburbanized young man of our time, a third-generation Italian American, "the real miracle is the web, the net" (808), and the old Bronx neighborhood is an "American gulag" (807) that repels him: Web, Net, and gulag are all metaphors for entrap-ment. But Nick, yearning for lost spirituality and drawn back to the Bronx, pursues on his own the mysteries of the screen.

The 827-page novel's final 17 pages are mainly a report off the Web, punctu-ated by keystrokes and "filtered" through Nick's mind.[68] Sisters Edgar and Gracie had searched in vain for Esmeralda whose death unleashed a wild out-pouring of grief. A graffiti artist paints the child's picture on a large mural, which becomes widely known. Most sensationally at night, every eight minutes the beam of light from a passing commuter train briefly illuminates a section of a billboard advertising Minute Maid Orange Juice, revealing the maid Esmer-alda. It is an accidental epiphany of the divine light *(lux sancta)* upon the re-deemed and redeeming Eternal Maid, except that there are no accidents in a world where everything connects.[69] People come to pray at the billboard, the frenzied crowds grow larger and larger, like the cult scene in Fellini's *La Dolce Vita* (a possible influence). Whereas Sister Gracie rejects cultism, which she denounces as "tabloid superstition," old Sister Edgar, as if recalling Pope Gregory the Great's defense of icons, admonishes her: "Don't pray to pictures, pray to saints" (819).[70] Edgar sees the mysterious face beneath the "rainbow of bounteous juice" and feels "someone living in the image, an animating spirit" (822). Eventually, the advertisement is removed, and interest tapers off.

Osteen questions whether the Esmeralda cult is a "genuine spiritual manifestation": "DeLillo remains studiously neutral; his narrator refrains from spoonfeeding us either irony or credulousness, instead just posing questions in the second person that invite our active participation."[71] The way out of this impasse is "transcendence" and "renewal": "Emblems of capital [the Minute Maid advertisement] are transmuted into an economy of grace" (258). Osteen's is a modernist stance: ideological neutrality (neither belief nor nonbelief), authorial impersonality, ironic juxtaposition, art. But, though he adopts some of their devices, DeLillo moves beyond opposition and works by analogy toward assertions of belief and conduct. Surely, for the conclusion of his epic novel he gives and asks for more than neutrality. The emblems of capitalism remain what they are, untransmuted; by analogy, however, the particulars and the orders of being to which they belong are linked together and impart new meaning.

Thematically dense, *durch-komponiert,* and symphonic in its majestic sweep, the epilogue of *Underworld* brings together many characteristic features of Italian American ethnicity and Catholicism: immanence and the analogical image, home, the child, memory, spectacle, cult, Tame Death and the afterlife. Surfing the Web, Nick discovers that his grammar school teacher Sister Edgar had died soon after joining the Esmeralda cult. As he plays on the keys, he imagines himself in contact with her; she, too, must feel the "billion distant net nodes" with their "lustrous rushing force" (825). Although cyberspace is "not heaven," there is a secular afterlife in which "everything is connected" if one performs the ritual action: "a keystroke, a mouse-click, a password—world without end, amen" (825). Global technologism with its advertised fantasy of human interconnectedness is the dark Other of an objective spiritual order of the mystical community on earth and heaven. Another keystroke enters the "H-bomb home page," at once remote and cozily familiar: apocalyptic mushroom clouds appear; Sister Edgar "sees God" or else she "sees" the largest nuclear device ever exploded, a Soviet test bomb over the Arctic Ocean in 1961, the utter denial of God. Which is it? J. Edgar Hoover also dies in the novel. Another click: in neither exactly space nor time, but in cyberspace, Sister Edgar is "hyperlinked at last" to Hoover, whirling within some purgatorial circle.

Perhaps, as David Cowart notes drily, it is the only afterlife she deserves.[72] "Is cyberspace a thing within the world," Nick wonders, "or is it the other way around?" (826). Will he find a way through his impasse, his unfulfilled desire for a spiritual life, by the help of this new machine?

For James Annesley, Sister Edgar is absorbed into an "internet nirvana" in which "science, economics, and mysticism intersect": "Why this should be the case is, however, never explained, nor is there any sense of the ways in which the complex and troubling trajectories of the novel can be resolved into this feeling of 'peace.' The author may feel a fusion of mysticism and technology washing through these final pages, but . . . others remain unconvinced." Yet DeLillo does not aim at "fusion"; he works by analogy, so opposites do not have to "resolve" to convey their meaning. There is neither Internet nirvana nor fusion of mysticism and technology because, as Nick himself says, these "intersecting systems help pull us apart"; they leave us "drained, docile"; they are "easy retreats, half-beliefs" (826). So much for the religion of technology! Tanner thinks *Underworld* "deliquesces into something close to sentimental piety" and "easy intimations of transcendence," and James Wolcott claims DeLillo's novels "have flubbed to mystification before."[73] These critics want rational explanations ("the case is . . . never explained") for what in DeLillo is supernatural intervention; since they show little awareness of his theological underpinnings or the subtleties of his religious vocabulary, they interpret as "sentimental piety," escapism, and "mystification" what are classical *pietas*, immanence, and hope.

The final pages of *Underworld* present an unveiling, an act of grace (826–27). With another keystroke a word floats across the screen, "in Sanskrit, Greek, Latin and Arabic, in a thousand languages." What and where is the word? Before disclosure, three commands appear: "Fasten, fit closely, bind together," that is, prepare to bind up the soul as if one were tying up, say, the garbage.[74] DeLillo, a Latinist, knows that the English word *religion* derives from *re-ligare*, to bind back or fasten, to bond. Like the paradisiacal vision of Dante who sees "bound in one volume that which is scattered through the universe" (*Paradise* 33.85–86), *Underworld* binds together its own world of being; it transforms the consumption and waste of contemporary civilization into a work of art. Nick turns away from the screen to look out the window; children play a "made-up" game, not a bought one or a computer game, "under the glimmerglass sky"; as if blessed by light, they play like the children of his youth. He glances around his study filled with "sunlit ardor." *Lux sancta* descends in "drenching noon," symbolic of the noonday entrance of divine plenitude into the natural world; it falls on the "monk's candle reflected in the slope of the phone," linking the Catholic Middle Ages and the scriptorium with technological modernity and communication; it makes the "tissued grain of the deskwood alive in light" and intensifies "the yellow of the yellow of the pencils" (826–27), where the hyperrealized ("alive") grain and glowing yellow signify a visionary moment. In the theology of light, the images suggest the divine inspiration visiting the writer at work. Like a "whisper of reconciliation" the word appears on the screen, in the "lunar milk of the data stream" (a metaphor of nourishment), a word that is more of a prayer uttered pianissimo than a claim that has been fulfilled: "Peace." The single-word paragraph, which is like "a blaze of calm," brings the novel to a close.[75] In the light shed around the home, and illuminating the gathered mysteries of the quotidian, Nick intimates the Underworld and the Divine World within everyday life.

# Notes

## Introduction

1. Walter E. Houghton, *The Victorian Frame of Mind, 1830–1870* (New Haven: Yale University Press, 1957), chap. 1; Nicholas Capaldi, *John Stuart Mill: A Biography* (Cambridge: Cambridge University Press, 2004), 133–37.

2. A generation is "the interval between birth and reproduction, here assumed to be 20 years" (Chris Bright, "A History of Our Future," in *State of the World: 2003* [New York: Norton, 2003], 179). Sherry Turkle, *Life on the Screen: Identity in the Age of the Internet* (New York: Simon and Schuster, 1995), 77. "Computers are more than screens onto which personality is projected. They have already become a part of how a new generation is growing up. For adults and for children who play computer games, who use the computer for manipulating words, information, visual images, and especially for those who learn to program, computers enter into the development of personality, of identity, and even of sexuality" (Turkle, *The Second Self: Computers and the Human Spirit* [London: Granada, 1984], 6). Cf. Eugene F. Provenzo Jr., *Video Kids: Making Sense of Nintendo* (Cambridge: Harvard University Press, 1991).

3. ". . . the increasing practice of bodily adornment through tattooing and the wearing of ever more jewelry on ever more parts of the body" (Stephen K. Sanderson, *Social Transformations: A General Theory of Historical Development* [1995; reprint, Lanham, MD: Rowman and Littlefield, 1999], 379).

4. Mario Rigoni Stern, introduction to *Un anno sull'Altipiano,* by Emilio Lussu (Turin: Einaudi, 2000), 3; *Guardian,* October 29, 2000, cited in James Heartfield, *The "Death of the Subject" Explained* (Sheffield: Sheffield Hallam University Press, 2002), 215. In the presentism of journalistic reality, what other comment might one expect? As Heartfield says in a chapter titled "The Retreat of the Elite," "The underlying response to the accusation of dumbing down is not to rebut the charge, but to suggest that maybe intelligence is overrated anyway" (215).

5. *Reading at Risk: A Survey of Literary Reading in America,* Research Division Report no. 46 (Washington, DC: National Endowment for the Arts, 2004), vii, ix, xi.

6. Study Group on the State of Learning in the Humanities in Higher Education, report to the National Endowment for the Humanities, *Chronicle of Higher Education* (November 28, 1984): 16–21; *Chronicle of Higher Education* (January 13, 1995): A30, cited in David Simpson, "Prospects for Global English: Back to BASIC?" *Yale Journal of Criticism* 11:1 (1998): 306. Even their film culture is woeful: they cannot appreciate the black-and-white film or, for that matter, the masterpieces of earlier cinema, confusing technological spectacle with genuine technique.

7. G. W. F. Hegel, *The Phenomenology of Mind,* trans. A. V. Miller (Oxford: Clarendon, 1977), 103 (A.3: final paragraph); Marshall McLuhan, *Understanding Media: The Extensions of Man* (Toronto: McGraw-Hill, 1964), 19. "Are we living life *on* the screen or life *in* the screen? . . . The traditional distance between people and machines has become harder to maintain" (Turkle, *Life on the Screen,* 21).

8. This stage "is already beginning to become a reality" (Peter Weibel, "The World as Interface: Toward the Construction of Context-Controlled Event-Worlds," in *Electronic Culture: Technology and Visual Representation,* ed. Timothy Druckrey [New York: Aperture, 1996], 339); Stelarc, "Towards the Post-Human," in *Cyber Reader: Critical Writings for the Digital Era,* ed. Neil Spiller (London: Phaidon, 2002), 264; Donna Haraway, *Simians, Cyborgs, and Women: The Reinvention of Nature* (New York: Routledge, 1991), 150–51.

9. Douglas S. Robertson, the author of *New Renaissance* (New York: Oxford University Press, 1998), asserts with the naive wonder and cultural deformation of a scientific projector in Swift: "The advantage of [voice-recognition] technology is that we can speak words at a rate that is several times faster than we can write or type them. After all, we have had several million years to adapt to the use of voice technology, compared to only a few thousand years to adapt to writing, and only a hundred years or so to adapt to the use of typewriters. The effect of voice-recognition technology will be to increase the productivity of writers by factors of two to five" (152–53). Just think, we could have had three *Brothers Karamazov* instead of one.

10. Allucquère Rosanne Stone on "the dawn of the virtual age" in *The War of Desire and Technology at the Close of the Mechanical Age* (Cambridge: MIT Press, 1995), 183. It is as if Rip Van Winkle had fallen asleep in the twilight of the West and awoke afresh twenty years later in early technoculture. Hugh Kenner, *The Mechanic Muse* (Oxford: Oxford University Press, 1987), 101. In 1983 Kenner predicted that "computers will have an impact on education equal only to that of the invention of the alphabet that made writing possible, and to the impact of movable type that made printed books possible" (cited in Eric Johnson, "The Awakening: Education, Writing, and Computers," *TEXT Technology* 3:6 [November 1992]: 3). In his zeal for electronic invention Kenner went so far as to say that Beckett's prose is "close to the languages of digital computers" (*The Mechanic Muse,* 92).

11. Alan C. Purves, *The Web of Text and the Web of God: An Essay on the Third Information Transformation* (New York: Guilford, 1998), vi. "Is God the network? the hypertext itself? the set of connections among spaces as well as immanent in those spaces?" (218). See David F. Noble's polemical attack on such works in *The Religion of Technology: The Divinity of Man and the Spirit of Invention* (New York: Alfred A. Knopf, 1997).

12. Marvin Lister, Jon Dovey, Seth Giddings, Iain Grant, and Kieran Kelly, *New Media:*

*A Critical Introduction* (London: Routledge, 2003), 10, 194–96. For Raymond Williams, *post*industrialism is a misnomer because it refers to the climax, not the aftermath, of industrial capitalism: "The system of rationalized production by increasing applications of technology, within a system of regular wage labour hired by the owners of the means of production, is not weakened but in its immediate terms strengthened when smaller and smaller numbers of workers are required to operate it" (*The Year 2000* [New York: Pantheon, 1983], 93).

13. The FCC approved a cellular phone system only in 1982, nine years after its invention.

14. Kenneth Flamm, *Creating the Computer: Government, Industry, and High Technology* (Washington, DC: Brookings Institution, 1988), 239.

15. Florence Olsen, "10 Challenges of the Next 10 Years," *Chronicle of Higher Education* (January 30, 2004): B1. "The mid-1980s was a turning point in the history of the computer culture. The Macintosh was introduced. [William Gibson's] *Neuromancer* was published [1984]. There was a new interest in introducing computing into elementary and secondary education, as well as into general pedagogy at the university level. Networked computing was becoming increasingly important" (Turkle, *Life on the Screen*, 322).

16. The Internet developed rapidly between 1983 and 1989 (Gene I. Rochlin, *Trapped in the Net: The Unanticipated Consequences of Computerization* [Princeton: Princeton University Press, 1997], 44). "The video game, . . . first marketed by American firms in the early 1970s, reached its full cultural significance in the early 1980s through the success of the Japanese firm Nintendo" (Michael Thomas Carroll, *Popular Modernity in America: Experience, Technology, Mythohistory* [Albany: SUNY Press, 2000], 24).

17. Don DeLillo, *Underworld* (New York: Scribner, 1997), 805.

18. Lister et al., *New Media*, 11–13, 63, 97.

19. José Ortega y Gasset, *Man and Crisis,* trans. Mildred Adams (New York: Norton, 1958), 59–66; Fernand Braudel, *On History,* trans. Sarah Matthews (Chicago: University of Chicago Press, 1980), 29–31, 50–52. In Braudelian terms, the communications revolution of the 1980s might be taken as an "intercycle" such as Ernest Labrousse saw in the depression of 1774–1791, "one of the prime launching pads of the French Revolution" (30).

20. Pitirim A. Sorokin, *Social and Cultural Dynamics* (Boston: Porter Sargent, 1937–1941), 3:535; 4:775; foreword to one-volume abridgement [Boston: Porter Sargent, 1957], iv). In passages such as these Sorokin foreshadows his Russian compatriot Aleksandr Solzhenitsyn—for example, his commencement lecture at Harvard, "The Exhausted West" (June 8, 1978). Arnold Toynbee, *A Study of History* (London: Oxford University Press, 1934–1961), 4:52, 275; Toynbee, *Civilization on Trial* (New York: Oxford University Press, 1948), 45. Cf. Marvin Perry, *Arnold Toynbee and the Crisis of the West* (New York: Lanham, 1982), 83–93.

21. Carroll Quigley, *The Evolution of Civilizations: An Introduction to Historical Analysis* (1961; reprint, Indianapolis: Liberty Press, 1979), 127, 413; Quigley, *Public Authority and the State in the Western Tradition: A Thousand Years of Growth, 976–1976,* Oscar Iden Lectures (Washington, DC: School of Foreign Service, Georgetown University, 1977), 26, 30, 36, 40. Cf. David Wilkinson, "From Mesopotamia through Carroll Quigley to Bill Clinton: World Historical Systems, the Civilizationist, and the President," *Journal of World-Systems Research* 1:1 (1995): 45–49.

22. Matthew Melko, *The Nature of Civilizations* (Boston: Porter Sargent, 1969), 163; Sanderson, *Social Transformations,* 379, 380. In an afterword to the expanded edition Sanderson did not alter his judgment, citing Albert Somit and Steven A. Peterson to the effect that "democracy may be only a fleeting phase that is destined to disappear in the near future"; "I fear they are correct" (424).

23. Quigley likens this possible future to the Holy Roman Empire at the end of the medieval period, a loose confederation with a titular leader (*Tragedy and Hope: A History of the World in Our Time* [New York: Macmillan, 1966], 1287). The West "believes in diversity rather than in uniformity, in pluralism rather than in monism or dualism, in inclusion rather than in exclusion, in liberty rather than in authority, in truth rather than in power, in conversion rather than in annihilation, in the individual rather than in the organization, in reconciliation rather than in triumph" (1227).

24. Robert A. Heilbroner, "Technological Determinism Revisited," in *Does Technology Drive History? The Dilemma of Technological Determinism,* ed. Merritt Roe Smith and Leo Marx (Cambridge: MIT Press, 1994), 74. There are two main types of technological determinism: "a 'soft view,' which holds that technological change drives social change but at the same time responds discriminatingly to social pressures, and a 'hard view,' which perceives technological development as an autonomous force, completely independent of social constraints" (Merritt Roe Smith, "Technological Determinism in American Culture," in ibid., 2).

25. Jacques Ellul, *The Technological Society,* trans. John W. Wilkinson (1954; English translation, 1964; reprint, New York: Alfred A. Knopf, 1973), 5. "Technique has enough of the mechanical in its nature to enable it to cope with the machine, but it surpasses and transcends the machine because it remains in close touch with the human order. The metal monster could not go on forever torturing mankind. It found in technique a rule as hard and inflexible as itself" (5).

26. Jacques Ellul, *Propaganda: The Formation of Men's Attitudes,* trans. Konrad Kellen and Jean Lerner (New York: Alfred A. Knopf, 1965), 22, 30–31, 290, 303–5, 308–10. "Education," notes Kellen, "is the absolute prerequisite for propaganda." Ellul considers "intellectuals as virtually the most vulnerable of all to propaganda, for three reasons: (1) they absorb the largest amount of secondhand, unverifiable information; (2) they feel a compelling need to have an opinion on every important question of our time, and thus easily succumb to opinions offered to them by propaganda on all such indigestible pieces of information; (3) they consider themselves capable of 'judging for themselves.' They literally need propaganda" (vi). Sebastian De Grazia points out that advertisers "gladly greet the news that college enrollments will be on the increase" because studies have "led them to expect that 'At every income level there is a general tendency by the college group to spend about twice as much as households whose heads did not finish grade school'" (*Of Time, Work, and Leisure* [New York: Twentieth Century Fund, 1962], 525). Ellul, *The Technological Society,* 5; Ellul, *The Technological System,* trans. Joachim Neugroschel (New York: Continuum, 1980), 171.

27. Cited in W. Terrence Gordon, *Marshall McLuhan: Escape into Understanding; A Biography* (New York: Basic Books, 1997), 183; Matie Molinaro, Corinne McLuhan, and William Toye, eds., *Letters of Marshall McLuhan* (Oxford: Oxford University Press, 1987), 261 (letter to David Reisman, February 18, 1960); Marshall McLuhan, *Counterblast* (New York: Harcourt, Brace, and World, 1969), 14; McLuhan, *Understanding Media,* 23 (see also Gordon, *Marshall McLuhan,* 200, 201). In *The Passing of Traditional*

*Society* (1958), Daniel Lerner also considers "advanced communications as the key to making societies modern" (Michael Adas, *Machines as the Measure of Man: Science, Technology, and Ideologies of Western Dominance* [Ithaca: Cornell University Press, 1989], 414). Cf. Elena Lamberti, *Marshall McLuhan: Tra letteratura, arte, e media* (Milan: Mondadori, 2000), 60–66, 80–90.

28. Cited in G. E. Stearn, *McLuhan: Hot and Cool* (Toronto: Signet, 1969), 331. "Media effects are new environments as imperceptible as water to a fish, subliminal for the most part" (McLuhan, *Counterblast*, 22). *The Medium Is the Massage* appeared in 1967. See James van der Laan, "Temptation and Seduction in the Technological Milieu," *Bulletin of Science, Technology and Society* 24:6 (2004): 509–15.

29. Samuel P. Huntington, *The Clash of Civilizations and the Remaking of World Order* (New York: Simon and Schuster, 1996), 4. "Avoidance of a global war of civilizations depends on world leaders accepting and cooperating to maintain the multi-civilizational character of global politics" (4). Dieter Senghaas, *The Clash within Civilizations: Coming to Terms with Cultural Conflicts* (London: Routledge, 2002), 77.

30. Langdon Winner, *Autonomous Technology: Technics-Out-of-Control as a Theme in Political Thought* (Cambridge: MIT Press, 1977), 202, 314, 323–24; Winner, *The Whale and the Reactor: A Search for Limits in an Age of High Technology* (Chicago: University of Chicago Press, 1986), 55, cited in M. R. Smith, "Technological Determinism," 32–33.

31. Peter C. Perdue, "Technological Determinism in Agrarian Societies," in *Does Technology Drive History?* ed. Smith and Marx, 188. "The more we discover about human and natural processes, the more potential power we seem to have and the less real control. Once we recognize that our choices are limited but not totally determined by the natural and social orders we live in, in both industrial and agricultural production systems, we can either surrender to despair or, in a new humility, discover appropriate roles for ourselves in the interrelated structures that humans, natural forces, and their tools create" (196–97).

32. Albert Borgmann, *Technology and the Character of Contemporary Life: A Philosophical Inquiry* (Chicago: University of Chicago Press, 1984), 41, 42, 189, 196, 207, 210, 220, 246, 247; advertisement for Borgmann, *Power Failure: Christianity in the Culture of Technology* (Grand Rapids: Brazos Press, 2003), in *Discerning Reader* (http://www.discerningreader.com). Echoing Borgmann, Charles Taylor believes that the claims of those who believe the technological system has us "totally locked in" are "wildly exaggerated"; their view "simplifies too much and forgets the essential." A great forgetting, indeed! Trying to steer a middle position, awarding claims to both the knockers and the boosters of technology, he believes that one can practice a benevolent technology (helping victims of hurricanes and famine), but Ellul says as much—the point is that this entails more technology. Although Taylor admits the "slide" toward technological domination, he is hazy and abstract on how to deal with it: "Instead of seeing our predicament as fated to generate a drive for ever-increasing technological control, which we will then either rejoice at or bemoan depending on our outlook, we understand it as open to contestation, as a locus of probably unending struggle." The resistance to atomistic individualism and instrumental reason since the romantic period "has made some dent"; "if we could uncover those moral sources we could doubtless make more of a dent; we do not have to live technology the way we do"; "the other modes are open," and so on. But such a transformation requires a far greater historical force than Taylor envisages; it is not going to be settled in a debating hall (*The Ethics of*

*Authenticity* [Cambridge: Harvard University Press, 1992], 73, 98–99, 107). One may contrast his well-intentioned wishful thinking with the savage realism of Ellul.

33. Cf. Winner, *Autonomous Technology:* "The dynamism that Ellul uncovers at this level is based on a series of contingencies. It is based on an if . . . then kind of logic": *if* the following three conditions are present—"(1) the universal willingness of people to seek and employ technological innovations, (2) the existence of organized social systems in all technical fields, and (3) the existence of technical forms upon which new combinations and modifications are based"—*then* the "expansion of technology is assured" (65–66).

34. Ellul, *Propaganda,* 6. "American sociologists scientifically try to play down the effectiveness of propaganda because they cannot accept the idea that the individual—that cornerstone of democracy—can be so fragile; and because they retain their ultimate trust in man. Personally, I, too, tend to believe in the pre-eminence of man and, consequently, in his invincibility. Nevertheless, as I observe the facts, I realize man is terribly malleable, uncertain of himself, ready to accept and to follow many suggestions, and is tossed about by all the winds of doctrine. . . . If I am in favor of democracy, I can only regret that propaganda renders the true exercise of it almost impossible" (xvi).

35. Berta Sichel, "New Hope for the Technological Society: An Interview with Jacques Ellul," *ETC.* 40:2 (Summer 1983): 194–95. In the early post–World War II period Ellul said he was pessimistic with regard to technology while his audience was optimistic. Later, he grew more hopeful while his audience turned negative (206). Cf. I. A. Richards, no enemy of scientism, in his later years (interview with Bruce Boucher and John Paul Russo, in *Complementarities: Uncollected Essays,* ed. Russo [Cambridge: Harvard University Press, 1976], 238).

36. Jacques Ellul, "The Search for Ethics in a Technicist Society" (1983), trans. Dominique Gillot and Carl Mitcham, *Research in Philosophy and Technology* 9 (1989): 31; Ellul, "How I Discovered Hope," *Other Side* 16:3 (March 1980): 29–30. "Events occurring since [Ellul] wrote *The Technological Society,*" comments C. A. Bowers, "provide optimism that the global spread of technological development, while perhaps irreversible, can be limited" (*Let Them Eat Data: How Computers Affect Education, Cultural Diversity, and the Prospects of Ecological Sustainability* [Athens: University of Georgia Press, 2000], 144). See also Carl Mitcham, *Thinking through Technology: The Path between Engineering and Philosophy* (Chicago: University of Chicago Press, 1994), 57–61.

37. Sichel, "New Hope," 206. Larry A. Hickman argues that Ellulian hope is an antimyth to confront the myth of the human loss of control amid technique. When, however, Ellul counsels "the hopeful Christian to *do* something creative, to *work* diligently for control within the interstices of the technological society," his religious myth contains a "subordinate technological myth: a covert story of control . . . a component that he cannot avoid if he is to propose any action at all" (*Philosophical Tools for Technological Culture: Putting Pragmatism to Work* [Bloomington: Indiana University Press, 2001], 150–51). One fails to see how Ellulian resistance, reason, limit, and self-control in the humanistic sense have anything to do with technological organization. Hickman's commentary on Heidegger mixes two meanings of control.

38. Romano Guardini, *Letters from Lake Como: Explorations in Technology and the*

*Human Race,* trans. Geoffrey W. Bromiley (Grand Rapids: William B. Eerdmans, 1994), 6. The elderly Goethe kept abreast of the growth of industrialism, commenting on the stark intrusion of factories in the Swiss mountain landscape in *Wilhelm Meisters Wanderjahre* (1829). "Riches and rapidity are that which the world admires and for which everyone strives," he wrote in 1825. "Railways, fast mails, steamships, and all possible facilities for communications are the field which the civilized world has in view that it may over-educate itself and thereby continue in a state of mediocrity. And it is, moreover, the result of universality that a mediocre culture should become common" (cited in Benjamin C. Sax, *Images of Identity: Goethe and the Problem of Self-Conception in Nineteenth-Century Germany* [New York: Peter Lang, 1987], 118).

39. Guardini, *Letters from Lake Como,* 7, 46. "The means were always integrated into the interplay of the human unit, and a limit was always set to make possible direct and living execution" (66). Goethe lamented the loss of the classical sense of limit: "The humblest individual can be complete, provided he moves within the limits of his talents and accomplishments," he said in 1829, "but even high deserts are obscured and annulled when this indispensable balance is absent. Cases of such disharmony are bound to multiply in our epoch; for who can do justice to the demands of an age so intense and so rapid in its movement?" (cited in Sax, *Images of Identity,* 118–19).

40. Romano Guardini, *The End of the Modern World* (Wilmington, DE: ISI Books, 1998), 53, 55. In his analysis of Giovanni Bellini's *St. Francis in Ecstasy* (Frick Collection, New York), Anchise Tempestini speaks of the "extraordinary synthesis with which the artist succeeds in presenting a landscape animated by the human presence, by various species of animals, and by plants, which grow scantily among the rocks but are luxuriant in the fertile plains and on the hills in the background. It is nature in which humans have intervened without disturbing its harmony and balance; for us, it is a nostalgic vision of a way of life within the natural environment that we see as lost and irretrievable" (*Giovanni Bellini,* trans. Alexandra Bonfante-Warren and Jay Hyams [New York: Abbeville, 1999], 114).

41. Guardini, *End of the Modern World,* 51, 56, 59, 88.

42. Ibid., 56; Guardini, *Letters from Lake Como,* 83, 85. Resembling Guardini in both his philosophic sensibility and his faith in the future, Gilbert Germain emphasizes the need to remain aware of our "living connection with the world we inhabit" in response to the so-called disenchantment of nature by technology (*A Discourse in Disenchantment: Reflections on Politics and Technology* [Albany: SUNY Press, 1993], 151).

43. Lewis Mumford, *The Urban Prospect* (New York: Harcourt, Brace, and World, 1968), 5; Mumford, *The Myth of the Machine,* vol. 2, *The Pentagon of Power* (New York: Harcourt Brace Jovanovich, 1970), 432–35.

44. David Solomon, "MacIntyre and Contemporary Moral Philosophy," in *Alasdair MacIntyre,* ed. Mark C. Murphy (Cambridge: Cambridge University Press, 2003), 144; Alasdair MacIntyre, *After Virtue: A Study in Moral Theory* (Notre Dame, Ind.: University of Notre Dame Press, 1981), 263. One of MacIntyre's notoriously bad analogies is between the totalitarian Soviet state and Borgia papacy (261–62). Ellul distrusted such analogies because the problems of earlier societies (monarchies, despotisms, democracies, and so on) were essentially sociopolitical and more or less amenable to intervention, whereas in the contemporary world the technological system is the governing force that blocks human attempts to alter its mandates (Sichel, "New Hope," 199).

45. Johan Galtung, Tore Heiestad, and Erik Rudeng, "On the Decline and Fall of Empires: The Roman Empire and Western Imperialism Compared," *Review* 4 (1980): 91–153, cited in Sanderson, *Social Transformations,* 378–79; see also note 3 above. The description recalls Vico's prophecy at the end of *New Science* (1744) on the "barbarism of reflection" that would overtake modernity (see Chapter 3). Matthew Melko, "The Contributions of Carroll Quigley to the Comparative Study of Civilizations and to the Study of Civilizational Interactions," *Comparative Civilizations Bulletin* 1 (Spring 1977): 6–7; Quigley, *Public Authority and the State,* 40. Cf. Livy on the decline of Rome (made astonishingly early, around 27 BC): "Of late years wealth has made us greedy, and self-indulgence has brought us, through every form of sensual excess, to be, if I may so put it, in love with death both individual and collective" (*The Early History of Rome,* trans. Aubrey de Sélincourt [London: Penguin, 1965], 3).

46. MacIntyre, *After Virtue,* 263. "The good life for man is the life spent in seeking for the good life for man, and the virtues necessary for the seeking are those which will enable us to understand more and what else the good life for man is" (219). Terry Pinkard, "MacIntyre's Critique of Modernity," in *Alasdair MacIntyre,* ed. Murphy, 180–81; MacIntyre, *After Virtue,* 223.

47. Nicola Chiaromonte, *The Worm of Consciousness, and Other Essays,* ed. Miriam Chiaromonte (New York: Harcourt Brace Jovanovich, 1976), 33. Gregory D. Sumner discusses Chiaromonte's "simple virtues," sense of limit, "solidarity," and the "Mediterranean genius for small-scale informality" in *Dwight Macdonald and the Politics Circle: The Challenge of Cosmopolitan Democracy* (Ithaca: Cornell University Press, 1996), 27–31, 158–67. Malraux drew the character of Scali after Chiaromonte in *Man's Hope.*

48. Chiaromonte, *Worm of Consciousness,* 64, 65. Rejecting abstract notions of history and progress, he decries an age of "bad faith," "the belief that material (industrial, technological, and scientific) advances go hand in hand with spiritual progress." He urges "conversion" to "the immediacy of nature and experience, to contact with things, one by one, in their primal disorder," for "cosmic piety" (the phrase is Bertrand Russell's) and respect for "the 'divine' inherent in all things and in every impulse of the spirit" (*The Paradox of History* [Philadelphia: University of Pennsylvania Press, 1985], 145, 147–48).

49. Sichel, "New Hope," 195; Michael Storper, "Lived Effects of the Contemporary Economy: Globalization, Inequality, and Consumer Society," *Public Culture* 12:2 (2000): 400.

50. A member of the Cambridge Heretics, founded by his collaborator C. K. Ogden, I. A. Richards published his theoretical studies on belief in the 1920s and '30s and was contributing to the topic as late as 1974, in his book *Beyond.* Much of this book was written during what has been called the "greater secularization decade" (1956–1973) in the Atlantic world. "Britain in the 1960s experienced more secularisation than in all the preceding four centuries put together," notes Callum G. Brown. "Never before had all of the numerical indicators of popular religiosity fallen simultaneously, and never before had their declension been so steep" ("The Secularisation Decade: What the 1960s Have Done to the Study of Religious History," in *The Decline of Christendom in Western Europe, 1750–2000,* ed. Hugh McLeod and Werner Ustorf [Cambridge: Cambridge University Press, 2003], 29). Brown notes that the change appears to be perma-

nent, not cyclical. This was the era of the Beatles and the emphasis on immediacy (for example, John Lennon's "Imagine there's no heaven"). Mainstream Christian church membership fell from 8 million in 1975 to 6,720,000 in 1992 (Heartfield, *"Death of the Subject,"* 163).

51. Charles E. Passage, trans., *The Complete Works of Horace (Quintus Horatius Flaccus)* (New York: Ungar, 1983), 5.

52. Coventry Patmore, cited in Walter Lippmann, *The Public Philosophy* (London: Hamish Hamilton, 1955), 11, and the title of a book by Sir Ernest Barker (1948). One of civility's traditions, which Lippmann sees in transcendent terms, is *openness*. Fed by many streams, Western humanism has refused to adopt a single, reductive explanation of human nature; this virtue may be less welcome if, as in the present, one or another system of explanation claims legitimacy. Even when thinkers decry closed systems or grand narratives, their antitotalization is too often pursued in the very dogmatic spirit that they elsewhere deplore.

## I. The Future of the Humanities in a Technological Society

1. The simile is adopted from Ruskin, on tourism and the new cult of speed: "All travelling becomes dull in exact proportion to its rapidity. Going by railroad I do not consider as travelling at all; it is merely 'being sent' to a place, and very little different from becoming a parcel." To *see*, it is necessary to slow down: "A turn of a country road, with a cottage beside it, which we have not seen before, is as much as we need for refreshment; if we hurry past it, and take two cottages at a time, it is already too much" (*Modern Painters*, vol. 3, *The Works of John Ruskin*, ed. E. T. Cook and Alexander Wedderburn [London: Unwin, 1903–1912], 5:370).

2. Eugenio Garin, *L'educazione umanistica in Italia*, 9th ed. (Bari: Laterza, 1975), 11. "It is not a *logos* and an historic commonality that should constitute the horizon of reference," says Gianni Vattimo in what may supplement Garin, "but the idea of an indefinite enlargement of *logos* before a community-always-in-the-making" (cited in Maurizio Ferraris, "Etica e ermeneutica," *Aut Aut* [Milan], n.s., 228 [1988]: 87–95). The allusion is to Heraclitus, "It is the *logos* of soul to increase itself."

3. At least the triumph of the humanities is much further off than he envisaged.

4. Andrew Feenberg, *Critical Theory of Technology* (New York: Oxford University Press, 1991), 7.

5. John R. Searle, *Is There a Crisis in American Higher Education?* Founder's Day Pamphlet Series no. 1 (Cheney: Eastern Washington University Press, 1995), 17–18.

6. "Whether the end accomplished is wise or unwise, beautiful or hideous, beneficial or harmful, must be determined independently of the instrument employed" (Winner, *Autonomous Technology*, 27).

7. Feenberg, *Critical Theory of Technology*, 6.

8. Ibid., 8.

9. As for "extreme": Stephen Rose says that Ellul is "just a frustrated man who [has] never been accepted and who [spends] most of his time railing against this fact." More sympathetic, Mumford still disapproves of Ellul's "ingrained fatalism." For Rupert Hall, "Ellul lives on black bread and spring water. . . . The prophet whose cry is only

'Woe, ye are damned' walks unheeded. Ellul is such a prophet. . . . If he is right, his book is useless" (cited in Clifford G. Christians, "Ellul on Solution: An Alternative but No Prophecy," in *Jacques Ellul: Interpretive Essays,* ed. Clifford G. Christians and Jay M. Van Hook [Urbana: University of Illinois Press, 1981], 147).

10. Ellul, *The Technological Society,* xxv.

11. Jacques Ellul, *The Humiliation of the Word,* trans. Joyce Main Hanks (Grand Rapids: William B. Eerdmans, 1985), 151. The concept of "least effort" to which I also allude is a way of putting Jacques Ellul's formula; according to Jeffrey Robbins, the phrase was originally employed by George Kingsley Zipf in *Human Behavior and the Principle of Least Effort* (Cambridge: Addison-Wesley, 1949) and traces to the principle of least action in physics, which in turn is related to the principle of economy. Whether Ellul knew of Zipf's work remains unclear (Chapter 2, note 23).

12. Robert Kanigel, *The One Best Way: Frederick Winslow Taylor and the Enigma of Efficiency* (New York: Viking, 1997), 441. The first efficiency expert and founder of scientific management, Taylor wrote that "the same principles can be applied with equal force to all social activities; to the management of our homes; the management of our farms; the management of the business of our tradesmen, large and small; of our churches, our philanthropic institutions, our universities, and our governmental departments" (*The Principles of Scientific Management* [1911], cited in Kanigel, *One Best Way,* 438–39).

13. The "fundamental law" of the instrumental theory of technology is "You cannot optimize two variables": one inevitably proves more efficient. Meanwhile, political, social, and religious trade-offs may introduce nontechnical values (Feenberg, *Critical Theory of Technology,* 6).

14. Ellul, *The Technological System,* 209.

15. C. George Benello, "Technology and Power: Technique as a Mode of Understanding Modernity," in *Jacques Ellul,* ed. Christians and Van Hook, 92. "Once the technical orientation has been adopted, an automatic cycle begins which brings into existence all possible results of technique" (92).

16. On the forces propelling an information economy Anthony Smith points out: "Information crises became endemic within the capitalist system from the middle of the last century. For example, keeping track of freight wagons in the massive US railroad system brought in its wake problems of managerial control—what we would call problems of information processing—that would have prevented further growth had not separate systems for handling the information itself evolved. Managing the handling of containers within a shipping operation, booking tickets for planes, ships and trains, running the timetabling of transportation systems, manufacturing the spare parts for mass consumer goods ranging from pianos to motor cars: all gradually became, or would have become, impossible without paratechnologies for collating the information" (*Software for the Self: Technology and Culture* [New York: Oxford University Press, 1996], 78).

17. Maurice Roche on the new capitalist world order echoes Ellulian self-augmentation ("Mega-events and Micro-modernization: On the Sociology of the New Urban Tourism," in *The Sociology of Tourism: Theoretical and Empirical Investigations,* ed. Yiorgos Apostolopoulos, Stella Leivadi, and Andrew Yiannakis [London: Routledge, 1996], 318).

18. Ellul, *The Technological Society,* 97.

19. Robert Merton, introduction to ibid., vi.

20. For Harry Braverman, Ellul is a bourgeois ideologist, "fetishizing" technology, treating it independently of social relations, and not seeing it as a weapon in the hands of capitalists (*Labor and Monopoly Capital: The Degradation of Work in the Twentieth Century* [New York: Monthly Review Press, 1974], 229). But Ellul points out that technology had won over not only the capitalists but also the workers; that "a common will developed to exploit the possibilities of technique to the maximum, and groups of the most conflicting interests (state and individual, *bourgeois* and working class) united to hymn its praises" (*The Technological Society,* 54–55). Moreover, he concedes that technique had improved the lot of labor in many ways, such as by reducing the working day and revolutionizing medicine. However, Ellul's whole argument is that if the workers were suddenly to come to power, their state would not want any less technology than the one they overthrew, so the problem of technology would not disappear. The state is the major supporter of the technological system, and hence a frequent target of Ellul's; it does not so much matter what kind of state *from a strictly technological standpoint,* as long as its ideology does not interfere, or interferes as little as possible, with the technological imperatives. Among reasons given for the collapse of the Soviet Union was its inability to keep up with the technological revolution.

John McMurtry defends Marx's belief in technology as an extension of human nature against Ellul's position that the technological system *as a whole* is in contradiction with it: Marx would construe such "neo-Luddite . . . distress at technology as, demystified, distress at the capitalist law of utilization of technology" (*The Structure of Marx's World-View* [Princeton: Princeton University Press, 1978], 224). But he never gets to the core of Ellul's critique any more than Braverman.

21. Ellul, *The Technological Society,* 132; Ellul, *The Technological System,* 171.

22. Cf. Jacques Ellul, *The Betrayal of the West,* trans. Matthew J. O'Connell (New York: Seabury, 1978): "No one today can claim to follow an autonomous path. And yet we see our intellectuals hugging the illusion that China has found 'another way.' Is it not perfectly clear, however, that this 'other way' is really not other at all and that everything about it—the Marxism, the rational methods, and above all, the very movement itself—is Western in its inspiration?" (31).

23. Ellul, *The Technological System,* 170. "Technique cannot be otherwise than totalitarian. It can be truly efficient and scientific only if it absorbs an enormous number of phenomena and brings into play the maximum of data" (*The Technological Society,* 125).

24. Winner, *Autonomous Technology,* 13.

25. Ellul, *The Technological System,* 125. The past sixty years have witnessed the decline in the number of wading birds in the Florida Everglades by 90 percent. Who would not support efforts to clean up and protect the Everglades? Yet technology is an indispensable means to accomplish this goal.

26. Ellul, *The Technological Society,* 82. "This can be said only of the *ensemble* of techniques, of the technical phenomenon, and not of any particular technique" (90).

27. Ellul, *The Technological System,* 125; Ellul, *The Technological Society,* 86, 92–93, 135. "At the present time, technique has arrived at such a point in its evolution that it is being transformed and is progressing almost without decisive intervention by man" (*The Technological Society,* 85). Technoevolutionism has a history with arguments on all sides of the question. Shortly after Darwin's epochal discoveries, Samuel Butler fan-

tasized that the machine was a step forward in the evolutionary process. Capable of doing what human beings could not, machines ultimately would dominate their inventors. "Day by day, the machines are gaining ground upon us . . . more men are daily bound down as slaves to tend them, more men are daily devoting the energies of their whole lives to the development of mechanical life. . . . that the time will come when the machines will hold the real supremacy over the world and its inhabitants is what no person of a truly philosophic mind can for a moment question" (*Notebooks,* cited in Mumford, *Myth of the Machine,* vol. 2, *The Pentagon of Power,* 194–95). Mumford credits Butler with launching the concept of automation, Norbert Weiner with the possibility of a machine producing another machine. Since machines will do everything better, "the transposition of life into mechanical organizations will, Butler pointed out, eliminate man's most serious difficulty: that of developing his own capacities to become human" (194).

At the same time, technoevolutionism has its proponents. "In the past the man was first; in the future the system must be first," wrote Frederick W. Taylor (cited in Kanigel, *One Best Way,* 438). "Can the synthesis of men and machine ever be stable," asks Arthur Clarke, "or will the purely organic component become such a hindrance that it has to be discarded? If this eventually happens—and I have . . . good reasons for thinking that it must—we have nothing to regret and certainly nothing to fear." Paraphrasing this argument, Winner says that "man should be pleased to have played even a small walk-on part in this much larger drama. To complain that humans have been left out of the final scenes is merely an example of outdated species chauvinism." In some views, notes Winner, machines are becoming more and more human, and human beings are becoming more and more like "cybernated organisms" surrounded by machines, but many theories of technoevolution suffer from the flaw that they presume the eclipse of free conscious agents (*Autonomous Technology,* 58–59).

28. Martin Heidegger, *Discourse on Thinking* cited in Winner, *Autonomous Technology,* 14.

29. Franco Piperno, "Technological Innovation and Sentimental Education," in *Radical Thought in Italy: A Potential Politics,* ed. Paolo Virno and Michael Hardt (Minneapolis: University of Minnesota Press, 1996), 123, 126.

30. Mumford, *Myth of the Machine,* vol. 2, *Pentagon of Power*, caption to fig. 21, between pp. 340 and 341.

31. See, for example, Gordon, *Marshall McLuhan,* 193–218.

32. Don Ihde, "Image Technologies and Traditional Culture," *Inquiry* (Oslo), 35 (1992): 378. "Images are the chosen form of expression in our civilization—images, not words" (Ellul, *Humiliation of the Word,* 126). Ours is "the century of the screen" (Paul Levinson, *The Soft Edge: A Natural History and Future of the Information Revolution* [London: Routledge: 1997], 162).

33. Ellul, *Humiliation of the Word,* 115–16, 127–28.

34. Ihde, "Image Technologies," 382, 383.

35. Ellul, *Humiliation of the Word,* 134, 211. "Impression and image take precedence over logic and concept," notes Sven Birkerts on the differences between print culture and electronic imaging (*The Gutenberg Elegies: The Fate of Reading in an Electronic Age* [London: Faber and Faber, 1994], 122).

36. Opened in 1983, Tokyo Disneyland was meant to be an "exact replica" of the original; its producers wanted Japanese visitors "to feel they were taking a foreign va-

cation." It became the top attraction in Japan within five years (fifty million visitors by 1988), where a visit "now replaces traditional outings to shrines and temples for graduation and new year celebrations." The French Press initially disparaged Disneyland Paris by calling it a "cultural Chernobyl." Yet when Disney managers made some concessions to give the complex a more European look and feel, the Europeans reacted negatively: they "came for an American experience." As a result, Disney returned to its original plan, and Disneyland Paris was on its way to success (Susan C. Schneider and Jean-Louis Barsoux, *Managing across Cultures* [New York: Prentice-Hall, 1997], 66).

37. Giuli Liebman Parrinello, "Motivation and Anticipation in Post-industrial Tourism," in *Sociology of Tourism,* ed. Apostolopoulos, Leivadi, and Yiannakis, 85. In "VR Means Virtual Reconstruction: Cluny Abbey Has Been Rebuilt" (*Wired* 2:1 [January 1994]), Andrew Joscelyne numbers contributions from Medialab, IBM, and France's Telecom ISDN bandwidth to the Institute National de l'Audiovisuel and the notes of the late Harvard architecture professor John Kenneth Conant: "You can't tour the Abbey of Cluny televirtually from your hot tub in Malibu yet, but real visitors can try out the on-site head-mounted-display version or view the video of the computer-generated mock-up via an interactive terminal."

38. Ihde, "Image Technologies," 383, 385–86.

39. Ellul, *Humiliation of the Word,* 117, 150–51.

40. Robert D. Putnam, "The Strange Disappearance of Civic America," in *Ticking Time Bombs: The New Conservative Assaults on Democracy,* ed. Robert Kuttner (New York: New Press, 1996), 281, 282. Disputing Putnam, Michael Schudson argues: "If people who formerly joined the YMCA to use the gym now go to the local fitness center, Putnam's measures will show a decrease in civic participation when real civic activity is unchanged" ("What If Civic Life Didn't Die?" in ibid., 287). It is not my intention to be anecdotal, but I visited a local fitness center and found it quieter than a church. In one room about twenty men and women were lined up doing treadmill exercises, each watching his or her own television hooked up with earphones. Might this support Putnam's argument that privatism is increasing, that "real civic activity" *has* changed? I am indebted to Anthony Lewis's commentary on Putnam in the *New York Times.*

41. Among the most litigious people in the world, Americans are fascinated by endless legal procedures ("Technicism is compatible with an increasingly legalistic interpretation of the American civic tradition," contends Manfred Stanley in *The Technological Conscience: Survival and Dignity in an Age of Expertise* [New York: Free Press, 1978], 206).

42. Ithiel de Sola Pool, *Technologies without Boundaries: On Telecommunications in a Global Age,* ed. Eli M. Noam (Cambridge: Harvard University Press, 1990), 261–62; Stanley, *Technological Conscience,* 44.

43. Thomas Sprat, *The History of the Royal Society* (1667), 113; Philippe Roqueplo and Marcel Jousse cited in Jacques Ellul, *The Technological Bluff,* trans. Geoffrey W. Bromiley (Grand Rapids: William B. Eerdmans, 1990), 143.

44. Ellul, *Humiliation of the Word,* 152. "Just as it was the agent of humanity's formation in the midst of the animals, so the word in our day is the agent of the great refusal" (176).

45. Heir to the concept of memory training in classical tradition, Vico advocated the teaching of languages in childhood, "when reason is much weaker while memory is so much stronger" (oration 6, in *On Humanistic Education [Six Inaugural Orations,*

*1699–1707],* trans. Giorgio A. Pinton and Arthur W. Shippee [Ithaca: Cornell University Press, 1993], 135). "Let their imagination and memory be fortified so that they may be effective in those arts in which fantasy and the mnemonic faculty are predominant. At a later stage let them learn criticism, so that they can apply the fullness of their personal judgment to what they have been taught" (*On the Study Methods of Our Time,* trans. Elio Gianturco [Indianapolis: Bobbs-Merrill, 1965], 19; see also Robert J. Di Pietro, "Humanism in Linguistic Theory: A Lesson from Vico," in *Giambattista Vico's Science of Humanity,* ed. Giorgio Tagliacozzo and Donald Phillip Verene [Baltimore: Johns Hopkins University Press, 1976], 349).

46. Ellul, *Humiliation of the Word,* 162. Cf. John Naisbitt, *Megatrends* (1982): "More than 60 percent of us work with information as programmers, teachers, clerks, secretaries, accountants, stockbrokers, managers, insurance people, bureaucrats, lawyers, bankers, and technicians" (14), cited in William Wresch, *Disconnected: Haves and Have-Nots in the Information Age* (New Brunswick, NJ: Rutgers University Press, 1996), 6.

47. Richards labored for many years to counter any such tendencies and to connect the study of Basic English with a development of intellectual skills.

48. Ellul, *Humiliation of the Word,* 161, 166.

49. "The language of international business is the language of the customer," observes T. Bruce Fryer. "Chinese, Hindi, English, and Spanish will be the most widely used languages of international trade in the future" ("The Language of Business," in *Global Business Languages: Pedagogy in Languages for Specific Purposes,* ed. Christiane E. Keck and Allen G. Wood [West Lafayette, IN: Purdue Research Foundation, 1996], 9).

50. Daniel Bell, *The Reforming of General Education: The Columbia College Experience in Its National Setting* (New York: Columbia University Press, 1966), 39.

51. *General Education in a Free Society: Report of the Harvard Committee* (Cambridge: Harvard University Press, 1946), 108, 112, 114, 205. Having become "technicians," we have lost the art of "general conversation" (69).

52. Gerald Graff, *Professing Literature: An Institutional History* (Chicago: University of Chicago Press, 1987), 173.

53. Frank Lentricchia, *After the New Criticism* (Chicago: University of Chicago Press, 1980), 342.

54. Ellul, *Humiliation of the Word,* 170, 176.

55. Alexander Dru, trans., *The Letters of Jacob Burckhardt* (Westport, CT: Greenwood Press, 1975) (July 24, 1889), 220.

56. Cf. Robert Casillo, "Techne and Logos in Solzhenitsyn," *Soundings* 70:3–4 (1987): 519–37. "There remains the hope that the art of the word, an incurably semantic art, will sooner or later make its repercussions felt even in those arts which claim to have freed themselves from every obligation toward the identification and representation of truth" (Eugenio Montale, *Poet in Our Time,* trans. Alastair Hamilton [New York: Urizen Books, 1972], 62).

57. Michael R. Real, "Mass Communications and Propaganda in Technological Societies," in *Jacques Ellul,* ed. Christians and Van Hook, 119–20. Cf. Clifford G. Christians, "Jacques Ellul and Democracy's "Vital Information" Premise," *Journalism Monographs* (Association for Education in Journalism), no. 45 (August 1976): 23; and George Cotkin, "The Tragic Predicament: Post-war American Intellectuals, Acceptance, and Mass Culture," in *Intellectuals in Politics: From the Dreyfus Affair to Salmon Rushdie,* ed. Jeremy Jennings and Anthony Kemp-Welch (London: Routledge, 1997), 248–70.

58. A. Smith, *Software for the Self,* 107, 115. For Smith, the main problem is "regulation," which is yet another technique.

59. Ellul, *Technological Bluff,* 144.

60. Mumford, *Myth of the Machine,* vol. 1, *Technics and Human Development* (New York: Harcourt Brace and World, 1967), 3; ibid., vol. 2, *The Pentagon of Power,* 435; Andrew Feenberg, "Subversive Rationalization: Technology, Power, and Democracy," *Inquiry* (Oslo), 35:3–4 (1992): 316; Langdon Winner, "Citizen Virtues in a Technological Order," *Inquiry* (Oslo), 35:3–4 (1992): 355. The latter two are reprinted in Andrew Feenberg and Alistair Hannay, eds., *Technology and the Politics of Knowledge* (Bloomington: Indiana University Press, 1995). Putnam, "Strange Disappearance," 284–85.

61. Immanuel Wallerstein, *After Liberalism* (New York: New Press, 1995), 144.

62. Christians, "Ellul on Solution," 148–56.

63. Gregory S. Butler, "The Political Moralism of Jacques Ellul," *Humanitas* 7:2 (1994): 43.

64. For the exemplum of the ascetic, always in training, see Burckhardt (Dru, trans., *Letters of Burckhardt* [December 31, 1872], 157), and also Ortega y Gasset, *The Revolt of the Masses,* (London: Allen and Unwin, 1951), chap. 7.

## II. The Great Forgetting: Library, Media Center, and Las Vegas

1. A single broadsheet, *Always* was published by Philemon Press in 1983. The poem was subsequently collected in Mark Strand, *The Continuous Life* (New York: Alfred A. Knopf, 1990), 30–31; numerous alterations dulled some of the fineness of the poem, making it less effective than the original version (cited here).

2. Harold Bloom, *Wallace Stevens: The Poems of Our Climate* (Ithaca: Cornell University Press, 1977), 1; Ralph Waldo Emerson, "Art," in *Essays, First Series,* in *Works* (New York: Walter J. Black, n.d.), 201.

3. David Lowenthal, *The Past Is a Foreign Country* (Cambridge: Cambridge University Press, 1985), 376, 377; cf. 94–96. See also James Fentress and Chris Wickham, *Social Memory* (Oxford: Blackwell, 1992); Janet Coleman, *Ancient and Medieval Memories: Studies in the Reconstruction of the Past* (Cambridge: Cambridge University Press, 1993); and Patrick Geary, *Phantoms of Remembrance: Memory and Oblivion at the End of the First Millennium* (Princeton: Princeton University Press, 1994). Geary comments that "the history of memory has suddenly become a very fashionable topic in historical research" ("The Historical Material of Memory," in *Art, Memory, and Family in Renaissance Florence,* ed. Giovanni Ciappelli and Patricia Lee Rubin [Cambridge: Cambridge University Press, 2000], 17). It is one of the contemporary ironies that memory should become fashionable at a time when the fact of forgetting is overwhelming.

4. Matthew Arnold, "Toast to Literature," May 1, 1875, in *The Complete Prose Works of Matthew Arnold,* ed. R. H. Super (Ann Arbor: University of Michigan Press, 1962–82), 8:374.

5. Richard W. Southern, "Aspects of the European Tradition of Historical Writing: 4. The Sense of the Past," *Transactions of the Royal Historical Society,* 5th ser., 23 (1973): 262.

6. Poggio Bracciolini to Guarino da Verona, *Two Renaissance Book Hunters: The*

*Letters of Poggius Bracciolini to Nicolaus de Niccolis,* trans. P. W. G. Gordan (New York: Columbia University Press, 1974), 194; Myron P. Gilmore, *Humanists and Jurists: Six Studies in the Renaissance* (Cambridge: Harvard University Press, 1963), 37; Southern, "European Tradition," 244–45. "The cultivation of a sense of the past now appears rather as a private luxury than as the medicine for the universal ill. But a hundred years ago, the study of history offered a sense of stability, permanence, and the gentleness of change, in place of a long vista of meaningless and inhuman errors. Hence it became the most cultivated area of intellectual activity for the better part of a century. Historical study has now lost this position" (245).

7. Caroline Winterer, *The Culture of Classicism: Ancient Greece and Rome in American Intellectual Life, 1780–1910* (Baltimore: Johns Hopkins University Press, 2002), 183.

8. Alvin B. Kernan, ed., *What's Happened to the Humanities?* (Princeton: Princeton University Press, 1997), 5–6.

9. David Damrosch, "Can Classics Die?" *Lingua Franca* (September–October 1995): 64.

10. Christopher Stray, *Classics Transformed: Schools, Universities, and Society in England, 1830–1960* (Oxford: Clarendon, 1998), 1.

11. Victor Davis Hanson and John Heath, *Who Killed Homer? The Demise of Classical Education and the Recovery of Greek Wisdom* (New York: Free Press, 1998), 3.

12. E. H. Gombrich, *Tributes: Interpreters of Our Cultural Tradition* (Ithaca: Cornell University Press, 1984), 21.

13. Damrosch, "Can Classics Die?" 65.

14. Kenneth F. Kitchell Jr., *Prospects: National Committee for Latin and Greek Newsletter* (Summer 1994): 1–6; see also his "The Challenge of Living 'in Interesting Times,'" *Classical Outlook* 72:2 (1995): 49–53.

15. Donald Phillip Verene, *Philosophy and the Return to Self-Knowledge* (New Haven: Yale University Press, 1997), 36, 37.

16. David Marc, *The Bonfire of the Humanities: Television, Subliteracy, and Long-Term Memory Loss* (Syracuse: Syracuse University Press, 1995), 26. "If educated people were, generally speaking, better at these skills a hundred years go than they are today, it is probably because they had more practice at them. The telephone, for example, turned letter writing from an organic necessity of middle-class life into an antiquarian art form, much as the camera turned painting from a practical documentary technique into an aesthetic ordeal. During this same period, broadcasting and film subsumed the routine storytelling functions of the culture, both journalistic and fictional, mostly at the expense of print forms such as newspapers and books" (ibid.).

17. *Reading at Risk,* vii, xii, xiii, 7.

18. Putnam, "Strange Disappearance," 281, 282.

19. Myron C. Tuman, *Writing with Norton Textra: A Guide for Composing Online* (New York: Norton, 1991), vii.

20. Anne Frances Wysocki, Johndan Johnson-Eilola, Cynthia L. Selfe, and Geoffrey Sirc, *Writing New Media: Theory and Applications for Expanding the Teaching of Composition* (Logan: Utah State University Press, 2004), 71, 89, 123. As Robert Alter says about "privilege": "Literature, in this view, is ultimately an arm of politics and as such it can be anything that politics decrees; its status as a specially valued kind of writing—'privileged,' presumably, like the privileged classes with their undeserved

wealth—is conferred by the values that regulate the flow of power in a society" (*The Pleasures of Reading in an Ideological Age* [New York: Simon and Schuster, 1989], 26).

21. I refer to the exceptionally fine handbook of this title by Harold C. Martin (New York: Rinehart, 1959).

22. Wysocki et al., *Writing New Media,* 89, 92–93, 113, 123, 126; César Graña, *Fact and Symbol: Essays in the Sociology of Art and Literature* (New York: Oxford University Press, 1971), 109.

23. See Ellul on the increase in visual orientation of textbooks (*Humiliation of the Word,* 117). For a full analysis of this principle, see Jeffrey Robbins, "Technology, Ease, and Entropy: A Testimonial to Zipf's Principle of Least Effort," *Glottometrics* 5 (2002): 81–96. See also Richard Feynman, Robert B. Leighton, and Matthew Sands, "The Principle of Least Action," chap. 19 in *The Feynman Lectures in Physics* (Reading, MA: Addison Wesley, 1964); Thomas J. Allen, *Managing the Flow of Technology* (Cambridge: MIT Press, 1977), 184; and Thomas Mann, "The Principle of Least Effort," *Library Research Models: A Guide to Classification, Cataloging, and Computers* (New York: Oxford University Press, 1993), 94. I am indebted to Jeffrey Robbins for this information.

24. Damrosch, "Can Classics Die?" 64.

25. Alter, *Pleasures of Reading,* 10–11; George Steiner, "Books in an Age of Post-literacy," *Publisher's Weekly* (May 24, 1985): 44.

26. Terry Eagleton, *Literary Theory* (Minneapolis: University of Minneapolis Press, 1983), 11.

27. Clara Hesse, "Books in Time," in *The Future of the Book,* ed. Geoffrey Nunberg (Berkeley and Los Angeles: University of California Press, 1996), 31–32; M. A. Rafey Habib, *The Early T. S. Eliot and Western Philosophy* (Cambridge: Cambridge University Press, 1999), 16.

28. Jacques Ellul, *The Political Illusion* (New York: Alfred A. Knopf, 1967), 61–63; Charles Taylor, *Sources of the Self: The Making of the Modern Identity* (Cambridge: Harvard University Press, 1989), 465.

29. Mark C. Taylor and Esa Saarinen, *Imagologies: Media Philosophy* (London: Routledge, 1994), October 10, 20, 1992.

30. Ibid., September 4, 1991.

31. Marc, *Bonfire of the Humanities,* 38, 42. Antimedia arguments are criticized by Kathleen E. Welch, in her attack on Aristotelian rhetoric, as "wizened, dull, uncommunicative, elitist" in a culture of "slavery, rape, and imperialism." Welch favors the Sophists for a rhetorical approach that is "performative, democratic, and open to all kinds of symbol systems." Since television involves "fragmentation, nonlinear juxtaposition, and ironic appropriations of the past," we should learn from the Sophists and not neglect these "chopped up, repetitive, formulaic" texts (*Electric Rhetoric: Classical Rhetoric, Oralism, and a New Literacy* [Cambridge: MIT Press, 1999], 9, 106, 109).

32. Neil Postman, *Amusing Ourselves to Death: Public Discourse in the Age of Show Business* (New York: Viking, 1985), 50, 80.

33. Marc, *Bonfire of the Humanities,* 39, 43.

34. Cicero, *Selected Political Speeches,* trans. Michael Grant (London: Penguin, 1969), 156.

35. Marc, *Bonfire of the Humanities,* 43, 137.

36. D. W. Fenza cited in Peter Barry, *English in Practice: In Pursuit of English Studies* (London: Arnold, 2003), 195.

37. Marc, *Bonfire of the Humanities,* 28; Richard Stivers, "The Computer and Education: Choosing the Least Powerful Means of Instruction," *Bulletin of Science, Technology, and Society* 19:2 (April 1999): 103.

38. Arnaldo Momigliano, "The Rhetoric of History and the History of Rhetoric: On Hayden White's Tropes," in *Comparative Criticism: A Yearbook,* ed. Elinor Shaffer (Cambridge: Cambridge University Press, 1981), 3:259–60.

39. Haraway, *Simians, Cyborgs, and Women,* 151; George Lipsitz, *Time Passages: Collective Memory and American Popular Culture* (Minneapolis: University of Minnesota Press, 1990), 5.

40. Jacques Ellul, *The Betrayal of the West,* trans. Matthew J. O'Connell (New York: Continuum, Seabury, 1978), 19–20.

41. James Y. Holloway, review of *The Betrayal of the West,* by Ellul, *Theology Today* 36:1 (April 1979): 107. "The genius of Western civilization, Ellul believes, has turned on itself. Western civilization—hence civilization itself—is on a suicidal track: reason becomes 'raving rationalism,' without self-restraint in its literature and art; freedom has turned into nihilism; respect for the person is simply license for one and all to-do-it-if-it-feels-good."

42. Ellul, *Betrayal of the West,* 33, 81. See Peter Novick's treatment of hyperobjectivism and hypersubjectivism in modern historiography (*That Noble Dream: The "Objectivity Question" and the American Historical Profession* [Cambridge: Cambridge University Press, 1988], 599ff).

43. J. H. Plumb, *The Death of the Past* (Boston: Houghton Mifflin, 1970), 14, 15, 16, 20, 39, 51, 57; Lowenthal, *Past Is Foreign,* 364.

44. Zygmunt Bauman, *Liquid Modernity* (Cambridge: Polity, 2000), 3.

45. Zygmunt Bauman, *The Individualized Society* (Cambridge: Polity, 2001), 158.

46. Bauman, *Liquid Modernity,* 82–83. "Liquidity extends to the organs of state control . . . authorities too numerous for anyone of them to stay in authority for long. . . . It is the infinity of chances that has filled the place left empty in the wake of the disappearing act of the Supreme Office" (61–64). Bauman thinks that state power is on the wane, but does not consider the expansion of technology as a controlling power. According to Andrew Feenberg, Bauman's *Intimations of Postmodernity* fails to appreciate the role of technology ("Modernity Theory and Technology Studies: Reflections on Bridging the Gap," in *Modernity and Technology,* ed. Thomas J. Misa, Philip Brey, and Andrew Feenberg [Cambridge: MIT Press, 2003], 55).

47. Bauman, *The Individualized Society,* 153.

48. Frederick A. Lerner, *The Story of Libraries: From the Invention of Writing to the Computer Age* (New York: Continuum, 1998), 14.

49. Ernest Albert Savage, *The Story of Libraries and Book Collecting* (New York: Burt Franklin, 1969), 3.

50. One research university library turned down, for lack of space, the gift of a twenty-year run of the journal *Sumer,* which has been described as "fundamental for the history of the region." Such is our *pietas* toward the first librarians.

51. Ernest Cushing Richardson, *Biblical Libraries: A Sketch of Library History from 3400 B.C. to A.D. 150* (Princeton: Princeton University Press, 1914), 161.

52. Rudolf Pfeiffer, *History of Classical Scholarship: From the Beginnings to the End of the Hellenistic Age* (Oxford: Clarendon, 1968), 27.

53. Lerner, *Story of Libraries,* 201.

54. Elmer D. Johnson, *History of Libraries in the Western World,* 2d ed. (Metuchen: Scarecrow, 1970), 118.

55. Quoted in Lerner, *Story of Libraries,* 47.

56. The first name I saw on arriving at the Verona airport was VALERIO CATULLO in big letters; the Italians had honored the memory of their great poet by naming an airport after him. When will we name an airport after a poet?

57. Edward H. Levi, *Point of View: Talks on Education* (Chicago: University of Chicago Press, 1969), 182.

58. William Y. Arms, "Relaxing Assumptions about the Future of Digital Libraries: The Hare and the Tortoise," *D-Lib* (April 1997), cited in Michael Gorman, *The Enduring Library: Technology, Tradition, and the Quest for Balance* (Chicago: American Library Association, 2003), 29, 32.

59. Alvin B. Kernan, *The Death of Literature* (New Haven: Yale University Press, 1990), 135–36.

60. For Atkinson, librarians of the future will have to instruct us all over again in the ancient art of browsing ("Managing Traditional Materials in an Online Environment," *Library Resources and Technical Services* 42 [January 1998]: 98).

61. Bonnie Nardi and Vicki O'Day, *Information Ecologies: Using Technology with Heart* (Cambridge: MIT Press, 1999), 23–24.

62. William Y. Arms, "Automated Digital Libraries: How Effectively Can Computers Be Used for the Skilled Tasks of Professional Librarianship?" *D-Lib* (July 2000), cited in Gorman, *Enduring Library,* 28.

63. Atkinson, "Managing Traditional Materials," 98; Gorman, *Enduring Library,* 32; Eric Stange, "Millions of Books Are Turning to Dust—Can They Be Saved?" *New York Times Book Review* (March 29, 1987): 3.

64. Ian Reid, *Wordsworth and the Formation of English Studies* (Aldershot: Ashgate, 2004), ix; Bram Kempers, *Painting, Power and Patronage: The Rise of the Professional Artist in the Italian Renaissance,* trans. Beverley Jackson (London: Penguin, Allen Lane, 1992), 317.

65. Mark C. Taylor, *Disfiguring: Art, Architecture, Religion* (Chicago: University of Chicago Press, 1992), 7, 89, 317 (the word that should be underlined is *elsewhere*).

66. See Barnett Newman, "The Sublime Is Now" (1948), in *Barnett Newman: Selected Writings and Interviews,* ed. John O'Neill (New York: Alfred A. Knopf, 1990), 171–72. Newman said that, unlike Kant and Hegel, Burke had succeeded in separating the sublime from the beautiful; he "reads like a surrealist manual." For the Kantian versus the Burkean sublime, see Giuseppe Sertoli, "Edmund Burke," in *Johns Hopkins Guide to Literary Theory and Criticism,* 2d ed. (Baltimore: Johns Hopkins, 2005), and his introduction to Edmund Burke, *Inchiesta sul Bello e il Sublime,* ed. Giuseppe Sertoli and Goffredo Miglietta (Palermo: Aesthetica edizioni, 1985), 9–40. Newman concentrated in philosophy at the City College of New York.

67. Cited in M. C. Taylor, *Disfiguring,* 89, 90.

68. Ibid., 11, 212, 226, 230, 317.

69. See Richard Shiff, "On Criticism Handling History," *History of the Human Sciences* 2:1 (February 1989): 63–87.

70. M. C. Taylor, *Disfiguring,* 8, 10, 317. "Disfiguring is an unfiguring that (impossibly) 'figures' the unfigurable" (8, 10). Taylor's notion may be influenced by (among

other sources) Jean-François Lyotard, whom he cites on "representing the unrepresentable."

71. Ibid., 6, 14, 157–58, 231; Thomas J. J. Altizer, *Total Presence: The Language of Jesus and the Language of Today* (New York: Seabury, 1980), 32–33. "There is no greater distance between Picasso and Leonardo than there is between Leonardo and Giotto" (33).

72. Newman, "The Object and the Image" and "The Sublime Is Now," in *Barnett Newman,* 170, 173.

73. As his friend Thomas Hess called him ("A Conversation: Barnett Newman and Thomas B. Hess," in *Barnett Newman,* 274).

74. Newman, "Statements," in *Barnett Newman,* 178. The implication is that Newman was not "in conversation with" formalists like Morris Louis or Kenneth Noland, nor with pop artists like Andy Warhol or Claes Oldenburg, nor even with his old abstract-expressionist comrades Mark Rothko and Willem de Kooning. See Newman, "Surrealism and the War," "Arshile Gorky," and "The New Sense of Fate," in *Barnett Newman;* and Richard Shiff, "Whiteout: The Non-influence Newman Effect," in *Barnett Newman,* ed. Ann Temkin and Richard Shiff (Philadelphia: Philadelphia Museum of Art and Yale University Press, 2002), 76–111.

75. M. C. Taylor, *Disfiguring,* 12, 50, 95, 113, 132, 184, 218.

76. Ibid., 84.

77. Jonathan Freedland, *Guardian,* December 2001; Peter Schjeldahl, "The Art World," *New Yorker,* May 30, 2004.

78. Wylie Sypher, *Literature and Technology: The Alien Vision* (New York: Random House, 1968), 69–70. "The aesthete pays lip service to *luxe,* but his Beauty is not Dinonysiac" (70).

79. Jacques Ellul, "Remarks on Technology and Art," *Bulletin of Science, Technology and Society* 21:1 (February 2001): 28; Richard Stivers, "Technology, Literature, and Art: An Introduction," *Bulletin of Science, Technology and Society* 21:1 (February 2001): 3–6; John Aldridge, *Talents and Technicians: Literary Chic and the New Assembly-Line Fiction* (New York: Scribner, 1992), 13; Josephine Gattuso Hendin, *Heartbreakers: Women and Violence in Contemporary Culture and Literature* (New York: Palgrave, 2004).

80. M. C. Taylor, *Disfiguring,* 205, 319.

81. Hester Thrale Piozzi, *Observations and Reflections Made in the Course of a Journey through France, Italy, and Germany,* ed. Herbert Barrows (Ann Arbor: University of Michigan Press, 1967), 216. The inscription refers to a lost play by Euripides.

82. Giovanna Franci, *Las Vegas and the Virtual Grand Tour,* with photographs by Federico Zignani, trans. Debra Lyn Christie, forthcoming. Cited with permission.

83. Michael J. Dear, *The Postmodern Urban Condition* (London: Blackwell, 2002), 204.

84. Eugene Moehring, *Resort City in the Sunbelt,* 2d ed. (Reno: University of Nevada Press, 2000), 268.

85. "So: It's Not Venice," http://www.reviewjournal.com/lvrj_home/1999/May-10-Mon-1999/opinion/11140092.html (May 10, 1999); Tom Price, "The ITF Marches Inland," http://www.ilwu.org/1099/itf_marches_1099.htm+Las +Vegas+protest+Venice &hl=en&ie=UTF-8.

86. Franci, *Las Vegas and the Virtual Grand Tour.*

87. Furio Colombo, *Mille Americhe* (Turin: La Stampa, 1988), 89–94; Edward C. Devereux Jr., cited in M. Downes, B. P. Davies, M. E. David, and Stone, *Gambling, Work,*

*and Leisure: A Study across Three Areas* (London: Routledge, 1976), 20. This recalls the negative pleasure (or "delight") of the Burkean sublime, one of numerous connections between gambling and the sublime (alea, thrill-seeking, etc. ).

88. Cited in Robert Casillo, "Pariahs of a Pariah Industry: Martin Scorsese's *Casino*," in *Screening Ethnicity: Cinematographic Representations of Italian Americans in the United States,* ed. Anna Camaiti Hostert and Anthony Julian Tamburri (Boca Raton: Bordighera, 2002), 162–65.

89. Shoichi Muto, *Las Vegas: 16 Hotels and Casinos, 5 Theme Restaurants* (Tokyo: Shotenkenchiku-sha, 1997), 62.

90. In Martin Scorsese's *Casino*, Ace fires a French showgirl who has not taken off enough weight—she is seven pounds overweight: more technicization.

91. Franci, *Las Vegas;* Umberto Eco, *Travels in Hyper Reality: Essays,* trans. William Weaver (New York: Harcourt, 1983), 40. This is the Las Vegas of the traveler who can say (as I once heard), "Venice is the same as Florence—[if you] forget the canals."

92. "The Sands, Dune, Aladdin, and Hacienda are all gone, replaced by grander successors" (Moehring, *Resort City in the Sunbelt,* 268). Hal Rothman, *Neon Metropolis: How Las Vegas Started the Twenty-first Century* (New York: Routledge, 2003), xxiii.

93. Franci, *Las Vegas.*

94. Eco, *Travels in Hyper Reality,* 40; Bruce Bégout, *Zeropolis: The Experience of Las Vegas* (London: Reacktion Books, 2003), 12.

95. Rothman, *Neon Metropolis,* xxvi.

96. Goffredo Parise, *L'odore dell'America* (Milan: Mondadori, 1990), 65–68, 112.

97. Robert Venturi, Denise Scott Brown, and Steven Izenour, *Learning from Las Vegas* (Cambridge: MIT Press, 1972), 6, 18–19; Herbert I. Schiller, *Culture, Inc.: The Corporate Takeover of Public Expression* (New York: Oxford University Press, 1989), 30–31, 99–101.

98. Sigfried Giedion, *Space, Time, and Architecture: The Growth of a New Tradition,* 4th ed. (Cambridge: Harvard University Press, 1963), xlvii. Eco also adopts Venturi's position on the "totally artificial" architecture of Las Vegas, which is "a 'message' city, entirely made up of signs, not a city like the others, which communicate in order to function, but rather a city that functions in order to communicate"; instead of following Venturi further, however, he turns to Giovanni Brino who has shown "how, though born as a place for gambling, [Las Vegas] is gradually being transformed into a residential city, a place of business, industry, conventions" (*Travels in Hyper Reality,* 40). Cf. Paolo Sica, *L'immagine della città da Sparta a Las Vegas* (Bari: Laterza, 1970), 320–21.

99. Venturi, Brown, and Izenour, *Learning from Las Vegas,* 7, 8, 18, 34, 117. "The Strip is virtually all signs"; "the sign is more important than the architecture"; "the freestanding signs on the Strip" are "like the towers at San Gimignano" (9, 13, 106). Although Venturi does say that he is only concerned with the form of architectural communication, not its content or its context (3–4), he often trades on both content and context in his Italian analogies. The neon signage of the Strip at night partakes of the same "amorphous space" and dematerialization of Byzantine ornament in the "Matorama" [*sic*] in Palermo; "the Strip by day is a different place, no longer Byzantine" (116). But how can one compare the religious imagery hovering in the space of the cupola of the Matorana to an ad for a casino or beer? I am indebted to Richard Shiff for the discussion of signage.

100. Venturi, Brown, and Izenour, *Learning from Las Vegas,* 161.

101. Rothman, *Neon Metropolis,* xxvi.

102. *New York Times,* December 19, 2003, D5.

103. Guido Piovene, *De America* (Milan: Garzanti, 1953), 341.

104. Ibid., 344, 349.

105. Belden C. Lane, *The Solace of Fierce Landscapes: Exploring Desert and Mountain Spirituality* (London: Oxford University Press, 1998), 44, 45, 46, 124, 125; Lane, *Landscapes of the Sacred: Geography and Narrative in American Spirituality* (Baltimore: Johns Hopkins University Press, 2002), 125. See also Richard V. Francaviglia, *Believing in Place: A Spiritual Geography of the Great Basin* (Reno: University of Nevada Press, 2003), 1–19, 206–27. Rudolf Otto, *The Idea of the Holy: An Inquiry into the Non-rational Factor in the Idea of the Divine and Its Relation to the Rational,* trans. John W. Harvey (London: Oxford University Press, 1923), 12–13, 18, 25, 71–72, 82.

## III. The Circle of Knowledge: Science and the Humanistic Curriculum from Petrarch to Trilling

1. David L. Wagner, "The Seven Liberal Arts and Classical Scholarship," in *The Seven Liberal Arts in the Middle Ages,* ed. Wagner (Bloomington: Indiana University Press, 1983), 9–10. See Robert A. Nisbet on the uses of "cycle" in Greek thought (*Social Change and History: Aspects of the Western Theory of Development* [New York: Oxford University Press, 1969], 30). For the Greco–Roman educational ideal, see Werner Jaeger, *Paideia,* trans. Gilbert Highet, 2d ed. (New York: Oxford University Press, 1943), 1:xxii, 299–300, 2:59, 64, 68–70; and Garin, *L'educazione umanistica in Italia,* 7–8.

2. A. Dwight Culler, *The Imperial Intellect: A Study of Newman's Educational Ideal* (New Haven: Yale University Press, 1955), 182–83. "The core of the Platonic *paideia,* as Werner Jaeger has shown, is not simply the ingathering of the heterogeneous branches of knowledge but the education of the soul, which is understood as the restoration of unity and harmony to man's fragmentary existence" (Giuseppe Mazzotta, *Dante's Vision and the Circle of Knowledge* [Princeton: Princeton University Press, 1993], 4).

3. Cicero, *Tusculan Disputations,* trans. J. E. King, Loeb Classical Library (London: Heinemann, 1927), 4.26.57; Cicero, *De Officiis,* trans. M. T. Griffin and E. M. Atkins (Cambridge: Cambridge University Press, 1991), 1.153. In Socratic *paideia,* intellect and ethics alike have their source in the Highest Good, so that there is no dichotomy of knowledge and virtue that would trouble later thinkers like Newman. For Socrates' answer to the Sophists, outlining a *paideia* centered on God as "measure of all things," and not man, see Werner Jaeger, *Humanism and Theology* (1943; reprint, Milwaukee: Marquette University Press, 1980), 52–53. On character, see Gertrude Himmelfarb, *Poverty and Compassion: The Moral Imagination of the Late Victorians* (New York: Alfred A. Knopf, 1991), 8.

4. John W. O'Malley, S.J., "The Jesuit Educational Enterprise in Historical Perspective," in *Jesuit Higher Education: Essays on an American Tradition of Excellence,* ed. Rolando E. Bonachea (Pittsburgh: Duquesne University Press, 1989), 15.

5. Edward Leigh on "trivial" Eton (1663) (quoted in Foster Watson, *The Beginnings of the Teaching of Modern Subjects in England* [1909; reprint, Wakefield, Yorkshire: S. R. Publishers, 1971], xxii).

6. Charles G. Nauert Jr., *Humanism and the Culture of Renaissance Europe* (Cambridge: Cambridge University Press, 1995), 48. Vittorino da Feltre's students at La Giocosa "stayed till twenty-one" (A. F. Leach, *The Schools of Medieval England* [1915; reprint, New York: Barnes and Noble, 1969], 271).

7. Sir Ernest Barker, *Traditions of Civility: Eight Essays* (Cambridge: Cambridge University Press, 1948), 136. In the *Book Named the Governour* (1531), however, Sir Thomas Elyot recommends beginning the second stage at about seventeen.

8. Remigio Sabbadini, *Il metodo degli umanisti* (Florence: Le Monnier, 1928); David A. Lines, *Aristotle's "Ethics" in the Italian Renaissance (ca. 1300–1650): The Universities and the Problem of Moral Education* (Leiden: Brill, 2002), 7. As Stray says of public school instruction, "The Modern Sides [where the sciences are emphasized] badly need study" (*Classics Transformed*, 86).

9. Vivian Ogilvie, *The English Public School* (London: Batsford, 1957), 142. Cf. T. W. Bamford, *Thomas Arnold* (London: Cresset Press, 1960), 117–27.

10. Sheldon Rothblatt, "The Limbs of Osiris: Liberal Education in the English-Speaking World," in *The European and American University since 1800: Historical and Sociological Essays*, ed. Sheldon Rothblatt and Björn Wittrock (Cambridge: Cambridge University Press, 1993), 22. "For the Greek, dire consequences follow from playing the flute too well. The self inevitably becomes fascinated by the skill, which is then regarded as an end in itself" (23). Rothblatt cites Henri Marrou on specialization: "Any particular technique tends by its own inner logic to develop exclusively along its own line, in and for itself, and thus it ends by enslaving the man whom it should serve" (*A History of Education in Antiquity* [Madison: University of Wisconsin Press, 1982], 225).

11. Michael Masi, "Arithmetic," in *Seven Liberal Arts*, ed. Wagner, 158.

12. Marie Boas, *The Scientific Renaissance, 1450–1630* (New York: Harper, 1962), 19.

13. Quoted in Robert E. Proctor, *Education's Great Amnesia: Reconsidering the Humanities from Petrarch to Freud* (Bloomington: Indiana University Press, 1988), 17.

14. Cicero, *De Oratore*, trans. H. Rackham, Loeb Classical Library (London: Heinemann, 1948), 3.32.127; Cicero, *Tusculan Disputations*, 5.36.105, cited in Proctor, *Education's Great Amnesia*, 16, 20.

15. Quoted in Paul Lawrence Rose, *The Italian Renaissance of Mathematics: Studies on Humanists and Mathematicians from Petrarch to Galileo* (Geneva: Droz, 1975), 16.

16. Quintilian, *Institutio Oratoria*, trans. H. E. Butler, Loeb Classical Library (London: Heinemann, 1920), 1.10.

17. Eugenio Garin, *Italian Humanism: Philosophy and Civic Life in the Renaissance*, trans. Peter Munz (New York: Harper and Row, 1965), 24.

18. Pamela O. Long, "Humanism and Science," in *Renaissance Humanism: Foundations, Forms, and Legacy*, vol. 3, *Humanism and the Disciplines*, ed. Albert Rabil Jr. (Philadelphia: University of Pennsylvania Press, 1988), 492.

19. Eric Cochrane, "Science and Humanism in the Italian Renaissance," *American Historical Review* 81 (1976): 1050; Rose, *Italian Renaissance of Mathematics*, 9. Besides denoting the recovery of ancient texts, the "Renaissance of mathematics" indicates a "fundamental change in the attitude of mathematicians who adopted the metaphor of restoration as an image of the advancement of mathematics" (294).

20. Petrarch, *Letter on His Own Ignorance*, cited in Garin, *Italian Humanism*, 23; Paul Fussell, *The Rhetorical World of Augustan Humanism* (Oxford: Clarendon, 1965),

8, cf. 18; Milton, *Paradise Lost* 8.173–75; Jonathan Swift, *Gulliver's Travels*, bk. 3; Samuel Johnson, *Life of Milton;* Jacob Burckhardt, *The Civilization of Italy in the Renaissance*, trans. S. G. C. Middlemore (London: Phaidon, 1960), 171–216.

21. Garin, *Italian Humanism*, 3–4.

22. Long, "Humanism and Science," 496.

23. Cochrane, "Science and Humanism," 1050; Long, "Humanism and Science," 492.

24. Aldo Schiavone, *The End of the Past: Ancient Rome and the Modern West*, trans. Margery J. Schneider (Cambridge: Harvard University Press, 2000), 144.

25. Rose, *Italian Renaissance of Mathematics*, 7. See also Douglas Biow, *Doctors, Ambassadors, Secretaries: Humanism and Professions in Renaissance Italy* (Chicago: University of Chicago Press, 2002), 71–98. The most important humanist physician of the sixteenth century, Girolamo Fracastoro (1478–1553) of Verona, was a pioneer of epidemiology in *De contagione et contagiosis morbis* (On contagion and pestilent fevers) (1546), and the author of the Lucretian medical poem *Syphilis sive morbus Gallicus* (Syphilis or the French disease) (1530). Like his younger contemporary Sperone Speroni, if not as explicitly, Fracastoro distinguishes science from poetry: "As for myself, in the poem which I dedicated to Pietro Bembo *[Syphilis]*, I did, indeed, touch on all these questions, but only so far as the poetic form allowed. . . . I was obliged to pass over many points in regard to the whole subject" (75). The gap between science and poetry widens in the following century as, for example, in the writings of the poet-physician Francesco Redi.

26. Robert Mandrou, *From Humanism to Science: 1480–1700*, trans. Brian Pearce (Atlantic Highlands, NJ: Humanities Press, 1979), 48. Cf. "Modern science began when ancient scientific texts were collected and edited" (Charles Whitney, *Francis Bacon and Modernity* [New Haven: Yale University Press, 1986], 9). "If it is true that Humanism consisted in a renewed confidence in man and his possibilities and in an appreciation of man's activity in every possible sense, it is only fair to give Humanism credit for the new methods of scientific investigation, the renewed vision of the world and the new attitude towards objects with a view to using them and to dominating them" (Garin, *Italian Humanism*, 221).

27. Boas, *Scientific Renaissance*, 18, 26.

28. Paul Oskar Kristeller and John Herman Randall Jr., introduction to *The Renaissance Philosophy of Man*, ed. Ernst Cassirer, Paul Oskar Kristeller, and John Herman Randall Jr. (Chicago: University of Chicago Press, 1948), 13.

29. Cochrane, "Science and Humanism," 1057. He was "if not the last of the humanists, at least a faithful heir of the humanist tradition" (1057). Galileo, who wrote on literary subjects, was "a humanist before he was a mathematician" (Rose, *Italian Renaissance of Mathematics*, 280).

30. Proctor, *Education's Great Amnesia*, 10. "The narrowing of the *studia humanitatis* from all the branches of learning to the Renaissance disciplines of grammar, rhetoric, history, poetry and moral philosophy, with the specific exclusion of geometry," writes Proctor, "is in essence the result of a radical change in the understanding of what it means to be human" (16).

31. Cochrane, "Science and Humanism," 1050. Cf. "When the humanist attacked medieval science, he was attacking an intellectual attitude that seemed to him oversubtle and sterile; he was emphatically not attacking science as such" (Boas, *Scientific Renaissance*, 27). "Nobody today would wish to maintain that science and philosophy

developed in *opposition* to the men of letters" (Eugenio Garin, *Science and Civic Life in the Italian Renaissance*, trans. Peter Munz [Garden City, NY: Doubleday, 1969], viii). See also Stephen Jay Gould, *The Hedgehog, the Fox, and the Magister's Pox: Mending the Gap between Science and the Humanities* (New York: Harmony, 2003), chap. 2.

32. Benjamin G. Kohl, "Humanism and Education," in *Humanism and the Disciplines*, ed. Rabil, 16.

33. William Harrison Woodward, *Vittorino da Feltre and Other Humanist Educators* (New York: Teachers College, Columbia University, 1963), 42–43, 236. Before the age of printed books, "poetry and prose were read aloud to the students, and then every word was defined, the rhythm of the passage was analyzed, its allusions noted, and a moral judgment made about the characters involved" (John D. Schaeffer, *Sensus Communis: Vico, Rhetoric, and the Limits of Relativism* [Durham: Duke University Press, 1990], 27).

34. Cited in Rose, *Italian Renaissance of Mathematics*, 16.

35. Bartolomeo Fazio quoted in ibid., 13; Vergerio quoted in Woodward, *Vittorino da Feltre*, 108. As far as faculty talents and rewards were concerned, "most of us, too," he said, "must learn to be content with modest capacity as with modest fortune" (109).

36. Matteo Palmieri, *Vita Civile*, cited in Garin, *L'educazione umanistica in Italia*, 129.

37. John W. Donohue, S.J., *Jesuit Education: An Essay on the Foundations of Its Idea* (New York: Fordham University Press, 1963), 35.

38. Françoise Waquet, *Latin, or, the Empire of a Sign: From the Sixteenth to the Twentieth Centuries*, trans. John Howe (London: Verso, 2001), 10. Cf. Anthony Grafton, "The New Science and the Traditions of Humanism," in *Bring Out Your Dead: The Past as Revelation* (Cambridge: Harvard University Press, 2002), 103, 109.

39. M. L. Clarke, *Classical Education in Britain: 1500–1900* (Cambridge: Cambridge University Press, 1959), 3–4. "The curriculum of the endowed grammar and public schools at the end of the eighteenth century was still much the same as it had been at the time of the Renaissance" (H. C. Barnard, *A History of English Education* [London: University of London, 1961], 14–15).

40. Ralph Waldo Emerson, *The Journals and Miscellaneous Notebooks*, ed. Susan Sutton Smith and Harrison Hayford (Cambridge: Harvard University Press, 1978), 14:339–40. Emerson was graduated from Boston Latin School, the "first transatlantic 'secondary' school" (1635), with a curriculum of Latin and Greek (Waquet, *Latin*, 22; cf. Pauline Holmes, *A Tercentenary History of the Boston Public Latin School, 1635–1935* [Cambridge: Harvard University Press, 1935], 252–53). Patrick Leigh Fermor, *A Time of Gifts* (New York: Harper and Row, 1977), 74

41. Woodward, *Vittorino da Feltre*, 239. "The darkness of our ignorance of the curriculum in our ancient schools," notes A. F. Leach, "is lightened for us first in 1528 by Wolsey's statutes"—but these covered only the eight levels of Latin (*Schools of Medieval England*, 300–301). On fifteenth-century humanism in England, Leach notes that "like mathematics [dialectic] presented too severe a study for those who found the whole end of life, literature and education in *belles lettres* and the art of expression" (271).

42. Grafton, *Bring Out Your Dead*, 102, 103.

43. Charles Webster, "Science and the Challenge to the Scholastic Curriculum, 1640–1660," in *The Changing Curriculum* (London: Methuen, 1971), 22, 23.

44. Ibid., 27–29. "In essence natural philosophy and mathematics could play an important role in the humanistic programme; it was even tolerant of the experimental approach" (27).

45. Ibid., 30.

46. Cited in Watson, *Beginnings of Teaching,* 103–4, xxiii, 197.

47. Ibid., 317, 351.

48. Cited in Grafton, *Bring Out Your Dead,* 101.

49. Quoted in R. M. Ogilvie, *Latin and Greek: A History of the Influence of the Classics on English Life from 1600 to 1918* (Hamden, CT: Archon, 1964), 8–9.

50. Webster, "Science and the Challenge," 33. "With their knowledge of the rapidly advancing and fluctuating world of the physical sciences and mathematics, the Oxford circle came to regard science as a subject apart from the fixed body of knowledge, which was the province of scholastic education. It was therefore more suited to mature scholars, gifted individuals and private societies" (31–32).

51. Locke cited in Waquet, *Latin,* 214–15; Gaisford cited in Grafton, *Bring Out Your Dead,* 99

52. V. Ogilvie, *The English Public School,* 85–86. "Otherwise the endowed schools remained wedded to their traditional curriculum and impervious to new ideas" (86).

53. Stray, *Classics Transformed,* 185–86.

54. Descartes, *Selections,* ed. Ralph M. Eaton (New York: Scribner's, 1927), 7, quoted by Vico in *On the Most Ancient Wisdom of the Italians (De antiquissima italorum sapientia),* ed. L. M. Palmer (Ithaca: Cornell University Press, 1988), 183; hereafter cited as *AW.*

55. Grafton, *Bring Out Your Dead,* 100.

56. Nicole cited in Félix Cadet, *Port-Royal Education,* trans. Adnah D. Jones (New York: Scribner's, 1898), 23, 26.

57. Anthony Kenny, *Descartes: A Study of His Philosophy* (New York: Random House, 1968), 6.

58. Vico, *On Humanistic Education,* 129, hereafter cited as *OHE.*

59. George Mora, "Vico and Piaget: Parallels and Differences," in *Vico and Contemporary Thought,* ed. Giorgio Tagliacozzo, Michael Mooney, and Donald Phillip Verene (Atlantic Highlands, NJ: Humanities Press, 1979), 49.

60. *The Autobiography of Giambattista Vico,* trans. Max Harold Fisch and Thomas Goddard Bergin (Ithaca: Cornell University Press, 1963), 146, hereafter cited as *AU;* Vico, *On the Study Methods of Our Time (De nostri temporis studiorum ratione)* (1709), x, hereafter cited as *SM.* Franco Rella treats the debate between Descartes and Vico in *La battaglia della verità* (Milan: Feltrinelli, 1986), 51–55.

61. Giambattista Vico, *De mente heroica* (On the Heroic Mind) (1732; hereafter cited as *HM*), trans. E. Sewell and A. C. Sirignano, in *Vico and Contemporary Thought,* ed. Tagliacozzo, Mooney, and Verene, 230.

62. Donald Phillip Verene, *The New Art of Biography: An Essay on the Life of Giambattista Vico Written by Himself* (Oxford: Clarendon, 1991), 130, 175–76.

63. Robert C. Miner, *Vico: Genealogist of Modernity* (Notre Dame: University of Notre Dame Press, 2002), 3; Talcott Parsons, "Vico and 'History,'" in *Vico and Contemporary Thought,* ed. Tagliacozzo, Mooney, and Verene, 224.

64. The certitude of Descartes is the *mathema* of Plato, in Franco Rella's words, "victory over the vertiginous impermanence of reality which ends by translating itself into a theology" (*La battaglia della verità,* 63). See John Paul Russo, "Ovidian Tales of the Modern: Franco Rella's Racconto Method of Criticism," *Italian Quarterly* 27:106 (1986): 63.

65. Descartes, *Discourse on Method,* in *Selections,* ed. Eaton, 11–12; cf. Remo Fornaca, *Il pensiero educativo di Giambattista Vico* (Turin: G. Giappichelli, 1957), 53.

66. James Robert Goetsch Jr., *Vico's Axioms: The Geometry of the Human World* (New Haven: Yale University Press, 1995), 102.

67. Henry J. Perkinson, "Vico and the Methods of Study of Our Time," in *Vico and Contemporary Thought,* ed. Tagliacozzo, Mooney, and Verene, 95. Vico may owe a debt to Bacon's distinction between Anticipations of Nature based on opinion, tradition, and dogma and the Interpretation of Nature based on induction *(Novum Organum)*.

68. For Franco Rella, *diversiloquium* combines logos and mythos (Russo, "Ovidian Tales," 64).

69. Fausto Nicolini, quoted by Fornaca, *Il pensiero educativo,* 67.

70. Leon Pompa, *Vico: A Study of the "New Science"* (Cambridge: Cambridge University Press, 1975), 74.

71. Norman Douglas, *South Wind* (London: Martin Secker, 1934), 176. "Our young men, because of their training, which is focused on 'natural sciences,' are unable to engage in the life of the community, to conduct themselves with sufficient wisdom and prudence; nor can they infuse into their speech a familiarity with human psychology or permeate their utterances with passion" *(SM,* 33–34).

72. In his critique of the *Port-Royal Logic,* Félix Cadet said that its ideal of deduction should have been supplemented by the Baconian ideal of induction *(Port-Royal Education,* 31).

73. "Doctrines must take their beginning from that of the matters of which they treat" (Vico, *The New Science of Giambattista Vico,* trans. Thomas G. Bergin and Max H. Fisch [Garden City, NY: Doubleday, 1961], para. 314, hereafter cited as *NS* followed by the paragraph number in Nicolini's standard ordering). Arnaldo Momigliano questions various a priori approaches to historical investigation (Marxism, racialism, and so on) *(Studies in Historiography* [New York: Harper Torchbooks, 1966], 107–8, 110).

74. As Henry J. Perkinson comments, "Whatever man creates—his theories, his behavior, as well as his institutions and his social arrangements—are all modifications of what he has previously created" ("Vico and the Methods of Study," 102).

75. As Antonio Aliotta comments in *Disegno storico della pedagogia: Dal punto di vista filosofico* (Rome: Perella, 1941), "The learner must not find truth either outside himself, adopting it passively (a process which can be likened to pouring a liquid through a funnel into a container), nor must he find it in himself by accepting it as an initial datum, as a gift, without contributing anything of his own. The learner, instead, should take an active role, a dynamic initiative, in the construction of knowledge. Only thus will he be able to attain a true possession of it" (227–28).

76. Arnold, "A Liverpool Address," in *Complete Prose Works,* ed. Super, 10:88.

77. Fornaca, *Il pensiero educativo,* 167.

78. On the rationale for copiousness, cf.: "The difference between science and prudence is that in science you need to eliminate all causes except one, whereas in prudence you need to find the greatest number of possible causes, probable causes and their interrelations" *(SM* 34); "Tacitus descends into all the counsels of utility, whereby, among the infinite irregular chances of malice and fortune, the man of practical wisdom brings things to good issue" *(AU* 138). One also notes that in the Socratic method, the first part is dialogue/dialectic or the gathering ideas; the second part lies in exhortation to moral action.

79. Vico cites Socrates to the effect that "the virtues and the disciplines were one and the same, and totally denied that any one of them was ever genuine unless all the others were present also" (*HM*, 233). As Verene comments, eloquence is "the quality a speech needs to be complete, to encompass all the dimensions of a subject . . . to make a beginning and to speak through to an end that takes each listener through all the relevant aspects of the subject, including digressions, but brings the listener always back to the point and brings the whole topic well into view" (*OHE*, 7); cf. Verene, *New Art of Autobiography*, 130–36.

80. Giambattista Vico, *Il Diritto universale*, vol. 2, *De Constantia Iurisprudentis* (1721), ed. Fausto Nicolini (Bari: Laterza, 1936), 2:320 (pars posterior, caput 2: "De Principiis Humanitatis").

81. Cf. *OHE*, 132–33 and 138–39 for Cicero's definition of wisdom as "the knowledge of all things natural and divine" (*Tusculan Disputations* 4.26.57; *De Officiis* 1.153). According to Vico's *verum-factum* principle, the arts of language are the chief means of making history and civil institutions, and also of comprehending them.

82. Quoted in Fornaca, *Il pensiero educativo*, 39–40. Fornaca portrays Vico as not fully appreciating the import of the new study methods taking root in European universities (197–98). Vico, *Selected Writings*, trans. Leon Pompa (Cambridge: Cambridge University Press, 1982), 264 (para. 1106). By barbarism of reflection Donald Phillip Verene interprets Vico to mean the reliance on instrumental reason and a purely functional language, differentiation of roles or specialization, demotion of imaginative myths and universals, and the loss of community (*Vico's Science of Imagination* [Ithaca: Cornell University Press, 1981], 194–95). Vico's generation was one of the first to sustain the impact of intellectual modernity.

83. Peter Burke, *The Art of Conversation* (Ithaca: Cornell University Press, 1993), 46.

84. Vico, *Selected Writings*, 2–3. D'Alembert, a mathematician by training, wrote in his *Encyclopédie* article on "college" that Latin was essential to understand writers like Horace and Tacitus; however, "we should limit ourselves to understanding them, and the time spent composing in Latin is time wasted. This time would be better spent in learning the principles of our own language" (quoted in Waquet, *Latin*, 11). *Enkuklios paideia* had taken on a very different meaning from that in Isocrates, Cicero, and Quintilian.

85. G. M. Young, *Victorian England: Portrait of an Age* (London: Oxford University Press, 1936), 160. George Eliot's thoughts on education gleaned from her novels and essays would make a rewarding study, given her training in Greek and Latin and her interest in science. In *Daniel Deronda* (1874) she mentions the debate over science and literature in education, and the estimable Sir Hugo Mallinger claims that, though he has forgotten his Greek, he applauds its influence: "It formed my taste. I dare say my English is the better for it" (chap. 16).

86. John Stuart Mill, *Essays on Literature and Society*, ed. J. B. Schneewind (New York: Collier, 1965), 358; Walter Hobhouse, *The Theory and Practice of Ancient Education* (1885; reprint, New York: Stechert, 1910), 54. "Study science is the cry of another party: the hopes of mankind lie in the increase of that knowledge of nature which alone is power. And a third voice is heard—the voice of poverty, suggesting that it will be best to study whatever subject is most marketable,—for life has become more complex and the struggle is harder, and the strugglers more numerous" (54).

87. Cited in Newman, *The Idea of a University Defined and Illustrated*, ed. Martin J. Svaglic (Notre Dame: University of Notre Dame Press, 1986), 121, 128.

88. Svaglic, introduction to ibid., xiii.

89. Cited in Culler, *Imperial Intellect,* 188; Newman, *Idea of a University,* 38, 54, 55, 76. "Viewed altogether, [the sciences] approximate to a representation or subjective reflection of the objective truth, as nearly as is possible to the human mind, which advances towards the accurate apprehension of that object, in proportion to the number of sciences which it has mastered" (35). "The trivium and quadrivium are so called because they are the roads *(viae)* by which the living mind enters into philosophy, and 'they so hang together . . . that if even one were absent, the others would not be able to make a philosopher'" (Culler, citing Hugh of St. Victor, *Imperial Intellect,* 184).

90. In Bernard Bosanquet's words, "It is that employment of the mind in which by great thoughts, by art and poetry which lift us above ourselves, by the highest exertion of the intelligence, as we should add, by religion, we obtain occasionally a sense of something that cannot be taken from us, a real oneness and centre in the universe"; this oneness restores us from the transitory and the fragmentary (cited in Irving Babbitt, *Literature and the American College: Essays in Defense of the Humanities* [1908; reprint, Washington, DC: National Humanities Institute, 1986], 204–5).

91. Newman, *Fifteen Sermons Preached before the University of Oxford* (London: Longmans, 1892), 287 (amended slightly in *Idea of a University,* discourse 6, 101, cited here); in Culler's commentary, "the integrity of all knowledge and the need of the human mind to reflect that integrity" (*Imperial Intellect,* 174).

92. Newman, *Idea of a University,* 108–9, 125.

93. Culler, *Imperial Intellect,* 219. "The real issue, therefore, between Newman and the utilitarians is the question, what is the chief good, the final end of man? Bentham said that it was happiness, but Newman (the religious answer apart) said that it was the full development of man's own nature" (223).

94. Newman, *Idea of a University,* 118, 124, 125. "The man who has learned to think and to reason and to compare and to discriminate and to analyze, who has refined his taste, and formed his judgment, and sharpened his mental vision, will not indeed at once be a lawyer, or a pleader, or an orator, or a statesman, or a physician, or a good landlord, or a man of business, or a soldier, or an engineer, or a chemist, or a geologist, or an antiquarian, but he will be placed in that state of intellect in which he can take up any one of the sciences or callings I have referred to, or any other for which he has a taste or special talent, with an ease, a grace, a versatility, and a success, to which another is a stranger. In this sense then . . . mental culture is emphatically *useful*" (125).

95. Ibid., 91. For the portrait of a gentleman, see 8.10 (pp. 159–60).

96. John William Adamson on F. W. Farrar's *Essays on a Liberal Education,* cited in Lionel Trilling, *Beyond Culture: Essays on Literature and Learning* (New York: Viking Press, 1965), 209. For the almost simultaneous debate going on in the United States, see Winterer, *Culture of Classicism,* chaps. 4–5. In 1867 E. L. Youmans, the founder of *Popular Science Monthly,* wrote that education should be brought "into better harmony with the needs of the times. . . . In place of much that is irrelevant, antiquated, and unpractical in our systems of study, there is needed a larger infusion of the living and available truth which belongs to the present time" (Winterer, *Culture of Classicism,* 105).

97. Stray, *Classics Transformed,* 95.

98. Henry Sidgwick, "The Theory of Classical Education," in *Essays on a Liberal*

*Education,* ed. F. W. Farrar (London: Macmillan, 1867), 86–89, 95, 96, 100, 101, 103, 108, 109, 113, 119–21, 124, 132.

99. Charles Horton Cooley, "Genius, Fame, and Race," *Annals of the American Academy of Political and Social Science* 9:3 (May 1897): 28. This was a common trope: in *Six Months in Italy,* George Stillman Hillard notes that "the image of Italy dwells in our hearts like that of a women whom we have loved" (Boston: Ticknor, Reed, and Fields, 1853), 2:450. For gender and classics, see Stray, *Classics Transformed,* 13–14, 80–82.

100. Sven-Eric Liedman, "General Education in Germany and Sweden," in *European and American University,* ed. Rothblatt and Wittrock, 78.

101. Proctor, *Education's Great Amnesia,* 102. For Proctor, classical humanism performs the indispensable task of showing the relation of the self to the community in a way that modern texts with their emphasis on the self cannot; modern humanism is a contradiction in terms. One might reply to Proctor that numerous texts of the past two centuries (Dickens, Eliot, Tolstoy, Mann . . .) involve the relation of self to community in a way no less central than in Sophocles, Cicero, Horace, and Marcus Aurelius.

102. Sidgwick's proposals were not adopted immediately. Status-conscious bourgeois parents wanted their children to receive the same education as the upper-class students. Greek was dropped as a compulsory entrance requirement at Oxford and Cambridge in 1918, Latin in 1959 (Stray, *Classics Transformed,* 265–69).

103. Pierre Bourdieu, *Distinction: A Social Critique of the Judgment of Taste* (London: Routledge, 1984), 83; Stray, *Classics Transformed,* 20–21, 217, 270. "In a society where the ideology of ascription has given way to that of achievement, the locus of social distinction shifts from the boundary between dominant and subordinate cultural content, to that between context-bound everyday knowledge and the context-free discipline which enables professional academics to transcend the everyday. This maintains hierarchy but marginalizes the classical and weakens its authority" (270).

104. De Grazia, *Of Time, Work, and Leisure,* 377–78. A similar sentiment was expressed by Nicola Chiaromonte commenting on Ortega y Gasset and the loss of values (such as self-mastery, freedom, reason): "The error of the elites is to have turned into mass, along with the masses or even before the masses. The 'revolt of the masses' cannot mean merely an increasing number of individuals progressively forgetting certain moral exigencies. It must be connected with the degradation of 'noble' values under the pressure of a phenomenon, or a complex of phenomena, stronger than the collective habit of individuals to respect a certain body of traditional values." These values inform Western humanism, "which, as late as 1914, could still legitimately be considered the basis of the moral life of Europe" (*Worm of Consciousness,* 238–39). Chiaromonte argues that, traditionally, the ideal humanist was to leave Plato's Cave of moral confusion and darkness, experience the higher truths, then return to it and help the masses; Marx upset the humanist tradition by claiming that one should lead the masses out of the Cave with them. But to lead them the intellectual "must develop a mass consciousness and must think and act *as if* he were simply one element of the great number" (242).

105. *The Letters of Matthew Arnold to Arthur Hugh Clough,* ed. Howard Foster Lowry (London: Oxford University Press, 1932), 124 (October 28, 1852). "But the language, style and general proceedings of a poetry which has such an immense task to perform,

must be very plain, direct and severe: and it must not lose itself in parts and episodes and ornamental work, but must press forwards to the whole" (124).

106. Matthew Arnold, preface to *Poems* (1853), in *Complete Prose Works*, ed. Super, 1:1; sonnet, "To a Friend." Cf. Douglas Bush, *Mythology and the Romantic Tradition in English Poetry* (Cambridge: Harvard University Press, 1937), 162.

107. Matthew Arnold, *Schools and Universities on the Continent*, in *Complete Prose Works*, ed. Super, 4:292. In "A Liverpool Address" (1882) Arnold, speaking before a medical convocation, urged that Latin remain an essential component of a "proper secondary school" (10:81). Arnold was opposed to the institutionalization of English studies in higher education (Franklin E. Court, *Institutionalizing English Literature: The Culture and Politics of Literary Study, 1750–1950* [Stanford: Stanford University Press, 1992], 116–17).

108. Thomas Henry Huxley, *Science and Culture, and Other Essays* (New York: Appleton, 1884), 14–16, 20–21.

109. Ibid., 13–14, 25.

110. Matthew Arnold, "Literature and Science," in *Complete Prose Works*, ed. Super, 10:56, 60, 67–68. Citing Arnold's "criticism of life," Paul Shorey wrote: "The chief Latin classics—Cicero, Virgil, Livy, Horace—in their lucid rationality and precision, their urbanity, their sanity, their common sense, their humanized and humanizing emancipation from 'primitive foolishness,' parochialism and fanaticism, are singularly well adapted for the initiation of the youthful mind into literature, criticism of life, and the historic sense" (*The Assault on Humanism* [Boston: Atlantic Monthly, 1917], 25).

111. Matthew Arnold, "On the Study of Celtic Literature," in *Complete Prose Works*, ed. Super, 3:330. Stray mocks the idea of the touchstone in the parlor game "the Golden Urn" played by Gilbert Murray, Logan Pearsall Smith, and the Berensons, in which quotations written down and dropped in an urn are taken out and identified. "In a way, this game sums up many of the ideological resonances of the defence of classical studies" (*Classics Transformed*, 265). Although the use of reference and quotation can signal nothing but class distinction, in a way Stray's comment sums up his own ideology according to which classics exhibits almost nothing but class distinction.

112. Babbitt, *Literature and the American College*, 88, 110, 125, 130, 140–44, 152.

113. William Giese, in *Irving Babbitt: Man and Teacher*, ed. Frederick Manchester and Odell Shepard (New York: Putnam's, 1941), 4; Babbitt, *Literature and the American College*, 125, 132, 141, 143–44, 163. It was said of Babbitt that he hated what other people only genteelly disliked.

114. Stray, *Classics Transformed*, 86.

115. Cited in Winterer, *Culture of Classicism*, 105–6. Eliot was not alone: one thinks of Andrew Dickson White, the first president of Cornell University (1868), and Daniel Coit Gilman, first president of Johns Hopkins University (1876); see Reid, *Wordsworth and English Studies*, 14–19.

116. Charles W. Eliot, *Educational Reform*, cited in Babbitt, *Literature and the American College*, 95. See Henry James, *Charles W. Eliot* (Boston: Houghton Mifflin, 1930), 1:230, 350–52.

117. Babbitt, *Literature and the American College*, 94, 96, 119, cited in Nevin, *Irving Babbitt*, 27. At odds with his colleagues in the French Department and his president, Babbitt did not receive tenure till he was forty-seven. Meanwhile, he soldiered on. His

New Humanism movement, cofounded with Paul Elmer More, enlivened academe until the 1930s, though his main influence was highly personal, in such students as T. S. Eliot, Walter Lippmann, Granville Hicks, David Riesman, and Ralph Kirkpatrick.

118. Babbitt, *Literature and the American College,* 130, 209. "When books like the Greek and Latin classics have survived for centuries after the languages in which they are written are dead, the presumption is that these books themselves are not dead, but rather very much alive—that they are less related than most other books to what is ephemeral and more related to what is permanent in human nature" (114–15).

119. Trilling, "The Leavis-Snow Controversy," in *Beyond Culture,* 145–77.

120. See David Laurence, "Notes on the English Major," *ADE Bulletin* 133 (Winter 2003): 3–5.

121. Harry Levin, who sympathized with student protest, pleaded with undergraduates on the steps of Harvard's Memorial Church to know the difference between "horizontal" relevance (such as they were exhibiting) and "vertical" relevance. Levin had been one of Babbitt's last students and held the first Irving Babbitt Professorship of Comparative Literature (his inaugural lecture, "Irving Babbitt and the Teaching of Literature," was published by Harvard University [November 1960]).

122. Lionel Trilling, "The Uncertain Future of the Humanistic Educational Ideal," in *The Last Decade: Essays and Reviews, 1965–75* (New York: Harcourt Brace Jovanovich, 1979), 166–67; Trilling, "Mind in the Modern World," ibid., 108–10.

123. Trilling, *Last Decade,* 126, 160–61, 171–74. See also Max Weber, "Science as a Vocation," in *From Max Weber: Essays in Sociology,* trans. H. H. Gerth and C. Wright Mills (New York: Oxford University Press, 1948), 129–59; and Jaeger, *Paideia,* 1: 297. As for "mystique of mind," Trilling's gift for Arnoldian phrase making failed him.

124. Trilling, *Last Decade,* 154. Trilling would doubtless have been pleased that the famous Humanities A syllabus remained remarkably constant from 1937–1938 to 2003–2004 and that five titles had never been off the list: *The Iliad,* the *Oresteia, Oedipus the King,* Dante's *Inferno,* and Shakespeare's *King Lear* (Timothy Gross, "250 Years: An Inner Life of Sufficient Richness; From General Honors to Literature Humanities," *Columbia College Today* [May 2004]: 24–30).

125. Trilling, *Last Decade,* 166, 175–76. In 1970 there was a party for Trilling in Cambridge on the night of his final Charles Eliot Norton lecture, "Sincerity and Authenticity"; it happened to coincide with the last of the big Vietnam demonstrations, which had gotten quite out of hand. We discussed the safer ways of returning home through the riot, and I recall his Olympian calm as he plunged into the night.

126. Bauman, *Liquid Modernity,* 3, 61, 82–83.

127. Ibid., 31–32. The classical idea of a "rounded education, confined as it was to the formation of culture and wisdom, stands in sharp opposition to the idea of an encyclopedia of sciences, that is, to a knowledge which is arrayed alphabetically like a dictionary or encyclopedia" (Friedrich Georg Juenger, *The Failure of Technology: Perfection without Purpose* [Hinsdale, IL: Henry Regnery, 1949], 92–93).

128. Plumb, *Death of the Past,* 56–57. The classics were rejuvenated, though not in the way Arnold had hoped, by their interdisciplinary relations with many fields in the later twentieth century (see G. W. Bowersock, "The New Old World," *New Republic* [November 4, 2002]: 27–31).

129. *A Report on the Harvard College Curricular Review* (Faculty of Arts and Sciences, Harvard University, April 2004).

130. Hans Ulrich Gumbrecht, "Live Your Experience—and Be Untimely! What Classical Philology as a Profession Could (Have) Become," in *Disciplining Classics*, ed. Glenn W. Most (Göttingen: Vandenhoeck and Ruprecht, 2002), 253–54, 265–67.

## IV. Belief and Sincerity

1. Lionel Trilling, *Sincerity and Authenticity* (Cambridge: Harvard University Press, 1972), 6; I. A. Richards, "Poetry and Beliefs," in *Principles of Literary Criticism* (London: Kegan Paul, Trench, Trubner, 1924), 272–87, hereafter cited as *PLC*; Richards, "Poetry and Beliefs," in *Science and Poetry* (1926; rev. ed. 1935; reprinted as *Poetries and Sciences* (London: Routledge and Kegan Paul, 1970), 57–66, hereafter cited as *SP;* Richards, "Doctrine in Poetry," in *Practical Criticism: A Study of Literary Judgment* (London: Kegan Paul, Trench, Trubner, 1929), 271–91, hereafter cited as *PC* (8th ed. published in 1956 by Routledge and Kegan Paul); Richards, "The Boundaries of the Mythical," in *Coleridge on Imagination*, 2d ed. (1934; reprint, London: Routledge and Kegan Paul, 1950), 164–86; Richards, "The God of Dostoevsky" (1927), "Belief" (1930), and "Between Truth and Truth" (1931), in *Complementarities: Uncollected Essays*, ed. Russo, 148–58, 24–36, 37–48, hereafter cited as *C;* Richards, "What Is Belief?" (1934), in *Poetries: Their Media and Ends*, ed. Trevor Eaton (The Hague: Mouton, 1974), 234– 41, hereafter cited as *P.*

2. For the intellectual context of agnosticism and rationalism, see Noel Annan, *Leslie Stephen: The Godless Victorian*, 2d ed. (London: George Weidenfeld and Nicolson, 1984), 234–99.

3. Matthew Arnold, "Dissent and Dogma," in *Complete Prose Works*, ed. Super, 6:212, 403.

4. David Hume, *An Enquiry Concerning Human Understanding* (Chicago: Open Court, 1924), 49; James Mill, *Analysis of the Phenomena of the Human Mind* (1829), ed. Alexander Bain et al., 2d ed. (London, 1869), 1:351; John Stuart Mill, commenting on James Mill (ibid., 402); John Stuart Mill, *A System of Logic Ratiocinative and Inductive*, ed. J. M. Robson, vol. 7 of *Collected Works of John Stuart Mill* (Toronto: University of Toronto Press, 1973), 574. Mill obviously did not think we change beliefs the way we change addresses. The debate had been adumbrated in Spinoza's critique of Descartes on suspension of judgment (*Ethics* 2, prop. 49, scholium).

5. J. S. Mill, *Analysis*, 423.

6. John Stuart Mill, *An Examination of Sir William Hamilton's Philosophy*, ed. J. M. Robson, vol. 9 of *Collected Works of Mill* (Toronto: University of Toronto Press, 1979), 61, 63, 65n.

7. See "An Interview" (*C*, 256); see also *SP,* 63.

8. Walter Bagehot, "On the Emotion of Conviction" (1871), in *Literary Studies*, ed. Richard Holt Hutton (London: Longmans, Green, 1903), 3:193, 200; Alexander Bain, *The Emotions and the Will* (London, 1859), 583, 578, 569, 571; Arthur Hugh Clough, "With Whom Is No Variableness," in *The Poems and Prose Remains of Arthur Hugh Clough* (London, 1869), 2:91.

9. Bain, *Emotions and Will*, 583; 3d ed. (London, 1875), 505. See also A. H. Murray, *The Philosophy of James Ward* (Cambridge: Cambridge University Press, 1937), 9–10.

10. Newman, "The Tamworth Reading Room," in *Victorian Prose*, ed. Frederick William Roe (New York: Ronald Press, 1947), 175–77.

11. Newman, *An Essay in Aid of a Grammar of Assent*, ed. I. T. Ker (Oxford: Clarendon Press, 1985), 75, 221, 228, 231–32, 74.

12. *The Works of William James*, ed. Frederick H. Burkhardt (Cambridge: Harvard University Press, 1981), 2:913–15, 948.

13. W. James, *The Will to Believe, and Other Essays in Popular Philosophy*, vol. 1 of ibid. (Cambridge: Harvard University Press, 1979), 29.

14. James Ward, *Psychological Principles*, 2d ed. (Cambridge: Cambridge University Press, 1920), 347. Ward notes that "certainty" is confusingly applied to both knowledge and personal belief. Hence, he stresses that "psychology is not interested in objective certainty or *truth* as such, but only in subjective certainty or *conviction*" (348).

15. Ibid., 358–59. Kant wrote, "I have therefore found it necessary to deny knowledge, in order to make room for faith" (*Critique of Pure Reason*, trans. Norman Kemp Smith, 2d ed. [London: Macmillan, 1933], 29).

16. James Ward, *The Realm of Ends; or, Pluralism and Theism* (Cambridge: Cambridge University Press, 1911), 113, 448, hereafter cited as *RE*; Ward, *Psychological Principles*, 355.

17. On Freud in England, see Francis Mulhern, *The Moment of "Scrutiny"* (London: Verso, 1981), 14.

18. See I. A. Richards, *The Philosophy of Rhetoric* (New York: Oxford University Press, 1936), 38–39, for his relating his theory of ambiguous meaning to the psychoanalytic "over-determined" meaning in dream symbolism.

19. This is abundantly clear from the topics raised in Frank E. Manuel, *The Eighteenth Century Confronts the Gods* (Cambridge: Harvard University Press, 1959), chaps. 2–4.

20. This is one of Richards's notorious statements on belief, often misconstrued when taken out of context, though he is surely in part to blame. It is probably statements like this one that led Charles Taylor to criticize Richards for treating beliefs as "irrelevant," an exaggeration when one takes his larger work on belief into account. Though objecting to Richards's psychologism with regard to belief as an inner ordering of the self, however, Taylor appreciated the fact that "Richards was on to something" in his assessment of the use of myth and dogma by modernist writers. Richards did not "factor out" the mythology or the dogma; he grappled with the historical problem, to the effect that "something has undoubtedly changed since the era of the great chain of being and the publicly established order of references." Yet Taylor treats these beliefs as epiphanic moments and not just as a "tentative" reordering of the psyche: "The metaphysics or theology comes indexed to a personal vision, or refracted through a particular sensibility" (*Sources of the Self*, 490–91).

21. Review of *Time and Western Man*, by Wyndham Lewis, *Cambridge Review* (March 9, 1928): 325–26.

22. For commentary on the belief question and the *Divine Comedy*, see Richards, *Beyond* (New York: Harcourt Brace Jovanovich), 112.

23. Richards revised his estimate of Homer's gods as they affect belief (ibid., 32–38).

24. Richards refers to Spinoza's scholium to *Ethics* 2, prop. 49.

25. For Richards, following classical British psychology, a "need" is a temporary imbalance in an organism striving toward equilibrium.

26. Samuel Taylor Coleridge, *Anima Poetae* (London, 1895), 291.

27. What applies to the modern reader also applies to the poet. In 1956 Richards told

Stephen Spender that "what the poet believed inside his poetry, need have no—indeed must have no—authoritatively rational connection dictated by outside belief. The curious thing about poetry is that anything can happen inside its peculiar world without commitment to what goes on outside'" (Spender, *The Thirties and After: Poetry, Politics, People (1933–75)* [London: Macmillan, 1978], 185). But this does not mean that poetry has no effect on personal behavior. Richards submits that it is not this or that idea in a poem, but the poem's total attitude as it finally affects one's emotional belief that is all-important. However, such statements, shorn of their context, could be easily misinterpreted and taken to license an uncompromising formalism.

28. The *success* of the belief is not measured in merely personal terms, "ordering the growth of the personality," but in public terms, "in aiding the good life" (*C*, 33).

29. John Paul Russo, *I. A. Richards: His Life and Work* (Baltimore: Johns Hopkins University Press, 1989), 638–39, 811.

30. *Works of William James,* ed. Burkhardt, 2:913.

31. Richards's own writings are clearly responsible for stirring a modest interest in the problem of belief for several decades. For bibliographies, see Robert Wooster Stallman, ed., *The Critic's Notebook* (Minneapolis: University of Minnesota Press, 1950), and M. H. Abrams, ed., *Literature and Belief: English Institute Essays, 1957* (New York: Columbia University Press, 1958).

32. William Wimsatt Jr.'s and Monroe Beardsley's "intentional fallacy," first articulated in 1942, stipulates that an author's recoverable or inferred design, intention, or belief could not serve as the standard for judging a poem. Though possibly the cause, it cannot be the standard because the relevant materials for such a search are either unrecoverable or available in uneven ways. The intentional fallacy was meant to be a bulwark against expressionist theories, psychologism, "spontaneity," "originality," Richards's "sincerity," and romantic and Victorian concepts of genetic criticism. See Wimsatt, *The Verbal Icon: Studies in the Meaning of Poetry* (Lexington: University Press of Kentucky, 1954), 3–5. For a critique, see William Empson, "Still the Strange Necessity," *Sewanee Review* 63 (1955): 467–77.

33. Peter Jones contends that Richards "anticipated" Collingwood on emotion and the definition of beauty, and that, regarding the latter, "perhaps Collingwood had taken more notice of I. A. Richards than he was wont to admit" ("A Critical Outline of Collingwood's Philosophy of Art," in *Critical Essays on the Philosophy of R. G. Collingwood,* ed. Michael Krausz [Oxford: Clarendon, 1972], 43, 62–63). Richards may also have influenced Collingwood on sincerity. "If art means the expression of emotion, the artist as such must be absolutely candid," Collingwood asserts. "Any kind of selection, any decision to express this emotion and not that, is inartistic not in the sense that it damages the perfect sincerity which distinguishes good art from bad, but in the sense that it represents a further process of a non-artistic kind, carried out when the work of expression proper is already complete" (*The Principles of Art* [Oxford: Clarendon, 1938], 115).

34. Arnold, *Complete Prose Works,* 6:351.

35. Tolstoy, *What Is Art?* trans. Charles Johnston (Philadelphia, 1898), 217–18.

36. Cf. Jean-Paul Sartre on the "pact of generosity" between author and reader: "Each one trusts the other; each one counts on the other" in the "dialectical going-and-coming" (*What Is Literature?* trans. Bernard Frechtman [New York: Philosophical Library,

1949], 55–56). In this respect, "bad faith" is betrayal of the pact and a failure of generosity (23).

37. I. A. Richards, C. K. Ogden, and James Wood, *The Foundations of Aesthetics* (New York: International Publishers, 1925), 74; William Wordsworth, *Preface to Lyrical Ballads*, quoted in *PLC*, 188–89.

38. After examining the biographical evidence, however, Maurice Lindsay concludes that "Ae Fond Kiss" is "lasting proof of the genuineness of his love for Nancy" (*Robert Burns: The Man, His Work, the Legend*, 2d ed. [London: MacGibbon and Kee, 1968], 233).

39. *The Doctrine of the Mean; or, Equilibrium and Harmony*, trans. James Legge, vol. 1 of *The Chinese Classics* (1861; reprint, Hong Kong: Hong Kong University Press, 1960), 283, 394, 407, 413; quotations from the *Chung Yung* are taken from this edition. Richards also used *The Chung-Yung; or, the Centre, the Common*, trans. Leonard A. Lyall and King Chien-Kün (London: Longmans, Green, 1927). Cf. Lippmann, *The Public Philosophy*, 137, 160. Lippmann also finds points of comparison between the Confucian doctrine of the "mandate of heaven" and the transcendent values of Western humanism with its "traditions of civility."

40. *Doctrine of the Mean*, 52. "Now we are astonished at the audacity of the writer's assertions" on sincerity, notes Legge, "and now lost in vain endeavours to ascertain his meaning" (50). Cf. his comment on sincerity as self-completion (418n25).

41. "What is it but extravagance," frowns Legge, "thus to fill man with the supreme Power?" (ibid., 416n22).

42. Max Weber believed that, for both political and social reasons, Chinese thought had remained attached to "pictorial" and "descriptive" forms and so resisted the logical trend of definition and reasoning that characterized Western thought and allowed it to advance. Chinese doctrinal emphasis was on the sententious remarks of the master, which have the "lapidar [*sic*] forcefulness" of "pontifical 'allocutions'" and prevent abstract questioning ("The Chinese Literati," in *From Max Weber*, 430–33).

43. T. S. Eliot, *The Use of Poetry and the Use of Criticism: Studies in the Relation of Criticism to Poetry in England* (London: Faber and Faber, 1933), 132n.

44. *Doctrine of the Mean*, 413. No oracle for Richards. In the *Chung Yung* one of the qualities of the sincere person is the ability "to foreknow": "When a nation or family is about to flourish, there are sure to be happy omens; and when it is about to perish, there are sure to be unlucky omens. Such events are seen in the milfoil and tortoise, and affect the movements of the four limbs" (417).

45. Ibid., 407, 414, 417.

46. Ibid., 418.

47. Ibid., 413. See also Richards, *Beyond*, 24–26.

48. Ezra Pound, "Mang Tsze: The Ethics of Mencius," in *Selected Prose, 1909–1965*, ed. William Cookson (New York: New Directions, 1973), 85. Pound translated the *Chung Yung* (*The Unwobbling Pivot* [1947]) and cited the ideogram *Chung* ten times in the Cantos: for example, canto 70, "I am for balance"; canto 84, "our norm of spirit / our [symbol] chung"; and canto 85, "thy mirrour in men" (*The Cantos of Ezra Pound* [New York: New Directions, 1972], 413, 540, 554). In "Mang Tsze," Pound defines the *"way"* as the "process of nature, *one*, in the sense that the chemist and biologist so find it. Any attempt to deal with it as split, is due to ignorance and a failure in the direction of the will" (87). The "Confucio-Mencian ethic or philosophy" projects a social vision

in sharp contrast to "the disorderly tendencies, the anarchy and barbarism which appear in poor christian teaching, fanaticism and superstition" (95).

49. *Doctrine of the Mean*, 419.

50. Ibid., 393.

51. *The Poetical Works of William Wordsworth*, ed. Ernest De Selincourt and Helen Darbishire, rev. ed. (Oxford: Clarendon, 1959), 5:286, 289; Arnold, *Complete Prose Works*, 6:31, 189.

52. *The Poetical Works of Robert Browning*, ed. Ian Jack and Margaret Smith (Oxford: Clarendon, 1983), 1:489, lines 766, 770–73.

53. Arthur O. Lovejoy, *The Great Chain of Being: A Study of the History of an Idea* (Cambridge: Harvard University Press, 1936), 24–25.

54. Spencer described the evolutionary process as "a change from incoherent, indefinite homogeneity, to coherent, definite heterogeneity"; life is "the continuous adjustment of internal relations to external relations"; "consciousness is the accompaniment of the increasing correspondence and the better adjustment" (quoted in W. B. Pillsbury, *The History of Psychology* [New York: Norton, 1929], 191). Richards found Spencer "too murky" a writer (*C*, 256).

55. On what better grounds to discuss nature versus nurture than those of evolutionary theory? Ward may have supplied Richards's clue in *The Realm of Ends*, which quotes Patrick Geddes and J. A. Thomson's *Evolution of Sex* (1890) on preformation (or "absolutist" or "singularistic") theory: "The germ was more than a marvellous budlike miniature of the adult, it necessarily included in its turn the next generation, and this the next—in short all future generations" (98). Against preformation, as we have seen, Ward set the pluralistic or emergent theory of "diverging lines," improved "adjustment" to environment, and the "process of integration and equilibration" (99, 101). "Which is the truer view it is impossible, of course, to decide while the issue between pluralism and absolutism is still itself undecided" (101).

56. See Stephen Jay Gould, *Ever Since Darwin: Reflections in Natural History* (1973; reprint, New York: W. W. Norton, 1979), 34–38; and Shelley R. Saunders, "The Inheritance of Acquired Characteristics: A Concept That Will Not Die," in *What Darwin Began: Modern Darwinism and Non-Darwinian Perspectives* (Boston: Allyn and Bacon, 1985), 149–50.

57. Richards, *Coleridge on Imagination*, 175. In this context the three qualities are virtually interchangeable: sanity is integrity is sincerity.

58. The Chinese "have had a deep, ingrained horror of violence" (*C*, 267).

59. *Doctrine of the Mean*, 418–19. "All this," notes Legge, "so far as I can see, is but veiling ignorance by words without knowledge" (419n25). Richards took a different view.

60. Eliot, *Use of Poetry and Criticism*, 132–33. See also John Constable, "I. A. Richards, T. S. Eliot, and the Poetry of Belief," *Essays in Criticism* 40:3 (July 1990): 222–43; and Richards, *I. A. Richards and His Critics: Selected Reviews and Critical Articles*, in *Selected Works of I. A. Richards: 1919–1938*, ed. John Constable (London: Routledge, 2001), 10:x–li.

61. Theodor Adorno, *Minima Moralia: Reflections from a Damaged Life*, trans. E. F. N. Jephcott (London: Verso, 1978), 152. Hereafter cited as *MM*.

62. Theodor Adorno, *The Jargon of Authenticity*, trans. Knut Tarnowski and Frederic Will (Evanston: Northwestern University Press, 1973), 9, 11.

63. In *Sincerity and Authenticity,* Trilling argues that "authenticity" implies "a more strenuous moral experience than 'sincerity' does, a more exigent conception of the self and of what being true to it consists in" (11). But Trilling has rigidified or reified the terms of *sincerity* and *authenticity* in this stark confrontation, treating them in effect as two separate categories instead of comprehending just the one categorical self, the atomic unit of the bourgeois epoch: the wild nephew is the *honnête homme* in self-alienation. For this reason, "authenticity" is never fully analyzed (via role-playing and so on).

64. See also *MM,* 35–37, on the "dialectic of tact" as the Goethean strategy of survival for alienated human beings in an inhospitable social world.

65. John Fekete, *The Critical Twilight: Explorations in the Ideology of Anglo-American Literary Theory from Eliot to McLuhan* (London: Routledge and Kegan Paul, 1972), 32–34. For Richards on history and biography, see my *I. A. Richards,* 201–25.

66. Richards and Adorno show most agreement on the importance of the work of art itself. Adorno reveres artists who express a "dynamically unfolding totality" in their historical moment (Beethoven, Goethe), and "this oneness" that is "more than just formal" challenges our "damaged," incomplete lives (quoted by Martin Jay, *Adorno* [Cambridge: Harvard University Press, 1984], 142–43); see also Theodor Adorno, *Aesthetic Theory,* trans. C. Lenhardt (London: Routledge and Kegan Paul, 1984), 169–71. Richards speaks of the "wider [that is, ever widening] equilibrium" that follows a proper reading, and of the "best life" that "feels like and is the experience of [great] poetry" (*SP,* 36, 39).

## V. The Tranquilized Poem: The Crisis of the New Criticism

1. Evan Watkins, *The Critical Act: Criticism and Community* (New Haven: Yale University Press, 1978), 5. Paul de Man states, "It can legitimately be said, for example, that, from a technical point of view, very little has happened in American criticism since the innovative works of New Criticism" ("Semiology and Rhetoric," in *Allegories of Reading: Figural Language in Rousseau, Nietzsche, Rilke, and Proust* [New Haven: Yale University Press, 1979], 4).

2. John Crowe Ransom, "Poets and Flatworms," review of *The Enjoyment of Poetry,* by Max Eastman, *Kenyon Review* 14 (1952): 159; Ransom, "The Concrete Universal: Observations on the Understanding of Poetry," in *Poems and Essays* (New York: Vintage, 1955), 180.

3. Frank Lentricchia, *After the New Criticism,* xii–xiii.

4. The *later* Pound advocated didacticism, statement in poetry, antimetaphorical language, antiambiguousness—all of which were at odds with New Critical assumptions.

5. John Crowe Ransom, *The New Criticism* (Norfolk, CT: New Directions, 1941), 3. According to William R. Elton, Richards is the "Father" of New Criticism, Ransom is the "Apostle" ("A Glossary of the New Criticism," *Poetry* 73 [1948–1949]: 153–63, 232–45, 296–307).

6. Lentricchia, *After the New Criticism,* xii.

7. René Wellek argues that the New Critics are "extremely anglocentric, even provincial" ("The New Criticism: Pro and Contra," *Critical Inquiry* 4 [1978]: 623).

8. Grant Webster, *The Republic of Letters: A History of Postwar American Literary Opinion* (Baltimore: Johns Hopkins University Press, 1979), 112–23.

9. Fekete, *Critical Twilight,* 45; see also 64.

10. Douglas Bush, "Marvell's 'Horatian Ode,'" *Sewanee Review* 60 (1952): 364, 376; Cleanth Brooks, "A Note on the Limits of 'History' and the Limits of 'Criticism,'" *Sewanee Review* 61 (1953): 131; the debate is reprinted in W. R. Keast, ed., *Seventeenth-Century English Poetry: Modern Essays in Criticism* (New York: Oxford University Press, 1962), 321–58. See also Bush's MLA presidential address attacking New Criticism: "The New Criticism: Some Old-Fashioned Queries," *PMLA* 64, supplement, pt. 2 (March 1949): 20–21.

11. Daniel Bell, *The End of Ideology: On the Exhaustion of Political Ideas in the Fifties* (New York: Free Press, 1960), 404, 402; Robert Weimann, *Structure and Society in Literary History: Studies in the History and Theory of Historical Criticism* (Charlottesville: University Press of Virginia, 1976), 127.

12. Fekete, *Critical Twilight,* 91; Louis Hartz, *The Liberal Tradition in America: An Interpretation of American Political Thought since the Revolution* (New York: Harcourt Brace, 1955), 7.

13. Ransom, "Concrete Universal," 163, 180, 165, 166–67. See also William J. Handy, *Kant and the Southern New Critics* (Austin: University of Texas Press, 1963), 17, 34–35, 53–54, 80.

14. Ransom, "Concrete Universal," 167–68; John Crowe Ransom, *The World's Body* (New York: Charles Scribner's, 1938), 349.

15. John Crowe Ransom, "Humanism at Chicago," *Kenyon Review* 14 (1952): 658–59.

16. Ellul, *The Technological Society,* 5, 340–42.

17. Mario Corona, "Getting Ready for the Fifties; or, Criticism Anesthetized," *Rivista di Studi Anglo-Americani* 6 (1986): 283–93.

18. Ransom, "Humanism at Chicago," 658; Cleanth Brooks, *The Well Wrought Urn: Studies in the Structure of Poetry* (New York: Reynal and Hitchcock, 1947), 212–13; Archibald MacLeish, "Why Can't They Say What They Mean?" (1955), in *A Continuing Journey* (Boston: Houghton Mifflin, 1968), 207; C. K. Ogden and I. A. Richards, *The Meaning of Meaning* (London: Kegan Paul, Trench, Trubner, 1923), 247–48, 360, 378; *SP,* 2. Brooks said that the words' "unit meanings" are acquired from experience "outside the poem" and that "we are, of course, always forced to go outside the poem" for these unit meanings (*Well Wrought Urn,* 255). As Lee T. Lemon points out, however, the "admission . . . is tucked safely away in a footnote: Brooks makes no attempt to follow it to its conclusion" (*The Partial Critics* [New York: Oxford University Press, 1965], 110).

19. John Crowe Ransom, symposium "Literature and the Professors," *Southern Review* 6 (1940–1941): 235; Ransom, *The World's Body,* 329.

20. John Hardy, "The Achievement of Cleanth Brooks," *Hopkins Review* 6 (1953): 161. This passage is cited in Webster (*Republic of Letters,* 99), but actually may be entered as evidence against Webster's main thesis that the New Critics are essentially "Tory Formalists," that is, "men who believe in or wish for a social and intellectual world and a literature that express belief in tradition, order, hierarchy, the fallen nature of man, the war of good and evil, and the ultimate union of warring dualisms in the Word of God and the metaphor of poetry" (63). This is the "ideological" side of the

New Criticism, but, as we have seen, there is the other "nonideological" side, which stresses the movement's instrumentality, technicism, ahistoricism, autonomy, and indeterminacy.

21. Ransom, "Criticism, Inc.," in *The World's Body*, 327–50.

22. Louis Simpson, "The Southern Recovery of Memory and History," *Sewanee Review* 82 (1974): 5. Still, of Pound's *Cantos*—heavily laden with references to history, sociology, philosophy, fascism, and Nazism, and marked by anti-Semitism—Tate would say that they are "not about anything. But they are distinguished verse" (*Reactionary Essays on Poetry and Ideas* [New York: Scribner, 1936], 45).

23. Robert Penn Warren, "Pure and Impure Poetry," in *Selected Essays* (New York: Random House, 1958), 22-23, 31, 26. At the same time, though Warren argues for "impurity," it is not for the sake of "impurity" per se, but for an enriched equilibrium, a poetry of "inclusion," a more highly charged conflictual interaction between "purity" and "impurity" that provokes formal "complexities," "ironies," "self-criticism." In this spirit he would praise Coleridge's *Ancient Mariner* as a poem of "pure imagination" (198) and, in a highly revealing example, contrast John Crowe Ransom's "Bells for John Whiteside's Daughter" with James Russell Lowell's "After the Burial," which is "identical in situation": "But in Lowell's poem the savagery of the irony is unqualified. In fact, the whole poem insists, quite literally, that qualification is impossible" (12–16). The loss of the child is simply inconsolable. As a result of Lowell's "not attempting to do anything about the problem," the poem lacks "'insides'" and "conflict"; "it tries to be a pure poem, pure grief," and such "purity" is poetically self-defeating. The fact that the bereavement is "historically real makes it an embarrassing poem, as well." If Warren were arguing for "impurity" faithfully rendered, he would not find in Lowell's mourning over a real death—the ultimate "impurity"—either a poetic failure or a source of embarrassment. By this standard Ransom's complexification of the mourning process is either false to the facts of mourning or only true to them at a much later stage, when the ego has recuperated and become "free and uninhibited again"—that is, when mourning has become memory. In sum, Warren's representative example of a "pure poem" has the effect of overturning his argument for "impurity," for Lowell's "pure poem" is a strong representative of "impurity" and rejected as such; every act on Warren's part to show that the poem is purifying itself by *eliminating* impurities only reinstates them at a deeper level of psychic action. "Purity" *is* "impurity"—a real death is at issue. Finally, the "impure" poem is "embarrassing" and a poetic failure because it cannot protect itself, via closure, from the reader's irony, his fastidiousness confronting the stark experience of the impure. Embarrassment is the breaking in of the nonaesthetic, the index of that Wittgensteinian "horror of mixing."

24. Edward Wasiolek, introduction to *The New Criticism in France*, by Serge Doubrovsky, trans. Derek Coltman (Chicago: University of Chicago Press, 1973), 14–15; Eliseo Vivas, *Creation and Discovery: Essays in Criticism and Aesthetics* (New York: Noonday Press, 1955), xi; Watkins, *Critical Act*, 25.

25. Murray Krieger, *A Window to Criticism: Shakespeare's Sonnets and Modern Poetics* (Princeton: Princeton University Press, 1964), 22–23; Ransom, *The World's Body*, 135; Warren, "Pure and Impure Poetry," 3, 31; Christopher Norris, *Deconstruction: Theory and Practice* (London: Methuen, 1982), 13–14; Walter J. Ong, S.J., "Wit and Mystery," in *The Barbarian Within* (New York: Macmillan, 1962), 90.

26. Ransom, *The World's Body*, viii; Tate quoted in Webster, *Republic of Letters*, 141–

42; Wimsatt, *Verbal Icon,* 268–69; R. Blackmur, "Irregular Metaphysics," in *A Primer of Ignorance,* quoted in Norris, *Deconstruction,* 13; Bell, *End of Ideology,* 310–11.

27. William Empson, "The Darling in the Urn," review of *The Well Wrought Urn,* by Cleanth Brooks, *Sewanee Review* 55 (1947): 697. "The anti-emotional bias, which is so often obscurely present, could make it very arid" (697).

28. Lionel Trilling, *The Liberal Imagination* (New York: Viking, 1951), 183–87.

29. Ibid., 46, 49 (italics added), 55–56, 129.

30. Wimsatt, *Verbal Icon,* 3–5; Richards, *Coleridge on Imagination,* 208; Wimsatt, *Verbal Icon,* 5; Cleanth Brooks, "My Credo," *Kenyon Review* 13 (1951): 74.

31. William Empson, *The Structure of Complex Words* (London: Chatto and Windus, 1951), 34–35.

32. Christopher Norris, *William Empson and the Philosophy of Literary Criticism* (London: Athlone Press, University of London, 1978), 131. Thus, when Empson weighs in on Marvell's Cromwell, he takes into account biographical reasons for possible ambiguities, "his real-life situation, idling and equivocating his way through the Civil War period: " 'Unemployment" is too painful and normal even in the fullest life for such a theme to be trivial' " (135).

33. Empson, *Complex Words,* 303–4, 369.

34. Norris, *William Empson,* 136.

35. Empson, "Still the Strange Necessity," 476–77.

36. Wimsatt, *Verbal Icon,* 269.

37. Norris, *William Empson,* 133.

38. Empson, "Still the Strange Necessity," 476.

39. William Empson, "The Intentional Fallacy, Again," *Essays in Criticism* 23 (1973): 435.

40. See note 10.

41. Walter Jackson Bate, *Prefaces to Criticism* (New York: Harcourt Brace, 1959).

42. Walter Jackson Bate, *Criticism: The Major Texts,* 1st ed. (New York: Harcourt Brace, 1952), 277.

43. Walter Jackson Bate, *The Achievement of Samuel Johnson* (New York: Oxford University Press, 1955), 62.

44. Leslie A. Fiedler, "Archetype and Signature: A Study of the Relationship between Biography and Poetry," *Sewanee Review* 60 (1952): 253–73.

45. Ibid., 265.

46. Ibid.

47. Gerald Graff, *Poetic Statement and Critical Dogma* (Chicago: University of Chicago Press, 1970), 65–86; Northrop Frye, *The Well-Tempered Critic* (Bloomington: Indiana University Press, 1963), 149.

48. Northrop Frye, "The Archetypes of Literature," *Kenyon Review* 13 (1951): 92–110.

49. Ibid., 104, 107–8.

50. Weimann, *Structure and Society,* 125.

51. Cited in ibid., 123. See also Roderick Seidenberg, *Posthistoric Man: An Inquiry* (Chapel Hill: University of North Carolina Press, 1950).

52. Gerald Graff, *Literature against Itself: Literary Ideas in Modern Society* (Chicago: University of Chicago Press, 1979), 129–49; Lentricchia, *After the New Criticism,* xiii, 157–58; Paul A. Bové, *Destructive Poetics: Heidegger and Modern American Poetry* (New

York: Columbia University Press, 1980), 30–48; Christopher Norris, *Deconstruction*, 5–14; Henry Staten, "Language and Consciousness in Richards and Wittgenstein," *Western Humanities Review* 36 (1982): 67, 73; Remo Ceserani, *Breve viaggio nella critica americana* (Pisa: ETS, 1984), 5–16; Barbara Foley, "From New Criticism to Deconstruction: The Example of Charles Feidelson's *Symbolism and American Literature*," *American Quarterly* 36 (1984): 44–64; Stephen W. Melville, *Philosophy beside Itself: On Deconstruction and Modernism* (Minneapolis: University of Minnesota Press, 1986), 115–38. A breach in the history of criticism in this epoch would be conveniently closed by an essay on the pivotal figure of Reuben Brower. Brower, who had studied with Richards at Cambridge in 1931–1932, had moved from Amherst to Harvard in the early 1950s, where he introduced Humanities 6, an undergraduate course in the New Critical method of close reading. He soon gathered a circle of younger colleagues, section leaders in the course, and graduate students among whom were numbered Paul de Man, J. Hillis Miller, Richard Poirier, David Kalstone, Niel H. Hertz, Edward Said, Paul J. Alpers, Helen Vendler, and Anne Ferry.

53. Foley, "From New Criticism to Deconstruction," 45, 56, 57 (Dauber cited on 57).

54. Lentricchia, *After the New Criticism*, 342.

55. Ibid., 166; Wyndham Lewis, *Men without Art* (London: Cassell, 1934), 69ff.

56. Barbara Foley, "The Politics of Deconstruction," *Genre* 17 (1984): 129, 133. "Both deconstruction and the New Critical method with which it is in part genetically connected are fundamentally formalistic and idealist schools of criticism that would negate—or at least drastically marginalize—the referential power and historical significance of literary discourse" (Foley, "From New Criticism to Deconstruction," 64).

57. Paul de Man, *Blindness and Insight: Essays in the Rhetoric of Contemporary Criticism*, 2d ed. (Minneapolis: University of Minnesota Press, 1983), 28.

58. Richards, *The Philosophy of Rhetoric*, 92, 94; Cleanth Brooks, "I. A. Richards and the Concept of Tension," in *I. A. Richards: Essays in His Honor*, ed. Reuben Brower et al. (New York: Oxford University Press, 1974), 153, 151.

59. Brooks, *Well Wrought Urn*, 207, 203, 209.

60. Lemon, *The Partial Critics*, 144; William K. Wimsatt Jr. and Cleanth Brooks, *Literary Criticism: A Short History* (New York: Alfred A. Knopf, 1957), 652–53. In 1960, in an essay called "Intentional Structure of the Romantic Image," Paul de Man wrote: "The word is always a free presence to the mind, the means by which the permanence of natural entities can be put into question and thus negated, time and again, in the endlessly widening spiral of the dialectic" (*The Rhetoric of Romanticism* [New York: Columbia University Press, 1984], 6). Years later, reviewing the book in which the essay was reprinted, René Wellek commented that this "sounds almost like Derrida" ("Criticism in the University," *Partisan Review* 53:4 [1986]: 527). But equally it sounds like Richards, who said "a word by itself apart from an utterance has no meaning—or rather it has too many possible meanings" (*Coleridge on Imagination*, 101)—who spoke of the work of difference as more significant than likeness in tenor-vehicle relations (*Philosophy of Rhetoric*, 127), and who described the interplay of feed-forward and feedback mechanisms in the production of meaning and wrote dialectical studies in multiple definition.

61. Lemon, *The Partial Critics*, 130–31; Wimsatt and Brooks, *Literary Criticism*, 648.

62. Ransom, *The World's Body*, 347–49; Ransom, *The New Criticism*, 281, 335.

63. Giuseppe Sertoli, "Umanesimo e Formalismo," in *Quaderno, no. 13*, ed. G. Cianci and J. P. Russo (Palermo: University of Palermo, 1981), 85–88.

64. Ibid. The theme of silence is reinforced by MacLeish's insistence that the poem should be "silent as the sleeve-worn stone," "wordless / As the flight of birds," "motionless," and the poem is "equal to: / Not true," that is, having no equivalent in external reality, in sum, the Emersonian unity of subject and object, mind and matter.

## VI. The Disappearance of the Self: Contemporary Theories of Autobiography

1. Roy Pascal, *Design and Truth in Autobiography* (London: Routledge and Kegan Paul, 1960), 5; cf. A. J. O. Cockshut, *The Art of Autobiography in Nineteenth- and Twentieth-Century England* (New Haven: Yale University Press, 1984), 2; René Wellek and Austin Warren, *Theory of Literature* (New York: Harcourt, Brace, 1949), 70–72; Stephen A. Shapiro, "The Dark Continent of Literature: Autobiography," *Comparative Literature Studies* 5 (1968): 421–54.

2. Cited in Heidi I. Stull, *The Evolution of Autobiography from 1750–1850: A Comparative Study and Analysis* (Berne: Peter Lang, 1985), 24–25.

3. Georges Gusdorf, "Conditions and Limits of Autobiography," in *Autobiography: Essays Theoretical and Critical,* ed. James Olney (Princeton: Princeton University Press, 1980), 31, 37, 38, 43, 48.

4. Pascal, *Design and Truth;* David Levin, "*The Autobiography of Benjamin Franklin:* The Puritan Experimenter in Life and Art" (1964), in *In Defense of Historical Literature: Essays on American History, Autobiography, Drama and Fiction* (New York: Hill and Wang, 1967), 58–76; Francis R. Hart, "Notes for an Anatomy of Modern Autobiography," *New Literary History* 1 (1970): 485–511. For bibliographies, see Philippe Lejeune, *Le pacte autobiographique* (Paris: Seuil, 1974) and *Je est un autre: L'autobiographie de la littérature aux médias* (Paris: Seuil, 1980); G. Thomas Couser, *American Autobiography: The Prophetic Mode* (Amherst: University of Massachusetts Press, 1979); William C. Spengemann, *The Forms of Autobiography: Episodes in the History of a Literary Genre* (New Haven: Yale University Press, 1980) (annotated); Albert E. Stone, ed., *The American Autobiography* (Englewood Cliffs, NJ: Prentice-Hall, 1981); "Recherches actuelles sur l'autobiographie," *Romanticisme: Revue du dix-neuvième siècle* 56 (1987): 111–25, with bibliographical notes on the 1980s by Philippe Lejeune (France), Hans-Jürgen Lüsebrink (Germany), Heinz Blaumeiser (Austria), Guy Mercadier (Spain and the Hispanic world), Eva Martonyi-Horváth (Hungary), Paul John Eakin (United States), and Yvan Lamond (French Canada); and Sidonie Smith and Julia Watson, *Reading Autobiography: A Guide for Interpreting Life Narratives* (Minneapolis: University of Minnesota Press, 2001), 227–67.

5. "In 'Autobiography as Narrative,' Alfred Kazin had implied a broader definition in saying that 'autobiography, like other literary forms, is what a gifted writer makes of it,'" comments Robert F. Sayre. "Kazin was most interested in the large number of modern books like Hemingway's *A Moveable Feast* and Robert Lowell's *Life Studies* which use fictional techniques yet 'deliberately retain the facts behind the story in order to show the imaginative possibilities inherent in fact.' That kind of writing . . . is hard to approach as traditional autobiography. It doesn't tell us the same kind of story;

its chronology is likely to be fragmentary or shuffled, inventive and exploratory; it approaches fiction" ("The Proper Study: Autobiographies in American Studies," in *The American Autobiography,* ed. Stone, 14).

6. Smith and Watson, *Reading Autobiography,* 123.

7. Wylie Sypher, *The Loss of the Self in Twentieth-Century Literature and Art* (New York: Random House, 1962), 14.

8. Burckhardt, *Civilization of Italy,* 81–84, 279; Steven Lukes, *Individualism* (Oxford: Blackwell, 1973), 45–73, cited in Michael Mascuch, *Origins of the Individualist Self: Autobiography and Self-Identity in England, 1591–1791* (Stanford: Stanford University Press, 1996), 20.

9. Robert F. Sayre, *The Examined Self: Benjamin Franklin, Henry Adams, Henry James* (Princeton: Princeton University Press, 1964), viii, 34.

10. Ibid., 13, 23.

11. Ibid., 23, 25, 27.

12. Ibid., 3, 195, 200, 202.

13. Ibid., 204.

14. Ibid., 198. Cf. the historical contextualizing of Augustine by Robert Elbaz (*The Changing Nature of the Self: A Critical Study of the Autobiographic Discourse* [Iowa City: University of Iowa Press, 1987], 32, 36).

15. Sayre, *Examined Self,* 93–94, 130, 133.

16. Couser, *American Autobiography,* 118.

17. Gordon O. Taylor, *Chapters of Experience: Studies in 20th Century American Autobiography* (New York: St. Martin's Press, 1983), 18.

18. Sayre, *Examined Self,* 164, 203. Cf. James on aesthetic theory: "Really, universally, relations stop nowhere, and the exquisite problem of the artist is eternally but to draw, by a geometry of his own, the circle within which they shall happily appear to do so" (James E. Miller, ed., *Theory of Fiction: Henry James* [Lincoln: University of Nebraska Press, 1972], 171–72).

19. James Olney, *Metaphors of Self: The Meaning of Autobiography* (Princeton: Princeton University Press, 1972), 3, 4, 6. "In the beginning . . . was Georges Gusdorf" (Olney, "Autobiography and the Cultural Moment: A Thematic, Historical, and Bibliographical Introduction," in *Autobiography,* ed. Olney, 8).

20. Olney, *Metaphors of Self,* 3, 8–9, 32; W. K. C. Guthrie, *A History of Greek Philosophy* (Cambridge: Cambridge University Press, 1962), 1:425; cf. G. S. Kirk, "Flux and Logos in Heraclitus," in *The Pre-Socratics,* ed. Alexander P. D. Mourelatos (Garden City, NY: Doubleday, 1974), 212–13.

21. Olney, *Metaphors of Self,* 6, 23.

22. Gould, *Ever Since Darwin,* 261.

23. Olney, *Metaphors of Self,* 9.

24. Ibid., 12, 15–16, 46; G. E. Moore, "The Refutation of Idealism," in *Philosophical Studies* (London: Kegan Paul, Trench, Trubner, 1922), 27. "Merely to have a sensation is already to *be* outside that circle. It is to know something which is as truly and really *not* a part of *my* experience, as anything which I can ever know" (27).

25. Karl J. Weintraub, *The Value of the Individual: Self and Circumstance in Autobiography* (Chicago: University of Chicago Press, 1978), 67. Unlike Burckhardt, Weintraub sets Dante closer to the Augustinian-medieval pole than to the modern one (Renaissance and after), the evidence being the "conventions of high medieval poetic

art, the intensive use of symbolism, the scholastic mentality, and the fundamental realities of an unquestioned metaphysical-religious ethos: the same characteristics that can be seen in self-revelations of such troubadours as Wolfram von Eschenbach and Ulrich von Lichtenstein" (67). For an opposing view, see Frank Kermode, "Dante," in *Continuities* (New York: Viking, 1968), 233–38.

26. Weintraub, *Value of the Individual,* xv–xvi. "To be sure, no two knights were ever the same, there are interesting differences between Achilles and Odysseus, and no 'imitator' of Christ ever duplicated his life. But the all-important point is that, despite all variation, the men who sought to follow such models saw virtue in approaching and fulfilling an exemplary way of being human while placing very little value on idiosyncratic difference—if at all" (xvi).

27. Ibid., xvi.

28. Ibid.

29. Cf. Francesco Guicciardini on the particular over the general in *Maxims and Reflections of a Renaissance Statesman (Ricordi),* trans. Mario Domandi (Gloucester, MA: Peter Smith, 1990), 42, 88, 105, 125.

30. Friedrich Meinecke, *Historism: The Rise of a New Historical Outlook,* trans. J. E. Anderson (London: Routledge and Kegan Paul, 1972), lv–lviii, 334. As Benjamin C. Sax writes, *Bildung* signified "the growth process of the individual, the historical continuity of the world, and the interaction between the two. *Bildung* spoke to the inner cultivation of one's talents, the development of humanity, and the education of humanity to the level of humanity. This development moreover involved neither a notion of an unfolding of some inner, determining germ nor the idea of the fulfillment of some external goal. The result of *Bildung* was not achieved in the manner of a technical construction, but supposedly grew out of the inner process of formation and continual cultivation and therefore remained in a constant state of further *Bildung*" (*Images of Identity,* 40).

31. Weintraub, "Autobiography and Historical Consciousness," *Critical Inquiry* 1 (1975): 827. As Georges Gusdorf notes, "The artist and the model coincide, the historian tackles himself as an object" ("Conditions and Limits," 31).

32. Cited in Meinecke, *Historism,* vi, 334.

33. Weintraub, *Value of the Individual,* 94–95, xvi.

34. Olney, "Autobiography and the Cultural Moment," 19. "Much of the early criticism of the autobiographical mode was directed to the question of the *autos*—how the act of autobiography is at once a discovery, a creation, and an imitation of the self" (19).

35. Avrom Fleishman, *Figures of Autobiography: The Language of Self-Writing in Victorian and Modern England* (Berkeley and Los Angeles: University of California Press, 1983); G. O. Taylor, *Chapters of Experience;* Paul John Eakin, *Fictions in Autobiography: Studies in the Art of Self Invention* (Princeton: Princeton University Press, 1985).

36. Susanna Egan, *Patterns of Experience in Autobiography* (Chapel Hill: University of North Carolina Press, 1984).

37. Elizabeth W. Bruss, *Autobiographical Acts: The Changing Situation of a Literary Genre* (Baltimore: Johns Hopkins University Press, 1976); Fleishman, *Figures of Autobiography;* Spengemann, *Forms of Autobiography.*

38. Luther H. Martin, Huck Gutman, Patrick H. Hutton, eds., *Technologies of the Self: A Seminar with Michel Foucault;* Robert Folkenflik, ed., *The Culture of Autobiography:*

*Constructions of Self-Representation* (Stanford: Stanford University Press, 1993), particularly John Sturrock, "Theory versus Autobiography" (21–37).

39. Elbaz, *Changing Nature*, 8, 10.

40. Lejeune, *Je est un autre;* Robert Folkenflik, "The Self as Other," in *Culture of Autobiography*, ed. Folkenflik, 215–35; Jan Campbell and Janet Harbord, eds., *Temporalities, Autobiography, and Everyday Life* (Manchester: Manchester University Press, 2002).

41. Arnold Krupat, "American Autobiography: The Western Tradition," *Georgia Review* 35 (1981): 307–17.

42. Stull, *Evolution of Autobiography,* 182; Smith and Watson, *Reading Autobiography,* 183ff.

43. Mascuch, *Individualist Self,* 6; "demonization" of Gusdorf in Paul John Eakin, *How Our Lives Become Stories: Making Stories* (Ithaca: Cornell University Press, 1999), 51. "Gusdorf regards autobiography as a cultural monument to the individual subject of Western culture—inevitably white, male, and highly literate," claims Julia Watson ("Toward an Anti-Metaphysics of Autobiography," in *Culture of Autobiography,* ed. Folkenflik, 59).

44. Folkenflik, introduction to *Culture of Autobiography,* 11.

45. Francesco Petrarca, *Secretum,* in *Prose,* ed. Guido Martellotti, in series *La Letteratura italiana, Storia e Testi* (Milan: Ricciardi, 1955), 7:255 *(nusquam integer, nusquam totus).*

46. For the debate on objectivity, see Novick, *That Noble Dream.*

47. Michel Foucault, *The Order of Things: The Archaeology of the Human Sciences* (London: Tavistock, 1986), 387; on Paul de Man's "Autobiography as De-Facement," see Watson, "Toward an Anti-Metaphysics of Autobiography," 62; Jeffrey Mehlman cited in Fleishman, *Figures of Autobiography,* 32; Michael Sprinker, "Fictions of the Self: The End of Autobiography," in *Autobiography,* ed. Olney, 342; Stephen K. White, *The Recent Work of Jürgen Habermas: Reason, Justice and Modernity* (Cambridge: Cambridge University Press, 1988), 4–5; Genaro M. Padilla, "The Mexican Immigrant as *:* The (de)Formation of Mexican Immigrant Life Story," in *Culture of Autobiography,* ed. Folkenflik, 131.

48. Heartfield, *"Death of the Subject";* Eduardo Cadava, Peter Conner, and Jean-Luc Nancy, *Who Comes after the Subject?* (New York: Routledge, 1991); Rei Terada, *Feeling in Theory: Emotion after the "Death of the Subject"* (Cambridge: Harvard University Press, 2001) (cited from the dust jacket).

49. This dire situation is not universal. In Holocaust studies, for example, Susan Gubar, Shoshana Felman, and Ranen Omer-Sherman have examined the power of the contemporary witness. Ethnic and feminist studies have greatly stimulated the theory of the memoir, as in the work of William Boelhower, Sandra M. Gilbert, Fred Gardaphé, Edwige Giunta, and Louise De Salvo.

50. Roy F. Baumeister and Jean M. Twenge, "The Social Self," in *Handbook of Psychology: Personality and Social Psychology,* ed. Theodore Millon and Melvin J. Lerner (New York: John Wiley and Sons, 2003), 5:345–46.

51. Susan M. Andersen and Serena Chen, "The Relational Self: An Interpersonal Social-Cognitive Theory," *Psychological Review* 109:4 (October 2002): 2.

52. Michael Fitzpatrick, *Spiked* (2003), available through http://www.audacity.org. Counseling figures are cited from Heartfield, *"Death of the Subject,"* 236.

53. Heartfield, *"Death of the Subject,"* 20–21, 147–50, 203, 224. The boundless et-cetera is the "bad infinity of the endless sequence that can always be expanded by the addition of another forgotten or excluded social movement" (149).

54. Ibid., 203, 208–9, 214, 217–18, 223–23. Like many other writers on cultural de-cline, Heartfield does not entertain the extent to which the technological system has engendered the sense of helplessness. I do not mean to contribute to this loss of self-esteem by pressing the case elsewhere in this book that technology is in almost total control. The only way to overcome the crisis is by first gaining one's bearings on the problem—Thomas Hardy's "if way to the Better there be, it exacts a full look at the Worst" ("In Tenebris—II"). Donald Drew Egbert, *Socialism and American Art in the Light of European Utopianism, Marxism, and Anarchism* (Princeton: Princeton University Press, 1967), 148.

55. Seyla Benhabib, *Situating the Self: Gender, Community and Postmodernism in Contemporary Ethics* (New York: Routledge, 1992), 218. "The involuntary individual-ism of a Robinson Crusoe and the voluntary individualism of a Henry David Thoreau show obvious debts to society. If Crusoe had reached the island as a baby, and if Thoreau had grown up unattended on the shores of Walden Pond, their stories would have been different" (B. F. Skinner, *Beyond Freedom and Dignity* [New York: Bantam, 1971], 118).

56. Ulric Neisser, "Five Kinds of Self-Knowledge," *Philosophical Psychology* 1 (1988): 35–36. See Isaiah Berlin, "A Note on Vico's Concept of Knowledge," in *Giambattista Vico: An International Symposium,* ed. Giorgio Tagliacozzo and Hayden V. White (Baltimore: Johns Hopkins University Press, 1969), 375–76.

57. Eakin, *How Our Lives Become Stories,* 25; Neisser, "Five Kinds of Self-Knowledge," 35, 55, 56.

58. Andersen and Chen, "Relational Self," 2, 3, 6, 7, 30, 33, 34.

59. Baumeister and Twenge, "The Social Self," 327–28, 345–46.

60. MacIntyre, *After Virtue,* 208, 214–16, 219. Cicero placed the *narratio* of an ora-tion—the story containing the facts of the case—in the second position, immediately after a brief exordium. He knew that if one can compose a good story and thereby con-vince jurors that one's own version of the facts is more plausible than one's opponent's, one locked up the case even before the *divisio, confirmatio,* and *refutatio.* Lawyers ever since have followed suit, at least successful ones: a defense attorney's emphasis in both opening and closing statements falls on the story. Both Adorno and MacIntyre share a strong distaste for the Enlightenment project with its championing of instrumental ra-tionality. Perhaps they forget that the Peace of Utrecht ended a hundred years of reli-gious wars.

61. C. Taylor, *Sources of the Self,* 38–39; C. Taylor, *The Ethics of Authenticity,* 2, 4, 22, 29, 35. Albert Borgmann says that the promise of technology had degenerated into the "procurement of frivolous comfort" (*Technology and Contemporary Life,* 39). The orig-inal ideal of subjectivity was not regressive; it has a civic component as in Ciceronian and Renaissance humanism.

62. C. Taylor, *Sources of the Self,* 34–38, 46–47, 49, 507; C. Taylor, *The Ethics of Au-thenticity,* 17, 33, 82, 127. "Today the individual has been taken out of a rich commu-

nity life and now enters instead into a series of mobile, changing, revocable associations, often designed merely for highly specific ends. We end up relating to each other through a series of partial roles" (C. Taylor, *Sources of the Self,* 502). Taylor relies on Earl R. Wasserman, *The Subtler Language* (Baltimore: Johns Hopkins University Press, 1968), for his analysis of "cosmic syntaxes" at the end of the eighteenth century. Mascuch draws interesting parallels between MacIntyre and Taylor on selfhood (*Individualist Self,* 21–22); both "highlight narrative competency as the essential characteristic of the person" (22).

63. C. Taylor, *Sources of the Self,* 489–90; C. Taylor, *The Ethics of Authenticity,* 58, 60.

64. Bruss, *Autobiographical Acts,* 4–6, 9. "Authors like Daniel Defoe, who had exploited the devices of autobiography while stripping them of their religious connotations, had taught the reading public to isolate and appreciate the representational density, emotional vitality, and illusion of authenticity these devices could produce" (61).

65. Ibid., 10–11.

66. Pascal, *Design and Truth,* 148, 158, 160.

67. Bruss, *Autobiographical Acts,* 98, 103, 112, 125.

68. Ibid., 18, 163–64; Elizabeth Bruss, "Eye for I: Making and Unmaking Autobiography in Film," in *Autobiography,* ed. Olney, 296–97.

69. J. Hillis Miller, "Postscript: 1984," in *Romanticism and Contemporary Criticism,* ed. Morris Eaves and Michael Fischer (Ithaca: Cornell University Press, 1986), 124–26; Sacvan Bercovitch, *The Puritan Origins of the American Self* (New Haven: Yale University Press, 1976), 17–18.

70. Elbaz, *Changing Nature,* vii, 120, 1–3, 10–11.

71. Ibid., 1, 16. "Only a leisure class can afford to devote so much time, energy and money to self-exploration," says Edwin M. Schur. "Far from inciting a break with our dominant patterns of competitive consumption (as some awareness-oriented idealists had hoped would happen), the 'new consciousness' has itself become a commodity. . . . [A]ttention is diverted from the more serious social problems that plague our society—poverty, racism, environmental decay, crime, widespread corporate and governmental fraud" (*The Awareness Trap: Self-Absorption instead of Social Change* [New York: McGraw-Hill, 1977], 7).

72. Elbaz, *Changing Nature,* 13–14, 152.

73. Ibid., 119, 120, 126, 128.

74. Eakin, *How Our Lives Become Stories,* ix–x, 43, 55, 61, 93.

75. Ibid., ix, 3, 4, 43, 50–51.

76. Ibid., 43, 55, 56, 59, 63–64, 85–86. As Eakin summarizes Shotter: "Possessive individualism, functioning as the dominant social 'text' to which we are held 'accountable,' masks the contribution of the 'practical social processes going on "between" people' toward making us what we are" (63). One cannot simply say "individualism"; it is necessary to add the pejorative "possessive," as if there were no other kind. For Eakin, Shotter is "one of the most recent in a long line of commentators seeking to undo the conceptual legacy of a culture of individualism that has blinded us to the relational dimension of identity formation" (63–64).

77. Watson, "Toward an Anti-Metaphysics of Autobiography," 57–58, 61, 69–70.

78. Ibid., 74–75; Eakin, *How Our Lives Become Stories,* 94. Cf. Lucy Noakes's commonsensical remark that autobiography "is a clear, material reminder of the links that exist between the past and the present" ("Women and the War That Never Happened:

British Women, Autobiography and the Memory of the Gulf War," in *Temporalities,* ed. Campbell and Harbord, 219).

79. Michael Renov, "The End of Autobiography or New Beginnings?" in *Temporalities,* ed. Campbell and Harbord, 280–81, 285–86, 288. I have not been able to accept Walter Benjamin's theory that art loses its aura when it becomes (over)reproduced mechanically. The cathedrals of Modena and San Zeno in Verona do not lose anything when I visit them in contrast to the photograph I have of them in my office. The Bach Suites are even more powerful in concert than when I hear them on a recording, and so on. It is true that by overhearing, say, a particular concerto, one can wear it out for a time. But that is quite different.

80. Turkle, *Life on the Screen,* 177, 263–64; Sarah Kember, "Kin or Clone: Contemporary Biotechnologies of the Self," in *Temporalities,* ed. Campbell and Harbord, 252–53.

81. Donna J. Haraway, *Modest_Witness@Second_Millennium: FemaleMan©_Meets_OncoMouseTM* (London: Routledge, 1997), 22; Haraway, *Simians, Cyborgs, and Women,* 149–51.

82. G. Stent, "Molecular Biology and Metaphysics," *Nature* (April 26, 1974): 77.

83. Maurizio Dardano and Pietro Trifone, *La lingua italiana* (Bologna: Zanichelli, 1985), 247.


## VII. Don DeLillo: Ethnicity, Religion, and the Critique of Technology

1. Gay Talese, "Where Are the Italian-American Novelists?" *New York Times Book Review* (March 14, 1993): 23; Dana Gioia, "Low Visibility: Thoughts on Italian American Writers," *Italian Americana* 12:1 (Fall–Winter 1993): 11.

2. That is, 10 percent Italian, 90 percent American. Letter from Frank Capra to Dominic Candeloro, October 22, 1978, *H-ITAM Digest,* July 17, 2001 (by permission). "I was so young (5) when my family moved from Sicily to California that I remember practically nothing about my life before coming to California. And since then I have had few contacts with Italian-Americans." What could Capra possibly mean that he had "few contacts" with Italian Americans since the age of five? What about his family? What about Little Sicily in Los Angeles where he grew up? For the ethnic dimension in Capra, see John Paul Russo, "An Unacknowledged Masterpiece: Capra's Italian American Film," in *Screening Ethnicity,* ed. Hostert and Tamburri, 291–321.

3. Daniel Aaron, "How to Read Don DeLillo," in *Introducing Don DeLillo,* ed. Frank Lentricchia (Durham: Duke University Press, 1991), 67–68; Christopher Durang, *Twenty-seven Short Plays* (Lyme, NH: Smith and Kraus, 1995), 376; Pearl K. Bell, "DeLillo's World," *Partisan Review* 59:1 (1992): 138.

4. Tom LeClair, *In the Loop: Don DeLillo and the Systems Novel* (Champaign: University of Illinois Press, 1987), 14, 34.

5. Thomas DePietro, "Where Are the Italian American Novelists?" *Italian Americana* 12:1 (Fall–Winter 1993): 26.

6. Joseph Tabbi, *Postmodern Sublime: Technology and American Writing from Mailer to Cyberpunk* (Ithaca: Cornell University Press, 1995), 173, 175, 191; Andrew Jude Price, *The Entropic Imagination in Twentieth-Century American Fiction: A Case for Don De-Lillo* (Ann Arbor: UMI, 1991), 117; Fred L. Gardaphé, *Italian Signs, American Streets:*

*The Evolution of Italian American Narrative* (Durham: Duke University Press, 1996), 190, 191. Still, DeLillo is "guided, if not haunted, by [Little Italy's] proverbial wisdom" (191).

7. Daniela Daniele, *Scrittori e finzioni d'America: Incontri e cronache, 1989–99* (Turin: Bollati Boringhieri, 2000), 116 (my translation).

8. Irvin Long Child, *Italian or American? The Second Generation in Conflict* (New Haven: Institute for Human Relations and Yale University Press, 1943), 71–72, 113–16, 146–49, 179–84. Some second-generation traits are shared by early third-generation ethnics. Given that his father was young when he emigrated with his parents, it may be that DeLillo (b. 1936) is closer to early third generation (those whose grandparents were born in Italy but whose parents were born in America).

9. Cited in John N. Duvall, *Don DeLillo's "Underworld": A Reader's Guide* (New York: Continuum, 2002), 9.

10. The "centro ideale" of Giovanni Verga's *I Malavoglia* is the "religione della casa" (*I Malavoglia,* ed. Piero Nardi [Milan: Mondadori, 1964], 176).

11. Richard D. Alba, *Italian Americans: Into the Twilight of Ethnicity* (Englewood Cliffs, NJ: Prentice-Hall, 1985).

12. Jonathan Little, "Ironic Mysticism in Don DeLillo's *Ratner's Star,*" *Papers on Language and Literature* 35:3 (1999): 315; James Annesley, "'Thigh bone connected to the hip bone': Don DeLillo's *Underworld* and the Fictions of Globalization," *Amerika-studien* 47:1 (2002): 92; Paul Maltby, "The Romantic Metaphysics of Don DeLillo," *Contemporary Literature* 37:2 (1996): 275; Daniel Born, "Sacred Noise in Don DeLillo's Fiction," *Literature and Theology* 13:3 (1999): 212; John A. McClure, "Postmodern/ Post-secular: Contemporary Fiction and Spirituality," *Modern Fiction Studies* 41:1 (1995): 143, 155, 159; Mark Osteen, *American Magic and Dread: Don DeLillo's Dialogue with Culture* (Philadelphia: University of Pennsylvania Press, 2000), 137–39; Anthony DeCurtis, "'An Outsider in This Society': An Interview with Don DeLillo," in *Intro-ducing Don DeLillo,* ed. Lentricchia, 55. As Paul Civello notes, Catholicism impressed upon him the "sense of mystery" and a concern for "discipline, ritual, and spectacle" ("Don DeLillo," in *American Novelists since World War II,* ed. James R. Giles and Wanda L. Giles, 5th series [Detroit: Gale Research, 1996], 15).

13. Richard Falk, "Religion and Politics: Verging on the Postmodern," in *Sacred Interconnections: Postmodern Spirituality, Political Economy, and Art,* ed. David Griffin (Albany: SUNY Press, 1990), 83.

14. McClure, "Postmodern/Post-secular," 142, 158; Suzi Gablik, "The Re-enchantment of Art: Reflections on the Two Postmodernisms," in *Sacred Interconnections,* ed. Griffin, 179.

15. Kurt F. Reinhardt attributes transcendent godhead principally to the Hebrew concept of divinity, immanent godhead to the "post-Platonist conviction that gods are projections of man" (*The Theological Novel of Modern Europe* [New York: F. Ungar, 1969], 6).

16. Guy E. Swanson, *Religion and Regime: A Sociological Account of the Reforma-tion* (Ann Arbor: University of Michigan Press, 1967), 2. "While in orthodox or Old-Protestantism there is this irreconciled and irreconcilable cleavage between the Creator and the creature, in Roman Catholicism [God is] simultaneously intimately present in the creature and in creation as an indispensable, sustaining, life-giving power" (Rein-hardt, *Theological Novel,* 5–6).

17. Michael Carroll, *Veiled Threats: The Logic of Popular Catholicism in Italy* (Baltimore: Johns Hopkins University Press, 1996), 69. The Italian practice of lighting candles caught on in America, much to the astonishment of the Church hierarchy that discouraged such displays. A Protestant himself, Enrico C. Sartorio says that his countrymen would never convert because "reformed Christianity in its cold and divided forms such as are found in Protestantism . . . will never appeal to an emotional, esthetic race" (*The Social and Religious Life of Italians in America* [Boston: Christopher, 1918], 98).

18. A. S. P. Woodhouse, *Puritanism and Liberty: Being the Army Debates (1647–9) from the Clarke Manuscripts* (Chicago: University of Chicago Press, 1951), 57–60.

19. David Tracy, *The Analogical Imagination: Christian Theology and the Culture of Pluralism* (New York: Crossroad, 1981), 410.

20. Malcolm Mackenzie Ross, "Ruskin, Hooker, and 'The Christian Theoria,'" in *Essays in English Literature from the Renaissance to the Victorian Age Presented to A. S. P. Woodhouse,* ed. Millar MacLure and F. W. Watt (Toronto: University of Toronto Press, 1964), 290.

21. William F. Lynch, S.J., *Christ and Apollo: The Dimensions of the Literary Imagination* (New York: Sheed and Ward, 1960), 152.

22. Victor Turner, *Dramas, Fields, and Metaphors: Symbolic Action in Human Society* (Ithaca: Cornell University Press, 1974), 6. "The paraded image of a saint or the Madonna encapsulates a sacred narrative of heavenly intervention or a Marian apparition and superimposes this mytho-historic time onto the everyday world of sidewalks and street corners" (Joseph Sciorra, "'We Go Where the Italians Live': Religious Processions as Ethnic and Territorial Markers in a Multi-ethnic Brooklyn Neighborhood," in *Gods of the City: Religion and the American Urban Landscape,* ed. Robert A. Orsi [Bloomington: Indiana University Press, 1999], 317). One recalls the street *festa* in Francis Ford Coppola's *Godfather II.*

23. "Religion dwelt not in temples," asserts Fustel de Coulanges, "but in the house" (*The Ancient City* [Garden City, NY: Anchor, n.d.], 38). For Robert A. Orsi, *festa* is the "most obvious declaration of what was unique" in Italian American Catholicism (*The Madonna of 115th Street: Faith and Community in Italian Harlem, 1880–1950* [New Haven: Yale University Press, 1985], 55). I place it second, behind the religion of the home and family.

24. The phrase is from Roy Ladurie cited in Orsi, *Madonna,* xx.

25. Simone Cinotto, *Una famiglia che mangia insieme: Cibo ed etnicità nella comunità italoamericana di New York, 1920–1940* (Turin: Otto, 2001), 120.

26. Richard Gambino, *Blood of My Blood: The Dilemma of the Italian-Americans* (Garden City, NY: Anchor, 1974), 16. "Food was the host of life, and not in any remote or abstract sense. It was the product of my father (or grandfather's, or uncle's, etc.) labor, prepared for us with care by my mother (or grandmother, or aunt, etc.). It was in a very emotional sense a connection with my father and my mother" (16). The immigrant deemed almost "sacrilegious" an American attitude "characterized in the extreme by the American food stand where one eats bland mass-prepared food on the run. . . . [T]o the Italian-American, food is symbolic of both life and of life's chief medium for human beings, the family" (16).

27. Philippe Ariès, *Western Attitudes towards Death* (Baltimore: Johns Hopkins University Press, 1974), 7, 14, 103, 105. Rudolph M. Bell describes a funeral procession

in Nissoria, Sicily, that commenced at the home of the deceased, wound through the town, passing relatives' houses, and ended at the family cemetery plot, all conducted "in complete silence, a public and communal display of inner strength" (*Fate and Honor, Family and Village: Demographic and Cultural Change in Rural Italy since 1800* [Chicago: University of Chicago Press, 1979], 45).

28. Leonard W. Moss and Walter H. Thomson, "The Southern Italian Family: Literature and Observation," *Human Organization* 18 (1959): 40; Ariès, *Western Attitudes towards Death,* 7, 105. In a review of Ariès's *Hour of Our Death,* George Steiner misinterprets the immigrant attitude to death, conflating the baroque and the romantic: against the cold modern view, "it is Mafia burials that preserve the flamboyant desolation of the romantics" (*New Yorker* [June 22, 1981]: 114). Yet with its elaborate religious rites, public spectacle, and emphasis on survival of the clan, the Mafia treatment of death is Tame and diametrically opposite to the inwardness of the romantic cult of the dead.

29. Nicholas J. Russo, "Three Generations of Italians in New York City: Their Religious Acculturation," in *The Italian Experience in the United States,* ed. Silvano M. Tomasi and Madeline H. Engel (Staten Island: Center for Migration Studies, 1970), 197. "To the Italian, the American-Catholic Church was predominantly an American-Irish Church and it was characterized as: (1) English-speaking; (2) Jansenistic; (3) overly reverential for and loyal to the clergy; 4) activistic; (5) conservative; (6) too concerned with fund-raising; (7) pervaded with a supernationalistic spirit, identified with all things Irish" (197).

30. With regard to the "Italian Problem," Richard A. Varbero comments that Irish American prelates, themselves only a generation or two away from forebears in Ireland who embraced popular and magical beliefs and practices along the lines of southern Italian peasants, may have seen the Italian immigrants as a revenant, thereby forcing them into ever stronger repression not only of the Italian devotional practices but also of "the scars of their own shameful past" ("Philadelphia's South Italians and the Irish Church: A History of Cultural Conflict," in *The Religious Experience of Italian Americans,* ed. Silvano M. Tomasi [Staten Island: American Italian Historical Association, 1975], 42–43). Southern Italian peasants were neither anti-Catholic nor anticlerical; as immigrants, they were not anti-Catholic but, given the response of the official Church, certainly did exhibit anticlericalism in self-defense.

31. In the years preceding its publication, DeLillo had been "expected to produce a masterpiece, a Great American Novel, the sort of work for which his entire career had prepared him and his readers"; "in general *[Underworld]* was widely recognized as DeLillo's best work, a significant literary event, a major contemporary American novel, perhaps the most widely heralded book of the decade" (Hugh Ruppersburg and Tim Engles, eds., introduction to *Critical Essays on Don DeLillo* [New York: G. K. Hall, 2000], 2).

32. Ellul, *The Technological System,* 171.

33. "More than any other Italian American writer living or dead," asserts James Periconi, "DeLillo can rightly lay claim to literary greatness at the same time that, against all expectation, he seeks to recover his personal and literary Italian past" ("DeLillo's *Underworld:* Toward a New Beginning for the Italian American Novel," *VIA* 11:2 [Spring 2000]: 142).

34. Daniele, *Scrittori e finzioni d'America,* 115.

35. DeLillo, *Underworld*, 696; hereafter page references are included in parentheses in the text and notes. Cf. 120, "Campobasso bread" and the "knife hand."

36. Duvall, *Don DeLillo's "Underworld,"* 10. I want to thank Lynn McInerney, of the Cardinal Hayes High School Alumni Office, for her assistance. The films of Martin Scorsese, who was graduated from Cardinal Hayes High School in 1960, have thematic points in common with DeLillo's novels: Little Italy, violence, cultism, immanence, *festa,* and the sacred.

37. O'Malley, "Jesuit Educational Enterprise," 20, commenting on the *Ratio studiorum* (1599), the "magna carta of the Jesuit tradition" (16).

38. Daniele, *Scrittori e finzioni d'America,* 116.

39. Paul Civello, *American Literary Naturalism and Its Twentieth-Century Transformations: Frank Norris, Ernest Hemingway, Don DeLillo* (Athens: University of Georgia Press, 1994), 123.

40. Robert Nadeau, *Readings from the New Book on Nature: Physics and Metaphysics in the Modern Novel* (Amherst: University of Massachusetts Press, 1981), 178.

41. LeClair, *In the Loop,* 181.

42. Richard Stivers, *Technology as Magic: The Triumph of the Irrational* (New York: Continuum, 1999), 73.

43. This camouflaged deflection of ethnicity may be informed by the residual distance of a second-generation ethnic on the part of DeLillo himself.

44. But see 409: Matt "looked slightly Jewish, a little Hispanic maybe . . . people said he looked a little everything. Mexican, Italian, Japanese even."

45. "Same reason as ever—the father, not the mother. The deep discordance, the old muscling of wills, that ungiving thing in the idea of brothers" (203); see 454 for Matt's defense of Nick's position.

46. DeLillo misfires with these arty titles: "The Triumph of Death," "Elegy for the Left Hand Alone," "Arrangement in Gray and Black."

47. Joseph Dewey, "A Gathering under Words: An Introduction," in *UnderWords: Perspectives on Don DeLillo's "Underworld,"* ed. Joseph Dewey, Steven G. Kellman, and Irving Malin (Newark: University of Delaware Press, 2002), 10; Jesse Kavaldo, *Don DeLillo: Balance on the Edge of Belief* (New York: Peter Lang, 2004), 105. In his analysis of the single-sentence paragraph ending the prologue, "It is all falling indelibly into the past" (60), Kavaldo comments that "the ink on all the paper thrown makes the moment 'indelible.'" He refers to the paper falling after the triumph of the Giants at the baseball game, yet the word also applies to the paper on which DeLillo is writing to preserve the past (105).

48. Gerald Howard, "The American Strangeness: An Interview with Don DeLillo," *Hungry Mind Review* 43 (1997): 16, cited in David Cowart, *Don DeLillo: The Physics of Language* (Athens: University of Georgia Press, 2002), 184–85.

49. Guardini, *End of the Modern World,* 197. "If we understand the eschatological text of Holt Writ correctly, trust and courage will totally form the character of the last [i.e., final] age" (108). Guardini counsels a "realistic piety" as a modus vivendi in the postmodern age, "a piety no longer operating in a separate realm of psychological interiority or religious idealism, but within reality, a reality which, because complete, is also the reality created, sustained, and willed by God" (205). Nick Shay's final meditations on morality are almost entirely private, stoic, and sad.

50. Osteen, *American Magic and Dread,* 221.

51. Pool, *Technologies without Boundaries,* 65.

52. Kavaldo, *Don DeLillo,* 105.

53. Robert A. Orsi quotes Sister Marty, an aid worker in the South Bronx: "Something in me comes alive when I come into this area. I feel God's presence more strongly here than anywhere else" (*Gods of the City,* 1).

54. Don DeLillo, *White Noise* (New York: Viking, 1985), 117; hereafter page numbers are within parentheses.

55. A desolate street scene in DeLillo's *Mao II* (New York: Viking, 1991) depicts a woman who lives in a plastic bag "and knew about bundling" (145), another who searches for "redeemable bottles" (152), a man who says "I have holes in my side" (145) (like Christ), "street people with their odd belongings bundled in a corner . . . things inside other things, some infinite collapsible system of getting through life" (152). The scene's almost biblical final line analogizes all that has gone before: "Only those sealed by the messiah will survive" (153).

56. Osteen, *American Magic and Dread,* 216.

57. As Kavaldo notes, Nick "sounds lifeless because he *is* lifeless, and the conditions that create the novel's world also create the sense of lifelessness that pervades Nick's character, the narrative, and the novel itself. DeLillo uses Nick's voice, in its wearing and flat texture, to show the effect, over fifty years, that the world of the novel has had on him, and by extension, on all of us" (*Don DeLillo,* 108).

58. Daniele, *Scrittori e finzioni d'America,* 116. DeLillo said he was trying to convey the "rich rude tang of the Italian-American vulgate" ("The Power of History," *New York Times Magazine* [September 7, 1997], cited in Cowart, *Don DeLillo,* 182). Italian and Italian American dialect and slang pervade these sections of the novel: *u'pazz* (214, 694) (crazy); *aiuto* (296) (help); *shnozzola* (676) (big nose); *sboccato* (680) (foul mouth); *animale* (687) (beast); *scucciament'* (695) (bore); *stunat'* (706) (stupid); *stroonz* (715) (shit); *Domani mattin'* (755) (sure); *malavita* (761) (underworld); *Madonn'* (761) (Madonna); *Mannaggia l'America* (766) (hell with America); *cafone* (767) (boor); *porca miseria* (768) (damn it all); *briscola* or *breeshk* in dialect (722) (card game); *tizzone d'inferno* or *tizoons* (768) (scoundrel). In one speech pattern, *ly* is dropped from the adverb: when the mother thinks of her husband or Nick of his father, "It did not happen violent" (208, 698, 700). Italian American phrases run through the narrative, often glossed by the narrator: *Whose better than me?* "This was a statement of the importance of small pleasures. A meal, a coat with a fake-fur collar, a chair in front of a fan on a hot day" (207, 700). *See what you're gonna do:* "This was a threat to a son or daughter who was not behaving. Straighten out. Change your attitude" (700). *I'm making gravy:* "Don't you dare come home late. . . . The pleasure, yes, of familiar food, the whole history of food, the history of eating, the garlicky smack and tang. But there was also a duty, a requirement. The family requires the presence of every member tonight" (698)—a manifestation of the religion of the family.

59. Paul Gleason, "Don DeLillo, T. S. Eliot, and the Redemption of America's Atomic Waste Land," in *UnderWords,* ed. Dewey, Kellman, and Malin, 140–42.

60. Douglas Keesey, *Don DeLillo* (New York: Twayne, 1993), 2.

61. Tony Tanner, *The American Mystery: American Literature from Emerson to DeLillo* (Cambridge: Cambridge University Press, 2000), 216.

62. Osteen, *American Magic and Dread,* 225. Nor do I agree with Osteen that, as against the artists who salvage waste into art, Nick "is content merely to recycle and

wallow in the waste of the past" (245). Nick is not an artist—what should one expect him to do? In fact, he does salvage memories and experience some epiphanic moments. In any case, DeLillo does not take this negative attitude toward the past.

63. "DeLillo's fiction," says Andrew Jude Price, "is full of characters who, in their paranoia, gradually withdraw from the world, become 'isolated systems'" (*Entropic Imagination*, 97). See also James Wood, "Against Paranoia: The Case of Don DeLillo," in *The Broken Estate: Essays on Literature and Belief* (New York: Random House, 1999), 180–91.

64. Matt calls it his "stature of danger and rage" (221), but it is always referred to, never portrayed to any large extent. Even the killing of Manza is an accident.

65. "Only violence, preferably as ransom and brutal as possible, can crack the slick surfaces of fetishized commodification and restore the connection and immediacy that embodiment entails" (N. Katherine Hayles, "Postmodern Parataxis: Embodied Texts, Weightless Information," *American Literary History* 2 [1990]: 411). But this statement, written of *White Noise*, does not fully reflect the moral attitude toward violence in *Underworld*.

66. A standard textbook in DeLillo's Fordham years was Walter Farrell's *Companion to the Summa* (New York: Sheed and Ward, 1968): "True habits are increased by only one medium. The medium is our own acts; not by every act, but acts which are more intense, more earnest than the habit itself" (2:168).

67. Mark Edmundson comments on the deliberate thinness of character: DeLillo is "in many ways nostalgic for the kind of strong self-identity whose demise he's busy chronicling" ("Not Flat, Not Round, Not There: Don DeLillo's Novel Characters," *Yale Review* 83:2 [April 1995]: 107, 122).

68. Duvall, *Don DeLillo's "Underworld,"* 68.

69. This is one of the novel's numerous moments of illumination, secularized versions of divine *lumen;* as in Saint Bonaventure's mystical theology of light, DeLillo treats light as both a physical and a metaphysical entity, "the original metaphor for a spiritual reality" (Umberto Eco, *Art and Beauty in the Middle Ages* [New Haven: Yale University Press, 1986], 46, 50).

70. In his letter to the Iconoclast bishop, Serenus of Marseilles, Gregory defended the use of sacred images for moral purposes: though an image must not be adored, neither must it be broken; rather, it should be venerated, "to learn from the appearance of a picture what we must adore" (*Ep.* 9.105), cited in Charles G. Herbermann et al., eds., *Catholic Encyclopedia* (New York: Appleton, 1910), s.v. "Images, veneration of."

71. Osteen, *American Magic and Dread*, 258.

72. "One reads her fate as a kind of poetic justice for a person whose devotional commitment seems to have been corrupted by a faith in the endlessly seen—movie stars—and in non-divine forms of the unseen: germs, radiation, Communists among us" (David Cowart, "'Shall These Bones Live?'" in *UnderWords*, ed. Dewey, Kellman, and Malin, 55). But perhaps her good deeds in the Bronx will save her. Osteen points out that in the end she does remove her latex gloves and embraces a person whom she suspects of having AIDS (*American Magic and Dread*, 258).

73. Annesley, "Fictions of Globalization," 92; Tanner, *American Mystery*, 220; James Wolcott, "Blasts from the Past," *New Criterion* 16 (1997): 66.

74. This echoes Eliot's "Datta, dayadhvam, damyata" (Give, sympathize, control) (*The Waste Land* V).

75. Robert Simpson's phrase describes the conclusion of Bruckner's *Eighth Symphony* (cited in Benjamin M. Korstvedt, *Anton Bruckner: Symphony no. 8* [Cambridge: Cambridge University Press, 2000], 49). *Underworld*'s conclusion deliberately recalls the end of Eliot's *Waste Land*, the Sanskrit "Shantih, Shantih, Shantih" ("the peace that passeth understanding").

# Index

294nn29–30; on death and afterlife, 217–18, 228–29, 293n27, 294n28; emphasis on family, 217–18, 234, 239; influence on *Underworld,* 222–23, 240; literature by, 211–12, 294n33; neighborhoods of, 214–15, 217, 220, 224, 231–36; religion of the home and, 222–23; themes in DeLillo's writing, 213–14
Italy, 87, 272n99; education in, 83, 101, 108–9; Las Vegas copying, 73–74, 77, 79–80

James, Henry, 44, 178–81, 286n18
James, William, 44, 122–24
*James Joyce* (Ellmann), 175
Japan: Tokyo Disneyland in, 254n36
Jesuits: curriculum of, 88, 93
*John Keats* (Bate), 175
Johnson, Paul, 1
Johnson, Philip, 72
Johnson, Samuel, 107
Jung, Carl, 167

Kant, Immanuel, and Kantians, 36, 276n15; New Criticism and, 152–54; sublime of, 67, 80
Kavaldo, Jesse, 295n47, 296n57
Kazin, Alfred, 285n5
Kellen, Konrad, 246n26
Kember, Sarah, 209
Kempers, Bram, 66
Kenner, Hugh, 4, 244n10
Kernan, Alvin B., 63
"Kin or Clone: Contemporary Biotechnologies of the Self" (Kember), 209
Kitchell, Kenneth, Jr., 46
Knowledge, 111, 116, 137; belief and, 122, 124, 276n15; circle of, 19, 82, 88, 102–3, 112–13; useful vs. liberal, 102–4
Krieger, Murray, 149, 157

Labor, 253n20, 256n46
Lanciani, Rodolfo, 78
*Landscape for a Good Woman: A Story of Two Lives* (Stedman), 205–6
Lane, Belden, 80
Language, 54, 57, 144, 146, 256n49; analogizing vs. metaphor and simile, 216–17;

devaluation of, 35–37, 39; in education, 83, 85, 93–94, 99–100, 255n45; effects of technology on, 41; emotive vs. referential, 155–56, 159–60; images vs., 30–33, 48–50; importance of, 41, 200, 270n81; of Italian Americans, 231–32, 296n58; types of, 161–62, 170, 272n105
Language majors: decline in, 25, 100–101, 114
Lasch, Christopher, 190
Las Vegas, 263nn98–99; compared to Rome, 77–78; lack of authenticity of, 73–75, 79–80; nature and, 80–81; symbolism of, 73–78
Latin. *See* Classical studies
Leach, A. F., 267n41
*Learning from Las Vegas* (Venturi), 76–81, 263n99
Leavis, F. R., 113
LeClair, Tom, 213
LeClerc, Jean, 62
Legge, James, 135–36
Legouis, Emile, 162
Leigh Fermor, Patrick, 89
Lemon, Lee T., 172
Lentricchia, Frank, 39, 149
Lerner, Daniel, 246n27
Lerner, Frederick, 62
*Letters from Lake Como: Explorations in Technology and the Human Race* (Guardini), 13–14, 249n39
Levi, Edward, 63
Levin, David, 175
Levin, Harry, 274n121
Lewis, Wyndham, 170
Liberal arts. *See* Humanities
Liberal education, 105–6, 113–16
*Liberal Imagination* (Trilling), 158
*Liberal Tradition in America, The* (Hartz), 152
Liberalism: antihistoricism in, 152
Libraries: decay of, 65–66; digital services of, 63–65; history of, 61–63; and need for librarians, 64–65, 261n60; vs. media centers, 61, 64
Lindsay, Maurice, 278n38
Lines, David, 84
Lippmann, Walter, 251n52, 278n39
Lipsitz, George, 57–58